THE CRIMINAL LAW SYSTEM
OF MEDIEVAL AND
RENAISSANCE FLORENCE

THE JOHNS HOPKINS UNIVERSITY
STUDIES IN
HISTORICAL AND POLITICAL SCIENCE
112th Series (1994)

1. *The Criminal Law System of Medieval and Renaissance Florence*
Laura Ikins Stern

Frontispiece for Angelo Aretino,
Tractatus de Maleficiis (1526)

THE CRIMINAL LAW SYSTEM OF MEDIEVAL AND RENAISSANCE FLORENCE

Laura Ikins Stern

THE JOHNS HOPKINS UNIVERSITY PRESS

Baltimore and London

© 1994
The Johns Hopkins University Press
All rights reserved
Printed in the United States of America
on acid-free paper

The Johns Hopkins University Press
2715 North Charles Street
Baltimore, Maryland 21218-4319
The Johns Hopkins Press Ltd., London

Library of Congress Cataloging-in-Publication Data
Stern, Laura Ikins.
The criminal law system of medieval
and Renaissance Florence / Laura Ikins Stern.
p. cm. — (The Johns Hopkins University studies in
historical and political science ; 112th ser., 1)
Includes bibliographical references and index.
ISBN 0-8018-4672-2 (hc : acid-free paper)
1. Criminal justice, Administration of—Italy—Florence—History.
I. Title. II. Series.
KKH9851.86.S74 1994
345.45'5105—dc20
[344.551055]
93-14557
CIP

A catalog record for this book
is available from the British Library.

TO GERDA SELIGSON

CONTENTS

Preface   xi

1.
Introduction: The Judicial System and the Territorial State   1

2.
Inquisition Procedure and the General Powers of the Foreign Rectors   20

    Inquisition Procedure   21
    General Powers of the Foreign Rectors   33
    Ecclesiastical Jurisdiction   40
    Comparison with Venice   43
    General Trends   45

3.
The Subordinate Officials of the Foreign Rectors   47

    The Subordinate Officials of the Podestà   50
    The Subordinate Officials of the Captain of the People   62
    The Subordinate Officials of the Executor of the Ordinances of Justice   71

4.
The Podestà and Other Officials with Judicial Powers Affiliated with the Podestà   74

    The Podestà   74
    The Consuls of the Guilds   86
    The Mercanzia   92
    The Officials of Grascia   101
    Territorial Jurisdiction and Other Spheres of Competence   107

5.
The Captain of the People   *115*

6.
The Executor of the Ordinances of Justice   *126*

    The Ordinances of Justice   *127*
    Executing the Ordinances of Justice—The Magnates   *130*
    Syndication   *137*
    The Executor and the Societies of the People   *149*
    The Executor's Jurisdiction over Prison   *153*

7.
The Executive Offices   *156*

    Powers over Election   *163*
    Powers over Legislation   *169*
    Powers of Direct Trial   *171*
    Bullectini   *176*
    The Tower Officials   *185*
    Otto di Guardia   *193*
    Other Executive Agencies   *198*

8.
The Cases: Philosophies of Prosecution and Profiles of Criminality   *200*

9.
Conclusion   *226*

Bibliographic Essay   *241*

Notes   *259*

Select Bibliography   *275*

Index   *281*

PREFACE

THIS BOOK is an investigation of the medieval and Renaissance criminal law system in Florence. It deals with this system primarily as a judicial institution and secondarily as a part of the central government, and, therefore, a political institution; that is, the processes of change, development, legislation, and revision made to the judicial system and law are seen to be motivated first by attempts to treat problems of crime more effectively, and failing this line of reasoning to have explanatory powers, by the interplay between the legal and political spheres. This latter area, in which the interplay between the legal and political spheres produces changes in the judicial system, supplies a great deal of information about politics. Although this information could be used to analyze politics in any part of this period, it is of particular value in analyzing the much-debated political situation of the early fifteenth century. I examine procedure, officials, and criminality and present a preliminary study of secular inquisition procedure based on the criminal cases and statutes. Up till now, the history of secular inquisition procedure, the procedure employed in Florence, has been either ignored or maligned because of its assumed close resemblance to ecclesiastical inquisition procedure. The judicial officials and their functions are central to my study: important conclusions can be drawn about the court system, the government, and society as a whole from information concerning the functions of these officials. As part of my investigation, I provide a profile of criminality by means of a statistical analysis of crimes.

The major officials of the Florentine criminal law system in the late Middle Ages and early Renaissance were the three foreign rectors: the Podestà, the Captain of the People (Capitano del Popolo), and the Executor of the Ordinances of Justice (Esecutore degli Ordinamenti di Giustizia). These rectors were foreigners, usually from other Italian city-states, who traveled from one Italian city to the next with an entire retinue of judicial officials, first reading the statutes and then administering justice for a set period of short duration—in Florence, six months. While the rectors themselves were not required to have legal training, their judges were professionals trained in the Roman law tradition. The types of officials that were required developed and changed as inquisition procedure developed and changed. Throughout this period, these officials gained greater responsibility in conducting trials as accusation-initiated procedure waned, inquisition- or state-initiated procedure gained predominance, and the statutes extended the *arbitrium* of judges and rectors, giving them more power to initiate cases independent of an accuser. The policing functions of the rectors and their subordinate officials increased as the initiation of criminal cases became a state responsibility. All three rectors reached a parity in authority and began functioning with a statewide purview, reflecting the greater organization and centralization of the state. Through examination of the statutes and court cases, the interlocking functions of a great many of the judicial officials and the officials of the more bureaucratic parts of the government can be observed. This system of checks and balances served to enforce the rules of government.

Criminal trials from the mid- to late thirteenth century until the early fifteenth century were conducted according to a fully expanded and fully articulated inquisition procedure. Inquisition procedure is that procedure in which the court system conducts most parts of the trial, either all of the proceedings except the initiation or all of the proceedings including the initiation. The court system investigates and establishes the substantive facts and objective truths and has the ability to initiate and prosecute cases *ex officio*. In Florence, the state courts became increasingly responsible for most parts of the procedure, initiating, gathering information, compelling witnesses, weighing evidence, sentencing, and executing sentences. The rules of this procedure were regulated by statute, with the lacunae in the statute law being supplemented by the vast literature of legal tracts of the Roman-canon jurists, especially the post-glossators. Statute law in Florence was closely followed in the courts, and the jurists were often consulted on correct interpretation of Roman law. Inquisition procedure was not borrowed wholesale and wholly developed in the midthirteenth century from canon law; it was continuously developing and adapting to suit the needs of the practical problems to which it was being applied. The use of a fully articulated inquisition procedure was diminished or arrested in the mid- to late fifteenth century when citizen-staffed courts invaded the criminal law system and undermined the traditional courts of the foreign rectors. Summary procedure, which lacked full assessment of evidence and safeguards for the defendant, then replaced the fully articulated inquisition procedure of the foreign rectors' courts. I am not as concerned with the citizen courts, which lacked a sophisticated procedure, as with the courts of the foreign rectors, which were closely affiliated with the Roman law tradition and used institutions and procedures of great sophistication.

I also examine criminality during this period through an analysis of samples of court cases drawn from various years. The profile of criminality depends on the government's philosophy of prosecution as well as on the nature of prevalent crime. Such an analysis can be used as a mechanism for examining government policy, social values, and class conflict. Criminality retained a traditional profile at least through the early fifteenth century. Statistical analyses of the court cases from the fourteenth and early fifteenth centuries point to the increasing effectiveness of the criminal law system, through indicators such as reductions in both the contumaciousness (flight from trial) rate and the reluctant witness rate. Public mechanisms for bringing cases to court, such as public fame initiation (i.e., accusation by people who had no direct knowledge but attested only to what was rumored in the neighborhood), were increasingly employed and increasingly effective. Torture was frequently employed to exact confessions, sometimes with preceding *inditia* (incriminating evidence) and sometimes without.

During this period, public authority increasingly predominated over private-corporate authority in the forum of politics until approximately 1434, when this trend was reversed and public authority became qualified and finally overwhelmed by Medici hegemony. I use judicial records first to examine the building of this public power and then to assess the status of attrition of republican institutions and the advance of patrician takeover of the criminal law system and the government as the Medici period approached. Despite the growth of an ensconced wealthy class, the vitality of the criminal law system demonstrates the continuation of the territorial state and republican institutions through the early fifteenth century. The aspects of the territorial state that can be demonstrated to have continued are its public-mindedness, accountability, bureaucratization, systematization, centralization, and care for legality, backed up by legal repercussions.

One of the great attractions in studying the criminal law material is its ability to throw light on many different facets of history. Because the criminal case records have both the potential for statistical analysis and a direct witnessing power through their narrative qualities, they provide valuable material in social history, particularly for the otherwise invisible lower classes and underclasses. The real incidents contained in the court cases are personal encounters with medieval and Renaissance attitudes and conventions. In order to be able properly to interpret the court cases for the information relevant to these other disciplines, the purposes of the court system in compiling this information must be known and taken into account. There is a critical need for concrete evidence to be interjected into a field in which speculation is abundant. Judicial material has been used for bolstering a variety of different arguments in social and political history without the law itself being examined or considered. Theories of patrician domination of the government have particularly borrowed piecemeal from the judicial material. A study of the judicial system in its own right refutes or validates theories in other fields. Records from the court system also illuminate the more hidden bureaucratic parts of the government, not just the deliberative branch, the machinations of the deliberative branch being much more evident. The continuous functioning of the bureaucracy was an important step in the direction of the modern state. The system of checks and balances formed by the bureaucracy helped protect the government from undue political influence. The judicial system, as a part of the political system, reveals a great deal about the political system, providing another reason to examine this judicial system. The court materials provide a perspective for looking at politics that differs from studies which center interest on the patrician network.

The period from the mid-thirteenth century until the early fifteenth century is a particularly important period in the development of law. It marks the foundation of the synthesis of a new Italian law, which emerged in the fifteenth century, forged from the mutual influence between learned law and local law. Traditionally, the glossators have been seen as the interpreters of Roman law, while the post-glossators have been seen as those who, after the interpretation of Roman law, brought it to bear on the problems of the extant legal systems. In reality, the post-glossators should be seen as a conduit between the learned law and the applied law, as the mechanism of mutual influence between the two. Learning and application stayed closely tied through their work. The jurists themselves dealt with issues such as banning that had an origin in local law, not Roman law. The litmus test in the formation of the law of the fifteenth century was practicality and practical application. Roman law became forged with practice to form a new Italian law. As Angelo Aretino stated, new *ius civile* should replace old *ius civile*. Tracts of jurists, such as the *Tractatus de maleficiis* of Angelo Aretino, were arranged in the order of a trial so that they would be useful to practicing judges; practical handbooks proliferated; and *consilia* (opinions of the jurists on actual cases pending) were most numerous in the fifteenth century. Practice stayed closely tied to learned law in cities such as Florence that were integrated into the system of the foreign rectors.

This period was especially important in the development of inquisition procedure, too. Inquisition procedure, in which the state was responsible for most parts of the trial, developed and changed throughout this period; it culminated in the period of highest development in Florence, the early fifteenth century. Inquisition initiation started as a special case used for a few select crimes; accusation was still the norm. By the early fifteenth century, inquisition had eclipsed accusation. Sources of information independent of the accuser, such as torture and public fame, became more important. The character of accusation-initiated cases changed to become more like inquisition-initiated cases. In the beginning, in accusation-initiated cases the litigants set up their own cases, naming the defendant, gathering the witnesses, and creating the *libellus* to which the witnesses responded. As the public nature of crime became more recognized, the judge took a greater part in the trial to assure that the case was properly prosecuted. The development of inquisition procedure in Florence, initiated in the mid- to late thirteenth century, was arrested when the citizen courts were created. The latter began claiming the most important cases, leaving the foreign rectors with the least important. Accusation again became the predominant initiation.

This period also witnessed the full development of inquisition in terms of effectiveness. Throughout this period, the state was becoming more organized, bureaucratized, centralized, and powerful. Greater control by the state over its constituency, manifested in greater powers of coercion, enhanced the effectiveness of inquisition procedure. When the state shouldered the major responsibility for prosecution, it began gathering information for the trial. Law went from being predominantly private to predominantly public. A much more active judiciary was possible under these conditions. The developments in the law were caused, or at least complemented, by developments in the state. As the state became more centralized and organized, so did the judiciary. The judicial system became so efficient that investigation made a transition into surveillance when the citizen courts permitted political influence to be decisive. But for the period preceding this, for the early fifteenth century, improved police techniques under the firm control of the rectors resulted in a fuller implementation of inquisition procedure.

In this book, I address several problems that have not yet received sufficient attention. I examine offices of the judicial system and the government in order to trace their functions and construct a precise institutional history. Some of these offices have been considered by historians such as Lauro Martines as instruments of patrician takeover of the government, as easily controlled and staffed by the patriciate, and as having vast influence over other segments of the government, such as the judicial branch, and great independence of action. A close examination of these agencies, such as the Office of the Tower, shows that they were not easily manipulated or electorily packed and that they were firmly ensconced in a system that interrelated them with other offices and limited their independent action. An examination of these government offices reveals a system of checks and balances which restrained undue power. Little work has been done in the study of applied law, and even less in the study of the relationship between applied law, statute law, and learned law. The law has been studied almost exclusively in its learned law aspects from the tracts of the Roman-canon law jurists. It is not known to what extent the learned law was an esoteric superstructure, a scholastic exercise, or to what extent it was useful to the court systems. Indeed, the relationship between learned law and applied law varied greatly from city-state to city-state; the quality of this relationship must be investigated for each city-state. The relationship between statute and applied law was discovered to be very close in Florence during this period, so close that we can almost equate the two. This situation was not true for all contemporary Italian city-states, for instance, Venice. I do not explore the relationship between learned law and statute law in Florence, but it, too, can be demonstrated to be close. Information contained in the practical tracts of the post-glossators was used in Florence to fill the gaps left in the statutes, although learned law and statute law did not always completely coincide—for instance, on the subject of torture. Knowledge of the applied law is critical in assessing the importance of statute and learned law. For legal historians, this study represents an in-depth exploration of an important inquisition-based court system, which can then be used for comparative purposes.

Another lack has been a study of inquisition procedure on the secular side. Few people are aware that inquisition procedure was used in the secular courts as well as in the ecclesiastical courts. Where its secular existence is known, it is popularly perceived to have been the same as ecclesiastical inquisition procedure, and, therefore, entirely pernicious. A similar presumption has been that in the mid-thirteenth century, ecclesiastical inquisition procedure, already fully developed, was adopted into the secular courts and remained fixed and changeless in the succeeding centuries. While secular and ecclesiastical procedure were similar, secular inquisition procedure was not concerned with the trial of heresy or witchcraft, but rather with crimes considered worthy of prosecution by most societies. The types of crimes treated in each court had a great effect on the procedure. The clandestine nature of heresy, witchcraft, and other ecclesiastical crimes made the unearthing of real evidence difficult and put special emphasis on confession, often obtained through torture. Trials conducted in the secular courts did not need to cope to the same degree with clandestine occurrences, so had a greater possibility of employing real information and proof, although torture was commonly used in secular inquisition procedure too. Secular inquisition procedure should be studied in its own right.

In introducing this book, a short historiographic essay places succeeding chapters in the general context of scholarship. A much more detailed historiographic essay appears as the Bibliographic Essay. The idea that inquisition procedure and the court system were established and then did not change appears implicitly in the six-volume work of Pertile, *Storia del diritto italiano*, and then explicitly in Kohler's commentary in Kohler and Azzi's *Das Florentiner Strafrecht des XIV Jahrhunderts*. Pertile treats the period 1200 to 1600 as one monolithic period, so that no analysis of change over time can be made and no developments traced. Kohler points to the statutes of 1284 as the first recorded time that the Podestà and his judges were permitted to initiate cases through inquisition in cases of theft, robbery, and murder, but he does not trace the expansion of this class of cases into subsequent centuries. He explicitly believes that the statutes of 1322–25 and those of 1415 were very similar and that the 1415 statutes were taken in large part from the statutes of 1322–25. According to Kohler, the statutes of 1415 were obsolete before their redaction and went unused. When transferred to the political system, this thought leads to the conclusion that the constitution of Florence was static and obsolete in 1415 and that creativity and change in politics were implemented from outside the normal channels of the government. Inquisition procedure and the court system changed greatly throughout this period. Although antique concepts of law did survive in the 1415 redaction, especially in the criminal code, changes in the law during the period from 1322–25 to 1415 were significant. The statutes of 1415 were employed and rules of legislation for emending the statutes were followed, at least until 1434.

Umberto Dorini's *Il diritto penale e la delinquenza nel sec. XIV* is a striking change from what went before and a masterful and entirely modern work. Dorini connects law with social conditions and recognizes the changing nature of criminality and law. His book was written partially as a corrective to Kohler's static concepts. Dorini illustrates change by comparing samples of criminal cases from the courts of the Podestà, the Captain, and the Executor for 1352–55 and 1380–83. He describes the initial phase of the change in the concept of law from private to public. By the time of the 1322–25 compilation, vendetta had come under the control of the state and was regulated and limited by the state. In 1355, a system of rewards was established for the rectors' police officials who captured culprits *in flagranti* (in the process of committing crimes); in 1373, it was expanded. The role of the state in interrupting crime and apprehending criminals was thus increasing.

My thesis, that republican government and the territorial state continued into the early fifteenth century, is most at variance with the theme of Lauro Martines' *Lawyers and Statecraft in Renaissance Florence*. Martines believes that in the 1380s and 1390s the Florentine political system changed from a republic into an oligarchy. According to him, the oligarchs used the device of creating new agencies within the government with extraordinary powers, in which they secured positions for themselves, in order to amass great powers. Further, their control of the state extended to controlling judicial process: the newly created agencies reserved the most politically crucial cases for themselves. Moreover, the rise of these agencies was encouraged by the atrophying of the regular judicial system of the foreign rectors. These agencies were dominating and stifling other parts of the government. The oligarchy came to own the government, while the idea of public good became an abstraction. By examining the agencies that Martines includes, I demonstrate that they were elected normally, did not try politically crucial cases, and did not act autonomously or without restraint. Furthermore, no attrition of the rectors' courts occurred until the mid-1420s, when war and a decline in population caused budget cuts in all parts of the government, including these courts.

Samuel Cohn, in *The Laboring Classes in Renaissance Florence*, presents another statistical analysis of court cases from different periods. He accents the effects of governmental philosophies of prosecution on the court system and consequently on all historical data collected from the court system. Cohn discovers that in the late fifteenth century, after the *popolo minuto* had lost their citywide distribution and lived, instead, in ghettos, the patrician government was better able to ignore crimes perpetrated against ghetto dwellers by other ghetto dwellers. The patricians in government dominated the court system and used it for their own benefit. In particular, they vigorously prosecuted crimes against property. Cohn's study does not directly assess material from the early fifteenth century, but he demonstrates that crime remained in its traditional patterns until at least 1374 and that the citywide distribution of the poor persisted until at least 1383.

More recently, Andrea Zorzi has investigated the Florentine judicial system. Zorzi is principally interested in how political power affected the judicial system. Because he accents political influence and corruption within the court system, he tends to deemphasize the everyday functioning of the courts. He is most interested in the Otto di Guardia and how it developed from being an agency within the government to being the court of the Medici. The Otto is the court in which the interplay between the political system and the judicial system was most direct, since it was often staffed by members of the patriciate and often sat in *balie* (assemblies with extraordinary powers) and assemblies of the government. His portrait of the disintegration of the court system of the foreign rectors and the takeover by the Otto in the mid- to late fifteenth century demonstrates exactly the opposite traits of the courts of the foreign rectors during their building period. The number of inquisitions *ex officio* plummeted as the percentage of accuser-initiated cases rose; the contumaciousness rate soared; the technical competence of the judges fell, as did sophistication of procedure; and the judicial system fragmented into specialized courts with specialized tasks.

Most of the information for this book has been drawn from the statute compilations, particularly the *Statuti della Repubblica Fiorentina* of 1322–25 and the *Statuta Popoli et Communis Florentiae* of 1415; the criminal cases from the courts of the foreign rectors; and the *provvisioni*, or enactments of the executive branch of the government in conjunction with the legislative councils. The statutes of 1415, including the preliminary version of 1408–9, were a wholesale revision and reorganization of former statutes, the statute compilations of 1322–25 and 1355. Paolo di Castro and Bartolommeo Vulpi, the two famous jurists who produced the statutes of 1415 from the confused and contradictory statutes and ad hoc provvisioni that preceded the 1415 redaction, were given great latitude in editing, revising, reforming, and eliminating obscurities, contradictions, and anachronisms from the statutes. Because of this revision, this compilation, which stayed in effect until 1530 and partly in use until the nineteenth century, can be expected to have been current when redacted.

In order to analyze change, I compared the statutes of 1322–25 to the statutes of 1415. While the statutes are, admittedly, a still shot of an ever moving picture, a momentary crystallization of norms, they incorporate changes made over many years and reflect a consensus of what is lasting and durable. The provvisioni, on the other hand, are the part of the system that is made today and torn down tomorrow. For this reason, I have used the statutes in preference to the provvisioni where available. I have examined the provvisioni from 1419, when the 1415 statutes came into effect, to 1434, when the Medici reentered Florence, the chronological terminus of this study. Additional information has come from the court cases, especially those of the Podestà for the years 1425–28. Information taken from the cases has enabled me to confirm conclusions drawn primarily from the statutes, as well as to formulate conclusions on procedure and crime.

Throughout this book, I use the terms for two concepts in a very specific and consistent way. First, *territorial state* indicates a state that is public-minded, accountable, impersonal, systematized, and centralized. The characteristics of the territorial state are sovereignty possessed by a central government, direct control of the constituency without intercessors, and a strong public sector promoting public interest above private interest. The government must be composed of more than one class. It must contain an accountable bureaucracy striving for efficiency. This concept is borrowed from Marvin Becker rather than Giorgio Chittolini, and the full implications of the difference are explained in the Introduction. Second, the terms *aristocracy* and *patriciate* are used in specific ways. *Aristocracy* refers to wealthy people who can be either successful or unsuccessful in gaining political power, desirous or not desirous of doing so. I recognize that this is not a homogeneous or legally defined group, and that people belonging to this group may come from a great variety of social, vocational, and economic backgrounds. *Patriciate,* on the other hand, refers to those wealthy people in society who have gained great political power either officially or unofficially. This group, likewise, is not homogeneous or legally defined, although it may be slightly more homogeneous because of clientele networks that assist certain groups of people in gaining power. When other historians use terminology that signifies related concepts, like oligarchy, I retain their terminology in describing their themes, leaving the definition of their concepts to be found in their work.

As stated earlier, the thesis of this book is that the growing strength of the criminal law system from the mid-thirteenth century to the early fifteenth century demonstrates the continuation of the territorial state through the early fifteenth century because it shows that the state, or at least this important part of the state, continued to develop. Developments within the criminal law system are posited to be symptomatic of developments within the state as a whole. Developments in inquisition procedure, such as the extension of *arbitrium,* gave the foreign rectors more power. The criminal law system became more effective during this period by gaining greater policing capabilities. The guilds and other corporations became more subordinated to the courts of the rectors. By the early fifteenth century, the citizen-staffed courts, which were vulnerable to private and patrician influence, had not taken away any significant areas of power or jurisdiction from the courts of the foreign rectors. Even political crimes remained in the rectors' courts.

The criminal law system continued to display the traits of the territorial state throughout this period up through the early fifteenth century. The rectors no longer served special constituencies but became uniform functionaries of the state. Private concepts of justice gave way to public concepts. The judicial system, as well as agencies of the government connected to the judicial system, such as the Office of the Tower, which was the part of the government in charge of communal goods and protecting them from private, especially aristocratic, incursion, continued to become more accountable. A comparison of statutes and cases shows that the statutes were constantly employed, and constitutionality was a matter of concern. The judiciary was kept separated from political machinations by a set of regulations designed for this purpose and by exterior Roman-canon law standards. The executive branch, the Signoria, although it had always possessed powers of interference in the judicial branch, was prevented from arbitrary interference by a system of regulations in use throughout this period. Few *bullectini* (executive mandates to the judicial system) were used. All officials in the government were contained within a system of checks and balances, which prevented one group of officials from seizing too much power. The profile of criminality from the early fifteenth century does not show use of the court system for the benefit of just one class. The Otto di Guardia, the executive agency that appropriated all judicial power in the late fifteenth century, did not yet try its own criminal cases.

The criminal law system, besides demonstrating the traits of the continuation of the territorial state, had the effect of keeping the government at large more republican by thwarting, or at least delaying, patrician takeover. The judicial system helped enforce the *divieti* laws, which forbade anyone to hold office concurrently, too frequently, or simultaneously with his relatives, and thus protected offices from coming under the exclusive dominion of the powerful. It enforced the syndication laws, which subjected all officials, even those of the executive branch, to a mandatory review of their performance in office, with possible prosecution for omissions or crimes. The judicial system ensured that changes made in the government had to be made constitutionally. The Councils of the People and of the Commune, bulwarks of republicanism, were not successfully neutralized in the early fifteenth century; their consent continued to be required. They continued to thwart attempts to dispose of constitutional forms. Election regulations, although increasingly favoring the wealthy, were upheld, as were regulations on legislation, as evidenced in the provvisioni records. The government chose to keep a judicial system tied into Roman-canon law and abstract notions of justice. No faction of the patriciate was successful in dominating; the policies of the Signoria changed constantly with its change in membership. Because procedural safeguards were present throughout the government, attempts at undue influence were forced to take subversive and clandestine channels, delaying patrician takeover.

One final, cautionary note: The territorial state in Florence was not the modern state. Anyone applying modern criteria for democracy, republicanism, organization, or sovereignty to the medieval and Renaissance Florentine state is bound to come away disappointed. Many of the concepts valuable in forming modern political theory were still hundreds of years from coming into existence. The Florentine state of this period can only fairly be compared with its contemporary states and can only fairly be judged by criteria of contemporary political theory. Otherwise, failure to meet modern standards is built in.

I wish to thank Marvin Becker for his provocative comments and patient criticism at all stages of the development of this book. His help, support, and encouragement have held me steadfast to its completion. Special thanks are due to Thomas Green for working on every facet of this book, for providing useful and incisive suggestions as well as encouragement. It has been a privilege and pleasure to work with him. My two closest friends in the academic world, Gerda Seligson and Gino Corti, have generously given my work their personal time and attention, for which I am deeply grateful. A still greater gift has been their friendship.

I am most grateful for the help and suggestions I have received from Diane O. Hughes. Thanks again to Sharon Krogman for her efforts in the mechanics of producing the original manuscript. I wish to thank Henry Y. K. Tom and the reviewer of the manuscript for the substantial contribution that they made in producing the final version. Warmest and deepest thanks go to my mother, Marion Ikins, who is always there when I need her, leaving her little time for anything else. Many thanks to my husband, Fred, for assistance and professional tips of all kinds. Last but not least, my children, David, Georgette, Noah, Marion, and Shirley, deserve my deepest gratitude for being wonderful and making life worth living.

In addition, I wish to thank the Renaissance Society of America and the American Commission for Cultural Exchanges with Italy (Fulbright Commission) for their generous support.

THE CRIMINAL LAW SYSTEM
OF MEDIEVAL AND
RENAISSANCE FLORENCE

I

INTRODUCTION: THE JUDICIAL SYSTEM AND THE TERRITORIAL STATE

IN THIS BOOK I use judicial material primarily to examine the judicial system and secondarily to examine the government of which the judicial system was a part. In particular, I use it to examine politics in the early fifteenth century, a time of intense interest to political historians because of the rise of the Medici. I intend, in this introduction, to elucidate the issues and controversies surrounding this topic. The difficulty lies in determining whether to treat the early fifteenth century as a culmination of the republican fourteenth century or as an antecedent of the patrician fifteenth century. The year 1434, when the Medici were invited to return to Florence and when they assumed some degree of control over the government there, was an important year in Florentine history. Because this event was so dramatic, it has had a great impact on the way in which historians have conceptualized and periodized the early fifteenth century. It is important to ascertain to what degree this event was really illustrative of the early fifteenth century, in order to evaluate both the state of survival of republican institutions and the progress of patrician takeover of these institutions preceding 1434.

Although I treat the judicial system mainly as a mechanism for law and order and not as a manifestation of a political system, no totally clear distinction can be made between the judicial and political spheres in the Middle Ages and the Renaissance. Thus, it is necessary to study this one crucial political issue. The assessments of republican institutions and patrician takeover must be made by examining the early fifteenth century in its own right. I shall examine the criminal law system and the way that it was affected by the government and society—and, conversely, affected government and society. The answer to the question of periodizing depends in part on whether the territorial state continued to develop or whether a state run by the patriciate and for the benefit of the patriciate was in existence before 1434. The strong judiciary of the early fifteenth century was symptomatic of the government as a whole and indicates the continuation of the territorial state.

Criminal Law System of Medieval and Renaissance Florence

The concept of the territorial state has been defined by Marvin Becker and added to by Giorgio Chittolini.[1] Becker has indicated that greater organization, centralization, accountability, and public-mindedness began to characterize the central government before the mid-fourteenth century. Chittolini has traced the characteristics of organization and centralization into the fifteenth century, especially as they pertain to the creation of a larger territorial state composed of smaller cities and their *contadi* (the surrounding countryside), as well as the Florentine *contado* and territory, and ruled by Florence. There are differences between these two concepts. First, these developments took place during two different but overlapping periods. The characteristics that Becker describes, of a public state responding to public needs and valuing participation from different classes, were formed in the 1340s and were eroded in approximately 1434, when the Medici returned to be Florence's first citizens. As Chittolini characterized it, dominance over the whole territory gained momentum in the early fifteenth century and continued well past 1434. Second, Becker's definition includes an element of republicanism and broad participation in government. Chittolini's territorial state spans a period of republicanism and then of patrician dominance. The process of the extension of Florentine dominance over the territory mainly profited the patrician class and became a part of the patrician program after 1434.

The uses of the term *territorial state*, therefore, can be quite different. This study explores the definition that pertains to the central government and the central judicial system. While the extension of the territory undoubtedly had an impact on the central judiciary, the traits described by Becker of accountability, public-mindedness, and republicanism are of more direct consequence. I define a territorial state as a sovereign state in which the central government controls most of the territory and the people in it. (No state in the Middle Ages or the Renaissance was capable of having more than a moderate level of sovereignty or control over its people or its territories.) The government is run by a bureaucracy that seeks to work efficiently with the public interest in mind. No one class controls the government for its own benefit, because the government holds public good to be superior to the rights of any person or any group. The constituents have a direct relationship with the state, instead of relying on a group to intercede for them. The government functions according to rules (the statutes) and is capable of enforcing its rules among its constituency. These are the main characteristics as defined by Becker and here traced into the early fifteenth century.

The medieval state in Florence, the commune, was decidedly not a territorial state. The Commune of Florence was composed of several corporate groups loosely held together by the government. Some people

3
The Judicial System and the Territorial State

within the state of Florence, such as certain feudal lords, did not have a direct relationship with the state, nor could they be compelled by it. Nearby cities vacillated between alliance with Florence and alliances with Florence's enemies, thereby endangering the stability and safety of the Florentine state. The medieval Florentine state was not sovereign; the corporate groups within it held the allegiance of their members. These groups, the Parte Guelfa, the guilds, and the Societies of the People, functioned as intermediaries between the individual and the state, rendering civic pride and concern for public good impossible. The members participated in the group, and the various corporate groups participated in the state. Thus, the government comprised such officials as the Priors of the guilds and the *Gonfalonieri* of the Societies of the People. Elections were organized so that each of these corporate groups, as a group, nominated people for office that it found suitable. The government was not successful in forcing its rule of law on its constituency; some of the groups, such as the guilds, had their own courts, and some, such as the Parte Guelfa, had too much to say in determining citizenship within the state. In the territory, the local cities were the intermediaries, the contadi and territories of these local cities communicating only indirectly with the government of Florence through these cities. Law was seen as a private matter between individuals in which interference by the state was viewed as improper. The concept of law as a force for public good was as yet little developed. The state was not centralized, nor was the bureaucracy articulated into a systematic, rational, and efficient organization.

But throughout the second half of the fourteenth century and the early fifteenth century, the state was in a process of change. For the fourteenth century, Marvin Becker has described this change as the development of the territorial state. Becker's views on the territorial state appear in *Florence in Transition* and "The Florentine Territorial State and Civic Humanism in the Early Renaissance."[2] In Becker's conceptualization, the movement in government toward a territorial state began in 1342. Previous to this time, laissez-faire government allowed privilege, laxity in law enforcement, and traditional immunities from taxation. But in the 1340s, when depressed economic conditions replete with bank disasters took their toll on the budget of the commune, the government was forced to take a more aggressive attitude toward its constituency. Aristocrats were forced to pay fair rents for the communal property they occupied. Immunities from taxation and from jurisdiction were rescinded. Law enforcement was tightened, partly to better control and protect the constituency and partly to collect penalties for communal coffers. It was sometimes necessary to resort to dictatorships or democratic regimes to conquer resistance, especially from the aristocratic class, to much-needed tax reforms. Popular government promoted reform and moderate democratization, while despotism promoted impersonal government. Both of these programs diminished the privileges of the guild patriciate that ruled in the 1330s.

The need for public law to prevail over private privileges initiated the era of the territorial state. When vendetta was the norm, an active judiciary was not desired. There was great resistance to the imposition of any measures fostering public good through law enforcement on a population that regarded private justice as a right. As fiscal demands pressed the government, the government became more accountable, rationalized, systematized, and centralized. The dictatorship of Walter of Brienne in 1342 was responsible for more rigorous law enforcement, reform of the fisc, greater centralization, and concessions to the lower orders. The government that followed Brienne's in 1343 overthrew the patriciate and carried on further democratization. At this time, a bureaucracy particularly effective in controlling the contado was established. Nobles who had usurped communal property were fined, greater stress being given to the recuperation of communal goods and rights. The syndication process—that process in which the performance of officials was judged and fines were levied for omissions or crimes committed in office—was strictly enforced to prevent officials from siphoning off communal funds. Capital flowed into the public sector. The strict enforcement of all the statutes started at this time. The *divieti* laws, which limited the length of term and frequency of officeholding of persons and families, were put into effect in 1343 to guard against any person or family becoming overly influential in government. The 1340s were thus the turning point from a medieval state to a Renaissance territorial state.

The next half century, the 1350s to the 1400s, saw the curtailment of the authority of private interest groups in the government. The Tuscan church, the Guelf party, the guilds, the confraternities, and the magnates were all brought under the power of the state. New men were becoming creditors of the Monte, the communal funded debt that paid substantial interest rates to its contributors, and were admitted to the ruling classes of the city. The number of citizens eligible for office increased in every decade from 1350 to 1400.[3] These citizens worked against patrician privilege. Because the government needed more money to fight expensive wars and to pay carrying charges on the communal debt, the creditor class had to be expanded to meet fiscal needs. Thus, an expanded political class deprived the privileged associations of public power. Correspondingly, allegiance became less parochial and more civic, contributing to the later development of civic humanism.

The development of the territorial state did not stop here but continued into the early fifteenth century. One of its aspects that underwent particularly rapid development was the consolidation of the territory and the neighboring cities into a unified Florentine state. The aggressive activities of the Visconti dukes of Milan, first Giangaleazzo in the late fourteenth century, then Filippo Maria Visconti starting in 1423, induced the larger cities of the Italian peninsula to secure their surrounding territories for defensive purposes. Territories left loosely annexed were destabilizing regions, which might possibly rebel and join enemy forces. Smaller nearby cities, likewise, had to be annexed and tied administratively, judicially, and militarily to the larger cities to act as secure buffer zones—in the process, suffering diminished autonomy, responsibility, and power. From 1385 to 1421, Florence acquired Arezzo, Pisa, Cortona, and Livorno.[4] The contadi of these cities and of already conquered but potentially troublesome cities, such as Pistoia, were severed from these cities and attached directly to Florence. *Ligae,* or groups of villages, were organized and then tied directly to Florence. This movement formed part of the general territorial state movement to organize and centralize.

This process affected the judicial area. All subject cities were required to have their statutes approved by Florence. Previous to 1400, the Florentine government had allowed its subject cities to rule their own contadi and have jurisdiction over them, despite protests from these regions. But in 1373, it began to foster direct dependence on Florence when it took away Pistoia's jurisdiction over its mountain area and made this area directly dependent on the Florentine court system.[5] By 1401, Pistoia retained only a limited civil jurisdiction over its contado. Throughout the territory, the podesteries and other local judicial offices, formerly held by local men, began to be staffed by Florentines designated by the Ufficio delle Tratte.[6] Increased qualifications for handling serious civil or criminal cases became required of the Florentine officials. A system of vicars was created above the *podestà* and captains (both local officials with judicial and administrative duties) of the territory to coordinate between the central government and the podestà and captains. The podestà, captains, and vicars that were dispatched from the central government with their judges, *milites* (military associates, heads of the police force) notaries, and *famuli* (police officials) were of a higher professional level than the podestà sent previously from the smaller cities. Most of these reforms appeared in the statutes of 1415, although some occurred subsequently. In the mid-1420s, additional reforms were made in order to reduce government spending during the financial crisis occasioned by war, such as reduction in the salaries of many of these officials and reduction in the number of these officials as jurisdictions were combined, the same kinds of changes that the central government made in order to reduce spending. However, the Florentine territorial state was not the modern state. It persisted in trading off recognition of Florentine sovereignty for concessions of privileges like local self-government, and having separate but coordinated treaties with each region under its suzerainty.[7]

The judicial system, likewise, continued to exhibit the traits of the further development of the territorial state. I will highlight the new facets of the statutes of 1415 and will demonstrate that these new developments contributed to the continued growth of a territorial state. These changes, especially the increasing vitality of inquisition procedure, indicate that a strong, centralized state existed in the early fifteenth century. An inquisition that could be initiated, conducted, and investigated by the state required a vast network of police officials to investigate crime and to coerce its citizens—for instance, to force witnesses to appear. The statutes of 1415 specified a cadre of investigating officials not extant in the 1322–25 period. The use of torture, however abhorrent, shows the state gathering its own evidence and not using private parties to do this job. The number of crimes that were allowed to be initiated by *ex officio* inquisition increased throughout the fourteenth century and into the early fifteenth century. Private accusation waned as the number of inquisition-initiated cases increased. The number of crimes initiated by public fame inquisition was substantial, showing a further erosion of the concept of crime as a private matter and an enhanced ability of the judicial system to investigate it. Public fame accusers were not required to have any relationship to the offended parties. Indeed, they need have no direct knowledge of the events in question, but need attest only to rumor. Inquisition procedure required a strong, centralized judicial system, the kind characteristic of a strong, centralized state.

The officials in the judicial system were undergoing processes of systematization aimed at increasing efficiency and nonpartisan justice. Two separate processes were at work. The foreign rectors, the major judicial officials, were becoming more similar to one another in authority. At the same time, through legislation, the areas of competence of all of the judicial officials were being sorted out and arranged in a more logical and consistent order, thus eliminating some of the confusion and overlap that had existed previously. Both of these processes contributed to a more efficient state.

Inquisition procedure was creating changes in the judicial system that increased the similarities among the rectors. As the rectors more frequently sent out officials to investigate crimes, the criteria for deciding who tried the crimes came to be based less on assigned areas of competence and more on first arrival at the scene of the crime. When the *famiglia* (the retinue comprising police officials and pages) of a certain rector either interrupted a crime or arrived at the scene to investigate a recently committed crime, the crime was tried in the court of that rector, despite any contrary divisions of competence (*Statuta* 3.3; hereafter abbreviated as *Stat.*). Besides this motive force toward uniformity, the rectors were becoming more similar because they no longer reflected different constituencies. Previously, each of the rectors had been part of one of the corporate entities that composed the Commune of Florence. A rector's area of competence reflected the nature of the corporate entity of which he was a part. By 1415, the corporate components of the government were weaker, and the rectors had become part of the government as a whole.

Simultaneously with the rectors losing their parochial character, the government of Florence was rearranging the tasks of the foreign rectors and of the other officials with judicial duties. When the judicial officials were freed from their old affiliations, the government imposed a new division of labor that was logical, dividing areas of competence by *materia*. The Tower Officials, for instance, subsumed under their authority all of the power over communal rights and goods that formerly had been exercised by separate officials with overlapping spheres of interest. Concomitantly, the whole system, freed from conflicting allegiances, was centralized. This centralization and bureaucratization is characteristic of a territorial state.

The rectors were becoming more uniform in still other ways. All three rectors were made equal in authority, and they had many of the same kinds of subordinate officials. The similarity in retinues bespoke a similarity of tasks supervised by the rectors. The criminal judges, although they sometimes had areas of specialization, could try cases involving any crime.

Another requirement of a territorial state is that it be administered, at least to some degree, with some benefit in mind for all groups, or at least not for the benefit of just one group. During the period of the medieval commune in Florence, the corporate entities that made up the commune and its government prevented the formation of a territorial state. In some period after 1434, the inroads that the patriciate, centered around the Medici, made into the administration of the state and the judicial system allowed the patriciate to rule the state in a way beneficial to itself. The territorial state ceased to exist after this takeover. In order to show that a territorial state existed in the early fifteenth century, it must be demonstrated that the power of the corporate entities had diminished so that they no longer held the allegiance of Florentines and no longer functioned as intermediaries between the people and the state. It also must be demonstrated that the patriciate did not yet control the state or the judicial system for its own benefit.

The judicial system was structured to remain autonomous from any group in Florentine society. Almost all the officials who staffed the judicial system—the three rectors and their judges, their police officials, and their notaries—were foreign. From earliest times, this was done specifically to separate the officials from factional conflict. The judicial officials continued to be chosen from among foreigners throughout the early fifteenth century; consequently, these offices were not greatly affected by the electoral manipulations of the patriciate. The short terms of office and the divieti laws for the foreign and citizen officials within the judicial system further thwarted any group from establishing real control. The foreign officials held office for only six months, and few other officials held office any longer. The divieti laws, which forbade the concurrent or consecutive holding of offices by members of the same family or *consorteria*, likewise prevented control by any group. These laws, which were initially unchangeable but became slightly more lax in the early fifteenth century (requiring thirty-six of the thirty-seven votes of the Signoria and the colleges, plus the approval of the councils), were still enforced.[8]

In addition, the syndication process continued to prevent the meting out of partisan justice. All of the judicial officials, foreign and citizen, and those officials adjunct to the judicial system with judicial powers, like the Priors and the Officials of Grascia, were subject to syndication, the mandatory process in which all of the officials were tried for any omissions or crimes committed by them during office. Even Lauro Martines, a historian who proposes the existence of oligarchic control in the early fifteenth century, admits that syndication put strong restraints on the judicial officials in this period to act according to statute and not according to factional interests. In his examples of conflict between the executive and judicial branches, the judicial officials refused to be coerced by the executive wing of the government for fear of the strict sanctions imposed by the syndication laws.[9] Syndication trials continued to be conducted regularly throughout the period under discussion. The basic structure of the judicial system kept it autonomous from illegitimate influences.

By the early fifteenth century, the corporate bodies that had formerly composed the government had lost and were continuing to lose power, both internally and in relation to the central government. It is universally agreed that the Parte Guelfa suffered a precipitous decline after its heyday in the 1360s.[10] The Parte Guelfa had been a very powerful force in Florentine politics as well as an independent and intractable one. At times the political actions of the Parte had been in direct and deliberate opposition to the official stance and foreign policy of the government. Previous to 1378, the allegiance of Florentines to the Parte had been so strong that the Florentine state shared its sovereignty with it. Through its power to *am-*

The Judicial System and the Territorial State

monire, to proscribe citizens as Ghibellines and thus strip them of their right to hold office, the Parte had held the power of bestowing and retracting citizenship. In 1378, a provision was enacted that restricted this power; henceforth, no one could be *ammonito* by the Parte without the consent of the Priors, Gonfalonier, colleges, Ten of Liberty, and twenty-one consuls of the guilds, who were obligated to accord anyone thus accused the right of defense. Previously, no defense had been allowed. This provision was reaffirmed by the more stable government of 1382.[11] In 1378, a commission of eighty-one men, appointed to investigate those who had been proscribed by the Parte, restored fifty-seven families (pp. 183–84). In 1393, the power to ammonire was taken away from the Parte altogether (p. 118).

Simultaneously, the state diminished the power of the Parte by changing the composition of the Parte's governing body and disenfranchising its noble elements. The Parte had always been predominantly composed of and directed by conservative nobles from old, even feudal, families. In 1358, the Commune of Florence sought to make the actions of the Parte, especially the use of its power to ammonire, more balanced and just, by requiring that two additional captains, who were to be of *popolano* status (commoners), be added to the already existing captains, the governing body of the Parte. In 1366, the commune required that of the nine captains, five must be popolani, two must be artisans, and only two could be nobles.[12] These changes weakened the power of the Parte to promote factional conflict through their power to ammonire because some consensus had to be reached among these captains to accord the imputation of Ghibellinism. In 1378, the government of Florence reactivated the Ordinances of Justice, the enactments from 1292 that restricted magnates from holding most offices, damaging the political effectiveness of the Parte. The constant interference of the state in the power and structure of the Parte diminished the Parte's independence and quashed its sovereign status. Any attempt by the Parte to regain its former power was suppressed summarily.[13] Buonaccorso Pitti reported that by the early fifteenth century, the Parte had become so weakened that "the captains had difficulty in recruiting citizens to accompany them on processions."[14]

The Societies of the People, the organizations of all the people of the different *gonfaloni* (the sixteen divisions of the city) into citizen militias, political bodies, and units of taxation underwent a similar loss of vitality and increasing subordination to the state. Together the men of the gonfaloni had formed a citizen militia, active throughout the fourteenth century, that was used particularly to put down factional conflicts and revolutions against the state started by magnates. During the revolt of the Ciompi in 1378, the militia of the Societies of the People, when called by the Priors to defend the government, did not convene. Many of these popolani were sympathetic to the Ciompi cause. After this period, the citizen militia was no longer viewed as a reliable source of protection for the government, so that foreign mercenaries were increasingly used even for this purpose. The citizen militia of the Societies of the People was never convened after 1393.[15]

In the 1280s, the gonfaloni had started to acquire great political importance, their elected officers, the Gonfalonieri, assuming a place in the central government. By the 1350s, these Gonfalonieri sat as a college adjunct to the Priors so that most of the activities of the Priors required the consent of the Sixteen Gonfalonieri. However, the rise of the Gonfalonieri did not increase the political importance of the societies of the gonfaloni. As the Gonfalonieri became more important in the central government, they became increasingly separated from the gonfaloni. The Gonfalonieri were no longer elected by the gonfaloni but were extracted from the *borse* (election bags from which the names of those who would serve were extracted) for the major offices, just as were the other major officials. Consequently, they no longer represented the interests of the gonfaloni.[16] Thus, the gonfaloni as military and political organizations atrophied.

There is, again, universal agreement that the guilds were also in decline in the early fifteenth century; however, the depth of this decline is debated, Marvin Becker positing a thorough deterioration and Gene Brucker a slight one.[17] John Najemy sets the date of the definitive quelling of the role of the guilds in the government at the end of the fourteenth century.[18] Guild revenues in the period from 1400 to 1434 declined sharply so that the state no longer could rely on the guilds for fiscal support.[19] Membership fell, particularly among the middle and lower guilds, resulting in the admission of foreigners to these guilds.[20] The communal courts began taking more and more criminal jurisdiction away from the guilds. In the communal statutes of 1355, the only rules extant pertaining to the guilds were those for electing the consuls. The statutes of 1415, on the other hand, have whole tracts devoted to the guilds, showing a more active regulation of them. By 1415, the consuls of the guilds were elected by the Priors, the Gonfalonier of Justice, and the colleges.[21] (It should be noted that the Gonfalonier of Justice was an executive official similar to the Priors, and not the same as the Gonfalonieri of the societies.) Laws prohibiting monopolies were applied to all of the guilds, including the seven major guilds. These laws allowed workers who were not in the guilds to carry on trades that had previously been performed within the guilds, thus weakening the control of the guilds and destroying their ability to drive up prices on their products. Foreign artisans not in the guilds were protected by the state.

II
The Judicial System and the Territorial State

In other ways, too, the state interfered in the guilds and diminished their power. The state fixed prices of necessary goods, including comestibles and building materials. Even more significantly, the state allowed recourse to the communal courts in any judicial matter. Previously, this had not been the case. For instance, the statutes from 1290 of the Ars Campsorum, the Guild of Changers, stated that a changer was required to move his case before the consuls of the guilds or he could be expelled from the guild.[22] However, the communal statutes of 1415 posed the communal courts as an alternative. A significant block of cases was barred altogether from the guild courts, including falsity (falsification of a product) and debt created through a public instrument—that is, a document drawn up by a notary and recognized by the state. Cases of defaulting and fleeing debtors were tried only in the courts of the foreign rectors and the court of the Mercanzia, the merchant court superior to the guilds. These restrictions on jurisdiction applied not only to the middle and lower guilds but to the seven major guilds as well. The foreign official of the Lana Guild, who served as the judge for this organization, had his power diminished. The state no longer supported the Lana Guild's control of the *sottoposti*, the various groups of workers who labored in the cloth industry as dyers, combers, and other manual laborers.[23] The foreign official of Lana could no longer order these workers to be tortured in judicial proceedings.

Just as all of the guilds became more subordinated to the state, so, too, did the Mercanzia. The Mercanzia had always been dependent on state support. After state recognition of this merchant court in 1308, the communal government had added more and more areas of jurisdiction to its sphere of interest. As the state's support of the Mercanzia grew, it gradually became an arm of the state. The Mercanzia was largely regulated by communal statute. State intervention in the Mercanzia was frequent—for instance, in 1399, 1401, and 1411, when the major offices of the commune intervened to approve extensions for the foreign officials of the Mercanzia who were in office at these times.[24] State recognition of the Mercanzia in 1308, almost from the time of its formation, prevented the guild courts from developing any areas of exclusive jurisdiction. The Mercanzia did not usurp areas of communal jurisdiction but increasingly took power away from the guilds. The Mercanzia, initially a court of international commerce, became a court of superior jurisdiction for all of the twenty-one guilds, just as it appears to be in the statutes of 1415. All guild members had recourse to the Mercanzia in any judicial matters concerning commerce. Cases that could not be tried by the guilds, such as falsity and debt aggravated by defaulting and fleeing, could be tried in the courts of the Mercanzia and the foreign rectors.

In the early fifteenth century, the guilds, formerly independent, also became more subordinate to the state as they became more reliant on the state to promote their interests. The state afforded the guilds protection through protective tariffs. Florence fought major wars, especially the one with Pisa in the early fifteenth century, to gain a port for its merchants, and funded a galley to promote trade. In 1393, the government of Florence began discouraging merchants from using foreign ships to carry their merchandise. Legislation prohibited taking gold outside the Florentine borders. In sum, the guilds were no longer corporate entities exercising great control over the state. The guilds were declining in power and independence as the ever-stronger territorial state subordinated them. Between 1382 and 1400, patrician and nonpatrician guildsmen embraced a consensus-based system of electoral politics, rather than a corporate-based system.[25] Merchants could no longer rely on the guilds for aid but increasingly sought aid from the larger forum, the communal government.[26]

Finally, the confraternities, religious groups that became politically active in the early fifteenth century, were supervised and then quashed by the state. The confraternities were a source of trouble for the state because they fostered factional conflict and private agreements on public matters properly regulated in public assemblages. In the late fourteenth century, the state sought to control these groups by appointing their officers and supervising their assets. In the early fifteenth century, the confraternities were forbidden to engage in any political activities.[27] In 1419, a provision was enacted prohibiting confraternities altogether. Some of the confraternities were reestablished but only those that gained the approval of the Signoria.[28] In 1443 officials of the three highest offices were forbidden to join confraternities.[29]

By the end of the fourteenth century, the sovereignty of the commune was no longer shared with the corporate entities that formerly composed it but was about to be threatened from another direction. An increasingly strong aristocracy was forming. After 1434, the Medici were successful in gathering a large group of clients and using changes in electoral procedure to assist in the election of Medici adherents to the highest offices. Extraordinary executive offices were created and given important duties in an attempt to circumvent the councils and operate without their consent. The patriciate used these offices to exercise control over other branches of the government. These changes in the government were foreshadowed by emergency measures necessitated by the financial crisis and altering the basis of power in the government. By the end of the period of prolonged war, by 1431–33, the top Florentine merchants and bankers were beginning to have a great deal of control over politics and institutions because the resources for the wars and government expenses were coming from this restricted class. The Medici, in particular, were floating the Florentine economy. While few were opposed to these wars, the erosion of constitutional liberties was a direct result of the wars and the financial dependence on the patriciate that they fostered.[30] The necessity of having experts to run the economy, politics, and the war effort began a process that later resulted in the division between the governed and the governing, a new element in Florentine government. Clientele relationships were forming that were able to circumvent the divieti laws for offices and gain continuity of officeholding, if not for one family, at least for a patronage network. However, another push for accountability in administration took place because of the financial crisis (p. 113). Laws were enacted aimed at creating a system so complex that personal influence, especially in tax assessments, was limited (p. 75). In the early fifteenth century, the patriciate was not yet in control of the government or the judicial branch. Some of the offices that were later powerful executive offices had been created but were either not functioning for the benefit of the patriciate or had not yet taken sufficient control to threaten the independence of the court system or the republican nature of the government. The court system had not been overrun by the executive branch in the early fifteenth century.

Many of the agencies that were close to the executive had judicial powers, but none of them were using these powers abusively to subvert or override the regular judicial system in the early fifteenth century. The regular judicial system was not showing signs of attrition except in the late 1420s, when, like every branch of government, it was adversely affected by spending cuts necessitated by the financial crisis. Even the allowance of the Otto di Guardia was cut to one-third.[31] The Otto di Guardia, the agency that would weaken the criminal courts and usurp their functions in the late fifteenth century, did not try criminal cases, except among *stipendiarii*, or mercenaries, and *conestabiles*, or domestic soldiers and guards, in the early fifteenth century. The Otto remained an investigatory body carrying on surveillance to detect subversion of the state. Information gathered about suspected traitors was turned over to the regular criminal court system, which apprehended the suspects and tried the cases. The only cases the Otto tried were infractions by stipendiarii and conestabiles, which normally had nothing to do with treason, were frequently conducted against foreigners, and usually resulted in small fines. The Otto gained broader powers of investigation but did not become a full trial court until the mid-fifteenth century. It was only granted the *balia* (full authority) to try political crimes in 1434, as is shown by its change in name from Otto di Guardia to Otto di Guardia e Balia and its activities in the trial of political crimes. The Otto possessed this balia temporarily and soon reverted to the status and name of Otto di Guardia. The Otto did not usually possess balia after 1434, although it did for six months in 1453 and for two years after 1458, these powers becoming more routine after this.[32] After 1434, the Otto did usurp jurisdictions that they were not legally authorized to treat. The Dieci di Guerra, the commission that was given balia over war and war-related activities, was sometimes formed out of the Otto plus two and was sometimes constituted independently. The office of the Dieci, likewise, was an important and independent executive office, but the Dieci was prohibited from intervening in internal politics.[33] Many of its tasks had to be approved by the Priors and the colleges.[34] Before 1434, the Dieci, like the Otto, had judicial powers only over stipendiarii, and probably only had these powers when the Otto became the Dieci in times of war.

The Tower Officials, other officials closely affiliated with the executive, possessed real political power but had no opportunity to use their power to benefit the patriciate. The Tower Officials supervised the lands and rights owned by the Commune of Florence, a large part of which was land confiscated from rebels and those who had been banned. The Tower Officials had judicial duties but were not in charge of deciding who the rebels and the banned were; either the foreign rectors or the Priors and the Gonfalonier decided this crucial question. The Tower Officials decided what property belonged to the rebels and the banned, but information concerning this was collected by a host of other officials and presented to the Tower Officials in the presence of the foreign rectors. Other officials under the foreign rectors were also involved in recovering communal lands. Anything but strict adherence to the procedures established by statute for the confiscation of goods would have been difficult because of this coordination in jurisdiction. The Office of the Tower was made increasingly systematic and efficient from the 1340s to the early fifteenth century, and efforts were still being made to reorganize and streamline the Office of the Tower as late as 1415. An efficiently run commission for the administering and renting of communal property acted against the interests of the patrician class, who sought to usurp communal land, and in the interest of the commune itself. Many of the 1415 rubrics pertaining to the Tower Office were aimed at making usurpation impossible. Great effort was expended in the recuperation of communal property, which became registered in one definitive list.

The office of the Conservatori delle Leggi, which investigated those extracted for communal office for some blemish that would disqualify them from office, such as illegitimate birth or tax delinquency, was undoubtedly used as a weapon of factional conflict among the oligarchs. However, since no faction clearly dominated before 1434, all factions

The Judicial System and the Territorial State

availed themselves of this vehicle of vituperation. This office was not established until 1429.

In the early fifteenth century, the only executive offices that had great powers of interference in the regular judicial system were the Priors and the Gonfalonier of Justice, that is, the Signoria. Their power was based not on *de facto* usurpation but on statute, and to a certain extent was logical and not necessarily abusive; it would be most unusual if a judicial branch staffed by foreigners had no supervision from the executive branch of the central government. Although the Priors and the Gonfalonier had great rights of interference, the early fifteenth century was not a period in which they frequently wielded these rights abusively. In the 1390s, the Priors accepted very few civil litigious petitions. In the cases of petitions that they did accept, they worked in conjunction with the regular court system. When they did intervene in a case being handled by the regular court system, their intervention took the form of consultation, not of decision. Records from the Deliberazioni dei Signori e Collegi, Ordinaria Autorità, show that the Signoria did not frequently settle disputes that had already been adjudicated by the regular court system until the 1460s. This trend of intervention began in the 1430s and 1440s, that is, after the Medici returned.[35] Court records from the early fifteenth century show little interference from the Signoria in criminal cases. Zorzi records no *bullectini*, mandates from the executive to the foreign rectors, in the year 1400–1401, and a sample of cases presented here from 1425 to 1428 from the court of the Podestà shows only two.[36] The only class of crime in which the Signoria frequently involved itself was tax delinquency. The extremely threatening behavior of the Signoria toward tax delinquents was mainly a ploy to secure payment. The Signoria threatened capital punishment, which could be commuted to no penalty at all with any sign that payment was forthcoming.[37] The offices of the executive branch were not nearly so concerned with gaining power for the patriciate or any certain patrician faction as they were with raising funds for defensive and offensive wars that secured trading rights and ports and protected Florence from the dukes of Milan.

In the fourteenth and early fifteenth centuries, few *balie*, emergency governments holding extraordinary power temporarily supplanting the normal legislative system and making decisions in times of crisis, were created. There was a balia in 1378 which lasted for one week and carried out the reforms promoted by the Ciompi revolt. The Balia of 1382 ended the Ciompi government and lasted for one month. The Balia of 1393 was occasioned by the discovery of the conspiracy of the Alberti, who apparently had plans to become the lords of Florence, and lasted for two weeks. The Balia of 1433, lasting for six weeks, signaled the defeat of Cosimo and the attempted entrenchment of the Albizzi in the government. In 1434, the situation was reversed, this balia exiling Rinaldo degli Albizzi and reinstating Cosimo.[38] The Balia of 1393 created the Council of Eighty-One, which was given extraordinary powers to circumvent the Council of the Commune and the Council of the People in imposing *prestanze* (forced loans to the government), hiring troops and electing the Dieci di Guerra. In other matters, the Council of Eighty-One voted at the side of the other councils. The legislative councils during the tenure of the Ottantuno reserved the right to review tax assessments and set interest rates.[39] Many safeguards were enacted to prevent favoritism and corruption in tax assessments. Although this council strengthened the position of the top officeholders and the top officeholding class because it included top offices in its membership, its main purpose was to give greater support to the war effort. All the balie of the fourteenth and fifteenth centuries were caused by real military crises, not by patrician machinations.[40] Power was still distributed among a large number of officials, whose membership changed frequently. The powers of the Eighty-One were rescinded in 1404 and the government returned to its constitutional form.[41] In 1411, the legislative councils passed a law curtailing the power of the executive branch to engage in military operations.[42]

During the late fourteenth and early fifteenth centuries, few irregularities in elections occurred. After the Alberti conspiracy in 1393, the government was anxious to weed out political opponents. The balia destroyed the scrutiny (list of eligible men) of 1385 and appointed *accoppiatori* (election secretaries) with authority to rearrange the existing borse and eliminate names from the borse of the Gonfalonier of Justice, putting the names instead in the borse of the Priors. In 1393 the election rules were suspended, when the accoppiatori, elected by the Priors, picked the succeeding Priors.[43] This was done because the new scrutiny for the *tre maggiori* (major offices) was not completed. The period from 1405 to 1414 was particularly free of election irregularities.[44] The period 1414–1423 was a tranquil and prosperous decade, also a period of regular elections.[45] The next *a mano* elections, that is, direct appointment of the executive magistracy by the accoppiatori, an emergency measure, occurred in October 1433.[46] The rules concerning elections, which called for scrutiny and extraction, normally were followed.

This regard for constitutionality, legality, and republican institutions in government was apparent not only before 1434 but to some degree after. The Medici based their regime on alterations in election procedure, fearing that greater changes in the constitutional form of the government would be unpalatable to all classes of Florentines, even the other patriciate and client families that supported Medici rule.[47] Values that Floren-

The Judicial System and the Territorial State

tine society held sacred, such as social mobility, rapid rotation of office, and shared rule at the top, were embodied in these constitutional forms. Despite the fact that the Medici regime did not gain full security from these electoral changes, no more could be changed without incurring insurmountable opposition. Opposition was keen enough to the changes that were made (pp. 23, 27–28). The Medici were not able to dispense with the Councils of the People and of the Commune until the 1470s, although they circumvented the councils by ruling through balie. However, the creation of these balie required the assent of the ancient councils, which they were not always inclined to give. In 1454, for instance, the councils dissolved the balia and returned to republican forms (pp. 22, 88). The Balia, or Council of One Hundred, was not made permanent until 1458, and even then, many of the decisions of the Balia required the assent of the ancient councils (pp. 114–15).

Thus, the executive agencies that had judicial powers were not claiming new areas of jurisdiction and forcing a process of attrition on the regular judicial branch. Also, these agencies were prevented from exercising undue power by a system of checks and balances between the judiciary and the agencies in which every judicial duty that was performed by the agencies was checked by a court within the regular judicial branch. Sensitive jobs continued to be entrusted to the foreign rectors and the members of their entourages. All officials in the government, including those in the agencies, were mandatorily syndicated by the Executor, that is, tried concerning their performance in office.

The performance of the Tower Officials was supervised in several ways. The areas of competence of the Tower Officials and of the governors of the gabelle (excise taxes), with whom they were closely affiliated, were checked by those of the judge of camera and gabelle, one of the judges under the Captain of the People. If the Office of the Tower had been unduly controlled by the Signoria or had been promoting justice for the benefit of the patriciate, the court of the judge of camera and gabelle would have supplied a regular court alternative. This judge tried many of the same cases as the Tower Officials and the governors of the gabelle. Likewise, other functions of the Tower Officials were shared and checked by functions of important notaries that existed under each of the foreign rectors, the notaries over the consignment of communal goods. As Marvin Becker has shown, from the time of Walter of Brienne, the regular judiciary was enlisted in the effort to prevent the siphoning off of communal goods.[48] The Tower Officials were also involved in this effort.

Other important officials in sensitive positions were also checked by the regular judiciary. The Officials of Grascia, officials with judicial powers whose predominant job was the prevention of famine in Florence, were monitored by all of the foreign rectors. Many of the duties performed by the Officials of Grascia were coordinated with those performed by the foreign rectors, particularly the Podestà. Likewise, the court of the Podestà carried out the same functions as the court of the Mercanzia. The Otto before 1434 turned over the cases it investigated to the foreign rectors for trial. The consuls of the guilds were monitored by the Podestà, his court also forming a court with superior jurisdiction to their own. He enforced monopoly and alimentary regulations on the guilds. The defaulting and fleeing debt proceedings carried out in the Podestà's court reexamined decisions made in the consuls' court. With this system of checks and balances still very actively in operation, the agencies were discouraged from acting in an extralegal or corrupt manner.

A case from 1420 against Johannes quondam Nicoli de Nursia illustrates how these checks and balances worked in practice in the court system. Johannes was a procurator for Magnificus vir Carolus quondam Bartolomei dominus magister de Tarlatus sive de Petramala, obviously an important person. Carolus had been condemned for an unspecified crime in the court of the Captain in 1408. Johannes was hired to get this condemnation canceled or annulled. First, Johannes went to the court of the Podestà and produced all sorts of allegations before him. When this did not work, he tried to persuade the Podestà's notary to cancel the condemnation. This failing, he proceeded to try to persuade the notary of the camera of the acts (the place where the court case records were stored during and after the trial), then made similar attempts before the Tower Officials, the Quinque Rerum, and the minor syndic to get the condemnation removed from the books and registers. At this point, criminal charges were initiated against him by inquisition of the Captain's court. He was contumacious and condemned to a fine of 1,000 lire. The many officials he approached demonstrates the difficulty of corrupting officials within the court system.[49]

What follows is not a fast-paced narrative of the territorial state but a detailed articulation of the officials of the judicial system and their functions, an institutional history. I undertook the study because it fills a gap in our historical knowledge and sheds light on the continuation of the territorial state. By tracing the functions of the judicial officials, I demonstrate three interrelated things. First, few islands of authority existed within the judicial system or the government which were not directly interrelated with the rest of the judicial system. Indeed, the judicial system seems to have been a coordinated and unified whole. Few, if any, officials were left on their own to make decisions without reference to other officials. This close interrelating made improbable the use of the judicial system as an instrument of patrician takeover, the very structure of the judicial system inhibiting patrician manipulation. The fully articulated system demonstrates a network of checks and balances which thwarted corruption and misappropriation of power. Second, only when the entire system is pieced together can the reader observe a bureaucracy at work. What seems like random activity to a casual observer coagulates into a working organization on closer examination. It is the working bureaucracy of the judicial system and of the government as a whole which is the basic creation and the primary trait of the territorial state. Third, only when the entire structure of the judicial system is fully revealed can the links between this system and the social life of Renaissance Florence be made. The way that the guilds, for instance, were regulated by the courts suggests conclusions about the characteristics and vitality of these social organizations. Emphasis placed on the prevention of certain crimes, often signaled by an official appointed to deal with these crimes, indicates important social problems. It is for the examination of these themes, which require a full explanation of the court system, that I have written such a detailed account. At every pertinent point, I have attended to the vicissitudes of political authority.

The coordinated, working bureaucracy made the corruption of one section of the government or one agency almost impossible. It was not easy to change or manipulate a large bureaucracy that was already in motion. However, once the Medici succeeded in taking over the system, the bureaucracy, acting almost with a life of its own, facilitated the rule of a prince. Once a prince was ruling, the tool of surveillance, which had been developed to aid law and order, promoted the continuation of the rule of the prince. All the forces of the government made opposition to the prince futile. The early and mid-fifteenth century witnessed the difficulty that the Medici faction had in assuming control of a fully operative system, while the late fifteenth century witnessed the difficulty that other segments of society had in getting rid of a prince once he seized control.

2

INQUISITION PROCEDURE AND THE GENERAL POWERS OF THE FOREIGN RECTORS

THE JUDICIAL SYSTEM of medieval and Renaissance Florence was headed by the three foreign rectors: the Podestà, the Captain of the People, and the Executor of the Ordinances of Justice. They came from outside Florence, mainly from other Italian cities, and brought with them retinues that included most of the officials manning the Florentine judicial system: the judges, the police officials, and some of the notaries. Aside from the regular court system, however, there were agencies that performed specific functions and had judicial powers over material pertaining to these functions. For instance, the Officials of Grascia guarded against grain shortages and tried cases of hoarding. The Tower Officials supervised communal lands, goods, and rights and tried cases in which communal lands, goods, and rights were usurped. The Otto di Guardia enforced the rules pertaining to the *stipendiarii* (mercenaries) and investigated offenses committed by stipendiarii and seditious activities. The judicial officials of these agencies were not autonomous from the regular court system; in fact, their duties were coordinated with the functions of the regular courts. Together these two systems formed the judicial system of Florence.

In this chapter, I discuss the powers and limitations of the foreign rectors. First, I examine the procedure according to which they ran their courts, since the judicial officials cannot be understood apart from the procedural framework that delineated their functions and tied their functions together. Second, I discuss the general powers and limitations common to all three rectors. I follow with short sections on the ecclesiastical court system, which channeled cases away from the secular court system and thus imposed limitations on it; and on the judicial system of Venice and how it compared with that of Florence. Once the general parameters of the criminal law system, especially the common characteristics of the three rectors, are drawn, the characteristics and functions of individual officials can be treated. In the chapters that follow this one, I discuss the subordinate officials of the foreign rectors and then each of the rectors in turn, including the history of each office.

I demonstrate how the criminal law system became more active and seized the initiative in regulating society as inquisition initiation became prevalent. These regulatory functions became institutionalized in police forces, methods of collecting proof, and rectors that could initiate any kind of criminal case. This system became more logically organized and efficient, which reflected the continued development of the territorial state. The strengthened public sector exercised greater control over the private sector, keeping it within legal bounds, containing vendettas and overbearing behavior, and posing greater resistance to private incursions on the government. The public sector was strong enough to carry out this program and was motivated by reasons of public utility to do so. The court system was very active in trying to maintain law and order throughout all ranks of society. One unified court system was much more accountable than several overlapping systems. Accountability was certainly a goal of the criminal law system—it was the purpose, for instance, of reading the condemnations in the councils. Attempts at fairness within the system, such as accurate recording of testimony and having officials that monitored sensitive parts of the procedure, worked toward greater equality and benefit for all classes. Adherence to statute, while it could not guarantee equality of social classes before the law, was the best available method of promoting equality and accountability.

Inquisition Procedure

The courts of the three foreign rectors conducted their criminal trials using inquisition procedure, a trial procedure in which the court system had the ability to initiate and prosecute cases *ex officio*, although it also could accept accusations. The state courts were responsible for most parts of the procedure: gathering information, compelling witnesses, weighing evidence, sentencing, and executing. Usually even initiating was conducted by the state. When a crime was committed and no accuser came forward to accuse, the courts initiated the proceedings. This characteristic of inquisition procedure, its lack of dependence on a private accuser, encouraged a transition from crime as a private matter to crime as a public matter. Likewise, in the proof stage of the trial, inquisition procedure encouraged the development of methods of independent investigation, such as sending out routine police forces with appointed rounds, gathering information and attaching of witnesses at the scene of the crime, and compelling these witnesses to appear in court. Unfortunately, the independent sources of information which were increasingly used included torture, public fame initiation and public fame proof.

I will explicate inquisition procedure here by moving chronologically through a hypothetical trial. The information presented is drawn from cases, from records of actual practice. A more sophisticated portrait of inquisition procedure could be extracted from the tracts of the learned law jurists, but this would not necessarily reflect actual practice and would prejudge results drawn from practice. Criminal trials were composed of several main parts: accusation or public initiation, citation, possible dilatory exceptions of the defendant, response of the defendant with possible exceptions, examination of the witnesses and presentation of other proof for both sides, publication of the witnesses, rebuttal of the witnesses, judgment, and execution. The proceedings were intended to move along at a quick pace; condemnation or absolution had to be reached forty days from the examination of the defendant (*Stat.* 3.2).

Cases were initiated in the courts of the foreign rectors in four major ways: private accusation, *ex officio* initiation, public fame initiation, and denunciation by a public official, usually a rector or syndic of the county and district. Private accusation was the only private method of initiation, the other three being public forms. *Bullectini* and *tamburazioni* were minor methods of initiation before 1434.

Despite the growing use of public initiation and the infringement of public initiation on traditional areas of private accusation in the late fourteenth and early fifteenth centuries, the Florentine court system continued to encourage private accusation (see Chap. 8). In cases initiated by private accusation, the accuser relieved the state of the effort and expense of the defense. The accuser had great responsibilities: paying court costs, such as the expense of the citations; paying gabelles (taxes); giving an oath that he justly accused and would prosecute the case to its conclusion; putting together the proof; and risking fines if the case failed. Most importantly, he named the culprit. If the accuser lost the case, he paid twenty soldi a day for each day the defendant was detained in prison (*Stat.* 3.111). He recovered the court costs only if he won—in which instance, the defendant paid them. However, by 1415 the state did not allow cases that would normally be initiated by private accusation or cases already initiated by private accusation to go unprosecuted. Crimes not privately accused became public matters and could be prosecuted *ex officio* by the rectors (*Stat.* 3.2).

Accusation changed character during this period. Initially, an accusation-initiated case had a very strong private character, almost like a civil case, in which the goal of the litigation was conflict resolution. The judge acted more like an arbitrator than a judge. The accuser was responsible for a great deal of the trial: naming the defendant, gathering the prosecution witnesses, and creating the *libellus* to which the prosecution witnesses responded. The defense witnesses, on the other hand, responded to the *exceptiones*, or *defensiones*, which were created by the defendant. The judge orchestrated the trial but interfered little in it.[1] Accusation-initiated trials were almost outside the inquisition system. But as the public nature of crime became more recognized, as the state became more interested in prosecuting crime for the public good, the judge began to interfere more in the trial of these cases, especially in the proof stage. The judge could call whatever witnesses he thought had information, elicit whatever testimony he liked, and ask whatever questions he thought to be relevant. The judge became more interested in seeing the criminal prosecuted. Accusation cases began to be conducted just like inquisition cases.[2] In fact, by 1432, the courts became so adamant that cases not go unprosecuted that a *provvisione* was passed that cases initiated by accusers resulting in absolutions would be initiated again by the state and retried. Accusers who did not want to see the culprit punished had been acting in collusion with the culprit, initiating the case but deliberately providing insufficient proof, thereby getting the culprit exonerated without paying for an instrument of peace and without risking that the state would initiate the case *ex officio.* Apparently, the state was very aggressive in initiating cases.[3]

For some crimes, only a restricted group of appropriate people was allowed to accuse, those who had a direct interest in the crime through their relationship with the victim. Accusations could be taken from any person related by blood to the injured person to the seventh grade of relationship. Also, a husband could accuse for his wife, a master for his apprentice, a lord for his serf or servant, a syndic for his corporation, and a tutor for his minor (*Stat.* 3.2).

The rules for private accusation varied considerably. In some cases, those of an entirely private nature, only the restricted group of accusers could accuse. In other cases, particularly cases against officials, anyone could accuse, provided that this person upheld all of the responsibilities of private accusation. In still other cases, accusations could be made with diminished responsibilities or by secret accusers. The names of secret accusers were known to the court, since sometimes secret accusers collected rewards for their accusations, but were never revealed to the defendant. Secret accusation was used particularly in crimes in which detection was difficult or in which the defendant was likely to be of such a powerful status that intimidation militated against personal accusation. Accusation was made easiest in cases in which the commune most desired information; these included crimes of officials, crimes of magnates, rebellion, sumptuary infractions, and sex infractions.[4] No crime of a serious nature required accusation by relatives (*Stat.* 3.2). Cases of diminished responsibility were also cases of diminished accountability. While the rectors were obligated to proceed in cases initiated by real private accusation, the rectors were less likely to find sufficient cause to proceed in cases initiated by a less accountable form of accusation. Even in most cases in which accusation was restricted to family, the state could initiate proceedings *ex officio.* In these cases, the rectors were required to request an accusation from the logical accusers, but if the logical accusers did not accuse, the state initiated a prosecution *ex officio* (*Stat.* 3.2).

The great variety of ways in which the court system would accept accusations shows that it encouraged and facilitated accusation, even in the later period. Whereas once the court system had been deferential to the honor and rights of the offended party, deference to these feelings was less of an issue in the early fifteenth century. The court system encouraged accusation because the responsibility and expense was transferred to the accuser.

The three other major forms of initiation, *ex officio*, public fame, and denunciation by an official, were all public forms. Public initiation was becoming more and more common throughout the fourteenth century and would become clearly preponderant over private accusation in the early fifteenth century (see Chap. 8). By 1415, public initiation was permitted in almost all cases.

Public fame initiation, transcending its origins in the prosecution of notorious crimes to become a general method of initiation, was the predominant form of public initiation by 1425. Although public fame was traditionally a kind of proof, it was used in the Florentine court system as both initiation and proof. The cases from the court of the Podestà from 1425 to 1428 show public fame being used as a case initiation, while the statutes very frequently prescribe the use of public fame witnesses in the proof stage of the procedure.[5] The same public fame accusers who initiated a case could also be used as witnesses at the proof stage, sometimes with the addition of information gleaned from torture. The accusers, like the witnesses, had no direct knowledge of the case, attesting only to what was rumored in Florence. Public fame initiation was a method of tapping the knowledge of the community or of a particular neighborhood. It was frequently used in cases in which other evidence was difficult to uncover, such as sodomy cases (*Stat.* 3.115). Public fame accusations could be gathered at the scene of the crime or at the bench if a general inquest was opened. These accusers did not have the responsibilities attributed to real accusers nor did they have to be accountable for their statements, since they were not attesting to any direct knowledge. Public fame accusers were not required to reveal the sources of their knowledge.[6] These accusers were not anonymous, since they were known to the court and since they gave a full account of whatever facts were rumored by the community.

Ex officio initiations were originated by the rector or judge when cases were not instigated through public fame or accusation. Crimes which were interrupted *in flagranti* came to court as *ex officio* cases. In these cases, the reports of the *berrovarii* (policemen) or other police officials were considered authoritative; the statements of one notary, one *miles*, or two berrovarii were sufficient to convict (*Stat.* 3.189). The usual crimes apprehended *in flagranti* were bearing prohibited arms, playing prohibited games, and going out at night past curfew, although all crimes had the possibility of being interrupted *in flagranti*. Each rector had berrovarii who went out routinely to patrol for crime. Even during the last eight days of a rector's office, when he did not carry out his other judicial duties, his retinues went out to catch criminals *in flagranti* (*Stat.* 2.7). A person could be captured at the scene, or chased and captured when those at the scene of the crime named a culprit (*Stat.* 3.3). Other cases initiated *ex officio* were those in which the appropriate accusers refused to accuse. Reticent appropriate accusers may still have been the source of much of the information in the trial. An inquisition could be carried out in someone's favor; that is, although a family member did not want to accuse, he urged the judge to begin an inquest (*Stat.* 3.30). An *ex officio* case could also originate as a general inquisition in search of a culprit.[7]

Many cases came into the courts of the foreign rectors through denunciations by the syndics and rectors of the county and district. Syndics and rectors were minor officials who had duties in connection with taxation, apprehension of criminals, and judicial matters. The rectors, along with the other men of the *popolo* or *plebatu*, were responsible for solving crimes in their locality (*Stat.* 2.79). When a crime was reported to the rector or syndic in the locality, he denounced the crime to one of the foreign rectors who formed the inquisition and investigated the crime. All parts of the trial, other than the denunciation, were carried out by the central court system.

A small percentage of cases entered the criminal courts as *tamburazioni* and *bullectini*. Tamburazioni were accusations made by placing anonymous slips of paper in boxes located near the palaces of the rectors, usually the Executor. Bullectini were executive mandates ordering the courts to initiate cases or to perform other procedures. In the medieval and Renaissance courts of the rectors, tamburazioni were allowed in a very limited number of cases. In the fourteenth century, they were used in cases of *popolani* accusing magnates, as well as anyone accusing officials of committing offenses in office. Since the statutes of 1415 abolished the use of tamburazioni in accusing officials, and special judicial treatment of the magnate class was waning by the early fifteenth century, tamburazioni were becoming less important in the regular courts of the rectors, in which accountability and preservation of safeguards for the defendant were goals. Proceedings rarely issued from tamburazioni, since few tamburi indicated strong enough cases to warrant recognition.[8] The rector proceeded upon a tamburo if it contained sufficient evidence, or indicated witnesses who could give sufficient evidence, on which to found a case. However, in the 1430s, tamburazioni became a major method of information gathering and case initiating in the citizen-staffed courts of the Conservatori delle Leggi, the Ufficiali di Notte, and the Onestà.[9] These courts concentrated on perfecting means of surveillance despite the lack of accountability or reliability of such information. The procedure in these courts lacked the substantiality and solemnity of law.

Cases could be initiated through bullectini, mandates from officials of the executive branch, such as the Priors and the Gonfalonier, or the Dieci di Guerra, to the rectors, instructing them to proceed, condemn, or mete out a particular penalty. These cases appeared as *ex officio* cases in the acts of the rectors. Bullectini initiated cases, for example, against those who revealed government secrets or those who were delinquent in their taxes for over three years (*Stat.* 3.58). Bullectini were not common in the fourteenth or early fifteenth centuries. As the Otto di Guardia subjugated the courts of the rectors, more bullectini emanated from the Otto instructing the rectors, sometimes to commence a proceeding and sometimes to reach a certain sentence. By 1478, 19.32 percent of the sentences in the rectors' courts emanated from bullectini.[10]

After the accusations were made or the inquisitions formed, the judge had the defendant cited two times by different *nuntii* (messengers) on different days, at the expense of the accuser. If the defendant was a foreigner from a state that bordered on the county and district of Florence, or even a vagabond from a bordering state, the judge cited him the first time by sending a denouncing letter to the head of that state, giving the person a term in which to appear to defend himself in the court in Florence. If he did not appear in this term, he was cited a second time, this time like a person who was a foreigner from a more distant place or a domestic or foreign vagabond. A distant foreigner or vagabond was cited by having a citation read in several public places in Florence, such as the Piazza of Saint John the Baptist, Or San Michele, and the new and old markets. A *cedula* (notification, sometimes containing a citation or subpoena) was posted on the door of the Palace of the Podestà. Distant foreigners and vagabonds were cited both times like this. A person from the city, county, or district of Florence was cited two times at his home (*Stat.* 1.70).

From the statements of private accusers, public fame accusers, witnesses to the crime, or police officials, a document of accusation or inquisition was drawn up. When a defendant answered the citation, he came to court to respond to the charges leveled in the accusation or inquisition. When a person was cited, he could respond in one of four ways: by denying, confessing, posing an exception, or fleeing. If he came to court to deny or confess, he was detained if the crime was one prescribed to be punished by a corporal penalty, but he could be released if the crime carried a pecuniary penalty and if he provided a suitable security, such as oathswearers (those who pledged to pay in the event that the defendant did not appear) (*Stat.* 3.2). No debtor could ever be released without the consent of the creditor (*Stat.* 3.111).

If the defendant posed an exception, there were several kinds that he could use: there were dilatory exceptions that delayed the trial, exceptions that changed the severity of the crime, and exceptions that canceled the trial by alleging some circumstance that made it invalid or unnecessary. The usual dilatory exception was one brought by a procurator or a friend of the defendant that alleged that the defendant was out of town, did not know he had been cited, and needed a delay so he could learn about the trial, return to town, and have an opportunity to defend himself. Another kind of exception contained the confession to the crime but called for a reduction of the charges. Usually the party was alleging that the crime did not occur at night, so that the defendant was not liable for the double penalty of night; did not occur within fifty *braccia* (arm's lengths) of a church or a public street, so that he was not liable for the double penalty of place; or that the assault did not leave a lasting scar, debilitate a member, or cause blood to flow, all circumstances that aggravated assault charges.

Other exceptions asked that charges be put aside altogether. There were several usual kinds of these exceptions. One alleged that the inquisition was obscure, not formed properly, inept, vague, did not proceed, did not conclude, and lacked all solemnities and substantialities. Another contended that several crimes appeared in one inquisition. Still another alleged that the victim had not paid his taxes so was not entitled to be protected by the law. But the predominant one stated that an instrument of peace had been contracted between the victim and the defendant within fifteen days from the day of the crime. Thus, this private agreement abrogated the public trial, which could be terminated at this point. While this would seem to demonstrate a triumph of private over public aspects within the court system and to embody an intermediary step in development between vendetta and state procedures, such was not the case. Thomas Kuehn has shown that instruments of peace in criminal cases and arbitrations in civil cases played a significant part in the development of law and the decline of self-help. Both procedures were carefully monitored and regulated by the state and evidenced a strong state that could develop many techniques of maintaining law and order and could extend its reach even into cases such as mutual assaults. Arbitrations and instruments of peace went through a period of development during the early Renaissance, aided by *consilia* of jurists such as Nello da San Gemignano.[11] These mechanisms mitigated the rigid structure of statute law and were thus a necessary accompaniment to the strengthening of the state courts.

After the defendant was cited, he had a certain term (the length of which depended on the distance that he lived from Florence) in which to appear and respond. If he did not do so within this term, he became banned, that is, he was pronounced contumacious but was not yet condemned. Being banned was an interlocutory sentence. His name and the crime with which he was charged were announced at the gates of the rector's palace and in his *popolo* by a public banner, or crier. If the defendant was from the *contado*, or district, a *nuntius* was sent by the foreign rector with a document of notification of the ban to the defendant's house or the house of the rector of the popolo. If the defendant was from the city, this document was taken to his house. In the ban, the judge set a new term, the term of the ban, within which time the defendant was again required to come to court. The length of this term was at the discretion of the judge, quite an important discretionary power, since when this term ended, the defendant became condemned on account of contumaciousness. The length of this term depended not just on the place but on the quality of the person and the quality of the crime. During this term, the defendant was not yet condemned: if he appeared and paid the gabelle stipulated by the ban, he could still defend himself in court. If he did not appear, he was considered to have confessed to the crime and was therefore condemned, except in cases of assassins and those hiring assassins (*Stat.* 3.125). A person could, therefore, be condemned in his absence. No one could be declared contumacious before twenty days from the first citation. If the defendant was absent from the city and did not receive the citation, he was required to take an oath to this effect. The time of *instantia*, the term from start to finish of the case, was considered not to have run. This absence could not exceed four months.

If, instead, the defendant came to court, he could confess or deny. Procurators or advocates were assigned by the judge to whoever needed them in civil and criminal cases, but knowledgeable counsel could not be sought in criminal cases, that is, the defendant could not ask for a *consilium* to be drawn up by a jurist (*Stat.* 2.10; 2.81). Confession led to conviction. Some confessions were motivated by a reduced fine, which was a benefit of confessing. A defendant who confessed as his first response paid a reduced penalty of three-fourths of the penalty. Likewise, people confessed if they thought conviction was inevitable, as in cases of crimes interrupted *in flagranti.* Confessions were often extracted under torture. In cases in which torture was used, the defendant originally responded with a denial. If there was some evidence of guilt but not enough to convict, the defendant could be tortured until he confessed. Sometimes public fame proof was combined with torture in order to convict. For instance, a person accused of price fixing or forming monopolies could be tortured by the Executor, if public fame information was given by one person against the defendant (*Stat.* 3.87). It was desirable from the judges' perspective to exact a confession, since confession was considered a sure proof of guilt. When the judgments of the judges and rectors were reviewed in the syndication process, enough proof had to be in evidence to warrant the conviction. Sometimes judges only condemned to partial penalties in cases in which confessions were missing.[12] Confessions and proof through two witnesses of sight, on the other hand, were considered to be such conclusive proofs that even if some formality of procedure was omitted, the trial and condemnation were still valid (*Stat.* 3.18). For a civil case involving less than 100 lire, even an extrajudicial confession before two witnesses was sufficient proof (*Stat.* 2.4).

Because of this need for certain proof, torture was frequently used. Torture was permitted in the trial of a limited but substantial number of crimes. Evidence contradicting the denial of the defendant was allegedly a precondition for the use of torture, but in the trials of certain crimes, this safeguard was allowed to be omitted. The judge made a pronouncement that the case was one suitable for the use of torture based on the kind of crime and preceding convicting evidence, if it existed (*Stat.* 3.110). Torture was used in cases of highway robbery, robbery at night, falsification, destruction of crops at night, rape of an honest or religious woman, transmission of information to an enemy, and homicide, only if preceding incriminating evidence existed. But in conspiracy, incitement to riot, sedition, usurpation of communal property, assault of a rector, abduction for ransom, and sodomy, all procedural safeguards were waived.[13] The courts had a free hand in extracting confessions by torture in these crimes.

Torture had wider use than its normal use for extracting confessions. If a culprit abducted someone, especially a child, in order to exact a ransom, the culprit or his relatives could be captured and tortured until the captive was released (*Stat.* 3.113). If someone took a Florentine official who had immunity to court, whether this court was in or out of the city, the accuser could be tortured until he retracted the molesting accusation (*Stat.* 3.82). Accusers could be tortured until they admitted that their accusation was false, and witnesses until they admitted to false testimony. The statutes specify that no popolano making an accusation against a magnate could be tortured, implying that other accusers could be subjected to torture under the right conditions (*Stat.* 3.110).

The judge was normally required to make a pronouncement that torture was appropriate and would be applied in the case. The defendant or his procurator had one day to refute the legality of the use of torture before the defendant was led off to be tortured. During torture, he was interrogated as to his knowledge of the alleged events contained in the accusation or inquisition. The judge was interested in collecting corroborative material as well as confessions. Because judges in the early fourteenth century apparently abused torture (if an abuse can be made more abusive), after 1346 foreign criminal notaries were required to be present at tortures to insure some adherence to procedure.[14] A confession given under torture was not valid; the confession had to be repeated at the bench. Consequently, all of the acts of the foreign rectors state that confessions were spontaneously given, whether in fact they were, or whether they were extracted by torture.

Torture was used in cases in which the defendant responded with a denial and the proof presented was sufficient to torture but insufficient to condemn without confession. Torture trials were contested litigations. However, most contested litigations consisted of denial by the defendant, preparation of the defense and prosecution, examination of witnesses for both sides, and a judicial decision by the judges and rector.

After the cited defendant responded, the defense and the prosecution had ten days to prepare their cases. The prosecution laid out its case, improving on the accusation, adding further statements, and creating the *capitula*, or chapters, the document containing the case that the prosecution would try to prove. In inquisition-initiated cases, the inquisition, often created from the preliminary inquest, the statements of public fame accusers, or the accounts of officials, formed the basis. The defendant, likewise, set up his witnesses and defense documents, usually called articles, but sometimes also called capitula. The prosecution witnesses were always said to respond to the prosecution's capitula (*Stat.* 3.2). The defense witnesses were said to respond to the defense articles in the statutes of 1322–25,[15] and similarly in the preambles to the cases in the *libri testium ad defensam*,[16] but in the statutes of 1415, they were also said to respond to the capitula of the prosecution (*Stat.* 3.2). Interrogation was a regulated but not a strictly formularized matter, despite its dependence on the capitula. The judge had a great deal of latitude in the way he proceeded. If criminal procedure was similar to civil, the judge had the power to make interrogations additional to the capitula whenever the interest of equity moved him. The witnesses could be examined over anything introduced or produced during the trial or over anything that the prosecution or the defense wanted (*Stat.* 2.14).

In any criminal case, the judge could call witnesses not gathered by either of the parties (*Stat.* 3.2). New witnesses and new capitula could be added during the ten days after the response, but the judge was prohibited from accepting any more witnesses or capitula during the ten days following this, using this ten days to examine the witnesses. Both the prosecution and the defense witnesses responded item by item to the capitula. The judge and the notaries received the witnesses and interrogated them about their aim in testifying, the source of their knowledge, the place of the crime, those present, and all other circumstances pertaining to the crime (*Stat.* 3.8). The freedom with which the judge could examine the witnesses was a feature of inquisition procedure which encouraged heavy reliance on testimony and promoted equitable resolution of cases. Witnesses could be compelled to come to court. The judges were required to cite the parties to be present for the examination of the witnesses, but the examination could proceed in their absence. The examining of a witness by the judge and the recording of his statements by a criminal notary were required to be carried on continuously without interruption and completed in one sitting, proceeding from the first capitulum to the last. The allegations of both parties, which the judge was required to hear, were made after the examination of the witnesses.

After the ten days for examining witnesses, the statements of the witnesses were published within the next three days—that is, copies of the statements were given to the two parties. After these three days, the parties had six days to rebut the witnesses. If any false testimony was discovered, no faith could be put in the statements of the witness. The responsibility for rebutting a witness for intentional falsification was left up to the opposing party and was not the responsibility of the judge (*Stat.* 3.2), although in this area, too, the judge undoubtedly became more independent and active.

Most crimes had a set amount of proof which was required to condemn—for example, two witnesses of sight and two of public fame. This would seem to limit the discretion of the judge and make his decisions automatic, again tending to give justice a formulaic character. However, judgments did not function like this in practice. If a litigation was contested, the proof was weighed by all the judges and the rector. In practice, there was a great deal of inexactitude concerning the quality of proof and the ways different qualities of proof could be combined. In the trials of many crimes, the judge was given a great deal of discretion, even in the proof stage.[17]

The amount of proof required to convict was based not only on the seriousness of the crime but on other factors as well. Little proof was required in cases in which proof would be difficult to acquire or in which the power of the defendant would discourage testimony. In crimes in which the court was anxious to convict, such as political crimes, the number of witnesses might be few and the quality of their knowledge less certain.

Condemnation or absolution had to be reached within twenty-five days from the day of the response. The judge conferred with the other judges and the rector to decide the case (*Stat.* 3.2). Condemnations and absolutions were read in the councils, copies of these condemnations and absolutions being retained in the camera of the acts (*Stat.* 3.25).

The Podestà, Captain, and Executor executed their own condemnations through their retinues. Those in custody who were condemned to corporal penalties were whipped through the streets, dismembered, burned, or decapitated, as specified in their condemnations. Those in custody who were condemned to pecuniary penalties were compelled to pay their fines or, if they failed to do so, were detained in the communal prison until they paid or until they received some kind of cancellation (*Stat.* 1.41).

If the culprit was not in custody at the time of condemnation, the rectors could try to capture him or could exact the penalties from his goods, if any existed. The *milites* and notaries of the foreign rectors patrolled the city, county, and district looking for the condemned and the banned. When they patrolled the county and district, they could take as many as twenty stipendiarii without obtaining a special license from the Priors and Gonfalonier (*Stat.* 3.189). The culprit himself was banned and, therefore, was always subject to arrest, and, in serious crimes, to assault with impunity by anyone. Penalties for sheltering the banned were severe (*Stat.* 3.156). Nevertheless, capturing condemned people once they had fled, especially if they had escaped outside the territory, was not normally successful. If the culprit was not caught, the rectors could try to exact the penalties from his goods, oathswearers, or relatives. Pecuniary penalties could be exacted in the culprit's absence by confiscating his goods to the amount of the penalty.[18] In cases of confiscation, the foreign rectors summoned the syndics or rectors of the popolo where the condemned person lived, who gave a report of the property owned by the condemned.[19] If oathswearers existed, as in cases of magnates or those who responded in court but freed themselves from custody by leaving security in the form of oathswearers, penalties could be exacted from the oathswearers. In very select cases, the family of the defendant was held liable for the penalty, usually in cases of crimes committed by magnates but also in cases of abduction of children, refusal to pay taxes, or crimes committed by clerics.[20] For some political crimes, the sons and descendants were banned for their fathers' crimes.[21] The rectors received rewards for executing or for exacting penalties. If the retinue of a rector captured a condemned person, the rector was rewarded with 25 or 50 lire, depending on the crime. Similar rewards were offered if the rector or his retinue captured culprits *in flagranti.* The rector received one-fifth of the penalty if the penalty was exacted through confiscation of goods.[22] There was no appeal from criminal condemnations given by the foreign rectors (*Stat.* 2.127).

General Powers of the Foreign Rectors

The offices of the foreign rectors were established at different times and initially fulfilled different functions. The office of the Podestà originated in 1193 as an executive office (head of the Commune of Florence) as well as a judicial office. The Podestà originally presided over the Council of the Commune. The office of the Captain of the People came into being around 1250 to provide protection and leadership for the popolano class, later adding to this function that of defending the guilds and guildsmen. The Captain, an executive and judicial official like the Podestà, presided over the Council of the People. The office of the Executor originated in 1307. The function of this office was outlined in the Ordinances of Justice, a code of law that regulated the magnates, that is, mainly the feudal families, and protected the popolani from the oppressive activities of the magnates. Each of these rectorates, created to head one of the ancient corporate groups that composed the government and society of Florence during the Middle Ages, had its own characteristics, functions, and constituency, although the functions and constituencies of these offices overlapped.

During the entire history of the offices of the rectors, the rectors had some civil and some criminal duties. They could try crimes committed in the county and district, or committed by or against people of the county and district, as well as crimes committed in the city by or against citizens. County and district officials were often limited in the seriousness of the crimes they could try. Crimes of greater seriousness were tried by the foreign rectors in Florence, as were some appeals from the decisions of the county and district officials (see Chap. 8). The Florentine rectors formed the highest rung in the hierarchy of the county and district officials. The foreign rectors were not limited in the seriousness of the cases they could try; however, they could not intervene in a case that was already being prosecuted in another court, nor could they instruct officials of the county and district as to how to proceed in their cases. For crimes committed in the city, the courts of the foreign rectors were always the proper courts unless the crime fell into one of the categories of crimes treated by an agency, in which case either the court of one of the rectors or the court of the agency was appropriate.

All of the rectors had mere and mixed *imperium*, power to act on behalf of the state. Imperium was the cornerstone of the relationship between the rectors and the judges. The judges, who were lawyers and jurists, had the expertise to try cases but not always the authority to transform their decisions into public acts. The rectors, who were not necessarily lawyers or judges, could not judge the cases but could supervise the trials conducted by the judges and wield the power of the commune to make these decisions public. While the Podestà and Captain were required to be of *miles*, or knightly rank, or even of count or marchese rank, the Executor was required to be a popolano but not a doctor or judge (*Stat.* 1.23).

Throughout the Middle Ages and the Renaissance, the judicial offices underwent many changes of function and switches of jurisdiction, emerging in the early Renaissance in a very different form than they had formerly assumed. By the redaction of the 1415 statutes, their traditional functions had little to do with what they really did. Despite this switching and changing, despite the complicated nature of jurisdictional limits within the judicial system in early Renaissance Florence, complete confusion did not reign. Samuel Cohn's contention that clear jurisdictional limits did not exist is somewhat mistaken.[23] Each rector did have an autonomous sphere of jurisdiction. There were guiding principles dictating to which court a particular case was sent. The delimitations between the courts had little resemblance to delimitations in the medieval world. Most of the exchanges of duties between these rectors were aimed at creating rational blocks of jurisdiction, consistent according to material. The systematization of these officials was an important process in the creation of the territorial state and an important step toward efficiency in the judicial system.

By the time that the 1415 statutes were enacted, three trends were in progress that were working subtle but important changes. Jurisdictions were sorted and switched throughout the fourteenth and early fifteenth centuries. The other two processes started only in the early fifteenth century and were apparent for the first time in the statutes of 1415. In one process, the jurisdictional delimitations between the rectors were disappearing altogether, and the rectors were achieving an approximate parity in authority and function among themselves. At least in criminal matters, all of the rectors were empowered to try all crimes for the first time. In the other new process, all of the rectors were becoming more powerful as the public aspect of crime gained greater ascendency over the private aspect. The sorting and switching of jurisdictions among all of the judicial officials, particularly the foreign rectors, will be discussed throughout this work, since familiarity with the officials is necessary to perceive this trend. The two new trends that gave the foreign rectors greater power are the subject of this section of this chapter.

In the statutes of 1415, a rubric appeared for the first time that gave the three foreign rectors an absolute parity of authority in criminal matters. All of the statutes and ordinances pertaining to the Podestà and his judges concerning criminal trials equally pertained to the Captain and the Executor, and to their judges (*Stat.* 3.6). Formerly the Podestà had been the major criminal authority, and the Captain and the Executor had possessed restricted and specific powers in criminal matters. Specific kinds of cases had been assigned to the courts of the Captain and the Executor, these courts being empowered to accept and try only these cases. For instance, the Executor's role had previously been completely circumscribed by the goals of the Ordinances of Justice. In 1415, the Executor's power was increased by endowing him with general criminal powers. All of the rectors were made equally powerful, all having the ability to deal with any crime and to wield the same tools (such as inquisition, torture, and corporal punishment) in dealing with these crimes. Nor could any rector step outside the framework of the statutes by claiming a greater *balia* (extraordinary power) in dealing with crime.

This parity of authority of the rectors contributed to the creation of the territorial state. The rectors were no longer products of separate governments within the government of Florence but were all equally officials of the state. This did not mean that each of the rectors fulfilled exactly the same function or treated exactly the same crimes; rather, each rector was capable of fulfilling any of the functions attributed to the other rectors and of trying any of the crimes usually tried by the others. That one rector could substitute for another, fulfilling the duties of the other under certain circumstances, provides further proof of their parity in authority. If one rector began a criminal trial but did not expedite the trial in the allotted amount of time, another rector who gained knowledge of this negligence stepped in and proceeded (Stat. 3.4). If the office of one of the rectors was vacant, all of its power, jurisdiction, and duties were transferred to one of the other rectors (*Stat.* 1.12). Even syndication, the trial of government officials, one of the clear-cut areas of jurisdiction of the Executor, could be performed by one of the other rectors if the office of the Executor was vacant.[24]

Although the rectors had the same authority, they often tried different crimes. In the statutes of 1415, there were many rubrics that assigned a specific duty to a specific rector. Each had a few areas of crime that were his special spheres of competence. The process by which jurisdictions were sorted and shifted was creating greater consistency in these special areas of competence. On the other hand, the statutes of 1415 assigned many crimes to all three of the rectors equally. In the statutes of 1322–25, crimes were never assigned equally to the three rectors, but mainly to one rector or another, or to the Podestà and the Captain. Before 1415, the position of Executor had never approximated the positions of the Podestà and the Captain.

Concomitant with this newly legislated parity of authority was a greater tendency to ignore special spheres of competence and allow any rector to treat any crime. By the early fifteenth century, case initiations relied more heavily on the rectors' retinues discovering crime than on private accusation. Inquisition procedure was effecting a revolution in traditional jurisdictional limits. In the past, crimes had come to court more through private accusation than through public means. Accusers went to the proper rector with cognition, so that crimes could be divided up neatly among the rectors.[25] In the early fifteenth century, the judicial system, which had a police force that could apprehend criminals *in flagranti* or rush to the scene of a crime recently committed, could not operate within traditional jurisdictional limits. A criminal could be apprehended by the retinue of one rector, although his crime would traditionally have been treated by another rector. The court of the official who discovered the crime, because this official had firsthand knowledge of the crime, was the natural court to try it. This breakdown of traditional jurisdictional limits is embodied in the rubric *De Praeventione Iurisdictiones* of the 1415 compilation (*Stat.* 3.3). Here the rector who captured the criminal or who first sent the inquisition or accusation concerning the crime to the camera of the acts (thus initiating the case) was preferred in trying the crime. Rectors were often given pecuniary bonuses for interrupting crimes and for successfully prosecuting a crime to condemnation. This encouraged them to investigate actively for crime, to gather sufficient evidence to warrant condemnation, and to terminate cases quickly. This system of rewards for officials and members of the retinues of rectors who captured malefactors *in flagranti*, established in 1355, contributed to the dominance of inquisition procedure and, consequently, to the breakdown of traditional jurisdictions.[26] The rector who interrupted a crime, or whose *famiglia* interrupted a crime, became the proper one to pursue the case.

Striking evidence of the increasing conformity and similarity among the rectors is the amalgamation of the formerly separate statute compilations dealing with each rector into one unified compilation dealing with all three rectors. The statutes of 1322–25 were organized into two separate codes, one dealing predominantly with the Podestà's duties, the other with the Captain's duties. Most of the duties of the Executor were outlined in the Ordinances of Justice, which was separate. The 1415 compilation was organized according to subject matter and not according to rector, many rubrics empowering all three rectors indiscriminately. Of the three rectors, the Executor remained the most distinct because the duties attributed to him in the Ordinances of Justice were more easily kept discrete than those assigned to the Podestà and the Captain in the statutes of 1322–25.

All three rectors were empowered to act in many instances and to recognize concerning many crimes, but sometimes only one rector was called on to act and to recognize. If different rectors did not try different crimes, there would be no need for a rubric requiring one rector to substitute for another. If all of them functioned identically, there would be no need for one rector to take over the duties of another. Many rubrics in the statutes of 1415 imply that an appropriate rector existed for different crimes. Crimes belonging to the office of Podestà should be denounced to the Podestà just as crimes belonging to the office of Captain should be denounced to the Captain.[27] Cases should be sent to the rector to whom cognition was given according to material.

One rubric aptly demonstrates the conflicting tendencies of uniformity of power and differentiation of function. When an accusation was extended or an inquisition was formed against a magnate, no one rector could proceed completely by himself. All of the rectors had to meet to deliberate whether the accusation or the inquisition should be pursued and the magnate tried. If they decided the case needed to be tried, the rector to whom the accusation was extended or by whom the inquisition was formed had to proceed, expedite, and terminate. If the rectors decided not to proceed, they were required to notify the Priors and the Gonfalonier of Justice, who convoked the Gonfalonieri and the Dodici Buonuomini (the two colleges), the captains of the Parte Guelfa, the Otto di Guardia, the six counselors of the Mercanzia (merchant court), and the twenty-one captains of the guilds, who then deliberated the same question, whether the case should be tried. If they decided that trial was necessary, they returned the case to the rector to whom it belonged for him to proceed. Competence in magnate crimes was distributed among all three of the rectors, accusations over such matters being accepted by all of them, but the case was returned to the rector who had jurisdiction over the particular crime committed by the magnate.[28] The division of jurisdiction was preserved despite the ability of any of the rectors to handle the case.

While some historians have theorized that some areas of crime were becoming separated from the regular court system and attributed to the courts of the agencies in the early fifteenth century, the 1415 rubric empowering all rectors to try all crimes suggests that the opposite process was taking place. The regular court system was not atrophying in favor of the agencies but instead was acquiring more power to deal with crime. The regular court system was interlocked with the agencies, the agencies gaining very few areas of exclusive jurisdiction that they could manipulate independently. The number of crimes that were actually being denied to the rectors were negligble and of inconsequential subject matter. The foreign rectors were no longer allowed to have any jurisdiction, not even in regular crimes, over prostitutes who worked out of the public brothels; only the Onestà, an agency of fifteenth-century vintage, had jurisdiction over them. Thus, prostitutes could not be arrested for any crime without the Onestà's permission. No rector nor any member of his retinue could harass a prostitute; if he did, he was fined (*Stat.* 5.2.34). Likewise, the foreign rectors were prohibited from investigating or trying infractions of the laws dealing with weights and measures without the permission of the Tower Officials.[29] These areas of exclusive jurisdiction of the agencies were not the kinds of crucial areas that an oligarchy seeking to expand its power would want to control.

The other new trend that appeared in the statutes of 1415 concerns the *arbitrium* (discretion) of the foreign rectors. In the statutes of 1415, all the rectors had arbitrium in recognizing and proceeding in cases of homicide; maiming body members, such as arms and legs; inflicting large wounds in the face from whence blood exuded, made with any kind of weapon; assassinating; sending assassins to assault a third party; sodomizing; conducting gambling games; and loaning money for gambling. The rectors had arbitrium in recognizing, proceeding, punishing, and condemning in cases of robbery on the streets; public theft; theft by highwaymen; falsification of instruments, court acts, or merchants' books; defaulting and fleeing with the money of another; impeding someone from possessing his home, lands, or possessions; injuring someone's agricultural laborers or renters of agricultural land; occupying someone's possessions by force; injuring of minors or guildsmen by magnates; disturbing the pacific state of Florence; rebellion; treason; extortion of money or property through threats or force; forcing someone into matrimony or engagement especially under the auspices of any dignity or office; offending someone going to or returning from a council, parliament, court, funeral, fire-extinguishing duty, or official duty of interrupting a crime; and giving false or fraudulent accusation or denunciation (*Stat.* 3.1). The power of arbitrium meant the rectors could take some liberty with the statutes and could do some interpreting according to their own discretion. For instance, the rectors could add together different levels of proof to make a whole proof. The statutes of 1415 witnessed a great extension of the arbitrium of the rectors. Arbitrium was generalized to all of the rectors, and the number of crimes in which the rectors were permitted to use their arbitrium increased. In the statutes of 1322–25, the Captain was permitted to use arbitrium in few crimes and the Executor in almost none. In these statutes, the Podestà was the only rector to possess the power of discretion over a good number of crimes, especially those of a serious nature. The 1415 statutes extended the power of arbitrium of the Podestà to all of the rectors and increased the number of crimes in which arbitrium could be applied. This extension of arbitrium was crucial because it broadened the areas of crime in which the rectors could initiate cases through inquisition.

Even by 1322–25, the Podestà had arbitrium over many crimes. The serious crimes named above for which the rectors had arbitrium only in recognizing and proceeding were the same in 1415 as they were in 1322–25.[30] But the crimes for which the rectors had arbitrium in recognizing, proceeding, punishing, and condemning had increased. The statutes of 1415 show new arbitrium in cases of extorting money through power or threats; forcing matrimony or betrothal, especially under the pretense of holding an office; offending those coming from or going to council, parliament, court, funerals, fires, or law enforcement duties; and accusing or denouncing falsely or fraudulently. When the specific rubrics that describe a specific crime and its remedy are examined, new areas of inquisition-initiated cases appear. The power of arbitrium of the rectors became extended to crimes involving the hoarding of foodstuffs and the impeding of those bringing foodstuffs into the city.[31] Further, the rectors could initiate *ex officio* cases against thugs who were hired by magnates to commit crimes and against people who slandered the Florentine guilds abroad.[32] Not only did greater use of arbitrium increase the use of inquisition initiation, it also increased the possibility of use of torture. In the statutes of 1322–25, arbitrium over torture was excepted from the general arbitrium given to the rectors in recognizing, proceeding, punishing, and condemning. But in 1415 this exception disappeared, paving the way for greater use of torture. Arbitrium also gave the judge the increased freedom to exact whatever testimony he thought appropriate and to call additional witnesses.[33]

The extension of inquisition initiation and of the use of torture had great impact on the judicial system, permitting the regular court system to gain greater control of initiation and evidence. Inquisition initiation increased the importance of preliminary investigation by court officials. Torture was a source of evidence that the judicial system could draw on without relying on the private sector. The judicial system was enriched in authority by the new powers attributed to the public sector. By 1415, the rectors had general arbitrium over a great many crimes, including homicide, serious assault, hiring assassins, sodomy, public theft, falsifying documents, defaulting and fleeing with the money of another, impeding entry into possessions, occupying another's possessions through force, assault by magnates, rebellion of all sorts,[34] extortion, offending those going to public functions, false accusation (*Stat.* 3.1), crimes committed by clerics (*Stat.* 3.16; 44), occupation of ecclesiastical property (*Stat.* 3.49), offenses against one of the foreign rectors (*Stat.* 3.101), assembling to influence elections (*Stat.* 3.56), usurpation of communal goods (*Stat.* 3.55), alienation or creation of bonds of servitude (*Stat.* 3.90; 89), and impeding the flow of foodstuffs into the city.[35] Some of these cases specifically allowed torture at the discretion of the rectors even without preceding incriminating evidence.

Ecclesiastical Jurisdiction

While these trends internal to the court system delineated the powers and limitations of the offices of the foreign rectors, external factors also affected them. By 1415, imperial power had no real impact on the judicial system, but the power of the Church continued to have effect. There were cases which were outside the purview of the foreign rectors and outside that of any other communal official. These were the cases that were tried in the ecclesiastical courts, either the bishop's or the inquisitor's court claiming them either by reason of person or by reason of material. Jurisdictional lines, which were never distinct, varied with political vicissitudes. Sometimes church and state handled different facets of the same case.

In civil and mixed cases, clerics were required by communal statute to respond in communal court when summoned. If they claimed clerical immunity, they were detained in prison until documents verifying their status as clerics arrived from the bishop. No one could decline the jurisdiction of the commune; clerics were required to come to communal court before they could be released. When a cleric accused of debt was released in this way, his creditors were *ipso facto* placed in possession of his patrimonial goods to the amount of the debt and related expenses (*Stat.* 2.18). Clerics could bring their claims of debt to the courts of the foreign rectors or the Mercanzia (*Stat.* 2.24). Civil and mixed cases moved by foreigners and clerics could be tried in Florentine courts, if the foreigners or clerics gave securities (*Stat.* 2.17). Marriage cases, that is, cases that centered on the question of whether a valid marriage existed or not, were tried in the Church courts. Cases of rape or harassment in which the assailant attempted to establish a valid marriage by creating a case of future consent plus intercourse could be tried in either the Church courts or the secular courts. Unless marriage was established, the assailant was fined (*Stat.* 3.112).

In criminal matters, the ecclesiastical courts controlled some kinds of cases and the communal courts others. Usury, for instance, was tried in the ecclesiastical courts, but the secular courts remained involved in this litigation. Although ecclesiastical legislation reserved usury cases for ecclesiastical courts, communal statute required that before a case of usury could be initiated in an ecclesiastical court, a deposit had to be left with the communal courts in the amount of the debt to be given to the creditor if usury was not proved in the ecclesiastical court in one month (*Stat.* 2.19). The commune required this method of dealing with usury because the secular government did not want usury proceedings to be used as a way of avoiding payment of debt.[36] Since charging an interest on loans and loaning money for pawned items were considered necessary evils by the state, communal courts sought to regulate but not to prevent such activities. Traditionally, this had been done by charging pawnbrokers a licensing fee and limiting the interest on loans to 30 percent.[37]

Jewish moneylenders and pawnbrokers were alternately invited to Florence and exiled from Florence depending on the availability or lack of availability of currency. While in 1406 the Jews were exiled from Florence because of their high interest rates, in 1430 they were invited back in order to lower the interest rates. They were limited to charging 20 percent at this time.[38] Although many merchants escaped usury charges during their lifetime, they were obligated to make some restitution in their last will and testament. Ecclesiastical legislation mandated that usurers who did not leave some restitution for their victims on their deathbed, if they were proved after death to have been usurers, could have their estates opened up to pay claims of usury.

The Church courts also had full power in heresy cases, although they relied on the state's courts to execute these condemnations. The foreign rectors arrested everyone indicated by the bishop and executed sentences of heresy pronounced in the court of the bishop or the inquisitor. The rectors and their retinues destroyed the meeting places of heretics. Convicted heretics were deprived of all political and civil rights and, along with their sons and grandsons, were excluded from public office. Heretics could not bring cases to court, nor could they testify. Their goods were confiscated and divided between the commune and the Church (*Stat.* 3.40). Particular interest centered on the treatment of the heresy of the Fraticelli, an order of spiritual Franciscans. Because this order had an inherent political philosophy, both church and state were interested in its regulation. The Fraticelli heresy, which championed poverty and was antipathetic to private property and rule by the wealthy, was a widespread belief among the *popolo minuto*. The Fraticelli were tolerated and protected by the Ciompi government of 1378 but outlawed by the more upper-class government of 1382, which cooperated with the efforts of the inquisitorial court to try the Fraticelli as heretics.[39] The statutes of 1415 continued to proscribe Fraticelli. All officials of the city, county, and district of Florence were required to give however many of their retinue as were requested to the inquisitor for the capturing and imprisoning of these heretics, under threat of penalty of 500 lire to the official (*Stat.* 3.41). While heretics were tried in the ecclesiastical court with the communal court system executing, flagellants were tried in the communal courts. The foreign rectors had balia in proceeding against those who went through the city beating themselves, even proceeding *ex officio* (*Stat.* 3.42).

The secular courts punished infractions of the sumptuary laws. However, to these secular penalties were added the onus of excommunication by the bishop, particularly in cases of wearing precious stones and metals.[40] Witchcraft cases could apparently be tried in either secular or ecclesiastical courts. Brucker cites cases from communal courts but admits that the roles of the inquisitorial and episcopal courts, courts that formerly tried sorcery, could not be assessed because of lack of records. Although the lacunae in the evidence do not permit an accurate assessment of the volume of cases, the volume appears to have been sparse but regular.[41]

Clerics had immunity from secular criminal prosecution as long as they could obtain documents of clerical status from their bishop. However, the secular courts had indirect ways to punish criminous clerics. For instance, if a cleric assaulted a Florentine, the rector could fine the cleric's relatives for the amount of the penalty (*Stat.* 3.44). Also, a cleric could be automatically disqualified from clerical status by committing certain crimes, such as homicide, theft, rape, arson, or any other enormity (*Stat.* 3.43). Once the cleric was disqualified from clerical status, he was tried in secular court.

Churches were forbidden to offer asylum to those committing homicide or assault, under penalty of loss of alms and loss of exemption from taxation for one year (*Stat.* 3.159). The bishops of Fiesole and Florence, the inquisitor of heretics, and the retinues of these ecclesiastical officials were prohibited from bearing arms unless the Priors and the Gonfalonier conceded licenses to them for this purpose (*Stat.* 3.190).

The struggle between church and state over competence continued to unfold. Although the Church courts did manage to exclusively try some important kinds of cases, such as usury cases, the Florentine judicial system continued to be involved in areas necessary for assuring the welfare of the state. The Florentine government cooperated with the Church courts only when they were acting in ways harmless or helpful to the aims of the state.

Comparison with Venice

This portrait of Venetian justice is posed as a worst case scenario, an example of a court system completely dominated by a nobility with a stranglehold on political power. The purpose of this section is to illustrate the methods used by an oligarchy to manipulate a court system, including the policing officials. This provides a contrast with the portrait of the Florentine court system drawn throughout the rest of the book. In the Venetian system, the nobles used the court system as a method of social control. The lack of adherence to statute gave class inequality before the law free rein.

As a consequence of the Serrata of 1298, which limited membership of the Major Council to certain specified aristocratic families, the government of Venice became controlled by a closed, hereditary oligarchy. The executive sector of the government dominated and constantly interfered in the judicial sector. The statutes were compiled in a random manner and were used in an approximate way, proceeding through analogy to the particular case, and if no analogy existed, through what seemed to be just and equitable to the judge. There was little adherence to statute, and statute and cases did not coincide. The unlimited ability to mold the law to the case at hand made the law readily susceptible to class-biased justice and political pressure.[42] Legislation of the Major Council was collected and filtered by the Avogaria, always the most important nobles of Venice, who gave this legislation their own stamp, impressing it with considerations of class and family. They also decided what legislation should be implemented.[43] In Florence, statutes were employed in the courts, restraining the influence of class and power. Legislation was enacted by the Priors, colleges, and councils, which were composed of men of varied social classes, and was recorded verbatim in the Provvisioni.

Most of the court system in Venice, both the investigating bodies and the adjudicating bodies, was composed of nobles. In the traditional system, the Cinque alla Pace were nobles who patrolled the streets with armed guards, providing summary justice on the streets for minor crimes and keeping the peace. The Avogadori, who investigated crime and presented cases before the Council of Forty, comprised the most important nobles of Venice. All of the Cinque alla Pace, the Signori di Notte, and the Capi di Sestieri, all patrolling and policing bodies in the fourteenth century, were drawn from nobles of lesser standing or young men of the upper families, because this job involved great danger. The Council of Ten was added to the traditional court system in 1310. At first it was an expedient to put down conspiracies and try state crimes, but soon it became a permanent body because the need to guard against conspiracies was permanent after the Serrata. The Council of Ten was composed of especially powerful nobles. In 1319, the Ten gained its own police force, the Capi di Sestieri, at first composed of one noble and four patrollers but soon increased to two nobles and eight patrollers per *sestiero* (geographic division of the city, of which there were six). The Council of Ten was composed for most of the fourteenth century of the twenty most important families in Venice. There were no *divieti* laws, so the same twenty families could dominate for long periods of time. Even the lawyers who worked in the court system, although not usually upper nobility themselves, fueled the class bias because they were sometimes involved with the nobility in client relationships. In Florence, the judges and many of the main policing officials were foreigners and thus distanced to some degree from Florentine political and class affiliations.

Nobles held a special relationship to the judicial system in other ways, too. Because nobles held so much control over the government and the judicial system, they conceived of themselves as above the law and frequently committed crimes against communal officials, for which they were treated with leniency at sentencing. Although, in Florence, the Ordinances of Justice were fairly successful in putting the overbearing behavior of nobles to rest, the nobility of Venice remained a very violent class, responsible for a disproportionate number of crimes, for example, 21 percent of assaults. Judgments made by nobles, such as the Council of Forty, reflected the attitudes of the nobility. Torture was more likely to be used in cases involving property. Class biases and political biases were often present in cases. Venetian criminal law enforced differences between classes, for instance, punishing those assaulting nobles more severely.

Procedures used in the Venetian court system left plenty of room for partiality in terms of class and politics. The Avogadori, who prepared cases to go before the Council of Forty, had no monitoring body sitting with them when they elicited testimony. The Forty tried assaults and most of the serious violent crime, especially when important families were involved. The Signori di Notte, also involved in collecting testimony, recorded this testimony in a very formulaic manner, presenting their version before the Giudici di Proprio. This formulaic testimony was very prejudicial to the defense. The Signori di Notte also patrolled and had extraordinary powers to capture and imprison robbers, rapists, fornicators, and other criminals for the most common violent crimes. The Signori handled some crimes summarily on the street. Their principal responsibility was to oversee the patrols of the city. During torture conducted by the Signori, no one could be present except the examiners.

In 1310, the judicial council with the greatest independence and arbitrium was created, the Council of Ten. The Ten were created to combat popular unrest occasioned by the monopoly of the nobility in the Major Council and, therefore, in the government. By 1320, the Ten had already gained a police force that could proceed from arrest to execution without external checks, if the case was a threat to public security. The Ten had no external controls, extended no safeguards to defendants, and offered no access to appeal or *gratia*. They did not have the limitation of working with a council that other police officials had. The Ten lacked the constraints of tradition and so could act more autonomously and creatively. The Ten accepted anonymous accusations. They supervised speech crimes, any kind of associations, and carrying arms in an attempt to stop conspiracy. All parts of their trials were kept secret, and their decisions were never reviewed.

The Venetian example presents a system in which there were no checks and balances between agencies, each agency working autonomously. This allowed the greatest amount of discretion and the freest rein of class bias. Nobles dominated policing, proof collection, judgment, and execution. The court system was openly employed in quelling lower-class unrest. No constitutionality or deference to procedure existed. Furthermore, the system was not part of the Roman–canon law tradition of the itinerant Podestà and Captains.

General Trends

The rectors' courts were vigorous and their jurisdiction wide. Inquisition procedure gave great responsibility to the state's courts, the responsibility of conducting most parts of the trial, even the initiation. The rectors could try any crime, the agencies taking very few cases away from the rectors' courts. Public initiation infringed on the traditional areas of private accusation. The whole system became geared to inquisition initiation; for example, the rector who interrupted a crime became the rector who rightfully tried the crime. The communal judicial system was successful in maintaining sufficient control over all cases that were important to the state in either a commercial or a political sense.

Because the state and its court system were strong enough to implement inquisition procedure, inquisition procedure became more developed and refined. More independent methods of investigation were implemented, some of them bad, such as torture, public fame initiation, and public fame proof, and some of them good, such as effective ways of eliciting good testimony and effective judicial safeguards for the defendant. There were checks within the system that insured greater fairness. Testimony was recorded without interruption and always in the presence of the foreign criminal notary. The written accusation or inquisition and capitula formed the established core of the testimony. Berrovarii investigated routinely for crime and served as witnesses. The combination of the strong state with inquisition procedure caused changes in the officials. All of the rectors became functionaries of one state, losing delimitations and reaching a parity in authority. Inquisition procedure made the divisions of competence less distinct. All of the rectors had the same arbitrium and the same wide judicial capabilities. The growing strength of the judicial system provides evidence that the territorial state continued to develop in the early fifteenth century.

3

THE SUBORDINATE OFFICIALS OF THE FOREIGN RECTORS

THIS STUDY is based in part on an examination of the functions of the various judicial officials, in order to discover who carried out the important functions in the Florentine judicial system and in the government as a whole. If the foreign rectors performed the important functions, this demonstrates that there was a centralized territorial state with an autonomous and sovereign judicial system. I investigated all officials with judicial power in order to rule out the possibility of strong competing jurisdictions outside the centralized system. These competing jurisdictions could have taken the form of courts of the old corporate entities (the guilds were the only corporate group to develop a court system) or the form of new courts of those agencies that became powerful through executive or patrician support. If I had discovered that agencies acting independently and without legal restraints had seized important areas of jurisdiction, especially agencies dominated by the patriciate, this would demonstrate patrician dominance of the court system. But this was not the case.

The first step is to examine the functions of the foreign rectors. This information can be gathered in various ways from the statutes of 1415. Some rubrics that are very general and describe the rectors and their general powers can be archaic and unreliable; thus, such rubrics need to be supported by other material to prove their currency. Many rubrics that describe a crime and designate a rector or rectors to prosecute it are often very specific and must be coordinated with other rubrics attributing similar crimes to the same rector in order to form an area of jurisdiction large enough to assure that the named rector currently treated the crime. Sometimes the divisions of tasks seem so narrow that doubt arises as to whether such petty divisions could be remembered, much less practiced. Another way of collecting information on the functions of the rectors is to examine the functions of the subordinate officials brought by the rectors. The rectors were closely involved with every task carried on by their officials. The jurisdiction of a rector subsumed all of the jurisdictions of the officials subordinate to him. When an official under a rector is entirely devoted to a task, we may be sure that this task was supervised by this particular rector, was carried out in practice, and was deemed to be an important one. All of the subordinate officials were foreign and came in the retinues of the rectors. Each of these officials had a particular purpose that formed part of the general function of the rector.

This chapter is organized as a mesh between two different organizational systems. It is organized both by rector and by type of subordinate official, whether judge, notary, or police official, according to a principle of nonrepetition. This division reflects the two major purposes of the chapter. While the descriptions of the subordinate officials are used to illustrate the principal duties of the foreign rectors, they are also used to demonstrate the duties of the subordinate officials in their own right to complete the articulation of the bureaucracy. Each rector is paired with his subordinate officials, but because many of the subordinate officials are common to more than one rector, a full description does not appear under each rector. If a subordinate official common to more than one rector is described under one rector, he is mentioned but not described under the other rectors. This has the unfortunate side effect of making the second rector discussed seem less important than the first and the last rector seem least important of all. This is not the case. Reference must be made to the earlier mentioned rectors for full information on subordinate officials.

When the subordinate officials are studied, several things surface. The subordinate officials that existed in 1415 were not the same as those that existed in the 1322–25 period. The changes in the subordinate officials between 1322–25 and 1415 demonstrate the same trends noted in the examination of the changes in the general powers of the rectors. In the 1415 statutes, many of the officials were common to all three of the rectors. All of the rectors had notaries over consignment, notaries of the *capsa* (a booth located inside or next to the door of the rector's palace), notaries over the goods of the banned, condemned, and rebels, and *milites socii* (military associates). Although each rector and his officials had some areas of specialization which were exclusively assigned to them, they demonstrated an inclination toward uniformity in 1415. No longer did they fulfill different functions in separate systems, as they did in the 1322–25 period; instead, they tended to work together in one centralized system. Even their distinctive functions were coordinated. Also, the number of police officials under each rector became similar. While, from 1322 to 1325, the disparity among the number of police officials under each rector was great, showing various levels of involvement in criminal apprehension and investigation, in 1415 disparity disappeared. All of the rectors became active in criminal matters.

While the number of judges of the rectors decreased from 1322–25 to 1415 proportionately to the decrease in population, the number of police

Subordinate Officials of the Foreign Rectors

officials increased in this period. In the 1322–25 period, the Captain and the Executor had barely any police forces, while by 1415 their forces were substantial. This is predictable, given the continued development of inquisition procedure in the early fifteenth century, which made rectors more active in criminal apprehension and investigation. Increased surveillance was performed by the regular court system, not by the agencies. Some police officials went out on routine rounds and some went on expeditions into the contado and territory, under the direction of the foreign rectors. The cadres of officials under the rectors, like the notaries of the capsa, had become completely geared to trial initiation through inquisition. The notaries of the capsa were also employed in monitoring the police officials. The increase in police officials commanded by the rectors militates against theories of attrition of the regular court system.

The functions of the subordinate officials often involved matters that were crucial to the commune and central to the control of power within the commune, demonstrating that these matters had not been alienated to the agencies. Areas in which one would expect to find patrician abuse, if patrician takeover was present, were controlled by the regular court system under the rectors. All of the rectors were involved in the recuperation of communal goods from illegitimate possessors and from communal officials that temporarily controlled them for the purpose of performing their offices. Appropriation of communal goods and lands was likely to be the practice of a patriciate, especially one that might feel it owned the commune through its substantial investments in the communal debt. Many of these communal possessions had been wrested from the patrician class in the mid-fourteenth century and were protected from infringement by the rectors and their subordinate officials. Likewise, the rectors controlled many areas of law that were susceptible to abuse by a patriciate growing more powerful. The Captain controlled appeals, considered to be the highest possible jurisdiction, through one of his subordinate judges, and all of the other rectors were likewise involved in appeals in some way. The collection of gabelles, an area of administration susceptible to corruption and usurpation, was monitored by a subordinate judge of the Captain, the same judge who monitored the treasury officials. The Executor and one of his judges syndicated the performance of communal officials in office—that is, reviewed their performance, which could result in possible prosecution for omissions, deficiencies, or crimes. The functions of the rectors' subordinate officials demonstrate that the rectors retained power over sensitive material. The rectors were held accountable for the activities of their courts; all parts of all trials were recorded and made ready for syndication. The foreign criminal notaries regulated the most sensitive parts of the procedure—the response of the defendant, testimony, and torture.

The rectors came from outside Florence to hold six-month rectorates in Florence, bringing their own retinues of judges, notaries, *milites,* and other officials. The Podestà brought four judges, two civil and two criminal, and fourteen notaries in all, including seven deputed to civil matters, four deputed to criminal matters, one placed at the door of the palace to write down the names of arrested suspects, one deputed to the consignment of communal goods to officials of the county and district, and one deputed to extraordinary matters and to registering the people who were condemned and banned (*Stat.* 1.4). He also had three *milites socii,* eight *domicelli* (pages), sixty *famuli* or *berrovarii* (armed police officials), and fourteen *equi* (mounted, armed police officials). The Captain had three judges, one deputed to criminal matters, one deputed to civil matters and appeals, and one deputed to matters of the treasury and gabelles. He had seven notaries, including two deputed to the criminal judge, one deputed to the judge of civil things and appeals, one deputed to the judge of treasury and gabelles, one deputed to the consignment of communal goods to the officials of the county and district, one situated outside the door of the palace to record those captured, and one deputed to extraordinary things and to registering the condemned and banned. Besides this he brought two milites, six domicelli, fifty berrovarii, nine equi, and one other equus who traveled with the notary deputed to consignment (*Stat.* 1.13). The Executor had two judges, one criminal and one civil. He had five notaries, one deputed to the civil judge, one deputed to the criminal judge, one deputed to the consignment of communal goods to the officials of the county and district, one deputed to extraordinary things and to registering the condemned and banned, and one situated outside the door of his palace to record those arrested. Besides these, he had one miles, four domicelli, thirty berrovarii, and seven equi (*Stat.* 1.23).

The Subordinate Officials of the Podestà

The most important officials under the rectors were the judges. Under the Podestà there were two criminal judges and two civil judges; under the Captain, one criminal judge, one judge of civil matters, appeals, and nullities, and one judge of camera and gabelle; and under the Executor, one civil judge and one criminal judge. A great deal can be learned about the rectors from the duties of the judges because the duties of the judges were specified by statute and were indicative of an area of jurisdiction subsumed by the rector. The sphere of jurisdiction of the judge was identical with that of the rector supervising him, except that the judge's jurisdiction only extended to one segment, one specialty, of the total jurisdiction of the rector. The judges could act only in cases where their supervising rector had jurisdiction according to statute (*Stat.* 1.6; 1.15). The identity of duties between the rectors and their judges was great, so great that when duties were ascribed by statute to a rector, one of his judges was intended as well. An examination of the role of the judges shows few duties that the rectors could perform that the judges could not. It is difficult to discern a difference in the capabilities of the rectors and the judges in their judicial roles.

The rectors were not always distinguished from their judges even by their possession of *imperium*, since the judges also had imperium in some instances. The collateral judges, or civil judges, were said to possess jurisdiction and mixed imperium in civil and mixed cases (*Stat.* 3.6). Mixed imperium was jurisdiction over civil and minor criminal cases, especially pertaining to the power of awarding possession of goods and of imposing pecuniary punishments. None of the judges was said to have possessed mere imperium; only the rector had it. Mere imperium was the highest jurisdiction, a power that properly belonged to a sovereign but could be delegated to a high-ranking official. It was the power of the sword, the ability to punish with corporal and capital punishments. Sometimes it was defined by jurists as the power over persons, citizenship, and liberty.[1] However, the judges possessed powers very close to imperium in serious criminal cases, since they carried out much of the trial and helped in deciding the case. After the trial was completed, the case was decided by the rector and all of his judges (*Stat.* 3.2). In civil and minor criminal imperium, the distinction between a rector and his judges was not clear-cut. In serious criminal cases, the judges and the rector together decided the case, but the rector had the power of sovereign sanction, the power to make the case publicly valid.

The rectors were not clearly distinguished from the judges by their possession of *arbitrium* (the power of discretion) either. While the rectors sometimes interceded in trials conducted by the judges to exercise arbitrium, the judges also could exercise it. The rector, for instance, could intervene in a trial and declare through his arbitrium that accusations concerning the crime would be accepted from anyone, not just from the relatives (*Stat.* 3.2). However, there were many instances in which the judge had arbitrium in recognizing, proceeding, and punishing. This meant that the judge, by himself, could initiate through inquisition, could leave out parts of the trial, and could change the penalties. An example of this is the power of the judge to shorten the period of citation. In certain crimes in which the judge or the rector was said to have arbitrium in recognizing, proceeding, and punishing, a person could be declared contumacious before the usual period of twenty days from citation had expired (*Stat.* 3.8).

The judges were involved in almost every part of criminal trials. There were few duties that the rector could perform that the criminal judge could not. For instance, both rectors and judges could receive accusations, but, more importantly, both could form inquisitions. Inquisitions could be formed by any of the rectors, or by the judges, or by the curia as a whole (*Stat.* 3.8). The judge cited the defendant, and if the defendant did not appear, banned him at the city gates. He pronounced whether the case was a suitable one in which to employ torture. The judge sat at the bench for rendering law and, with the criminal notary recording, interrogated the witnesses (*Stat.* 3.8). The rector, likewise, sat at the bench (*Stat.* 1.7). Both the rectors and the judges had the power to terminate, that is, to decide cases (*Stat.* 1.6). Both the rectors and the judges could recognize and terminate in the most serious crimes: theft, assassination, robbery on the streets, falsity, homicide, assault resulting in severe facial wounds, assault resulting in debilitation of a member, arson, rape, adultery, incest, disruption of the state, treason, and rebellion (*Stat.* 3.7). Even the responsibility of ordering executions was shared by the rectors and the criminal judges (*Stat.* 1.6). The often identical tasks and powers of the rectors and the judges led to the conclusion that in almost any passage of the rubrics that empowered a rector, his judges were also included, even if only the rector was named. The criminal judges could try any crime over which their rector had jurisdiction. Some of the other judges, like the judge of camera and gabelle, were more specialized.

Some features, however, did distinguish the rector from the judge. The judge was an expert in law, while the rector was either a *miles*, in the cases of the Podestà and the Captain, or a *popolano*, in the case of the Executor. The judge, who possessed legal expertise, was the one actually deciding the case, while the rector supervised the process and added official sanction. Still, the rector had a very active role in the process and helped form the judgment. The rectors made sure that the judges observed the procedural rules of the court (for instance, that they had the foreign notaries present during the examination of witnesses), and could remove a judge from office for infractions (*Stat.* 3.2). Likewise, the rectors monitored the performance of the criminal notaries (*Stat.* 3.8).

The criminal judges were experts in law, but they did not need to be doctors in civil law. Here civil law means Roman law as contained in the *Corpus Iuris Civilis*, including both civil and criminal law. Judges who were not doctors in civil law had still studied civil law in an Italian university for at least five years, following a curriculum called a *studio generale* in law.[2] These criminal judges attached to the rectors were foreign, so they were not members of the Florentine Guild of Judges and Notaries. To gain a doctorate, which was needed by the collateral or civil judges but not by the criminal judges, a judge attended law school for six to nine years. Judges who were legal experts but not doctors could make binding decisions in court.[3] The rectors could not have tried cases without the judges, particularly since the rectors and their retinues went from city to city serving as magistrates and heads of the judicial system. Only someone well versed in the principles of law could learn the various statutes of the various cities in the short time allotted.

The Captain's criminal judge had the same duties and powers as the Podestà's criminal judge, except that the Captain's judge handled those criminal cases over which the Captain had jurisdiction. Since there were many areas of crime in which any one of the rectors was capable of acting, the duties of the criminal judges attached to the Podestà, the Captain, and the Executor were similar. The Captain also had some routine crimes particularly assigned to him. The Executor's criminal judge was somewhat different: although he conducted the same trials in the main as did the criminal judges attached to the other two rectors, he had areas of specialization: the trial of crimes perpetrated within the communal prison and the trial of public officials in the syndication process. The jurisdiction of this judge over cases in prison will be discussed in this chapter in the section concerning the Executor's other subordinate officials, while the involvement of this judge in syndication will be described in Chapter 6, on the Executor himself. All of the criminal judges conducted trials of routine crime, even the Executor's judge.[4] There were routine crimes particularly ascribed to the Executor by statute that must have been treated by his criminal judge. Also, the trial of a great number of crimes was permitted to all three of the rectors, showing that a certain number of these crimes were expected to be tried in the criminal court of the Executor.

The Podestà also had two collateral judges, who were always doctors in civil law, to handle civil and mixed cases. The collateral judges could decide debt cases, which were considered to be mixed cases, and were sometimes said to handle even cases of defaulting and fleeing debt, the most criminal kind of debt, although these cases were usually attributed to the criminal judges (*Stat.* 1.6). The civil judge performed *staggimenta* and sequestrations; that is, if a plaintiff complained to the court that money was owed to him by another and the court affirmed that such debt was owed, the judge could order that the debtor's goods be seized and held by the court until the debt was paid. On the strictly civil side, the collateral judges of the Podestà gave *mundualdi,* or guardians, to widows and other women needing them, gave tutors and curators to minors, tried suits involving mundualdi, tutors, and curators, and removed these guardians if they acted improperly. The collateral judges of the Podestà could try and execute any civil cases in which the Podestà had jurisdiction (*Stat.* 1.6). Besides general civil duties, they accepted petitions for cases that would be tried before the Priors and the Gonfalonier of Justice, as did the collaterals of the Captain or the Executor. The crimes that were the subjects of these petitions were crimes committed by popolani that were of such a violent or heinous nature that the person petitioning felt the offender should be tried as a magnate and, as such, according to the Ordinances of Justice. Once received by the collateral judges, these petitions had to be handed over to the Priors and the Gonfalonier of Justice within three days.[5] Both the Captain and the Executor had collateral judges who were permitted to act in all civil and mixed questions in which the supervising rector had jurisdiction. The collateral judge of the Executor had only this general civil jurisdiction with no areas of special jurisdiction attributed to him. Although the collateral judge of the Captain had a general civil jurisdiction, the special sphere of civil jurisdiction assigned to him, the duty of trying appeals and nullities, was of greater importance.

Besides these judges, the Podestà brought with him a whole cadre of notaries. He had fourteen in all: seven deputed to civil matters; four to criminal matters; one to the recording of those coming into custody; one to the consignment of communal goods to the officials of the county and district; and one to extraordinary matters and the registering of people condemned and banned. The notaries deputed to civil matters recorded the acts of the collateral judges (*Stat.* 1.6). The rectors' criminal notaries kept five sets of books, each containing a separate part of the trial. One book contained accusations accepted and inquisitions formed by the Podestà, the Captain, and the Executor, and their judges and courts, although often accusations and inquisitions were recorded in separate books because they were compiled in different ways. In another book, the notaries recorded the testimony of witnesses for the defense and, in another, that for the prosecution. Another book was the book of the process, containing all of the acts of the court in bringing the case to litigation, such as the citations and the bans. The last book, containing the condemnations and absolutions, often repeated the significant parts of the trial. The criminal notaries recorded the statements of witnesses directly into the books of testimony while they were deposing. The accusations and denunciations, on the other hand, were copied into the book from accusations and denunciations received from outside sources. The criminal notaries were required to give copies of the acts to anyone seeking them. The judge and the notary interrogated witnesses concerning the deed, their intention in deposing, their method of having acquired knowledge concerning the case, the year, the month, the day, the hour of the day, the place, and those who were present. The notary was required to record the statements made by the witnesses concerning each *capitulum* in the accusation, denunciation, or inquisition, not in an abbreviated way, but just as the witnesses deposed (*Stat.* 3.8).

The criminal notaries discussed above, who were foreign, are not to be confused with the foreign criminal notaries. The foreign criminal notaries were elected differently, were fewer in number, and fulfilled a different function than the criminal notaries who were foreign. The foreign criminal notaries were indirectly chosen by the Priors, the Gonfalonier of Justice, and the colleges, while the criminal notaries who kept the books of the acts came with the rectors in their retinues. To choose the foreign criminal notaries, the Priors and the Gonfalonier of Justice picked a name of a commune, city, castle, or rural village which could not border on the county or district of Florence, out of a *borsa* (election bag). Then the commune or place was notified and asked to send four of its notaries to Florence. Each of the criminal judges was assigned one foreign criminal notary and two of the other kind of criminal notaries. The duties of the foreign criminal notaries were mainly to record the responses made by the defendants. They recorded all denials and confessions that the defendants made in the presence of a criminal judge concerning the accusations, denunciations, notifications, or inquisitions leveled against them. They also recorded the testimony of the witnesses (*Stat.* 1.61). When a defendant was being examined, the notary was required to identify himself as the foreign criminal notary and advise the defendant to tell the truth without fear. The foreign criminal notary had to inform the defendant if the crime for which he was being tried was one concerning which the judge had discretion in assigning the penalty. The entire accusation had to be read to the defendant before the foreign criminal notary could receive his responses. Confessions made under torture were not valid unless they were made again at the bench. The foreign criminal notary had to be present for both of these confessions, and he recorded the confession made at the bench. These foreign criminal notaries recorded the testimonies of witnesses just as the other kind of criminal notaries did. If the written records of the two kinds of notaries were discordant, the Priors, the Gonfalonier of Justice, and the colleges decided which acts were to be given credence (*Stat.* 1.61). Both sets of criminal notaries were part of the courts of the Podestà, the Captain, and the Executor. Their existence proves that all of these courts had a sizable regular and general criminal case load. It also shows an effort to introduce greater accountability and adherence to procedure into the taking of testimony and the applying of torture.

The foreign criminal notary was directly involved in redacting important documents on which the outcome of the trial was based: the response of the defendant and the testimony of the witnesses. However, it was the judge, not this notary, who directed the formation of these documents. The main purpose of the foreign notary of crime was to serve as a watchdog for the criminal justice system, keeping the judge's activities within legal bounds. These notaries were created to prevent judges from ignoring whatever procedural safeguards existed in the administration of torture. They were chosen from foreign cities, yet were separate from the retinues of the rectors, in order to avoid affiliations with any faction within Florence and with any of the other judicial officials. It was this notary who announced his presence to the defendant and told him to speak the truth without fear. His presence was mandatory at the response of the defendant, the depositions of the witnesses, the site of the torture, and the subsequent confession in the courtroom. His version of the acts acted as a check on the version of the other criminal notary. However, his impact on the formation of the documents was little; the judge directed the actual formation of the trial. It was the judge who formed the inquisition, compelled the witnesses, and directed the examination of the witnesses. The judge and the criminal notary thus counterbalanced each other.

Another notary of the Podestà, the notary of the capsa, was deputed to writing down the names and crimes of those coming into custody, at the fort of the Podestà. This notary came into existence in 1322. The capsa (as noted above) was a booth located inside or next to the door of the rector's palace, and the fort was the prison in the palace where suspects stayed before they were tried or transferred to prison. The Podestà's milites brought back many suspects to be registered at the capsa. They captured and led back to the fort those who bore prohibited arms, played prohibited games, went about at night past curfew, or committed other crimes. Also those who were already banned or declared criminals, even debtors, when they were captured, were led back to the fort by the conestabiles, the berrovarii, the Podestà, or other officials, for registration by the notary of the capsa and temporary incarceration in the fort (*Stat.* 1.7). The milites, who brought everyone they captured to the notary of the capsa, were closely affiliated with this notary. The milites reported the number of times and the hours that they went out to carry out their job to the notary of the capsa, who recorded this in his acts and assessed the diligence or negligence of the milites. Although the notary of the capsa registered anyone who was led to the Podestà's fort by communal officials, even if the suspect was accused by a private accuser, the mechanisms involving the notary of the capsa were established primarily for facilitating inquisition procedures. Mainly he registered those arrested by the milites and other policing officials. The cases that were processed by the Podestà's notary of the capsa demonstrate some kinds of cases tried in that rector's courts, such as those concerning bearing prohibited arms, playing prohibited games, and going about at night past curfew. Debt, in particular, is cited as a crime for which the Podestà's officials made arrests, thus emerging as a principal kind of crime tried in that rector's court.

The Captain also had a notary of the capsa who was stationed near the door of his palace to record those captured. This notary performed the same functions as the Podestà's notary of the capsa. The Captain also had a miles who investigated cases of bearing arms, going at night, playing prohibited games, and other crimes, demonstrating that the Captain similarly had jurisdiction over these violations. Although the notaries of the Executor are not as well explained in the statutes of 1415 as the notaries of the other rectors, he also had a notary of the capsa and a miles, and thus jurisdiction over bearing arms, going at night, and playing prohibited games. The development of this office and its spread to all three rectors demonstrates the necessity of processing a good number of people arrested by the retinues of the rectors, indicating an active and aggressive policing system.

All of the rectors had their own notary over consignment, and so shared jurisdiction over the duties that pertained to this notary. This notary was not just a *iudex ordinarius* (meaning that his writings carried official weight), he filled the function of a judge with a minor criminal jurisdiction. Notaries were important members of the hierarchy of officials and even had some legal training. Some filled posts in the county and district with minor criminal jurisdictions. The notary of consignment consigned horses, household goods, food, arms, equipment, armor, and other items necessary to guard the castles and lands and to perform the offices to the podestà, captains, *castellani* (officials in charge of the castles), and other officials of the county and district and their retinues, and collected them back again when these officials finished office (*Stat.* 1.10).

The scope of the consignment extended to all of the fortresses of the county and district and to all of the lands subject to the commune. Any of these podestà, captains, and castellani who did not return that which had been assigned to him; who committed any fraud, negligent act, or crime concerning these things; or who was negligent concerning the conservation or custody of the castles, was condemned by the notary of consignment. He executed and exacted the condemnations, which were pecuniary, by compelling payment from the convicted official or from this official's oathswearers. The notary of consignment had full arbitrium and all power in proceeding, recognizing, terminating, condemning, making definitive judgments, and even executing. He could proceed, recognize, punish, condemn and execute summarily, even with no legal writing preceding the condemnation. He needed only to record his writings pertaining to the crime, negligence, or fraud in the acts of the commune. His documents or acts of office were considered to have the presumption of law, to have the same value as full legal proof. However, the notary of consignment could not condemn anyone to a greater penalty than that specified in the statutes, so could only diminish penalties. Evidently, discretion in punishing and condemning in this case was not characterized by complete discretion in setting the penalty but was less grandiose than it sounded. Still, the notary of consignment was an important official who acted to prevent the appropriation of communal goods. Jurisdiction over this kind of usurpation remained squarely within the jurisdiction of the regular court system.

The podestà, captains, castellani, and other officials of the county and district, who ruled the lands, castles, forts, and villages in the county and district, and their retinues, were required to produce their communal goods for the notary of consignment at the request of the notary, immediately if he so requested, or they would be condemned to a 500-lire penalty. This penalty could be diminished according to the magnitude of the crime. The notary worked his way through all the lands, castles, forts, and villages, making the podestà, captains, and castellani produce their consigned possessions and retinues at least once a month. There were checks on the performance of this notary. Two witnesses from the place or castle—or, at least, men deputed through the officials of the castle—had to be present during such demonstration in order to prove that it had taken place. The notary reported to the officials of the castles (*offitiales castrorum*), Florentine officials of the central government who reviewed his performance. At least once a month the notary returned to the palace of the Podestà, Captain, or Executor to begin the trials against the officials of the county and district and to execute his sentences, although he was not permitted to stay in Florence more than six days. The Podestà, the Captain, and the Executor got a small bonus for any condemnations made by this notary. The notary of consignment was also charged with the consignments and inspections of the mercenary foot soldiers of the commune who were stationed in these castles or places. The fines exacted from these foot soldiers were given to the *offitiales defectuum* (*ufficiali de' difetti*, those officials who monitored the mercenaries for deficiencies, such as not bringing the agreed-on number of soldiers) of Florence (*Stat.* 1.10). This notary was first mentioned in the statutes of 1415.

The last notary, the notary over the banned, over the registers of the

Subordinate Officials of the Foreign Rectors

condemned and banned, and over extraordinary things, was an important official responsible for an essential part of criminal trials. Although the late fourteenth- and early fifteenth-century Florentine criminal justice system was very aggressive in capturing criminals, compared to medieval standards, many criminals remained at large. The judicial system resorted to condemning suspected criminals who were contumacious. It banned them, putting them outside the protection of the law so that anyone could commit offenses against them with impunity. The notary who kept track of such exiles was a vital part of the system of execution of penalties. He kept records on all those for whom the police forces were looking, those being cited to current litigation, and those against whom offenses could legally be committed. Only those committing serious crimes were banned.

The notary over the banned performed several other functions. Like the milites socii, he could investigate for those suspected of playing prohibited games or bearing prohibited arms. He sometimes performed just as a civil notary, writing down the acts of civil cases. He banned suspected criminals, that is, he announced in one of the councils the names of those who were contumacious from the courts, thus making them outlaws who could be offended with impunity. He also investigated for infractions of the sumptuary laws; that is, wearing garments that were prohibited because they were too expensive, or spending too much on weddings or funerals. Each of the rectors—the Podestà, the Captain, and the Executor—had a notary over the banned, showing that each of the rectors subsumed under his jurisdiction that notary's sphere of duties. The notary over the banned announced those condemned and contumacious from the court of whichever rector he served. Besides jurisdiction over extraordinary crimes, such as playing prohibited games and bearing prohibited arms, the important area of jurisdiction over sumptuary laws was shared by all of the rectors. Sumptuary infractions were investigated by the notary and tried by the criminal judges and the rectors. It is not accidental that this notary was the only one not attached to a judge that existed in the 1322–25 period as well as in 1415. The Podestà had a notary over the book of the banned in 1322–25 who dealt with contumaciousness, a problem that was more widespread in 1322–25 than in 1415, perhaps because less manpower was devoted to this activity in the earlier period. Efficient record keeping of the banned contributed to curbing the problem of contumaciousness and showed an active program of pursuit.

Both the milites socii and the notary over the banned investigated those playing prohibited games and those bearing prohibited arms. Only the milites investigated those going about at night past curfew because the notary over the banned only investigated during the day. Nor did this notary attempt to apprehend banned people, delinquents, rebels, or those harboring them. He only kept the records pertaining to them, and he investigated to determine what goods the banned person owned. The notary over the banned did arrest for the extraordinary crimes. He related the names of those he arrested to the notary of the capsa, who registered them.

The notary over the banned published in one council or another, within fifteen days from condemnation, all those condemned through contumaciousness in the court of his rector. After this, the condemned person was considered banned. No one could be banned who was condemned for debt or for a crime with a penalty of 100 lire or less, even if the person was condemned for several crimes totaling over 100 lire but with each crime having a penalty of less than 100 lire. The notary over the banned then gave the names of the banned to the custodians of the acts (Stat. 1.9). Those who were thus banned had their goods confiscated and could be offended by anyone with impunity while they were at large. This was a very severe sanction invoked against those who were contumacious. A culprit would presumably only be contumacious if the penalty he was facing was very severe and his condemnation or torture most certain. The possibility of unlimited imprisonment for nonpayment of a pecuniary penalty made the punishment for poor criminals severe, whatever the magnitude of the crime, and made contumaciousness a likely choice. The court cases show that this inequity was partly compensated for by the discretion of the judge.[6] If the defendant was known to be destitute, the judge limited the amount of time the culprit could spend in prison if nonpayment occurred, stating this to be the reason. The Signoria, too, abrogated this harshness with releases from prison as oblations (acts of mercy as offerings to God). Although contumaciousness was reduced in the early fifteenth century through increased police activity, it continued to be a problem for the judicial system.

The Podestà also brought with him three soldiers (milites) who were heads of the police force.[7] The milites were constantly going through the city, at least one of them at all times, day or night, searching for those committing the extraordinary crimes, committing any other crimes, fleeing the court system after having been banned or declared rebels, or harboring banned people and rebels. They investigated in the city, county, and district of Florence. Besides their routine rounds, they were sent on special expeditions by the Podestà to capture criminals. The milites worked in conjunction with the notary of the capsa, and their performance was evaluated by the number of arrests they recorded with the notary of the capsa. When the Podestà sat at the bench for rendering law, at least two of the milites assisted him and his judges. The statutes are vague as to the function of the milites in the court. Either they were used to present evidence against those they arrested, or they were used to execute the penalties, to take suspects away to be tortured, or to take criminals away to be imprisoned or executed. Most likely, an important investigatory official like the miles presented evidence. The emphasis that is placed on arresting for prohibited arms, prohibited games, and curfew violations in the job of this official and of the notaries refers more to a procedure of arrest than to specific crimes. These crimes are the most obvious crimes where arrest *in flagranti* and initiation *ex officio* would be used. All of the rectors had milites to serve their courts in 1415 (*Stat.* 1.7).

The rest of the Podestà's retinue was made up of minor officials, numerically great and cumulatively fulfilling an important function. The Podestà's court had eight domicelli, or pages, who did not bear arms and must have acted as errand runners. The sixty arms-bearing famuli or berrovarii of the Podestà, composing the largest retinue of berrovarii of any rector, were his police force. Like the milites, they sometimes investigated crimes themselves and sometimes accompanied a higher official to stop a rebellion or to arrest criminals. The berrovarii also provided proof in court: for some crimes, the report of one berrovarius was necessary to convict and for others, the reports of two berrovarii. The berrovarii captured debtors, receiving a small commission from the creditors (*Stat.* 1.40). The number of berrovarii serving the rectors had increased since 1322–25, despite the fact that the population had decreased sharply. The decline in the population was reflected in the decrease in judges. The number of judges attached to the Podestà fell from eleven in the 1322–25 period to four in 1415. The Captain's number of judges remained the same, three in each period, as did the Executor's number, two in each period. But the number of berrovarii increased markedly. The Podestà had the same number of berrovarii in each period, sixty, but the Captain, who had only twenty-four in the 1322–25 period (or thirty if we credit him with the six berrovarii serving the judge of appeals), had fifty in 1415. The Executor had only four berrovarii in the 1322–25 period but thirty in 1415.

Besides these berrovarii who were on foot, the Podestà retained fourteen horsemen, ten of whom bore arms. The arms-bearing horsemen must have functioned like the berrovarii, pursuing criminals fleeing from one *popolo* to another. One horseman without arms was attached to the notary of consignment when he went from castle to castle in the contado and district checking up on the officials staffing the castles. The horseman preceded the notary, announcing to the castle officials that they should prepare their *monstra* (demonstration of proper staff and communal goods) to display to the notary. Neither the Podestà nor the other rectors brought any *nuntii* (announcers, messengers) of which they made abundant use. The nuntii carried the citations to the defendants and witnesses, and the reports of the cases to the officials of the camera of the acts. The varieties of nuntii called the *precones*, or banners, announced the outlawing of people throughout the city. Although the rectors used these minor officials, the nuntii were provided by the commune of Florence from among the Florentine residents.

The Podestà brought an abundance of officials in his retinue to serve the purposes assigned to him. The tasks to which the different members of his retinue were devoted delineate some of his areas of responsibility in a very general but definite way. The Podestà's court tried cases of extraordinary crimes, infractions of sumptuary laws, debt, appropriation of communal goods by county and district officials, and negligence in providing for the security of castles by the county and district officials. More information on the Podestà's jurisdiction can be gleaned from the specific rubrics mentioning the Podestà as the acting official for specific crimes. These rubrics will be discussed later.

The Subordinate Officials of the Captain of the People

The Captain of the People was another foreign rector, equal in stature and authority to the Podestà and sharing some of the same functions but also performing distinctive ones. Studying the officials under the Captain proves to be an effective way to learn about that rector's functions. This is fortunate, since the specific rubrics mentioning the Captain as the acting official for specific crimes provide little useful information. The study of the specific rubrics produces the outlines of few large blocks of jurisdiction exclusively or mainly treated by the Captain. Additional knowledge must come from the rubrics describing his subordinate officials.

The Captain was also a foreign rector expected to bring with him a retinue of officials: three judges, two milites socii, seven notaries, six domicelli, fifty berrovarii, and ten horsemen, nine of which were arms-bearing. The one horseman who did not bear arms was attached to the Captain's notary of consignment (*Stat.* 1.13). Of the three judges serving the Captain, one was devoted to criminal matters, one to civil matters, appeals and nullities, and one to camera and gabelle. Only the judge treating civil matters and appeals needed to have earned a doctorate. Little is said concerning the criminal judge, but little need be said. The criminal judge tried all criminal matters that were assigned to the Captain and was able to impose penalties up to an unlimited amount, including capital punishment. The Captain was empowered to try any criminal case whatever, although there were certain kinds of crimes that he usually tried and that were usually reserved for him. However, the number of crimes that are ascribed specifically to the Captain are comparatively few. One must conclude that the Captain and his criminal judge treated general criminal matters, largely those in which his retinue made the arrest. If the retinue caught criminals *in flagranti* or investigated a crime recently committed, this would include any kind of crime. There were many crimes in which no rector was favored as the appropriate rector. The bulk of the cases tried by the Captain's criminal judge must have been of these kinds.

One of the three judges was deputed to the office of camera and gabelle. This judge handled civil cases up to a sum of only ten lire, a minor amount (*Stat.* 1.16). No written accusation was necessary to start such a case, nor was there any contested litigation; rather, the judge of the case expedited it as quickly as possible and according to his discretion. In fact, the judge was required to finish the case within fifteen days of the first citation or he was fined. One witness of sight or a written account in the book of the creditor or plaintiff, if he was a merchant or guildsman in one of the twenty-one guilds, was sufficient proof to win the case. There were no appeals from these sentences nor any kind of exceptions allowed, execution beginning immediately, even if this involved the capture of the defendant (*Stat.* 2.3).

Besides functioning as a small claims court, the court of the judge of camera and gabelle was the court in which controversies over communal indirect taxes, or gabelles, were aired. The commune levied gabelles on many items, from wine and oil to contracts, and from weights and measures to arguments.[8] The judge of camera and gabelle recognized, terminated, and executed concerning all cases, complaints, and controversies over communal gabelles and over all the things contained in and pertaining to the ordinances and provisions of these gabelles. These cases were conducted in much the same way as the small claims cases. The procedure was summary, appeal was not allowed, and execution was immediate. The judge was not obligated to give any reasons why he decided as he did, nor was he obligated to counsel the litigants on points of law.

In gabelle cases, the jurisdiction of the judge of camera and gabelle was coordinated with that of two other offices, the Office of the Tower and the office of the governors of gabelles. The Tower Officials tried cases of crimes perpetrated by gabelle collectors. The governors of gabelles declared those not paying their gabelles debtors and defaulters of the commune, and they seized the goods of tax debtors and sold them to cover the amount owed.[9] All of the rectors aided the governors of gabelles in seizing goods and capturing tax debtors. The coordination of the functions of the important agencies with the functions of the rectors of the regular court system was normal in the structure of the judicial system.[10]

Since the commune was very aggressive in collecting its gabelles, there were never any cases of the commune's taking people to court over their taxes. The judge of camera and gabelle heard cases of people wishing to have recourse against the seizing of their goods by the commune in cases in which they felt the taxation was unjustified. One example of a dubious instance would be when a foreigner contracted for the sale of any goods within the county and district of Florence. By statute, this foreigner was responsible for paying the gabelle of contracts. The judge of camera and gabelle heard cases of questions concerning the gabelle of contracts, a tax likely to generate questionable cases. If a question arose concerning payment of this gabelle, the party wishing to have his case heard placed a deposit in the amount of the gabelle with the governors of gabelles. Then the judge of camera and gabelle heard the case and decided promptly.[11]

More than handling litigation of those feeling themselves unjustly taxed, the judge of camera and gabelle handled crimes connected with gabelle collection, namely fraud, extortion, and bribery. Cases of extortion must mainly have involved gabelle collectors and gabelle officials as defendants, so that, in this regard, the work of the judge of camera and gabelle overlapped that of the Tower Officials. Fraud and bribery, tried by the judge of camera and gabelle, could have been committed by collector or tax payer. The judge of camera and gabelle, in these instances, was trying criminal cases (*Stat.* 1.16).

Another example in which the judge of camera and gabelle acted in a criminal case concerning gabelles was his treatment of infractions of the ordinances of weights and measures. The standardization of weights and measures was supervised by the same officials who handled true gabelle cases, the Tower Officials and the governors of the gabelles. Merchants who sold goods that needed to be measured out, like wine, or be of standard size, like barrels, were required to have official measures with communal seals at their shops. Any merchant who did not have such measures was tried and punished summarily by the judge of camera and gabelle. Trials could be initiated by inquisition by this judge, by denunciation, or by accusation.[12] The judge of camera and gabelle had two more spheres of competence in his piecemeal jurisdiction. He handled cases involving business of the treasury and treasury officials, and he took the oaths and securities from all citizen officials, especially the treasury officials and other officials handling communal money (*Stat.* 1.16; 1.19). What little is written about this judge's duties over treasury officials indicates that only the judge of camera and gabelle was permitted to initiate cases against treasury officials. Because the treasury officials were in charge of sending out salaries, money for household goods, and money for whatever else the rectors and officials needed, these rectors and officials were not given the power to threaten the treasury officials through any kind of

Subordinate Officials of the Foreign Rectors

judicial action. Thus, the Podestà, the Captain, the Executor, and the foreign officials could not capture or detain any treasury official unless there was a denunciation or accusation against this official for a crime, personal debt, or infraction of the laws against bearing arms. If any threat was made to a treasurer, the treasurer docked the official's salary without having to provide any kind of proof. The judge of camera and gabelle syndicated the treasury officials by reviewing their figures and tried treasury officials for inconsistencies in their books which signaled that they had given out too much money to officials they favored (*Stat.* 1.22).

The judge of camera and gabelle administered the oaths and took the securities from all treasury officials and all officials who were elected, extracted, or deputed, including county and district officials. A notary, called the notary of extractions, who was present at all extractions and elections, sent a list of those extracted, elected, or deputed to the judge of camera and gabelle, who kept a record of these officials, noting when they were elected. This judge then summoned them to take an oath that they would exercise their offices well and legally and to post their securities. These securities usually consisted of oathswearers who vouched to pay a certain amount in the event of the official's bad performance or criminal behavior. The oathswearers needed approval of the communal approvers, who evaluated the characters and funds of the oathswearers. If the approvers evaluated incorrectly, and the expropriation of communal money by the official was followed by the defaulting of his oathswearers, the approvers were held responsible for paying.

After the judge took the oaths and securities from the officials, he checked his records to make sure that all the officials of the commune were syndicated. He recorded the dates when the officials were syndicated and absolved in syndication and when they restored any communal money that they possessed. If he discovered any case in which termination of office was not followed by syndication and restoration of funds within one month, he reported this case to the Priors and the Gonfalonier of Justice. The official was fined for this infraction (*Stat.* 1.17).

In sum, the judge of camera and gabelle tried civil cases of less than ten lire, civil and criminal cases involving gabelles, and criminal cases involving the treasurers and treasury business. He collected the securities from treasury officials, county and district officials, and all other citizen officials, making sure these officials were syndicated. Thus, the judge of camera and gabelle had some criminal jurisdiction. His duties were part of the active program to prevent corruption and usurpation, and part of the system of checks and balances within the government.

The last of the three judges serving the Captain was the judge of civil questions, appeals, and nullities. Of the three judges serving the Captain, this civil judge was the only one required to have a doctorate in law. He tried all civil cases involving amounts of greater than ten lire that were within the Captain's jurisdiction, and appeals and nullities of cases from other courts. Not all cases were subject to appeal, and of those that were, not all were sent to the judge of appeals. He was not the only judge who participated in the appeals process; the civil judges serving the other two rectors also conducted appeals of certain kinds.

The most important cases that were not subject to appeal were criminal cases in which the condemnations were made by officials in the city of Florence, such as the foreign rectors.[13] No criminal cases from within the city ever went to appeal before the judge of appeals or anyone else. Therefore, appeals were only permitted from civil cases and arbitrations from the city of Florence, and civil cases, arbitrations, and some criminal cases from the county and district (*Stat.* 2.127). There were no appeals from the sentences of the consuls of the guilds unless the sentences violated communal statutory guidelines.[14] However, the consuls' jurisdiction over criminal matters was limited. There were no appeals from condemnations by the Tower Officials, in conformity with the prohibition against appeals from criminal condemnations reached in the city by communal officials.[15] When the Tower Officials condemned those who bought the rights to collect the gabelle but did not pay the commune for this privilege, appeal was not permitted.[16] There was no appeal from the judgments of the governors of the gabelle of contracts.[17] From the aspect of assessing the level of patrician control, it must be pointed out that not just the criminal condemnations of the officials of the agencies were above appeal, but the condemnations of the rectors as well. All of the officials that were part of the central government in Florence were considered important enough to make decisions that were not reviewed.

Because of the great complexity of civil cases, civil decisions given by the rectors were subject to appeal. The person appealing had to do so within ten days from the time of the original sentence or injunction. The appeal or nullity had to be brought forth in the presence of the judge who had rendered the sentence or in the presence of the judge of appeals, if the other judge was not available. If the appeal was brought forth to the judge who gave the first sentence, this judge took the appeal before the judge of appeals within eight days from the time he received it. The judge of appeals had twenty days to decide the appeal. The judge of appeals did more than review the records of the case; he retried the whole trial.[18] His trial included calling the witnesses who had appeared in the first trial (*Stat.* 3.17). Frequently the judge of appeals used knowledgeable counsel, as the advice of jurists was called, usually in the form of *consilia*, written opinions of famous expert jurists (*Stat.* 3.91; 2.1). If the judge of appeals overturned the original decision, the party favored in the first decision had an opportunity to appeal the appeal (*Stat.* 2.127).

Besides trying appeals from civil cases, he also recognized appeals from arbitrations, making reformations of arbitrations. Two different kinds of arbitrations existed in the Middle Ages and the Renaissance. An *arbiter* imitated procedural guidelines and issued a sentence that could not be appealed. An *arbitrator*, on the other hand, was usually a mutually agreed-upon party who made a less formal decision not according to set procedures but according to a vague notion of equity. The goal was conflict resolution, but if the compromise failed, the decision could be annulled.[19] The appeal from an arbitrated decision was called a reformation of an arbitration, or a *reductio ad arbitrium boni viri*.[20] The *boni viri* could be the judge of appeals, the Podestà, or a privately chosen party.

The rules governing appeals originating in the county and district were completely different from those governing appeals originating in the city of Florence. Both civil and criminal cases judged by officials of the county and district were sometimes subject to appeal. In cases from the county and district, the possibility of appeal was created if the case had originally been tried in a lower court by a minor official. Civil cases from the county and district were more likely to be subject to appeal than were criminal cases. The judge of appeals could nullify any case from the contado or territory in which an official without proper jurisdiction had given a sentence in a civil case. In theory, any sentence or injunction (*praeceptum*), definitive or interlocutory, in civil or mixed cases given by any rector or official of the county and district could be appealed to the judge of appeals in Florence (*Stat.* 5.4.59). In reality, where the official was of high rank, appeal was not allowed from civil cases of little moment. There was no appeal in civil cases involving less than fifty lire tried by the Vicar of Alpi Fiorentine. This vicar had civil jurisdiction over all people in his vicariate, not just over stipendiarii (*Stat.* 5.4.44). Appeals were not permitted from decisions made by the Podestà of Montecatini in civil matters involving amounts of less than 100 lire. From the civil definitions made by the Podestà of S. Stephano, no appeal could be made to the judge of appeals of Florence if the case involved less than fifty lire (*Stat.* 5.4.23). As always when dealing with the county and district, guiding principles were of limited application. Because every location came under Florentine dominion with its own separate treaty, the rules governing jurisdiction were frequently different for different locations. Despite greater uniformity of rule, the territories still remained particular cases laboriously coordinated during the period of the redaction of the 1415 statutes. The rules governing the territory were partially reformed in 1423–24, when podesteries were combined into larger units.[21]

Very frequently, no appeals were permitted from criminal condemnations given by officials in the county and district. The decisions of the Captain of Arezzo and the Captain of Pisa, both of whom had only criminal jurisdiction, were not subject to appeal or nullity (*Stat.* 5.4.19; 5.4.1). No appeals were permitted from criminal condemnations issued by the Vicar of Alpi Fiorentine (*Stat.* 5.4.44), nor by either the Podestà of Santa Maria a Monte (*Stat.* 5.4.79) or the Podestà of Massae and Cozzile (*Stat.* 5.4.80). For our purposes, it is more significant that some appeals were permitted to the judge of appeals in Florence from criminal condemnations issued by county and district officials. Thus, the judge of appeals in Florence had some involvement in the criminal process. Although the great bulk of cases must have been appeals of civil cases, since these could come both from within the city of Florence and from the county and district, some small number of criminal appeals were conducted by the judge of appeals.

While it is clear that most appeals must have been aired before the judge of appeals, necessitating his existence, appeals did go at times before the other civil judges, those of the Podestà and that of the Executor. The Captain's judge of appeals and nullities was the judge of first appeals. Any time the judge of appeals heard an appeal and reversed the decision of the first sentencing court, the party who won the first suit and lost the appeal had an opportunity to file a new appeal. Each party was allowed one appeal. This pertained only to civil cases, in which there were two opposing parties. The second appeal could not be tried by the same judge as the first appeal, so it was usually aired before the Executor's civil judge. There did have to be contingencies, rules for the instances in which the Captain's civil judge, who was the judge of appeals, or the Executor's civil judge had done the original sentencing. These judges could not then try the first or the second appeal. In these instances, all of the civil judges of the rectors became involved in the appeals process. When the judge of appeals sentenced in the original case, the Executor's civil judge tried the first appeal and the Podestà's civil judge tried the second. If the Executor's civil judge tried the original case, the Podestà's civil judge tried the first appeal and the judge of appeals tried the second (*Stat.* 2.127).

The civil judges attached to the other rectors were also involved in trying appeals coming from the courts of the county and district officials.[22] Appeal was permitted from all the criminal sentences of the Podestà of S. Gemignano and the Podestà of S. Miniato to the Podestà of Florence and his collateral judge (*Stat.* 5.4.39; 5.4.40). Appeals could be made only in civil cases from fifty lire up from the Podestà of Castro Pontenari, the Podestà of Chiusi, and the Podestà of Civitella Vald'ambra to the Podestà of Florence.[23] Appeal was frequently to the Podestà of

Subordinate Officials of the Foreign Rectors

Florence and his civil judges and never to the Executor and his civil judge. The Executor's civil judge apparently was mainly involved in appeals as the judge of second appeals and so did not handle many cases of first appeal, even from the county and district. The Podestà, on the other hand, bore as much of the burden of appeals coming from the county and district as did the judge of appeals. To the list of duties of the civil judges of all the rectors must be added some duties in the area of appeals.

One other quixotic sphere of jurisdiction belonged to the judge of appeals and nullities. It is difficult to see how his jurisdiction over sumptuary infractions at baptisms fit in with his other duties. Nevertheless, along with the rectors, the judge of appeals had cognition over such infractions, mainly the spending of too much money on the celebration of baptism.[24] The judge of appeals was supposed to depute notaries to investigate sumptuary infractions at baptisms.[25]

The judge of appeals had traditionally been a very important official possessing the highest sphere of competence, a sphere that in earliest communal history was not even possessed by any communal official, rather by an imperial official. In the statutes of 1322–25, he was an autonomous official who was elected separately and came from a foreign city-state with his own retinue.[26] At that time, the Priors, the Gonfalonier, the Sixteen Gonfalonieri, and the Twelve Buonuomini chose a suitable foreigner who was a doctor of laws. The office of the judge of appeals was subordinated to the Executor in 1412 but was transferred to the Captain in 1415, where it remained until 1477.[27] By subordinating the judge of appeals to the Captain, the judge was distanced from the Signoria's control. (The Signoria was composed of the Priors and the Gonfalonier of Justice.) In 1415, the Captain began bringing the judge of appeals in his retinue. The Captain was elected through electioners who were drawn from the borse by the Priors, the Gonfalonier, and the colleges.

The history of the judge of appeals is an example of jurisdictions of officials being shifted and switched between the time of the statute compilation of 1322–25 and that of 1415. Major switches occurred in the judicial system right up until the time of the 1415 redaction. Duties of one official were assigned to another in an attempt to coordinate similar functions and to simplify jurisdictional lines, a part of the movement that continued into the early fifteenth century of creating a systematized and efficient judicial system. When the judge of appeals went from being autonomous to being subordinate to the Captain, he did not become less powerful nor more influenced by the executive branch. His integration into the structure of the rectors is not an example of the attrition of the regular court system but rather an example of the regular court system being placed in control of a very influential set of responsibilities. The Captain was chosen to supervise the judge of appeals because his civil judge tried the fewest number of civil cases in the first instance. Both the Podestà and the Executor had civil judges with general civil duties as their main activity, while the Captain, on the other hand, before he supervised the judge of appeals, had only one civil judge, the judge of camera and gabelle, with very specific duties. Many of his decisions could not be appealed. If the judge of appeals had been subordinated to the Podestà or the Executor, many of the decisions which should have gone to the judge of appeals would have been barred, since the court of the same rector could not have tried both the original case and the appeal. The whole system of first and second appeal would have been thrown into chaos.

The Captain also brought with him seven notaries to serve his courts and assist in the fulfillment of his duties. Some of his notaries were the same and served the same purposes as the Podestà's. One was a notary of consignment who traveled throughout the county and district to check on the communal property consigned to the county and district officials. A second was a notary of the capsa who sat at the door of his palace recording the names and crimes of those arrested and detained at the palace, especially those caught for playing prohibited games, bearing prohibited arms, and going about at night after curfew. A third was deputed to extraordinary things and to the banned. This notary investigated cases of playing prohibited games and bearing prohibited arms. He registered and published the names of those whom the Captain had banned, that is, who were contumacious and declared to be outlaws who could be offended with impunity. He investigated the goods of the condemned and banned, and compelled the rectors of the county and district to do the same (*Stat.* 1.15). Two other notaries were deputed to criminal matters, to writing the acts of the criminal court and copying the acts for anyone seeking them. Together, one reading and the other listening and copying, they made another copy of all the acts so that one copy could be placed in the camera of the acts and the other could remain with the Captain. As did the Podestà's criminal notaries, the Captain's criminal notaries wrote down the parts of the trials in the acts, including directly recording the statements of witnesses.

Of the two remaining notaries, one was deputed to the judge of camera and gabelle and the other to the judge of civil things and appeals. The notary of the judge of camera and gabelle wrote the civil cases of ten lire or less that were aired in the judge's presence and recorded the securities and oaths of the officials of the commune that were handled by the judge of camera and gabelle. For the duties that this judge performed in connection with the treasury, he was given a notary from the Guild of Judges and

Subordinate Officials of the Foreign Rectors

Notaries of Florence (*Stat.* 1.16). The notary deputed to the judge of appeals wrote the acts of these appeals.

The Captain had two military associates (milites socii), one of whom went through the city every day once during the day and once at night accompanied by berrovarii. He investigated for all crimes, including the extraordinary crimes and the enormous crimes. Further, this soldier pursued and captured those who were already condemned and banned. He functioned exactly like the soldiers of the Podestà. The other soldier was deputed to pursuing the condemned and banned throughout the city, county, and district, with the aid of twenty berrovarii. When he worked outside the city, which he was required to do every ten days, he also commanded two horsemen. This miles operated in a slightly different manner than the Podestà's milites, in that he took regular trips outside the city for purposes of investigation and capture, while the Podestà's milites went where they were sent by the Podestà (*Stat.* 1.22).

Besides these officials, the Captain had six domicelli, fifty berrovarii, nine arms-bearing horsemen, and one horseman who traveled with the notary of consignment. The Captain was greatly involved in criminal matters, although perhaps not as much as the Podestà. His slightly smaller retinue indicates a slightly lesser capacity to investigate, pursue, and capture criminals and slightly less involvement in the criminal process as a whole. The Captain had one criminal judge as compared to the Podestà's two, showing a diminished criminal jurisdiction in comparison to the Podestà. This judge was completely devoted to ordinary criminal trials, that is, to trials of those crimes in which all of the rectors were instructed and empowered to proceed, and to trials of those few crimes uniquely treated by the court of the Captain. Both of the Captain's civil judges had some criminal duties. The judge of camera and gabelle tried infractions of ordinances pertaining to gabelles—in particular, fraud, extortion, and bribery. He also tried treasury officials when their accounts did not balance. The judge of appeals had little criminal involvement, but he did recognize criminal appeals originating in the courts of the officials of the county and district.

The Subordinate Officials of the Executor of the Ordinances of Justice

The Executor of the Ordinances of Justice, although he was not a noble like the Podestà and the Captain, but a popolano, was like the Podestà and the Captain in having to bring with him a retinue of officials to assist in carrying out his functions. Like the Podestà and the Captain, he was not a doctor of law or any level of judge. The Executor was supposed to bring with him two judges, one of whom was a doctor of civil law, one soldier (*miles socius*), five notaries, four domicelli, thirty arms-bearing berrovarii, and seven arms-bearing horsemen.

Unlike the Podestà's and the Captain's criminal judges, whose main jurisdiction was crimes in general, the Executor's criminal judge had important specialized functions as well as a general criminal purview. This criminal judge tried prison crimes and was involved in the syndication of officials. He was in charge of investigating and trying crimes perpetrated in the communal prison, the Stinche, either by the prisoners or by the administrators. Each month this judge toured the Stinche, probing crimes committed against the prisoners and duties neglected by the *superstiti* or other officials. *Superstiti* were prison officials in charge of releasing prisoners either on bail or after payment of their condemnations. They were in a position of great power in relation to the prisoners, a position which made them particularly prone to committing extortion, as were the provisors of the prison who supplied the prisoners with food and necessities and took care of any cleaning that was done. The Executor's criminal judge had authority over all cases of fraud or extortion that took place in the Stinche whether committed by *superstiti*, provisors, treasurers, other officials, or the prisoners, and could determine cases of debt between prisoners. Once a month he went before the Priors, the Gonfalonier of Justice, and the colleges to report if functions were being neglected or supplies were not being provided (*Stat.* 1.24). Besides his prison-related functions, he managed a regular criminal case load. He tried all the cases of crimes that were uniquely assigned to the Executor, the cases for which trial was permitted to any one of the rectors, and the cases in which the culprit was apprehended by the Executor's retinue, even if these crimes were formally assigned to another rector. He was also involved in syndication, the procedures against officials who committed crimes in office, which procedures were headed by the Executor. His duties in connection with the prison and with syndication must have taken up most of his time but not all of it, since there were routine crimes uniquely assigned to the Executor's court. The statutes describing the Executor's retinue contain no information on the function of the civil judge. He tried whatever civil cases were assigned to the Executor.

The Executor brought five notaries with him. One was a notary of consignment (*Stat.* 1.10), while another was a notary over extraordinary things, banned people, and the registers of the condemned (*Stat.* 1.9). Since the Executor had a miles, he must have had a notary of the capsa to whom the miles took culprits who had committed extraordinary and other crimes in order that they be registered outside the Executor's palace. Further, the Executor had one criminal notary and one civil notary.

Again, the size of the Executor's retinue would indicate that he had even less involvement in apprehending criminals than did the Captain. Still, the Executor's thirty berrovarii put him much closer to parity with the Podestà in criminal matters than he ever had been before. The Executor's new powers to treat any crime considerably broadened his influence in criminal matters. Before 1415, his involvement in criminal matters was much narrower.

In conclusion, all of the rectors had criminal judges who conducted trials of ordinary crime. The Podestà, with two criminal judges and sixty armed berrovarii, stands out as the rector most involved in criminal investigation and prosecution. The Captain, with two civil judges devoted to specific tasks, was immersed in civil matters but not in general civil matters to the same degree as the Podestà, who had two civil judges devoted to general civil matters. There seems to have been a great emphasis on apprehending culprits who had committed extraordinary crimes, that is, playing prohibited games, bearing prohibited arms, and violating the nighttime curfew, since each rector had a notary over extraordinary things, milites socii to interrupt these crimes, and a notary over the capsa to register them. While emphasis on these crimes cannot be denied, their visibility may reflect that they were the ones most likely to be interrupted *in flagranti* and most easily discovered by the berrovarii. Also, those bearing arms as well as those violating curfew show a predisposition toward committing other crimes. Since the rectors could investigate other crimes as well, their stated interest in the extraordinary crimes may indicate as much a method of investigation as a specialization. Their berrovarii could apprehend criminals committing any kind of crime, turning them over to a court system that would initiate trials through public methods. The statutes of 1415 gave all the rectors general powers in criminal matters. All of the criminal judges attached to the rectors devoted some of their time to a general criminal case load. The rectors no longer represented special interests or served particular constituencies.

4

THE PODESTÀ AND OTHER OFFICIALS WITH JUDICIAL POWERS AFFILIATED WITH THE PODESTÀ

The Podestà

IN CHAPTERS 2 AND 3, I examined the general powers and the subordinate officials of the rectors to determine some of the duties of the rectors. In order to uncover other duties, I will examine the specific rubrics that describe a crime and name a rector to handle it. For several reasons, these rubrics must be interpreted with care. Sometimes the divisions of jurisdiction described in these rubrics are so narrow that their translation into practice is doubtful. Some are anachronistic, harking back to times when the rectors headed different corporations within the government. In the process of switching jurisdictions, some of the rubrics were not properly changed to reflect current jurisdictional areas. Despite the great advances in organization in the statutes of 1415, anachronism, redundancy, and contradiction continued to exist. Therefore, in order to procure reliable information from the specific rubrics, only large blocks of duties consistently assigned to a rector should be heeded.

Most of the confusion in assignment of jurisdiction in the 1415 statutes is caused by rubrics that reflect vestiges of the rectors' former jurisdictions as heads of separate corporations within the state. In the thirteenth century, when the Podestà and the Captain headed different corporations, each rector conducted some duties within his corporation which were the same as the duties conducted by the other rector within his corporation. Both the Podestà and the Captain enforced city ordinances, thus performing some of the same functions. However, the corporations that the rectors headed were very different, imposing different requirements on their leaders. The Captain, who protected guildsmen in the thirteenth century, had different duties than the Podestà, who promoted the power of the urban patriciate over competing groups with sovereignty in that century. When all of the rectors became part of the same central government, confusion was created in the statutes that described their duties. The process of switching and changing jurisdictions which took place in the fourteenth century further confounded the statutes. Therefore, in order

The Podestà and Other Affiliated Officials

to gather reliable information from the statutes, care must be taken to sort out rubrics that reflect redundancy, anachronism, and confusion. The current rubrics can only be distinguished from the outdated rubrics when the previous functions of the rectors in connection with their obsolete corporations, as well as the changes that had taken place in their jurisdictions throughout the centuries, are known.

The Podestà was the major criminal rector in the thirteenth and fourteenth centuries. In the early fifteenth century, besides being connected with his subordinate officials, he was linked with a network of other officials that formed the judicial system as a whole. Some of the officials of the greater judicial system were more closely affiliated with the Podestà than with the other rectors. These officials will be discussed in this chapter along with the Podestà. Because of the coordination of functions between the Podestà and these officials, the discussions of the Podestà and of these affiliated officials become more comprehensible when they are treated together. The Podestà was closely connected to some of the officials suspected by some historians of being the vehicles of patrician takeover, such as the officials of the Mercanzia. Examination of the affiliations of these officials shows that their connection with the executive branch was distant, while their connection with the rectors was close, and that they were not vehicles of patrician takeover but accountable parts of the government. When officials of the greater judicial system were more closely aligned with one rector than with another, they are discussed along with the rector of closest affiliation. If officials were aligned most closely with the Priors and the Gonfalonier of Justice (the executive branch), they are discussed along with the Priors and the Gonfalonier.

Several aspects of the territorial state are demonstrated by changes in the Podestà's court, particularly the subjection of the guilds and the guild courts to the state and the goals of the state. The independent manipulation of the well-being of the workers by the guilds was diminished when some important kinds of cases were transferred to the rectors' courts in the early fifteenth century and when the foreign official of Seta was abolished and the foreign official of Lana reduced in power. The 1415 statutes contain many rubrics on the guilds and show a much more active regulation of them. The Mercanzia, the higher court for the guilds, did not foster the independent judicial status of the guilds but was an arm of the state that regulated them. The power of the Mercanzia throughout the fourteenth century was fostered by the state, when the state ceded jurisdictions to the Mercanzia, permitted it to use special procedures, and allowed it to generate law. By the early fifteenth century, the Mercanzia had lost its executive and diplomatic powers. It then acted as a superior court of the guilds and was constrained to apply the statutes of the commune. The Podestà's court acted as an alternate court to the Mercanzia, so that plaintiffs who felt they would receive biased justice under the Mercanzia could litigate their cases in the court of the Podestà. The Mercanzia had no exclusive sphere of jurisdiction; it was not an independent agency forwarding the goals of a patriciate but a less independent agency that had become watered down by the quotidian business of all of the guilds and firmly entrenched in the system of checks and balances. The alimentary and necessities guilds, which handled food and construction materials, were most directly affected by the movement to subjugate private to public interests through regulations assuring abundance, and fixing prices and salaries. The Officials of Grascia had a jurisdiction coordinated with and subordinate to the Podestà over these guilds.

The Office of the Podestà was created in 1193. Documents from 1193 record a Podestà at the head of a body of consuls composed of the consuls of the *milites*, the society of the knights that represented the neighborhoods, and the *consoli mercatanti*, representatives of the merchants.[1] The consuls performed both executive and judicial functions in the city of Florence at that time. The Podestà became involved in all political affairs and was first among the representatives of the commune.[2] Most of the important diplomatic documents of this era, such as recorded negotiations with foreign states and local magnates, began to bear the signature of the Podestà.[3] He also became a major judicial official. While the commune of Florence never included all of the population of Florence, not even at the height of the territorial state when participation was comparatively broad-based (that is, at no time was everybody enfranchised), in the twelfth and early thirteenth centuries the commune was a very restricted group. At the inception of his office, the Podestà, as head of the consuls, represented a very restricted group, a small part of the total population.

In these early days of the commune, the patriciate was composed of the landed nobility and the commercial upper class. These classes were represented first by the consuls and later by the Podestà. In the twelfth and early thirteenth centuries, *populus* meant the classes that were not represented in the commune, and commune meant the governing classes. These two classes corresponded to the *pedites* and milites of the military organization of the city. Only the milites enjoyed political participation and held consular seats. The milites were composed of the *cavalieri di corredo*, the high feudal nobility, often holding their authority directly from the Emperor, and the minor nobility, either minor feudal lords or citizens of whatever origin who became powerful through their successes in commerce. These merchants were often, but not necessarily, from noble families. Consular power was held by this very tight patriciate, while the borgese and popular classes were only indirectly represented by the heads of the major merchant organizations. These organizations had not yet acquired direct political representation, not even in the councils. The popular class was very indirectly represented by the Calimala Guild.[4]

Thus, when the Podestà came into existence as the head of the consuls, he represented very specific interests. At that time, the struggle for political power was between various urban patrician families sometimes affiliated with the Guelf and Ghibelline factions. Also, the *grandi popolani* of the city found their goals to be in conflict with the magnates who persisted in acting in a lawless manner.[5] Conflict between urban and *contado* patrician families was limited, however, because the patrician families of the commune were really the patrician families of the contado who had moved to the city. Concomitantly, as rural proprietors moved to the city, more land in the contado was becoming owned by *cittadini* (city residents). At the time of the advent of the Podestà, there were thus many ties between the city and the contado. The patriciate of the city were powerful before and after they immigrated to the city.[6] The nobles appear to have been the first group to immigrate in numbers.[7] It is this restricted group that the Podestà, as head of the consuls, represented.

Podestà appeared in most Italian communes in the period from 1150 to 1200, partially as an invention of Emperor Frederick I. Although some cities had podestà who were merely head consuls before the Diet of Roncaglia, after this diet, Emperor Frederick I sent imperial magistrates throughout Italy to head the administrative and judicial institutions. To cities that had rebelled against the reinstitution of imperial power, he sent his own podestà; but in cities that had been more cooperative, he allowed the choosing of domestic podestà. For those cities in which the podestà was chosen domestically, the podestà became a mediator between the communal government and the Emperor. These cities found their autonomy reinforced, not diminished.[8] Outside of the Imperial influence in creating the podestà, the cities themselves contributed to this political development both by creating hierarchical consulates with the nascent podestà as head consuls and by choosing dictators as provisional governors in times of emergency.[9] Florence was late in creating a podestà. In Florence, the Podestà emerged as head of the consuls and then replaced the consuls altogether.

The whole power of the state was not invested in the Podestà. Vittorio Franchini and Lorenzo Cantini, both experts on the Podestà, agree that the Podestà did not act alone but as a representative of the commune. While the Podestà as he evolved in Florence freed himself from the consuls, he often acted at the mandate of the Council of the Commune, which, like himself, represented the commune. When the Podestà carried out duties in international politics, he acted as a representative of the council that represented the commune.[10] In important decisions like constitutional reforms, international treaties, and declarations of war, he could execute or be consulted but had no place in making the decisions. All important acts were reserved to the major council. The Podestà convened the council and put the material in order for presentation, but the council did the deliberating.[11] The Podestà had greater independence in his judicial activities;[12] for instance, independent of any magistracy, he had the right to order all the laws of the commune to be executed,[13] and he could issue judicial decrees that were enforceable. Normally, he was required to follow the statutes in assigning penalties in the thirteenth century. His part in legislation was relatively unimportant. In the thirteenth century, he was head of public security, police matters, and attempts to put down rebellion.[14]

At some point in the long history of the office of the Podestà, the Podestà lost his political powers, including his power to head and convoke the Council of the Commune. There are many fourteenth-century documents showing the Podestà presiding at the Council of the Commune, just as there are many showing the Captain presiding at the Council of the People. The last document that Cantini has found showing these two rectors presiding at their councils dates from 1373.[15] After that, both the Podestà and the Captain became strictly judicial officials, as they appear in the statutes of 1415.

Some historians have seen the decline of the Podestà's political power as evidence of the decline of that office. While the political power of the Podestà declined, his judicial power did not. The loss of political power cannot be used to illustrate the attrition of the regular court system. The process by which the Podestà's political duties fell away in deference to his judicial duties should properly be seen as part of the sorting and shifting process. At this point in the creation of the territorial state, the bulk and complexity of administration forced a division between executive and judicial duties, the Podestà and the Captain becoming strictly judicial officials. The burden of cases in the judicial sphere was enough to occupy all of the time of the foreign rectors. The officials who remained predominantly executives, like the Priors and the Gonfalonier of Justice, found their executive duties to be so onerous that some of their tasks had to be diverted to other agencies. The Dieci di Guerra, for instance, was assigned the Priors' powers over war. After 1373, the Podestà and the Captain turned their attention exclusively to judicial matters. As initiation of cases by inquisition became more usual, the judicial duties of the Podestà, the Captain, and the Executor became more burdensome.

The Podestà was the major criminal official in the early fifteenth century, although the three rectors were near parity at this time. In previous centuries, the Podestà's ascendancy was much more marked. From 1193, when the office of the Podestà was created, until 1250, the Podestà, along with the consuls, formed the only criminal court. In 1250, the office of the Captain of the People was created and very specific criminal jurisdictions were subsequently assigned to the Captain, having to do with his position as head of the democratic organization of the *popolo*. Throughout the thirteenth century and well into the fourteenth, all serious crime was handled in the Podestà's court. The statutes of 1322-25 show the Podestà still in control of all serious crime such as theft, assault through hired assassins, highway robbery, robbery, falsification, homicide, serious assault, arson, rape, and adultery. The Captain had no jurisdiction in these areas, nor did the Executor.[16] During the fourteenth century, jurisdictional areas were continually being switched from one official to another in an attempt to set up coherent blocks of jurisdiction under systematically organized officials. Even more important was the process taking place in the fourteenth century by which the three foreign rectors became more and more alike in their functioning in the criminal law system. The motive force behind this convergence of function was the inquisition procedure used in the criminal courts. Although, by 1415, the three foreign rectors had a great deal in common, they also had functions that were uniquely their own. It is these differentiating functions that I investigate here and in the following two chapters.

In the statutes of 1415, the traditional occupation of the Podestà, the trial of serious crime, was assigned to all three of the rectors, while the traditional occupation of the Captain, the trial of cases pertaining to the guilds, was assigned to the Podestà. The jurisdiction over comestibles and the supervision of officials dealing with comestibles, as well as the jurisdiction over cases connected to the consuls of the guilds, were the mainstays of the Captain's court in 1322-25 but belonged in the Podestà's court by 1415.[17] Jurisdiction over simple debt, and defaulting and fleeing, was an important area for the Podestà in 1415, as it had been in 1322-25.[18] These spheres of jurisdiction were the ones most clearly attributed to the Podestà alone in 1415. The areas of jurisdiction uniquely attributed to the Podestà are emphasized below. It is well to remember that authority over serious crime was generalized to all three rectors. However, the Podestà's courts employed more criminal judges than the courts of the other two rectors, and remained the major criminal court.

One of the clearer areas of jurisdiction was the Podestà's authority over cases related to the guilds. The Podestà tried these cases and executed sentences imposed by guild consuls. The important jurisdiction over debt was assigned to the Podestà because debt litigation was closely tied to the guilds. There were three kinds of debt cases, and all could involve the court of the Podestà. The first, cases in which the debt was created through a public instrument, could involve merchants or regular people, and were tried by the Podestà because a public instrument was a communal document. The second, cases of debt created through a private document, such as a merchant's account book, were usually judged by the consuls of the guilds with the Podestà executing, but could be judged by the foreign official and six counselors of the Mercanzia, the Podestà, or either of the other rectors. The third, cases of defaulting and fleeing debt, usually involving merchants who were entrusted with the money of a partnership or who had money given to them to conduct mercantile business, were treated by all three of the rectors or by the foreign official and six counselors of the Mercanzia, sometimes being attributed to the court of the Podestà exclusively.[19] Defaulting and fleeing debt belonged to a higher jurisdiction than that possessed by the consuls. Other guild-related cases in a higher jurisdiction were sometimes assigned to all the rectors and sometimes, like falsity, specifically to the Podestà. In this regard, the Podestà possessed a jurisdiction superior to that of the consuls.

Debt cases hold a questionable position in any explication of criminal law. These three examples of different kinds of debt cases display a varying degree of criminality. The statutes themselves seem to be very flexible on this point, sometimes treating debt as a civil matter, sometimes as a criminal matter. As a debt extended through time, passing from one stage of attempted collection to another, it steadily became considered more and more criminal. If civil law pertains to the rights and duties of persons and criminal law pertains to the prosecution of willful wrongdoing, the growing suspicion of the refusal to pay made the debt considered more criminal. When the Podestà tried a debt case created by a public instrument, if the instrument did not contain a period of time in which the debt had to be paid and, therefore, had not passed into a judgment already presumed made on the expiration of this period, the trial went forth according to civil procedure (*Stat.* 2.57). If, on the other hand, the Podestà was trying a case of debt where the period stated in the instrument had already expired, the case was tried before a criminal judge and a fine was levied to be paid to the commune (*Stat.* 3.171). An instrument that contained a specific time period in which the debt had to be paid was called a guarantee. Also, if a sentence or a decision concerning the validity of the debt had already been made in another court, such as the court of the consuls of the guilds, and the case was then brought before the Podestà, criminal intent was assumed. If other periods of time had expired and the defendant had exhausted other chances to pay the debt or defend himself against the creditor, the case had very definitely become criminal, and the defendant became obligated not only to a two-soldi-per-lire fine but also to a large condemnation. Further, he was banned, and his sons also suffered for his crime.

The Podestà or his judge tried cases of debt in which no period of payment appeared in the public instrument. Discussion of this kind of debt is found in the civil code of the statutes. The creditor came to the Podestà's court when he wanted repayment, or at the time tacitly agreed upon by debtor and creditor for repayment. The Podestà cited the debtor, giving him fifteen days in which to put up any opposition, along with all of the extensions allowed in civil procedure to arrange his proof. If he defended at this point he was entitled to delays and extensions. After this he could be captured, detained, and compelled to pay, or his goods could be seized to pay the debt. After the fifteen days in which he could freely defend were past, if he was then captured by either the creditor or the Podestà's retinue, defense was more difficult. The debtor was required to leave a deposit in the amount of the debt if he wanted to contest it. If the creditor was alleged by the debtor to be suspect, then the deposit could be put up by a *campsor* (moneychanger) for the debtor. If the debtor made the deposit, he could be released. Then the proof on both sides was presented and the case was adjudicated. If the fifteen days was past and the debtor did not appear, he could be captured, as above. His goods could be confiscated by the Podestà and given to the creditor or sold, with the money given to the creditor to the amount of the debt. The Podestà had the sale of these goods announced so that others with claims against the debtor could come forward to place them (*Stat.* 2.57).

In cases of a more criminal kind of debt, debt in which the debtor was obligated through the public instrument to pay within a certain term, the debtor was considered to have defaulted but not to have fled when he exceeded the term of the instrument (*Stat.* 3.171). Discussion of this kind of debt is found in the criminal code, and cases were aired in the presence of a criminal judge. The debtor was condemned to a two-soldi-per-lire fine. Judgment and fining were immediate, since the judgment was presumed to be already made when the term in the instrument expired. A similar sequence of events occurred when a sentence of another court had already condemned the defendant as a debtor so that some presumption of guilt had already been made. Cases of debt created by private documents could be tried by arbitration, by the consuls, or by the foreign official of the Mercanzia. When a creditor brought such a case already judged in another court to the court of the Podestà, the Podestà condemned the debtor to the amount of the debt and to the two-soldi-per-lire fine. In both cases, the Podestà was responsible for collecting the debt and the fine.

When a debt was created through a private writing, such as a merchant's account book, either the consuls of the guild or the foreign official of the Mercanzia was eligible to try the resulting disputes. Any case that the consuls or the foreign official could try, the rectors could try; this offered an alternative to trials within the guild complex. Although in the past the guilds had tried to force their members to litigate exclusively in the guild courts, by 1415 communal statute forbade such compulsion.[20] The commune no longer permitted the guilds to have areas of exclusive jurisdiction. Instead, it extended more active regulation and perusal over the guilds, continuing to strengthen its own jurisdiction while diminishing that of the guilds.

The most criminal kind of debt was debt involving defaulting and fleeing. This kind of debt was considered heinous because it harmed manufacturing and trade. In such cases, the criminals were merchants who, because of their business, were entrusted with the money or goods of a partnership or trading company.[21] Defaulting and fleeing cases always involved debt of 100 lire or more (Tract. cess. fug. 16).

Any one of the rectors or the foreign official with the six counselors of the Mercanzia was permitted to act in cases of defaulting and fleeing debt (Tract. cess fug. 3; 5). However, there is some reason to believe that the Podestà predominated even here. All of the rectors were permitted to conduct defaulting and fleeing trials because it was desirable to have as many officials as possible looking for this kind of debtor, who could be anywhere inside or outside the territory. Since defaulting and fleeing debt posed a threat to trade, wide participation in apprehending these criminals was permitted. However, the procedure for handling this kind of debt was somewhat similar to the procedure by which the Podestà executed sentences given by the consuls of the guilds. The wording of the statutes suggests that when the Podestà held a trial in which he pronounced people to have defaulted and fled, he was really trying cases already tried by the consuls of the guilds and was adding many more means of execution and additional sanctions to those used by the guilds.[22]

The pronouncement of defaulting and fleeing was mainly a device by which the Podestà checked the decisions of the consuls and aided execution to assure payment to the creditors. The consuls did not have the resources available to the communal officials for investigating, apprehending, or punishing and so came to rely more and more heavily on communal officials. The foreign rectors could torture in defaulting and fleeing cases, a power of investigation not possessed by the consuls. The rectors had large retinues that investigated throughout the city, county, and district, and even outside. Besides imposing the 500-lire fine, the rectors could obligate the debtor's descendants to pay the debt and could put other pressure on them. When the communal officials condemned a debtor for defaulting and fleeing, his sons and masculine descendants were obliged to pay the creditors or leave Florence and were barred from his guild. The sons and other descendants through the masculine line born at the time of the defaulting were deprived of all offices and benefits in Florence.[23] A defaulting and fleeing debtor even had his picture painted on a wall of the Podestà's palace. Since the consuls could not levy these sanctions, it was reasonable that they would turn over important debt cases in which they had reached a sentence to the courts of the communal officials for retrial and execution. Since the crime was of such great moment, the foreign rectors retried cases in their own courts. The consuls tried the case for debt and the rectors tried for the successive crime of defaulting and fleeing. The primary rector in trying defaulting and fleeing cases was the Podestà because of his close relationship with the consuls. In the early fifteenth century, because the consuls were not permitted to try defaulting and fleeing cases, the court of the Podestà became a court of higher jurisdiction.

Samuel Cohn has presented some statistics on debt for the three periods he has studied, 1344–45, 1374–75, and 1455–66. He has noted a steady rise in the incidence of debt cases involving nonaristocratic debtors and aristocratic creditors from 14 percent to 21 percent to 31 percent. He also has noted that the percentage of debt cases brought to the foreign rectors' courts by corporate bodies, that is, by the courts of the guild consuls or by the Mercanzia, increased in relation to the percentage of cases brought by private individuals from 1 percent to 16 percent to 63 percent. This is a dramatic rise, particularly in the period 1455–66. He has concluded that the communal criminal courts were increasingly used by the guilds to reinforce their decisions and to aid in the collection of debts owed to merchants. According to Cohn, this change in the character of litigation shows that the wealthy controlled the court system and used it to oppress the poor in the period 1455–66.[24] But this change can be attributed to changes in the laws concerning debt.

The statutes of 1322–25 show that the guilds related differently to the commune in this period than they did in 1415. In the earlier period, the commune allowed the guilds a great sphere of independence and regulated them very little. For instance, the commune gave the foreign official of Lana great autonomy in exercising power over the *sottoposti* (workers performing menial tasks under the guild who were not guild members) of the Lana Guild, the Wool Guild. The statutes of 1415, on the other hand, show the commune taking power away from the guilds and installing it in communal officials such as the foreign rectors, who regulated the guilds. Cases of crimes such as fraud and falsity were removed from the guild courts and given to the communal courts. As the territorial state centralized, it took power and autonomy away from corporate groups and strengthened communal officials. A striking example is the change made in debt legislation during the period from 1322–25 to 1415.

In the 1322–25 period, the courts of the consuls of the guilds could try every kind of debt, except debt created through a public instrument, including the most criminal kind of debt, defaulting and fleeing.[25] In 1415, the consuls could still try cases of debt created through a private document but cases of debt created through a public instrument belonged in the court of the Podestà, and cases of defaulting and fleeing debt became the exclusive preserve of the foreign rectors and the foreign official of the Mercanzia. Most defaulting and fleeing debt cases in 1415 were not new cases aired before the foreign rectors but cases of debt created through a private document, which were tried first within the guild complex and then were brought to the communal courts in order to gain greater means of execution and more severe sanctions.[26] They were required to be cases between merchants involving more than 100 lire. When these cases were brought into communal court, they were not just executed at the request of the consuls, since they were frequently very important cases, they were entirely retried. The purpose of the new legislation, which transferred this kind of case from the guild courts to the courts of the communal rectors, was to gain greater control over these important cases. Because these cases damaged the public good by harming trade, the commune took charge of them. If the rectors had merely executed the sentences of the guilds in these matters, they would not have needed the power to torture and the *arbitrium* in investigating, proceeding, condemning, and punishing.[27] While the rectors had the power to torture and the arbitrium in proceeding in the 1322–25 period, at that time defaulting and fleeing cases in communal court were not retrials of guild cases but first-instance cases brought by individuals, which necessitated an assessment of the evidence. Since cases of this kind could be tried within the guild complex, most merchants preferred to take their defaulting and fleeing cases to the guild courts. During the earlier period, the guilds tried to compel their members to prosecute in guild courts.[28] In the 1415 statutes, the guilds were not allowed to prevent litigants from bringing their defaulting and fleeing cases to the court of a rector.[29]

In 1415, in cases of debt created through private documents, the consuls of the guilds delivered sentences and the Podestà was required to execute these sentences at the request of the consuls without overturning them. On the other hand, the procedure for trying defaulting and fleeing debtors was deliberately set up to give the rectors the power of retrial. Since debt was one crime tried in one court and defaulting and fleeing was another crime tried in the other court, the debtor was not being tried twice for the same crime nor could the commune be required to carry out such severe sanctions in cases in which the communal courts had not tried the case. The consuls of the guilds produced the proof of debt, and the commune decided whether the further crime of defaulting and fleeing had been committed.

The great increase that Cohn notes in the incidence of debt cases being transferred from the courts of the guilds into the courts of the foreign rectors reflects the addition of the defaulting and fleeing debt cases. In the early period, these cases were not found as frequently in the communal courts because they were also being tried in the guild courts. Defaulting and fleeing debt cases would almost never need to be transferred from the guild courts to the communal courts. The courts of the guilds could try the cases, and the communal officials would execute the sentences. The only defaulting and fleeing cases in communal courts would have been brought by individuals. In 1415, all defaulting and fleeing cases were tried in communal courts, and many of them were transferred there from the guild courts. This construction of the facts can be tested against Cohn's other statistics on debt. If Cohn's thesis were correct, one would expect to see a corresponding dramatic jump in the incidence of debt cases involving upper-class creditors and lower-class debtors. While these kinds of cases increased steadily, from 14 percent to 21 percent to 31 percent, they did not take a dramatic jump in incidence. This is because the great number of cases which Cohn sees being transferred from the guild courts to communal courts do not involve upper-class creditors and lower-class debtors. Defaulting and fleeing debt was debt between two merchants involving amounts of 100 lire and over. Cohn's thesis of the use of the court system by the rich to oppress the poor is not borne out by this example. Instead, public interest triumphed over private interest, communal institutions over particular corporate groups. The guilds were no longer self-determining institutions but were undergoing a process of subordination to the state and to the communal court system.

Defaulting and fleeing debt was considered a criminal kind of debt. A case against a principal debtor was conducted criminally, while if against his heirs, it was conducted civilly (Tract. cess. fug. 3). In regular private debt, the creditor or his heir was expected to accuse, but in defaulting and fleeing debt, anyone was allowed and encouraged to accuse. The case could even be initiated by inquisition, since the public aspect of defaulting and fleeing debt was prominent (Tract. cess. fug. 1). If the defendant was contumacious, this was considered as a confession, as in criminal cases. There was no appeal from condemnations in these cases, just as there was none in criminal cases (Tract. cess. fug. 3).

The public nature of defaulting and fleeing debt made trying these cases most suitable for communal court. Usually defaulting and fleeing cases were very simple: the supposed debtor was cited, was contumacious because he had fled, and, therefore, was pronounced guilty. If, on the other hand, he appeared in court, he was not treated as a regular debtor. He paid a deposit to have his defense heard or reached an agreement with his creditors by giving a security. If he would do neither of these, he was immediately put in prison and his goods were seized and held at the will of the creditors. A debtor not paying within three months from the day he was put in prison was pronounced a defaulting and fleeing debtor. If the debtor was cited and sent a procurator to court, the procurator would not be heard without a deposit. In these cases, it is clear that some presumption of guilt concerning the debt had already been made, either because of a former sentence or some other proof. But even with debt having been proved in another court, defaulting and fleeing still remained to be proved. It could be proved through four witnesses of public fame (Tract. cess. fug. 3).

The Consuls of the Guilds

The Podestà's court fulfilled several functions in relation to the courts of the consuls of the guilds. The Podestà executed the consuls' sentences, entrusting the consuls with the trial of the cases and following their mandates.[30] The Podestà tried cases brought by anyone, even guildsmen, who chose to pursue cases in the communal courts rather than the guild courts, which provided an option and even a corrective to the consuls' courts (Tract. Cons. Art. Merc. 34). The rectors could try any case that the consuls could try. The Podestà tried cases of crimes which were trade-related but were not within the jurisdiction of the consuls, such as falsity and defaulting and fleeing (Tract. Cons. Art. Merc. 33). Some of these cases specifically regulated the guilds. Thus, the Podestà acted as an aid, an alternative, a superior court, but never as an appeals court (Tract. Cons. Art. Merc. 27).

For some cases tried in the courts of the consuls, the Podestà, his civil judges, and the foreign official of the Mercanzia were required to execute the sentences of the consuls automatically without retrying the cases (Tract. Cons. Art. Merc. 27). Debt created through a private document, such as a merchant account book, was tried by the consuls and executed by the rectors. The guilds and their officials were responsible for seeing that merchants kept their account books properly. The familiarity of the members and officials of the guilds with the account books and with the financial status and the reputations of the merchants within their guilds made the guild complex the natural place to try cases of debt between merchants, when the debts had no public ramifications. Debt created by a public instrument had no connection with the documents of the guilds, so was tried in communal court. Defaulting and fleeing debt was a public crime, but the communal courts compelled the guilds to supply evidence.

Because the guilds were familiar with the account books of their merchants, the civil jurisdiction of the consuls remained wide. The consuls rendered law for their guildsmen and for people dealing in the materials and the business of the guild. The consuls had competence in cases brought by a *matriculus* (master, graduate, full member) of the guild against any citizen, county dweller, or district dweller who was not matriculated, if the *matriculus* stood to gain a benefit, even if the business transacted did not pertain to the guild. Under the jurisdiction of the guild were those not matriculated who trafficked in merchandise pertaining to the guild, either wholesale or retail. All the laborers and apprentices of masters belonged to the guild and were under the jurisdiction of the consuls. All the heirs of dead merchants who had been in the guild and the heirs of anyone obligated to guildsmen could be compelled to appear before the consuls. Jurisdiction was both civil and criminal. The consuls tried cases according to communal and guild statutes, the statutes of the guild having to be in conformity with communal statutes (Tract. Cons. Art. Merc. 10; 100; 27).

The consuls' familiarity with the account books allowed them to retain many duties in connection with them. The consuls decided what writings in merchants' books should be given credence. Credence was given to a private document written in the hand of the person who was disadvantaged by the document unless a contradictory document by the creditor signifying satisfaction of the debt or a public instrument signifying satisfaction of the debt existed. If an error in a merchant account book was alleged, the consuls decided if the document was in error. If a case of doubt or discord arose in the court of the Podestà, the consuls were called in to evaluate the account books. The consuls had such a strong hold on the evidence in cases where merchants books were involved that even in cases in communal court, the consuls assessed the evidence, the merchant books. When a doubt arose about a merchant's book, whether the case was being tried in the court of the consuls or in the court of the Podestà or Mercanzia, the consuls of the merchant's guild, along with the consuls of the seven major guilds, decided whether the merchant's records were accurate, unless the merchant or artisan belonged to the seven major guilds, in which case the consuls and the men of his own guild decided (Tract. Cons. Art. Merc. 12).

The guild courts could be biased in favor of their own merchants, particularly since they held power over the assessment of merchant books; therefore, it was necessary for the communal courts to serve as an unbiased alternative. Initially the guilds tried to prohibit their artisans and merchants from moving cases in courts other than the courts of the guilds. The Statutes of the Changers Guild of 1290, for instance, forbade members to move cases in other courts under penalty of expulsion from the guild and a fine.[31] In 1415, however, artisans and merchants who wanted to litigate in the courts of the foreign rectors of the commune could not be punished by their guilds even when their litigation involved someone in their own guild or pertained to the business of their guild. Even the foreign official and the six counselors of the Mercanzia could not punish a member of a guild for such an action.[32] The Podestà's court, as well as the courts of the other rectors, offered alternate courts to that of the consuls or even to that of the foreign official of the Mercanzia. The Podestà was specifically charged with enforcing all partnerships, contracts, promises, obligations, and pacts between artisans and merchants (Tract. Cons. Art. Merc. 15).

The spirit of this law shows a markedly different attitude on the part of the commune toward the guilds. Previously, the commune had wanted the guilds to take care of their own problems and manage their own artisans. This was particularly true in connection with the Lana Guild. The commune had fostered the power of the foreign official of Lana so that the Lana Guild could more effectively deal with its own artisans, particularly its sottoposti artisans. Previously, the government of the commune had allowed the Lana Guild to manipulate the economic status of the sottoposti workers in order to promote the well-being of the commune's most important guild. The thwarting of the autonomous authority of the guilds is evident in the diminution of the criminal powers of the foreign official of the Lana Guild and the disappearance of the foreign officials of the Seta Guild. The foreign official of Lana had formerly exercised judicial control over the sottoposti workers—the combers, tinters, weavers, and all the other workers who finished the cloth—making judgments and executing sentences. Since the Lana Guild had its own prison, the foreign official could execute sentences independent of the commune. One of the primary aims of the Ciompi revolt was to rid the workers of this official and his judicial relationship with the guild. In 1378, the position was abolished. In 1382, it was revived in a much diminished form. The foreign official now had no jurisdiction over many of the sottoposti workers, such as the tinters, shirtmakers, and shearers, except in cases in which the workers accepted cloth to finish from the wool manufacturers and pawned it instead. The foreign official was no longer allowed to use torture in judicial proceedings (Tract. Cons. Art. Merc. 45). The commune adopted a position of neutrality, no longer promoting the guild's control of the workers but mediating disputes between the two. The foreign official of Lana continued to exist in 1428 in this diminished form while the foreign official of Seta disappeared.³³ By 1415, the commune did not support the autonomy of the guilds. Regulation of the guilds by the commune was much more active in 1415, as witnessed by the great multiplication of the communal statutes regulating the guilds in the 1415 compilation. The posing of communal courts as alternatives to guild courts was part of this movement to undermine the autonomy of the guilds and, in general, part of the movement to pull all groups within the ambit of the communal government.

The Podestà's court, and sometimes the courts of the other rectors, acted as courts of higher jurisdiction to the guild courts, besides acting as aids and alternatives to the latter. The rectors, particularly the Podestà, tried cases that were related to trade but were outside the jurisdictional limits of the guilds. These cases belonged to a superior jurisdiction because they involved large amounts of money, involved serious crime, had a public nature, or conflicted with the interests of the guilds. The rectors also enforced statutes that regulated the guilds, promoting public good over the private good of the guilds or individuals within the guilds. The guilds dealing in necessary items, in particular, were regulated by communal officials.

Some crimes were deemed by the commune to be unsuitable for the guild courts, either because they touched on public matters or because they touched on matters in which the interests of the guilds would bias a trial. In the criminal area, more cases were passing over into the category of cases tried by the commune, instead of belonging as before to the category of cases tried by the consuls and executed by the commune upon the request of the consuls. The withdrawal of these cases from the guild courts shows that the commune was dissatisfied with the previous system of trial in the guilds and automatic execution without communal review. The weakness of the sanctions that the guild courts could invoke, mainly involving ejection from the guild, worked in favor of the transfer of cases to communal courts. In cases in which the consuls wanted to invoke more serious sanctions, they had to call on the commune and its police forces. The impetus in these cases was toward communal involvement, the commune gradually seeking more control over the cases that it executed.

Defaulting and fleeing debt and falsity belonged to the category of cases which once were tried by the consuls but became the exclusive domain of the foreign rectors and the foreign official of the Mercanzia. Fraud involving guildsmen was also frequently tried in the courts of the foreign rectors, particularly the court of the Podestà. In the early fourteenth century, not only were defaulting and fleeing cases tried in the courts of the consuls, but legislation regulating the trial of such cases in communal court was enacted by the guilds. Rubrics regulating the treatment of defaulting and fleeing appear in the statutes of the major guilds, such as the Lana Guild, the Seta Guild, the Guild of Changers, and the Calimala Guild. The statutes of the Calimala Guild give the consuls the capabilities of seizing and selling the goods of those defaulting and fleeing.[34] In the statutes of 1322–25, the twelve major guilds had the power to make ordinances over defaulting and fleeing debt, the Captain of the People being required to put these ordinances into effect as if they were communal statutes.[35] Their power extended beyond their own courts to control the manner in which the Captain of the People, the rector primarily affiliated with the guilds in the 1322–25 period, performed the cases that were litigated in communal court. Defaulting and fleeing debt cases were withdrawn from the guilds because of their public nature, and because of the magnitude of the sanctions that needed to be invoked.

Falsity was a very broad category of crime tried by the guild courts in the fourteenth century. In the statutes of 1415, the consuls of a guild were specifically forbidden to recognize in their court falsity committed in the guild.[36] Fraud committed by guildsmen was tried in the guild courts in the fourteenth century but increasingly in the court of the Podestà by 1415. Falsity and fraud were both broad categories of serious crime which were central to the fourteenth-century jurisdiction of the guilds. Both of these crimes were likely to be committed to the detriment of the guild or its merchants so that an unbiased trial in a guild court was unlikely. Falsity usually referred to the falsification of a product, for example, passing off one type of cloth as another, or putting the seal of the guild on a product not made by the guild and made of inferior material.

Falsity in the making of *croco* was making false yellow dye (*Stat.* 3.139). In the rubric on making impure wax, the crime is interchangeably called falsifying, fraud, and falsity (*Stat.* 3.140). Falsity in making dye and wax was recognized, condemned, and punished by the Podestà in 1415. It was the responsibility of guild officials to denounce falsity to the Podestà within five days.[37] The consuls were forbidden to try any cases of falsity, except for the proconsuls and consuls of the Guild of Judges and Notaries and the consuls of the Lana Guild. However, the Podestà was also charged with condemning guildsmen for falsity even if they were in the Lana Guild.[38] One example of a crime that was considered to be fraud arises in a rubric dealing with the masters and manual laborers working with wood, stone, or roof tile. If any of these workers committed fraud on the job, the Podestà, who took an oath to fulfill this duty, condemned.[39] Fraud in this context referred to the use of an inferior material passed off as the desired material or the use of inferior workmanship passed off as properly completed construction. This kind of fraud was very close to falsity, and both were considered major crimes.

The Podestà and Other Affiliated Officials

The loss of the consuls' power over falsity may have eroded their ability to try fraud cases. Fraudulent erasure was similarly punished by the Podestà, as was malicious entry. Fraudulent erasure was the erasure of a real obligation from a merchant's account book, and malicious entry, the entry of a fictitious obligation in an account book, in order to harass another merchant. Fraudulent erasure had always been tried by the communal courts because merchant account books were accepted as a kind of public proof.[40] For this reason, the Podestà and the Captain supervised the consuls in their duties of compelling merchants to write their books in a particular format. A merchant suspected of fraudulent erasure or malicious entry was tried and punished at the will of the Podestà.[41] If a merchant denied having a book he was said to have, the matter was investigated by four guildsmen with the Podestà or Captain condemning. The guilds supplied the evidence and the rectors condemned.

The Podestà also had a distinctive relationship with another group of artisans, those dealing in comestibles, building materials, or other necessary items. In this area his jurisdiction overlapped the jurisdiction of the Officials of Grascia, who supervised trade in these materials. Because these materials were vital for the life of the commune, the commune took an interest in regulating them and the people who worked with them. The Podestà carried out part of this regulatory process, monitoring the activities of guilds and guildsmen working with these materials. There were conflicts between the objectives of the commune and the objectives of these guilds. While the guilds dealing with construction might have wanted to increase the salaries of their guildsmen and decrease the availability of the materials, the commune, represented by the Podestà, kept salaries low and availability of materials high. For instance, masters who worked with wood, stone, or pavement were forbidden to form partnerships with those who sold these materials; if they did, the Podestà condemned them. The Podestà was required to summon the rectors of this guild and remind them of this prohibition (Tract. Cons. Art. Merc. 57). Anyone was allowed to work in the building trade, not just members of the guilds, which drove down salaries for construction workers. If the consuls tried to prevent anyone from working, the Podestà punished them (Tract. Cons. Art. Merc. 66). The Podestà compelled furnace makers to perform good work by sending out secret investigators to check it (Tract. Cons. Art. Merc. 59). The Podestà condemned any official who prevented people from freely selling *gallam*, an inferior kind of wine (Tract. Cons. Art. Merc. 79). Shoemakers using untreated leather were condemned by the Podestà (Tract. Cons. Art. Merc. 81). The Podestà and his criminal judges proceeded against anyone who impeded people bringing victuals from entering the city (Tract. Cons. Art. Merc. 149). In this way, too, his jurisdiction was superior to that of the guilds. Where public matters were at stake, the communal officials took charge of the trials.

Although the Podestà had a much greater sphere of jurisdiction in cases involving the guilds than did the other two rectors, he shared some important responsibilities with them. Both the Podestà and the Captain, along with the Priors and the Gonfalonier of Justice, were charged with settling any disputes that arose between the guilds (Tract. Cons. Art. Merc. 6). Both the Podestà and the Captain were responsible for compelling Florentine citizens who made contracts in foreign markets to pay off their obligations (Tract. Cons. Art. Merc. 21; 22; 23). The Captain, and even the Executor, had some responsibility in guild-related cases, but not to the same extent as the Podestà. The Captain acted in fewer cases involving the guilds in 1415 than he had in the 1322–25 period. In the process of sorting and shifting jurisdictions, the Captain's attention was directed to other problems, while the Podestà's focus became more centered on the guilds.

The Mercanzia

The way that the Podestà's court related to the guilds was similar to the way in which the Mercanzia related to them. The Mercanzia functioned as a court with a higher jurisdiction than the court of the consuls in the same material, much like the court of the Podestà. The foreign official of the Mercanzia, with the consent of the six counselors of the Mercanzia, could pronounce debtors defaulting and fleeing and execute these sentences even through the capture of the debtors, just as the Podestà could (Tract. Cons. Art. Merc. 26). Both officials were also involved in enforcing obligations, contracts, and partnerships. If some of the partners made a contract obligating money that belonged to the partnership, all the partners could be compelled to pay. If one of the partners made a contract, even without his partners' knowledge, and registered the contract in their books, all of the partners were obligated, and the foreign official of the Mercanzia enforced these obligations (Tract. Cons. Art. Merc. 16). The Podestà had a very similar role in enforcing the obligations of partnerships (Tract. Cons. Art. Merc. 17). The Podestà and the foreign official of the Mercanzia were in analogous positions in relation to the guilds. The foreign official of the Mercanzia, like the Podestà, was involved in supervising the elections of the consuls of the guilds. The foreign official of the Mercanzia notified the electors when a Ghibelline or a noncitizen was elected (Tract. Cons. Art. Merc. 3). If someone was elected consul of a guild that was not his major guild or was elected rector in two guilds, the Podestà condemned (Tract. Cons. Art. Merc. 2; 5). The sentences of the consuls could be sent to execution through the Podestà or the foreign official of the Mercanzia (Tract. Cons. Art. Merc. 27).

The position and characteristics of the Mercanzia in the early fifteenth century lend support to the existence of the territorial state. The Mercanzia formed an arm of the state regulating the guilds. Yet the Mercanzia was included in the system of checks and balances so was not an all-powerful institution with no limits or accountability. In the following pages, I discuss the manner in which the Mercanzia was incorporated into the state. Then I describe the manner in which the Mercanzia lost its autonomous and executive powers and became watered down and overburdened by its jurisdiction over the guilds, including the lower guilds. Finally, I assess the Mercanzia's position in the system of checks and balances.

The Mercanzia has been singled out as having possibly been instrumental in the oligarchic takeover, like the other executive agencies. However, the Mercanzia held a unique position in relation to the government of Florence. It was a powerful agency with judicial powers but had no similarities to the powerful executive agencies with judicial powers that were created at the end of the fourteenth century and the beginning of the fifteenth century. The historical development of the Mercanzia was very different from that of the executive agencies, leading it to relate differently to the government and to the groups that it regulated. Unlike the executive agencies, the Mercanzia originated outside the government as a voluntary association of the major guilds. Very soon the communal government began assimilating it and fostering its authority over international trade and over the Florentine guilds. The Mercanzia was entrusted with the government's diplomatic business concerning trade and with the creation of the international law used by the Florentine state. Furthermore, the government continually increased the Mercanzia's sphere of influence over the Florentine guilds until all of the guilds were under its supervision. In the early fifteenth century, the government of Florence took away the Mercanzia's power over the international politics and international commercial relations of the commune, delegating these powers to the executive branch where they properly belonged. The Mercanzia became an arm of the government that regulated the guilds. The Mercanzia of the early fifteenth century would have made a very poor vehicle of oligarchic takeover because it had no autonomous spheres of activity and exercised executive powers less and less. Its function became strictly to carry out the communal statutes that regulated the guilds. Thus, the Mercanzia of the early fifteenth century was a less political and less autonomous agency than the Mercanzia of the fourteenth century, particularly in international politics.

The Mercanzia initially was a court of arbitration where merchants in the top guilds could work out commercial disputes. At that time, the top guilds were joined together in a voluntary association to promote commerce and settle disputes. In the Balia of 1309, the Mercanzia was accorded a broader jurisdiction by the state, giving it the authority to proceed as an ordinary tribunal without the formality of an ordinary tribunal, so that tradesmen, especially foreign tradesmen, could get swift satisfaction for debt, fraud, theft, and other offenses. The Mercanzia was guided by *ius commune* and equity. In the Balia of 1309, it also acquired full jurisdiction over reprisal and connected material, even involving those who did not belong to the major guilds.[42] Because the Mercanzia was not a corporation like the guilds, it did not have jurisdiction over its members. Like the Mercanzia of Lucca, the Mercanzia in Florence had particular areas of jurisdiction accorded to it by the state in certain litigation concerning business (p. 9). In these areas, the Balia of 1309 conferred power on the Mercanzia that had up until then belonged to the state. At that time, the state first gave jurisdiction to the Mercanzia over reprisal because the Mercanzia's duty to render justice to foreigners was intended to forestall reprisal (p. 31). The Mercanzia started with personal jurisdiction over the members of the five top guilds but eventually had a jurisdiction on the basis of material when it took over all commercial trials (p. 21).

The cooperation between the state and the Mercanzia was very important for the development of the Mercanzia's power, especially over reprisal, because it increased the Mercanzia's ability to remedy the complaints of foreigners; that is, the state aided the foreign official of the Mercanzia in the execution of his sentences (p. 88). In order to be effective in promoting commerce, there was need for a body with jurisdiction over all merchants and with statutes that were not technical but instead concerned good faith and honesty. The Mercanzia eventually achieved this broadness of jurisdiction when the state encouraged its jurisdiction to spread not only over the members of all the guilds but over all people connected with commerce and all commercial material (p. 121). While the Mercanzie of some cities in their initial stage of development subsumed the individual guilds, thus gaining a broad base of power, the Mercanzia in Florence was rendered powerful by the state. The Florentine Mercanzia formulated rules concerning defaulting, selling stolen goods, altering commercial account books, and holding partners and apprentices liable. These regulations significantly contributed to the development of commercial law (p. 115). Further, the practice of the Florentine government in commercial matters was greatly influenced by the legislation of the Mercanzia.

In 1309, the Mercanzia was given the ability to proceed without the formality of an ordinary court. Summary procedure, in which all of the terms of proceeding were abbreviated (including the length of time assigned to the judge to sentence) and the amount of necessary proof was diminished, was the procedure common to all of the Mercanzie of the Italian cities. Summary procedure was desirable so that foreign merchants, as well as domestic merchants, would know that quick justice was available against Florentines dealing in bad faith. Proof of debt often consisted of some instrument of debt and the oath of the creditor, or one witness and the oath of the creditor. This was enough, at least, to secure sequestration of goods. Sometimes the judge could order that *berrovarii* seize goods without the defendant having been cited. Judges were given a very short period in which to decide cases, and either no appeal was allowed at all or execution was carried out despite a pending appeal.[43]

In the fourteenth century, the Mercanzia was a very important court, especially in international commercial cases. It functioned as a court with which foreign states and foreign merchants could deal, and it filled a diplomatic role that gave the Mercanzia the responsibility of meting out quick, consistent, fair, and powerful justice. As the Mercanzia gained jurisdiction over more and more of the guilds, first the most important and international guilds and then the less important and local ones, its function as an international court became more watered down. The fourteenth-century Mercanzia had several very important areas of jurisdiction. Almost from its inception it had jurisdiction over all cases involving foreigners. The Balia of 1309 gave the foreign official and the counselors the ability to handle cases in which a foreigner was robbed anywhere in the city, county, or district of Florence. In these cases, Mercanzia officials had the ability to recognize and condemn the local rectors and men of the place where the robbery was committed in order to satisfy the amount of damages fixed by the foreign official (p. 33). In 1309, the Mercanzia acquired from the state a related jurisdiction over reprisal and over connected material, even when the reprisal involved those who were not in the guilds under the Mercanzia at this time.

In the statutes of the Mercanzia of 1312, the Florentine government added more spheres of jurisdiction to the court of the Mercanzia, some of these spheres being of a rather quotidian nature, which detracted from its international business. Before 1312, the Mercanzia had executed the sentences imposed by the consuls of the five major guilds. In 1312, this duty was extended to executing the sentences of all of the guilds. The security of particular streets, those streets that foreign merchants used to cross the territory of Florence and enter the city, were attended to by the Mercanzia. The Mercanzia gained competence over questions concerning gabelles and gabelle collectors because reprisals could be provoked by unfair gabelles being charged or by abuses being perpetrated by gabelle collectors against foreigners trading in Florence. At this time, the Mercanzia began to hear complaints and develop policies and laws concerning the liability between partners. The statutes of 1312 gave the Mercanzia the very important duty of dividing the liabilities in cases of defaulting (pp. 38–39). The Mercanzia acquired the right to treat fraud (*ruberie*) committed not only against foreigners but also against people of the city, county, and district of Florence (p. 43).

In 1318, an important change in Mercanzia jurisdiction took place. The Mercanzia acquired all jurisdiction related *ratione materiae* to commerce. The foreign official could carry out not only the statutes and ordinances of the Mercanzia but also all the statutes of the consuls of the five major guilds and the statutes of the commune on material related to the jurisdiction already possessed by the Mercanzia. Previously the Mercanzia had only executed communal statutes concerning reprisal and defaulting and fleeing (p. 56).

The groups of people over which the Mercanzia had jurisdiction steadily increased. At its inception in 1309, the Mercanzia's jurisdiction was circumscribed by the five top guilds. Although in 1312 the Mercanzia acquired the duty of executing the sentences of the consuls of all of the guilds, by 1324 it had first instance jurisdiction only over the ten top guilds, and in many activities, its jurisdiction was restricted to the five original guilds or to seven guilds (pp. 37, 66). In 1340, the Mercanzia further increased its jurisdiction. At that time, the rules of admittance into the Mercanzia actually favored those who did not join a guild: those exercising a trade who were not in a guild could be plaintiffs before the Mercanzia but not defendants. In order to eliminate this advantage, each trade was assigned to a guild so that those exercising it could be cited before the Mercanzia even if they were not members of a guild (pp. 74–75). In 1372 the jurisdiction of the Mercanzia was increased to encompass all of the guilds, thus newly admitting the fourteen minor guilds (p. 83). The Mercanzia could deal with any citizen of Florence, even if he was not a guildsman or merchant when a foreigner was the plaintiff (p. 119).

The Mercanzia's most important area of jurisdiction was reprisal. Many of the other areas gravitated to the Mercanzia because they pertained to reprisal, in order to lend the Mercanzia greater authority in regulating reprisal. Reprisal was the right, conceded by the government to one of its subjects, to capture a citizen of a foreign state and seize his goods up to a certain sum, until the subject, who had suffered an offense at the hands of another citizen from that foreign state, had obtained the satisfaction that he deserved.[44] During the Middle Ages, reprisal frequently damaged commerce. The bad faith or insolvency of one Florentine citizen could cause the damage or destruction of the goods or business of another Florentine citizen, particularly of a citizen who held goods or conducted business abroad. The laws of Florence and of the other cities allowed reprisal in response to such abuses as debt, suretyship, robbery, highway robbery, undeserved incarceration, abusive taxes or tolls, or ill-gotten gains.[45] Reprisals could be conceded against individuals, corporations, or cities.[46] Execution of the reprisal usually took place in the territory that conceded it. Reprisal was only used if regular legal remedies were not available, so was not used by Florentines against other Florentines. Concession and regulation of reprisal was reserved to the highest magistrates in a state. With the passing of time, the power to concede reprisal was switched from official to official depending on what official was ascendant. In most communes, as in Florence, power was passed from a foreign official to an outside agency to citizen magistrates. In Florence, power was possessed by the Podestà in the thirteenth and early fourteenth centuries, by the Mercanzia in the fourteenth century, and by the Priors in the fifteenth century.

Jurisdiction over reprisal was first given by the state to the Mercanzia in 1309. The Mercanzia was supposed to render justice to foreigners against Florentine *cittadini* or *districtuali* or against places in the *contado*. When a letter denouncing a Florentine reached Florence, the foreign official of the Mercanzia was required to compel this citizen, his consorts, his partners, his brothers, or his sons still under his *patria potesta* to satisfy the debt or post a security to pay whatever amount the foreign official decided he owed. If the cited Florentine debtor did not appear before the Mercanzia, he was declared defaulting and fleeing and was thrown out of his guild. The foreign official also executed the penalty, determining the goods of the debtor and seizing them to the amount owed. At this time, the foreign official also satisfied any other creditors. The foreign official could also proceed against the debtors of the person defaulting and fleeing and against his *fittatioli, lavoratori,* and *inquilini* (all three were dependent agricultural tenants), obligating them to give their rents to the creditors or quit their lands.[47] If a Florentine suffered reprisal because of another Florentine, the Mercanzia proceeded against the one to blame to compel him to restore the amount of the damages and the interest, putting him in jail, if necessary. The commune of Florence empowered the Mercanzia to conclude treaties with foreign states that mutually limited the concession of reprisals, a power that demonstrates the Mercanzia's assimilation into the government (p. 40). The Mercanzia conceded reprisals to Florentines who had just cause, first writing to the offending foreign commune inviting a defense. The Mercanzia took care of reprisals requested by Florentines as well as reprisals in which Florentines suffered. If a Florentine demonstrated that a reprisal being carried out against him was unjust, the Mercanzia negotiated with the foreign land to have the reprisal removed (pp. 41–44). The Mercanzia had power over reprisal until 1408, when this power passed to the Priors (pp. 126–27). The power over reprisal made the Mercanzia a diplomatic bureau of the government.

The Mercanzia had important relationships with both the guilds and the communal rectors. However, the Mercanzia did not become powerful through its connection with the guilds but through its connection with the state. In the Mercanzia's formative period, the guilds were already politically established. In the fourteenth century, the Mercanzia did not subsume the guilds and become powerful in this way; rather, the state assimilated the Mercanzia and placed it over the guilds. The jurisdiction of the Mercanzia began to concur more and more with that of the guilds until it posed an alternate, as well as a superior, court to the guilds, like the court of the Podestà. In the fourteenth century, both the guilds and the Mercanzia had jurisdiction over defaulters, but the Mercanzia had more legal remedies. Both tried questions between masters, workers, and apprentices. Both tried counterfeiting and fraud, but the Mercanzia generally tried only those cases that had an important impact on trade, such as the sale of stolen goods and the alteration of merchants' account books (pp. 99–101). Beyond the jurisdiction of the guilds, the Mercanzia tried merchants who were not inscribed in any guild and judged cases that transcended one guild. In the early fifteenth century, the consuls lost their jurisdiction over defaulting and fleeing; now, the Mercanzia and the Podestà exclusively tried these cases.

The jurisdiction of the Mercanzia also concurred with that of the foreign rectors. An important area of coordination was reprisal, in which both the Podestà and the Mercanzia had jurisdiction in the fourteenth century. However, during that time, the authority of the Podestà concerning reprisal became subordinated and regulated by the Mercanzia and the Priors. Reprisals could be conceded by the Podestà or his collateral judge, but the Mercanzia had to be notified (pp. 54–55). Another case of concurrence between the competence of the Podestà and that of the Mercanzia was that in which a creditor of a corporation wanted to proceed against the individual members of the corporation. Similarly, a case in which a person who suffered damage not caused by his own doing sought compensation from the person on whose account he suffered was treated by both the Podestà and the Mercanzia (p. 108). The jurisdiction of the Mercanzia concurred with that of the rectors in defaulting and fleeing. The important legislation on defaulting and fleeing appeared in the 1322–25 statutes pertaining to the Captain and was used by the Mercanzia as well as the rectors. In the fourteenth century, the Captain was the executive who protected the guilds, a job also performed in some part by the Mercanzia. Although their authority partially concurred, the Captain protected the political aspects of the guilds, while the Mercanzia protected their commercial interests (p. 110). In the early fourteenth century, the Captain dealt with all the guilds, while the Mercanzia had particular interest in the most important guilds.

In the early fifteenth century, the Mercanzia diminished in importance both because it lost its sphere of influence in international trade and because it lost jurisdiction over reprisal and certain kinds of defaulting and fleeing cases. The Mercanzia, fostered by the state, remained subordinated to the state. Lauro Martines believes that the Mercanzia was one of the agencies through which the oligarchy was taking over the government in the early fifteenth century. He maintains that the Mercanzia was gaining power because it was acquiring exclusive jurisdiction in defaulting and in reprisal. According to Martines, the Mercanzia was given additional powers to compensate for the attrition of the regular court system.[48] While Martines believes that the Mercanzia became completely assimilated by the state, he sees the Mercanzia in an analogous position with the executive agencies that had been created in the late fourteenth century.

In the early fifteenth century, however, the Mercanzia did not possess exclusive jurisdiction in either defaulting or reprisal. Instead, the Mercanzia lost all of its power to regulate reprisal and affiliated cases and shared its jurisdiction over defaulting with the Podestà, who tried many such cases. Martines does not take into account the Mercanzia's loss of power in international affairs. In fact, the government of the territorial state took these powers back from the Mercanzia, giving executive power back to the executive branch. In short, agencies used for patrician takeover should be gaining power, not losing it. Guido Bonolis, an expert on the Mercanzia, blames the agency's dwindling power in the early fifteenth century on the development of a stronger central government.[49]

The statute compilation of 1415 reaffirmed that jurisdiction over the concession of reprisal had been transferred from the Mercanzia to the Priors, the Gonfalonier of Justice, and the councils.[50] All of the jurisdiction attendant on reprisal was also transferred. There is no more mention of the Mercanzia receiving letters from foreign states or of the Mercanzia creating treaties with foreign states concerning reprisal. After 1415, reprisals were conceded by way of petitions extended to and approved by the Priors, the Gonfalonier of Justice, and the councils. The removal of this jurisdiction from the Mercanzia greatly diminished its power and importance. Certainly reprisal had not become an insignificant and outdated remedy or it would not have become the exclusive dominion of the Priors and the Gonfalonier of Justice, the most powerful officials in the state. Reprisal appears to have remained important both in its private and in its public aspects, that is, both as a means for merchants to recover money from bad or fraudulent business deals made with foreigners and as a political statement of ill will from the Florentine commune to another government, a kind of miniature declaration of war. Private petitions continued to be a source of demands for reprisal so that the mercantile use of reprisal remained important (Tract. Cons. Art. Merc. 24). Further, the Priors and the Gonfalonier of Justice monopolized this power in order to control foreign policy and prevent individuals from creating ill will among political powers (Tract. Cons. Art. Merc. 25). In the Florentine territorial state, the central government gained exclusive control over its foreign policy.

The power that the Mercanzia possessed over cases of defaulting had always been closely tied to its power over reprisal. The Mercanzia saw to it that Florentine merchants did not default against foreign creditors who would seek reprisal. The 1415 statutes still attributed to the Mercanzia power over defaulting but not in cases that were likely to involve reprisal. The Balia of 1309 gave the Mercanzia the duty of carrying out two communal statutes concerning defaulting likely to provoke reprisal: "Qualiter procedatur contra illos, quorum de causa nundinis, vel alibi Florentini molestantur" (In what manner one should proceed against those on account of whom Florentines are damaged in the marketplace or elsewhere) and "De indemnitate communis Florentiae" (Concerning the invulnerability of the commune of Florence). Both of these rubrics involved the commune's duty to safeguard Florentine citizens from reprisals caused by other Florentine citizens and carried out by foreigners. The 1415 version of these statutes made no reference to the Mercanzia as an agent of performance; instead, it named the Podestà and the Captain. Both rubrics stated that if a foreign government sent a letter accusing a Florentine of defaulting, these rectors took a security from the person implicated and heard the defense (Tract. Cons. Art. Merc. 21; 22). However, in the 1415 communal statutes, the Mercanzia is frequently mentioned as handling simple cases of defaulting and fleeing but not as handling defaulting and fleeing cases of international involvement.[51] The Mercanzia heard claims against the goods of defaulters which goods had been confiscated and sold.[52] The Mercanzia divided up the goods of defaulters who settled their debts when they were bankrupt and then came into a richer state.[53] It decided the liability of partners and apprentices of defaulting merchants. By 1415, the Mercanzia had jurisdiction over all of the twenty-one guilds.

In 1415, the Mercanzia had become a higher court for the guilds and an alternate court to the courts of the consuls of the guilds, especially for important merchants. It still performed trials that the consuls could not perform because of a conflict of interest.[54] The Mercanzia executed the sentences of the consuls of the twenty-one guilds. Trials held in the consuls' courts that were not completed in forty days devolved to the foreign official and six counselors of the Mercanzia.[55] The Mercanzia examined the books of merchants in the Florentine guilds to determine their credibility.[56] It was in charge of keeping track of the emancipations severing liability between fathers and sons among Florentine merchants (*Stat.* 2.110). This involvement with the guilds further points to the phasing out of the Mercanzia's international connections and its placement in the Florentine judicial system as a higher court for the Florentine guilds. The acquisition of the power of reprisal by the executive branch and the continued involvement of the foreign rectors in the guilds shows that the Mercanzia remained an accountable part of the state.

The Officials of Grascia

The Officials of Grascia were another set of officials that tried guild-related cases and with whom the Podestà, in particular, was associated. Most of the information about these officials is contained in the Tractatus et materia Consulum Artium et Mercatorum of the statutes of 1415. The Officials of Grascia were not guild officials, like the consuls, but were communal officials limiting the interests of the guilds in favor of the interests of the commune. Their job was to prevent any famine or shortage of necessary materials in Florence by regulating prices of necessary materials and food, by limiting organizations, like the guilds, that sought to drive up prices for materials or work, by encouraging the flow of materials and food into Florence, and by prohibiting their dispersion out of Florence.

Thus, the Officials of Grascia had close dealings with only a few of the guilds, those that had anything to do with food and necessary materials. With these guilds, the Officials of Grascia were in an adversarial position, as was the Podestà, because they sought to keep food and materials cheap and abundant. All of the rectors were empowered to aid these officials, but the Podestà was most frequently assigned specific duties in this area. The possibility that infractions of regulations concerning necessary materials could occur anywhere in the territory, or even outside the territory, made their prosecution a natural duty for those officials with large retinues like the rectors. The Podestà's particular interest in the Officials of Grascia stemmed from his duties in supervising the guilds, to which these officials were intimately related. Sometimes the Officials of Grascia oversaw the consuls of the guilds, preventing them from forming monopolies and setting prices. For instance, the statutes concerning abundance allowed anyone to sell meat wholesale or retail, not just members of the butchers' guild. The guild could not have a monopoly over meat to drive prices up, nor could it interfere in its sale when conducted by those outside the guild. Anyone selling meat for eating, whether a member of the guild or not, was subject to the jurisdiction and coercion of the Officials of Grascia. The price of meat was set by these officials.[57] Likewise, anyone could make bread for sale. Those doing so were subject to the Officials of Grascia and could not be harassed by the consuls of the bakers' guild (Tract. Cons. Art. Merc. 186). The Officials of Grascia also established the prices of materials sold by guilds dealing in essentials, such as building materials. The Officials of Grascia could not set prices over goods pertaining to the seven major guilds, but none of these guilds dealt in necessary materials (Tract. Cons. Art. Merc. 139).

Despite the fact that the Officials of Grascia could make provisions and regulations concerning abundance and were obligated to make sure that they were observed, and despite the fact that for some infractions the likely culprits were members of the guilds, the Officials of Grascia were not allowed to recognize cases brought against the *matriculi* of any guild or those holding shops. The consuls were expected to expedite these trials of merchants and guildsmen. If they were not able to expedite in two months, the cases devolved to the Officials of Grascia (Tract. Cons. Art. Merc. 135; 136). There must have been many cases that were relatively unsuitable for the courts of the consuls. If guildsmen were tried for breaking the price regulations, the consuls of the guilds would not be likely to move quickly or punish severely. These cases were likely to end up in the court of the Officials of Grascia. The guilds first had the right to deal with their own members, but if they did not, the Officials of Grascia did. The Officials of Grascia had complete cognition over abundance infractions committed by those outside the guilds. Since the sale of comestibles was open to those outside the guilds, cases concerning these people were under the jurisdiction of the Officials of Grascia. Sometimes the Officials of Grascia were given exceptional jurisdiction even over members of the guilds. Anyone bringing beasts into the city for selling for meat, whether a member of the guild or not, was under the jurisdiction of the Officials of Grascia.

The Podestà had a higher jurisdiction than the Officials of Grascia concerning the supervision of comestibles. Here is another example of an agency checked by and subordinated to the foreign rectors and the regular court system. The Podestà was related to the Officials of Grascia in the same way that the Officials of Grascia were related to the consuls of the

The Podestà and Other Affiliated Officials

guilds. The Officials of Grascia had one month to expedite trials of abundance infractions before they devolved to the Podestà to terminate (Tract. Cons. Art. Merc. 135). The Podestà also had the power to condemn for crimes belonging to a higher jurisdiction than those of the consuls and the Officials of Grascia. He condemned guildsmen belonging to a guild dealing in necessary items who committed fraud, falsity, or extortion (Tract. Cons. Art. Merc. 66; 67; 70). Cases of abundance infractions that were unsuitable for both the courts of the consuls and the court of the Officials of Grascia were tried by the Podestà and other rectors. The Podestà condemned any person impeding those conducting victuals into Florence, having full discretion in proceeding, accusing, punishing, and sending to execution, including the power to initiate through inquisition (Tract. Cons. Art. Merc. 149). Those impeding were likely to be the consuls of the guilds or someone sent by the guilds so that the courts of the guilds would be unsuitable places for these trials. The Officials of Grascia were not allowed to try members of the guilds unless the cases devolved to them; thus, this task was left to the rectors.

The Podestà, as well as the other rectors, tried many of the same cases as the Officials of Grascia. The Officials of Grascia proceeded, punished, and condemned those committing infractions in buying or selling grain or vegetables, in taking or unloading them in prohibited areas, and in measuring them incorrectly. The rectors could do the same (Tract. Cons. Art. Merc. 275). All of the rectors, in fact, could try anyone breaking abundance statutes (Tract. Cons. Art. Merc. 141). The Podestà condemned for exactly the same kinds of crimes that the Officials of Grascia did. He attempted to prevent monopolies and enforced the free flow of necessary goods and the quality control regulations concerning necessary items (Tract. Cons. Art. Merc. 58; 79; 81; 120). The Podestà had spies that circulated every day in search of infractions pertaining to food and necessary items. Both he and the Captain could condemn those who did not obey the regulations that set prices of these goods (Tract. Cons. Art. Merc. 59). The Podestà had a larger jurisdiction than that of the Officials of Grascia, since he was able to try *matriculi* of the guilds.

The Officials of Grascia were known by a variety of names: the Officials of Piazza Or San Michele, the Officials of Wheat (de Blado), and the Officials of Corn (de Grano) (Tract. Cons. Art. Merc. 97; 135; 140). Amazingly enough, the Officials of Grascia were not the same as the officials of abundance. Nor were they the same as the officials over the abundance of meat and fish despite the fact that the Officials of Grascia made regulations concerning these comestibles and tried cases against those who carried on activities decreasing the abundance of meat and fish. The Officials of Grascia were not the same as the officials over the abundance of wheat and corn, despite the jurisdiction of the Officials of Grascia over wheat and corn, nor were they the same as the officials of mills, despite the jurisdiction of the Officials of Grascia over mills. The officials of abundance had a different function than the Officials of Grascia, mainly buying staples outside of Florence and bringing them back to Florence. The eight officials of abundance of wheat and corn were the same as the officials of mills (molendinorum). These officials were separate until the officials of abundance of wheat and corn were given the duties of the officials of mills, the governing of communal mills. There were six officials of the abundance of meat and fish (*Stat.* 5.2.24; 32).

The officials of abundance had complete authority over the purchase of comestibles outside of Florence and their importation into Florence. They could go for the purpose of buying whenever they liked and could buy for whatever price they liked. They could make contracts obligating the commune as if they were made by the Priors, the Gonfalonier of Justice, and the colleges (*Stat.* 5.2.26). They supervised the building of communal ovens in Florence, as many and where they liked, so that bread could easily be made in the city. They could make regulations, even penal regulations, connected with these spheres of competence. No Florentine was allowed to keep more grain than he needed for his family: anyone so doing had to appear before the officials over the abundance of wheat and corn to have the amount he bought recorded and to turn in the superfluous amount to these officials. If a person failed to do so, the Podestà, the Captain, or the Executor punished him.[58] The officials over the abundance of wheat and corn and the officials over the abundance of meat and fish did not have any judicial functions other than to make regulations about the selling of grain and meat. The Officials of Grascia, on the other hand, had substantial judicial duties.

The Office of Grascia was divided into two sets of officials: the citizen officials and the foreign officials. Although they served the same general function, to prevent famine, they had different judicial capabilities. The citizen Officials of Grascia could only decide cases involving amounts up to 100 lire. In cases involving less than 10 lire, they could act according to summary procedure. They must have had the power to initiate cases through inquisition, since they sent out spies to investigate. They could compel witnesses from the city, county, or elsewhere, condemning witnesses not appearing to a quantity of up to 25 lire. Further, they could make regulations concerning abundance (Tract. Cons. Art. Merc. 157; 274). The foreign Official of Grascia was capable of trying cases involving amounts greater than 100 lire. The lack of limits to his jurisdiction is indicated by his ability to administer torture (Tract. Cons. Art. Merc. 280). The foreign Official of Grascia had a larger retinue so that he could

The Podestà and Other Affiliated Officials

carry on special investigations at the request of the citizen Officials of Grascia and execute many of the condemnations made by himself and by the citizen officials (Tract. Cons. Art. Merc. 276; 280). He could investigate at his own initiative. He relied very heavily on the reports of his retinue for proof, sufficient proof being provided by the report of one of his notaries or two of his berrovarii who gave their oaths to support their testimony. Supposedly, he was allowed to condemn only in cases where proof was provided through confession, contumaciousness, or reports of his retinue; that is, he was not permitted to judge cases through evaluating the testimony of witnesses. However, this conclusion is mitigated by the equating of one witness of sight or three of public fame with one report from a retinue member. He must have relied mainly on the reports of his retinue but could evaluate testimony when this alone was available. His ability to torture separated him from the other Officials of Grascia and must be understood as an indication that he tried abundance cases of a very serious nature.

The Officials of Grascia supervised several groups of laborers whose jobs had bearing on the abundance and the price of comestibles and essentials. They could not recognize cases against those in the guilds, but they could recognize against artisans who were not in the guilds, such as the many foreign artisans, foreign laborers, and newly arrived artisans from the contado who lived and worked in Florence but were not part of the guilds (Tract. Cons. Art. Merc. 135; 136; 140). Labor outside the guilds was permitted in any field connected with necessary items. Some industries, particularly the silk industry, employed many foreign semiskilled and skilled laborers. These groups were under the control of the Officials of Grascia, both citizen and foreign. Outside labor forced salaries of laborers and artisans down. The Officials of Grascia protected these outside laborers from the wrath of the guilds but also oppressed them by keeping their salaries low. Both citizen officials and foreign officials had cognition over servants (Tract. Cons. Art. Merc. 144; 149). They could recognize, try, and sentence summarily in cases in which nurses, servants, domestics, and stewards brought cases against their masters and, conversely, where masters brought cases against their servants. This jurisdiction was assigned to the Officials of Grascia because servants were another class of worker whose wages were regulated.

The wages of agricultural workers were also regulated in order to keep the price of comestibles low. In the early fifteenth century, there was a shortage of agricultural workers so workers who rented land were forbidden to leave it and take it out of cultivation. The regulation of the salaries of these workers kept their salaries low and unable to follow the market when demand rose. The Officials of Grascia controlled these agricultural workers, keeping agricultural workers on the land and keeping land in cultivation (Tract. Cons. Art. Merc. 144). They had authority over those with annual contracts and those who labored for wages. In order to be able to enforce contracts between laborers and the people from whom they rented the land, the Officials of Grascia made judgments concerning the meaning and the terms of pacts that contained doubtful or unclear phrases.[59] The citizen Officials of Grascia compiled a list of all the agricultural laborers who rented land, worked by the job, or worked for wages in the city, county, or district. The syndics and rectors of the popoli of the city, county, and district reported all the laborers of these types in their popoli to enable the citizen Officials of Grascia to make such a list. The list was used to check on these laborers to see that they continued to cultivate the land according to their pacts. Abandoning land was a criminal offense.[60] The Judge of Grascia, who was the same as the foreign Official of Grascia, condemned those who violated the statutes concerning agricultural labor.[61]

The Officials of Grascia had cognition over pavement makers, oven makers, masters of stone and wood, tailors, shoemakers, leather treaters, merchants of old iron, butchers, meat sellers, fish dealers, poultry dealers, fishermen, corner merchants, bakers, millers, cooks, pasta makers, hotel owners, and washers and fullers of cloth.[62] They supervised the quality of their work, set prices and salaries, and punished violators of these regulations (Tract. Cons. Art. Merc. 57; 77; 125; 232). They recognized all cases connected with corn, wheat, wine, vegetables, flour, oil, and other comestibles (Tract. Cons. Art. Merc. 85). They functioned as a consumer protection service in making sure meat and fish were fresh and were what they were purported to be (Tract. Cons. Art. Merc. 107). They condemned people who took foodstuffs outside the city. Those who unloaded comestibles in places other than the regulated areas or measured dishonestly were condemned by the Officials of Grascia (Tract. Cons. Art. Merc. 275). Many of these crimes could also be investigated and prosecuted by the Podestà or the other rectors (Tract. Cons. Art. Merc. 59; 125).

The functions performed by the Officials of Grascia significantly decreased the powers of the guilds which they regulated. By allowing outside labor to work in the same capacities as artisans within the guilds, the Officials of Grascia decreased the ability of the guilds to control these vocations. Foreign artisans who were not members of the guilds were actually protected by the state. When the state fixed prices of certain goods, this further defeated the purpose of joining a guild. This state interference in the guilds diminished the power of these organizations.

The Podestà and Other Affiliated Officials

Territorial Jurisdiction and Other Spheres of Competence

Florence had had dominion over some of its surrounding territory in the communal period, but this territorial dominion underwent rapid accretion in the late fourteenth and early fifteenth centuries. The foreign rectors were very involved in the supervision of the courts of the county and district, and the Podestà was paramount among the three rectors in this supervision, especially concerning crime. An examination of the administration of justice of the contado and district in the early fifteenth century demonstrates that the foreign rectors and the regular judiciary were the cornerstone of the territorial judicial system during this formative period; a major movement toward centralization and organization was executed, consistent with the continuation of the territorial state; and the government tied the contado and district into the regular central administration and made its officials accountable, consistent with the continuation of the territorial state. The often aggressive wars of the early fifteenth century added large areas of territory to Florence, especially smaller cities and their contadi.

The challenge of administering this extended territory in the early fifteenth century was met by measures striving for greater centralization, greater systemization, and greater uniformity. These measures, although only partially successful, generated the institutions and offices that lasted through the Grand Ducal period and almost unaltered into the nineteenth century.[63] All of the county and district offices, formerly staffed by local people, became filled by Florentines.[64] These offices became sources of income and prestige for the aristocracy and minor aristocracy. Many of the offices were minor, but some were extremely powerful with wide jurisdictions in terms of area and *materia*. As the offices came to be uniformly staffed by Florentines, the powers of the officials were increased. Almost all of the reforms that aimed at greater centralization, organization, and uniformity were present in the 1415 statutes, although a few reforms occurred subsequently. In 1424, sixteen podesteries were abolished mostly being fused with other podesteries, a change that continued to manifest itself in the podestà having to hold court alternately in one seat and then the other.[65]

The organization laid out in the statutes of 1415 is very unusual because it is the first attempt to treat a territory as a consistent whole, even though there were many differences in the concessions, jurisdictions, and privileges extended to the different areas. The network of jurisdictions laid out in 1415 was more than merely a federation, being better coordinated than any other regional state in Italy: Milan gave greater concessions to feudal authority, and Venice greater concessions to local jurisdictional traditions.⁶⁶ Minor villages and rural areas with small population centers were organized into *ligae* (leagues), which communicated directly with the central government (*Stat.* 5.4.94). There was some attempt to create uniform jurisdictions for officials in the contado and territory: a new rule was instated that set uniform jurisdictions for local rectors inside ten *millaria* and outside ten *millaria* of Florence (*Stat.* 5.4.59). Differences in the manner in which towns and cities were administered and in the jurisdictions of officials administering them usually stemmed from what the original terms were in the acts of submission to Florence, how amicable to Florentine rule a town or city was, and what level of pacification was necessary to secure a particular area.⁶⁷

When this centralization of the judicial system of the extrinsic posts occurred, the foreign rectors in Florence were the cornerstone of the system. The rectors held the highest jurisdiction over cases from the contado and district, syndicated all the extrinsic officials, and tried the appeals of cases from the contado and district. The other central government officials that later controlled the judicial posts in the contado and district and became extremely powerful and independent agencies because of this control either did not exist or did not fill this function by the early fifteenth century. The Cinque del Contado existed, being established provisionally in 1418 and permanently in 1420, but controlled finances in the contado and district, not judicial matters.⁶⁸ The Conservatori delle Leggi, an extremely important agency in the contado and district, especially during the Grand Ducal period, was only established in 1429, when it took over the syndication of contado and district officials. In its early period, it was an enthusiastic proponent of accountability.⁶⁹ The Otto di Guardia, also extremely important later, monitored stipendiarii and exiles and banned people in the contado and district but had no regular jurisdiction in these areas. Statutes discussing the sending of bullectini to the courts in the contado and district mention the Signoria with the colleges as a possible source of bullectini, but they do not mention the Otto. The Otto di Prattica, also important later in the contado and district, only came into existence in 1471. The foreign rectors were in a powerful position in coordinating the judicial system of the county and district during this most important formative period.

The rectors had a higher jurisdiction than most of the county and district officials, that is, they had cognition over serious crimes that the officials of the county and district could not treat (*Stat.* 5.4.39; 5.4.47). Each of the rectors was assigned similar duties but over different locations. Despite efforts toward uniformity, different officials of the county and district related differently to the communal government. Some of the officials had very limited jurisdictions in constituency, land area, or de-

The Podestà and Other Affiliated Officials

gree of seriousness of the cases that they were allowed to try. Cases that were beyond their limits either according to constituency or degree of seriousness were deferred to the rectors in Florence. Cases beyond their limits in land area fell to other local officials of the county and district. There were no special places in the county and district in which the Podestà, the Captain, or the Executor had sole jurisdiction. Different county and district officials were supervised by different Florentine rectors; and even officials from the same place, such as the Podestà and the Captain of Pisa, were supervised by different Florentine rectors (*Stat.* 5.4.1). There were so many variations in the relationships between the supervised and the supervising officials that each of these relationships could almost be considered unique.[70] An example of the intermixing of jurisdictions which brought more serious cases to the courts of the Florentine rectors comes from the region of Anghiari. In Anghiari there was a vicar of very high standing with jurisdiction mainly over stipendiarii, as well as local rectors with minor civil and criminal jurisdictions. The vicar could try tumult and failure to honor the jurisdiction of the Florentine government committed by anyone, and could try civil and criminal cases involving stipendiarii, with the right to try capital crimes, initiate any kind of case through inquisition, and administer torture in his proceedings. He could not interfere in the minor civil and criminal jurisdictions of the local rectors in his district. Cases that did not involve stipendiarii or tumult, and were of greater seriousness than the local rectors' courts were permitted to try, devolved to the court of the Podestà in Florence (*Stat.* 5.4.22). Similar cases from other areas devolved to the Captain in Florence. The Podestà of Florence was sometimes called upon to punish county and district residents who were condemned by the officials of the county and district but had failed to pay their pecuniary penalties (*Stat.* 5.4.51; 17).

When the rectors in the county and district received notice of or discovered serious crimes, they were obligated to denounce the cases before the courts of the foreign rectors in Florence. The acts of the Podestà and Captain in Florence are full of cases initiated by denunciation of the rectors of the county and district. The local rectors compiled the evidence, gathered the witnesses, and made the denunciation to the foreign rector. People of the locale were obligated to pursue culprits committing crimes in their locale or fleeing through their locale. The Podestà of Florence could punish podestà of the county and district who did not pursue and turn in criminals wanted in Florence (*Stat.* 5.4.39; 40).

The Florentine rectors were in charge of syndicating all the contado and district officials. The crimes they examined and the process they followed are described in the section on syndication in Chapter 6. Here I will simply outline the broad extent of their involvement. The foreign rectors actually syndicated all of the officials of the contado and district twice: once at the location in the county and district, and once in Florence. During the last days that an extrinsic official was in office, a judge attached to the Podestà or the Captain traveled to the location in the county and district to syndicate him. Accusations and information were gathered there in a general mandatory inquest from those who believed themselves to have been harmed by the official. Offenses against local people, such as extortion, were best tried on location. The Podestà syndicated some of the most important officials of the county and district: the Captain of Pisa, the Captain of Arezzo, and the Podestà of Arezzo (*Stat.* 5.4.1; 20). Syndication in Florence occurred after the end of office when financial records, records of omissions, and court records were handed in for review. Then the contado and district officials were syndicated by the Executor's judge in the regular syndication process. All extrinsic officials were held accountable for their acts. Some of the syndication powers of the foreign rectors were transferred to the Conservatori delle Leggi in 1429. They were apparently very active in ferreting out crimes committed: 20 percent of the officials accused of crimes were condemned, for syndication, a high percentage.[71]

Appeals, too, were sent to the courts of the foreign rectors. Information on appeals from the contado and district is found in Chapter 3, under the Captain's judge of appeals. Appeals could be made from the county and district in some civil cases, some criminal cases, and some arbitrations, a larger group of cases than those considered appealable in the city of Florence, because the officials of the county and district were of lesser stature. Criminal cases were less often appealable than civil. Appeals from criminal cases went to the judge of appeals under the Captain or to the Podestà's civil judges. The Podestà took appeals in civil cases of 50 lire and up from the court of the Podestà of Pontenari, from the court of the Podestà of Civitella Vald'ambra, and from the court of the Podestà of Chiusi (*Stat.* 5.4.24; 25; 26). The Podestà received appeals from criminal cases from the court of the Podestà of S. Gemignano and the court of the Podestà of S. Miniato (*Stat.* 5.4.39; 40). Other appeals went to the judge of appeals in Florence. The Executor's civil judge was involved in appeals from the county and district as a judge of second appeals so handled no cases of first appeals. Thus, all of the rectors' courts were involved in this highest of jurisdictions for the county and district, the trial of appeals.

Rules for jurisdictions within the areas of the county and district were varied despite efforts at uniform handling. Any case involving a Florentine as either an actor or a defendant could be tried in Florence. Any case outside the jurisdictional limits of officials in the contado and district

III
The Podestà and Other Affiliated Officials

devolved to a higher court in the contado and district or to one of the Florentine rectors. Limits were constituted by worth of the goods being contested, if civil, or amount of possible penalty, a measure of seriousness, if criminal. As an attempt at uniformity, one rubric outlines the terms of jurisdiction in areas near Florence and then areas farther away. Podestà within ten *milliaria* have a civil jurisdiction of up to 25 lire, and those outside ten *milliaria* up to 50 lire. These rectors had a criminal jurisdiction of only 5 lire. However, those who possessed a greater jurisdiction before the rubric was redacted retained the higher jurisdiction in both civil and criminal matters (*Stat.* 5.4.59). The uniform jurisdictional limit for civil cases was raised in a subsequent *provvisione*.[72] Given the low jurisdictional limits, many criminal cases from the nearby contado must have devolved to the rectors. Debt posed somewhat of an exception; those who were detained in the county and district for debt were sent to the Stinche prison. Also as somewhat of an exception, those who were charged with receiving banned people could be condemned in the courts of any rector of the county and district to a fine of 25 lire (*Stat.* 5.4.59).

But despite the use of extrinsic offices by the aristocracy as income (sometimes substantial income), and despite the source of this income deriving from the county and district, in the early fifteenth century, officials of the county and district were not free to fleece their constituency. Efforts were made by the central government toward accountability, to tie county and district officials into the regular governmental structure. Condemnations made in the county and district were to be made through procedure, not through bullectini (*Stat.* 5.4.3). Copies of cases and condemnations above 50 lire were to be sent to Florence (*Stat.* 5.4.3). Every *liga* elected or deputed a *camerius* (treasurer) for receiving payments of condemnations made by the Podestà, and the books of the Podestà's notary were checked against the books of the *camerius*. Oblations extended to prisoners in Pisa were bestowed in the same way and with the same restrictions as they were in Florence, through a *partito* (winning vote) of two parts of the Priors, the Gonfalonier, and the colleges (*Stat.* 5.4.4). The statutes of 1415 forbid the Signoria to delegate powers to local rectors in order to raise the level of the cases they could handle (*Stat.* 5.4.59). However, from 1364 on, commissaries, or extraordinary officials, were sometimes sent out by the government to carry out special tasks, which were reason of state missions.[73] Sometimes, too, local rectors were delegated extraordinary powers to act almost as commissaries. At times, these commissaries and delegations were attempts to get outside the network of accountability and to create officials with greater independence or powers. A provvisione of 1415 attempted to quash the multiplication of less accountable powers by forbidding at least some officials, such as the Six of

Arezzo, the Officials of Castrorum, and the governors of the gabelle of gates, from creating *commissarii*.[74] Commissarii were usually men of patrician affiliation. In the early fifteenth century, the appointment of these men to fill needs in the contado and district, such as regulating relations between Florence and the subject jurisdiction and reviewing the statutes of subject cities, meant only that the patriciate had the common political goal of holding the contado and district under Florentine sovereignty. It did not indicate a more elaborate agenda of patrician consensus. In the 1420s, the reduction by one-fifth of podesteries, from which patricians derived honor and income, certainly speaks against the existence of a patrician consensus of agenda.[75]

The rectors and vicars were chosen by lot from a group of eligible citizens. Officials in the county and district were syndicated and were restricted through *divieti* regulations, such as the Captain of Pisa, who had a three-year divieto on his post. Offices were subjected to rapid rotation, lasting usually only six months. Connell posits that the county and district officials were heavily monitored for accountability until 1434. This then diminished because of political reasons permitting liberty of gain, then increased again after 1494.[76] There was thus continuity between the central institutions of the territorial state and territorial institutions in respect to a continued effort toward accountability. Centralization may have also followed a similar profile, with some decentralization occurring after 1450. In the 1415 statutes, the city of Pistoia was treated as if it was part of the contado of Florence (*Stat.* 5.4.31). However, after 1454 Pistoia was exempted from the control of many Florentine officials; and, by 1494, from Florentine law concerning the territory.[77]

Comitatini and *districtuali* (county dwellers and district dwellers) probably did not consider being under Florentine jurisdiction a benefit, although Florentine rule was not entirely harmful. The higher level of legal expertise among Florentine judicial officials improved justice in the county and district. In most areas, local customs and statutes were intended to be applied, as long as these customs and statutes were in conformity with Florentine law and were approved by Florence, a boon to comitatini and districtuali. Most officials and their retinues were entirely Florentine, however, and unversed in local customs. In rare instances, Florentine law provided that one of the officials in the judicial retinue be local (*Stat.* 5.4.23). Florentine citizens continued to hold privileges that comitatini and districtuali lacked, such as the right of Florentines to be actors or defendants in the courts in Florence, and therefore, always to be tried on friendly turf. Florentines could have death sentences commuted to pecuniary penalties, but comitatini or districtuali could not.[78] In the early fifteenth century, in cases of crimes committed against Florentines

The Podestà and Other Affiliated Officials

or their goods by comitatini or districtuali, penalties could not be diminished from the penalties prescribed by statute.[79] This was an improvement over the statute prescribing a double penalty for a comitatini or districtuali who had offended a Florentine. This rubric had been aimed mainly at magnate crime, at preventing disruption of city life by magnate lawlessness (*Stat.* 3.36). Chittolini cites the case in Pistoia in which people of the contado of Pistoia favored being removed from Pistoian jurisdiction and tied directly to Florence. When agricultural workers were involved in legal cases with their patrons who lived in Pistoia, they found the courts in Pistoia to be more biased in favor of these patrons than courts in Florence.[80]

The material contained in the 1415 statutes concerning the contado and district was certainly one area of the statutes that was not antiquated; rather, it was new, innovative, and in current use. Nor was it a part of the statutes that soon became replaced; the rules for the territory remained largely unchanged into the nineteenth century.

Another important area of jurisdiction of the Podestà was his jurisdiction over magnates. Although it is commonly thought that the Executor treated most magnate crimes, this was, in fact, not true. The Podestà was paramount in prosecuting crimes committed by magnates, especially crimes against persons, the central area of magnate crime. The Podestà's part in executing the Ordinances of Justice is discussed in Chapter 6.

A more petty but cumbersome jurisdiction was the Podestà's sphere of judicial duties combating infractions of city ordinances. The Podestà tried the majority of these crimes. For instance, he expelled lepers from the city, and he arrested those holding goats or hogs in the city or those running horses through the city.[81] He arrested those defacing or destroying city walls or destroying building walls and ditches, the destruction of which harmed neighbors. No one was permitted to dry clothes on the city gates nor to do anything that caused a bad odor inside the city.[82]

The Podestà was still the major criminal official in 1415. By this time, he was no longer the head of the corporation of the commune but an integral part of the central government. The change of the office of the Podestà from a political and judicial office to a strictly judicial office was part of the process in which the different arms of the government were separated but was not a diminution of his judicial power. The judicial duties of the Podestà became more burdensome as the state assumed more and more responsibility in criminal trials. The sorting and shifting into logical jurisdictions was part of the process of the formation of the territorial state. Although the Podestà had a general criminal purview, he still retained some areas of specialty in 1415. The Podestà's dominance in debt cases enforced his ties to the guilds. The communal courts in general, and the Podestà's court in particular, were regulating the guild courts more and seizing more of their jurisdiction—for instance, the jurisdiction over defaulting and fleeing debt. The commune no longer allowed the guilds to compel guildsmen to litigate exclusively in the guild court, thus undermining the independence of the guilds. The Mercanzia was part of the state system that regulated the guilds, as was the Podestà. The Mercanzia was rendered powerful by the state, was assimilated more and more by the state, and was increasingly placed in charge of the guilds, until the major function of the Mercanzia became to carry out communal statutes regulating the guilds. The Mercanzia was syndicated like other communal offices. The Office of Grascia worked to subordinate certain guilds to public needs in order to prevent famine. Greater subordination of the contado and district to the state provided the Podestà with a new set of judicial functions.

5

THE CAPTAIN OF THE PEOPLE

THE CAPTAIN is a model of the process of the formation of the territorial state. During his initial period of existence, he had a corporate and parochial constituency and tried crimes related to this constituency. Later he became a public functionary, a part of the centralized judicial system. He was also part of the process in which the branches of the government were separated, when his executive duties were removed and assigned to executive officials and his onerous judicial duties became his exclusive concern. His authority in criminal matters was greatly increased by the process through which all the rectors gained the same criminal powers. One of the most important jurisdictions that the Captain retained in 1415 was his duty to monitor the Priors and the Gonfalonier for adherence to constitutionality and procedure.

Although all three of the foreign rectors went through a transition from possessing specific jurisdictions related to their corporations to possessing general jurisdictions on a commune-wide basis, the Captain of the People illustrates this process best of all. The Podestà initially had a wide jurisdiction, which became even more general in the early fifteenth century. The Executor started with a very specific jurisdiction, and, even after he was given wide judicial capabilities when authority was generalized and equalized among the three rectors, he retained several areas of specific jurisdiction alongside his general criminal responsibilities. The Captain started with specific jurisdictions, lost most of these, and acquired a general jurisdiction. In the fourteenth century, his office extended over a conglomerate of specific criminal jurisdictions that he had acquired in the late thirteenth century. By 1415, some of these jurisdictions had been removed from him and assigned to the Podestà. Responsibility was transferred in cases when the subject matter of the jurisdiction fit well into the jurisdictions already possessed by the Podestà. These specific jurisdictions were replaced by a general criminal purview. The result was an increase in the Captain's involvement in criminal cases and an increase in his authority. When the statutes of 1415 are examined for crimes which were assigned exclusively to the Captain, very few crimes surface which belonged to his exclusive jurisdiction. The crimes that do emerge are vestiges of his criminal jurisdiction from past eras. If only the specific rubrics were available on which to base the characterization of the Captain, it would be difficult to ascertain what the Captain's functions were in the early fifteenth century. Fortunately, the rubrics naming the subordinate officials of the foreign rectors already have supplied information.

The office of the Captain of the People was created between 1244 and 1250, just before the period called *il primo popolo*, to head the corporation of the popolo. The popolo was the collectivity of all classes of Florentines other than the feudal aristocracy and the commercial aristocracy. At the time that the office of the Podestà was created, these aristocratic classes were the only classes that were really enfranchised in Florence: the popolo had no direct representation. By 1244, the classes that made up the popolo had gained some power; the popolo now had a double representation in the General Council of the commune through their military organization and the organization of the guilds. The heads of the *pediti*, in times of war, or the *buonuomini* (the heads of the sections of the city), in times of peace, were represented in the council. The upper guilds were directly represented in the council through the *capitudines*, one per guild, while the lower guilds sent representatives, or priors, from the federation of the minor guilds. The *militi* of the commune, the aristocratic military organizations, no longer held power in the commune, so divided by the Guelf and Ghibelline conflict was this class.[1]

Internal politics in Florence in this period were controlled to a great extent by external politics, specifically by the vicissitudes of the conflicts between Pope Innocent IV and Emperor Frederick II. As the armies of one or the other raged up and down the peninsula, the government of Florence found it necessary to walk both sides of the street, fearing to offend either pope or emperor. During the years from 1244 to 1250, Frederick II, although he may have been losing the propaganda campaign, was winning the military campaign. He began sending a legate to Florence to serve as Podestà, once even sending his son. The members of the popolo, who were in the main Guelf, not wanting to alienate themselves from the pope, withdrew their support from the Podestà and created their own leader, the Captain of the People.

In 1244, the armies of the emperor drove the pope out of Rome to Lyons, where he took up quarters. The pope responded by deposing the emperor in 1245, which set off a civil war in Florence. After the emperor had occupied the major part of the Papal States, the Florentine government consented to the imposition of an imperial legate. The members of the popolo, that is, the military organization of the pediti, took up arms, having at their head two Captains. As a response to the Ghibelline turn of the government, the popolo organized into religious societies, *societates fidei*, to which the pope extended protection. These religious societies, closely identified with the military societies of the pediti, were part of the mechanism that elected these Captains, whom they invested with military and judicial powers. Besides having a military command, the Captains were given civil authority by the popolo, similar to that of the Podestà. The General Council recognized the political authority of these Captains. The Captains had their own notaries and *nuntii*, and voted in the General Council, helping make the important decisions of state. During times of peace, the buonuomini represented the popolo in the government, but in times of war, the Captains of the People represented the popolo. Either the buonuomini or the Captains shared power with the Podestà and with the representatives of the guilds. Militarily the Podestà was head of the *cavalleria del commune*, which was constituted mainly by the Ghibelline aristocracy. Starting in 1245, the Podestà of Florence was an imperial legate. The General Council, motivated by desire for survival and political opportunism, allowed imperial intervention in order to assure the primacy of Florence in Tuscany. Before the pope was exiled to Lyons, the Podestà had been men of Guelf sympathies.

Almost immediately, controversies arose concerning the jurisdictional boundaries between the Podestà and the Captains of the People. Soon the documents mention the existence of one executive magistrate, the Captain of the People, instead of two Captains. By this process, the popolo withdrew from the power of the Podestà and became a city within a city under the protection of the papacy.[2] Henceforth, the signatures of both the Podestà and the Captain appeared on documents, such as the treaty with Siena made on August 20, 1245. In 1246, Emperor Frederick II sent his son, Frederick of Antioch, as papal legate and Podestà to Florence. To counter, the popolo stayed in arms to make its influence felt in the communal government and to safeguard the rights of the people.

After 1250, as a result of the movement called *il primo popolo*, the popular class gained fuller representation. The groundwork for this successful popular movement was laid in the period from 1245 to 1250. During the period of il primo popolo, the popolo was established as a permanent political society with statutes and an annually elected Captain who possessed the highest attributes of power. The popolo became parallel to the commune and became elevated to an important political status, further democratizing the government.[3]

The corporation of the popolo of which the Captain was head was an autonomous political unit, a city inside a city. It competed with other autonomous political units for political voice in a government forged out of the loose affiliation of these corporations. The political balance was determined by temporary alliances between the corporations. The autonomy of the popolo is underscored by the fact that the head of this corporation assumed full power, military, executive, and judicial, over its constituents. The Podestà and the Captain duplicated each other's duties in the prosecution of infractions of city ordinances, such as dumping garbage in the river, because they were parts of two almost separate governments.

Except for the period from 1268 to 1289, when popular movements in Florence were suppressed and when the Captain of the People was the same as the Captain of the Parte Guelfa, the Captain was the spearhead and embodiment of the popular movement and the defender of popular rights. The job of the Captain was to defend the nonmagnate classes from the magnates. As the office of the Captain advanced through time, it acquired additional functions. In 1280, the Captain of the People received the additional title of Conservator Pacis, Conserver of the Peace. At that time, the pope was very active in arranging peace settlements between the Ghibellines and the Guelfs and among magnates who were aligned with these two factions. The Captain was given the special duty of ensuring that the peace was kept.[4] The Office of the Defender of the Guilds and Guildsmen was created in 1282, when the Priors were created, and was merged with the Office of the Captain of the People in 1284.[5] Among all the classes of defenseless people protected by the Captain, the guildsmen became the foremost. By the beginning of the fourteenth century, the Captain had the conglomerate jurisdiction of Captain of the People, Conserver of the Peace, and Defender of the Guilds and Guildsmen.

Like the Podestà, the Captain of the People, besides being a judicial official, was a political leader. The vicissitudes of the Office of the Captain of the People paralleled those of the Office of the Podestà in their political aspects. The Captain of the People headed the Council of the People, the council made up of the more popular constituents, while the Podestà headed the Council of the Commune, the more aristocratic council. Throughout most of the fourteenth century, the Captain was a political leader, but in 1373, he is last seen to preside at the Council of the People.[6] At this time he became strictly a judicial official. Although the falling away of his political duties signaled a diminution of his total power, his power in the judicial area remained intact, and even increased. In this process, the executive branch was actually separating from the judicial branch, not attempting to engulf it. The separation of the different branches of government was part of the process of systematization of the territorial state. The judicial power of the Captain was greatly increased by the generalization of authority among the three rectors.

The statutes of 1322–25 show that the Office of the Captain to subsume a hodgepodge of duties. The criminal duties of the Captain, assigned to him at different times throughout the late thirteenth century, were very specific and piecemeal; his civil duties were equally disjunct. The Captain had three judges under his supervision. One of the judges, just as in the statutes of 1415, was the judge of camera and gabelle (treasury and taxes).[7] Another of his judges handled the collection of all of the condemnations made in the courts of the Podestà and the Captain and of all taxes owed to the commune. Concomitant with this duty, he carried out the confiscation and destruction of the homes and possessions of those condemned, banned, or owing taxes.[8] The system whereby a judge serving the Captain collected condemnations for both the Podestà and the Captain was soon eliminated. By 1415, each of the rectors, including the Executor, was responsible for the collection of his own condemnations, and the penalties were subtracted from his salary if they were not collected. Both of these judges had very narrow areas of jurisdiction. The third judge was left to try all the ordinary civil and criminal cases assigned to the Captain. It was impossible, therefore, for there to be very many duties for which the Captain was solely in charge, especially as compared to the number of duties which the Podestà with his three criminal judges was capable of fulfilling. Criminal cases strictly related to his functions as Captain of the People, Conserver of the Peace, and Defender of the Guilds and Guildsmen were assigned to his exclusive jurisdiction.

In the 1322–25 period, one very important notary supervised by the Captain was the notary over the goods of rebels. This official executed penalties against criminals, particularly political criminals and those guilty of extortion and corruption.[9] He had his own notary to record his activities and to record the goods of the criminals, as well as his own berrovarii to carry out investigations and confiscations. His job was to investigate, discover, and confiscate for the commune the goods of the condemned, the banned, and those defaulting on their taxes. His function was very similar to that of the judge over the collection of condemnations: the judge collected penalties in other ways than confiscation, the notary collected penalties through confiscation. The notary over the goods of rebels confiscated the goods of those who were unable to pay their condemnations or who committed crimes such as rebellion for which confiscation was automatic. He also heard claims against the goods that were being confiscated by the commune. This official did not survive very long under the Captain either. In the late fourteenth century, there was an entire agency devoted to this task, the officials over the goods of rebels, the condemned, and the banned. By 1415, the officials over the goods of rebels, the condemned, and the banned, along with other officials who supervised communal goods, rights, and gabelles, had been incorporated into the Office of the Tower. The Office of the Tower was an extremely powerful office that managed, maintained, and rented out communal goods, lands, and gabelles.

The Captain supervised the notary over the goods of rebels in the 1322–25 statutes because the people whose goods were being confiscated in the early fourteenth century were members of political factions involved in the Guelf-Ghibelline conflicts. Whichever political faction was being ousted from Florence was having their goods confiscated by the commune. In 1301, when the rubric treating the office of the Captain's notary over the goods of rebels was redacted, the majority of exiles were members of the Guelf Black Party, many of whom were being exiled for inciting castles to rebel against Florentine suzerainty. The Captain's duties as Conservator Pacis made him the natural official to direct the task of confiscating the goods of those involved in factional conflict. But soon the task of confiscating the goods of rebels, the condemned, and the banned had changed in nature and had taken on much greater proportions. Throughout the rest of the fourteenth century and in the early fifteenth century, possessions were mainly confiscated from those perpetrating serious crimes or those delinquent in their taxes, but not necessarily from those perpetrating political crimes. The people being banned in 1415 were those who were condemned to penalties of at least 100 lire for serious crimes such as disturbing the possession of immobile goods, committing homicide, inflicting facial wounds, kidnapping for ransom, committing grand theft, falsifying, or rebelling (Stat. 1.9). While the Captain was the most logical official to supervise the confiscation of the goods of rebels, the condemned, and the banned in the 1322–25 period, he was no longer logical in 1415 when those condemned were regular criminals. While the 1322–25 statutes placed the Captain in charge of holding the book of all communal goods including goods confiscated from the rebels, the banned, and the condemned, the Tower Officials were given this duty in 1415.[10]

The Captain, because he acquired the additional office of Defender of the Guilds and Guildsmen, was designated the main rector to protect the political rights and execute the judicial decisions of the guilds in the 1322–25 statutes. The Captain, in particular, was responsible for executing the sentences of the rectors and consuls of the guilds, although the Podestà was, on occasion, likewise responsible. The rubric describing the duty of the Captain in this regard assigns the consuls and rectors of the guilds an almost limitless jurisdiction. In the 1322–25 period, the Captain was obligated to execute sentences at the request of the consuls or the rectors. The only crimes expressly banned from the courts of the rectors and the consuls of the guilds were those involving comestibles and other necessary items; namely, meat, stone, and wood.[11] The Captain extended

The Captain of the People

special protection to the goods and persons of artisans who were subject to the Florentine guilds.

The guildsmen were not the only group defended by the Captain. The purpose of that office was to defend the classes in Florence that were hitherto defenseless, the nonmagnate classes that had been physically threatened and politically ignored by the magnates and the merchant nobility. The general description of his criminal duties highlights his ability to try crimes in which overbearing behavior, violence, force, or threat played a major role. The Captain could recognize cases of violent compulsion, violent expulsion, violent removal of possessions, disturbing the peace, and compelling of contracts through violence, threatening, or fraud. He could recognize cases of kidnapping made through abuse of power or threat. He could recognize cases in which powerful men prohibited agricultural workers from occupying or working their lands.[12]

The Captain also protected the popolo from famine. In the early fourteenth century, the Captain tried infractions of the laws that were established to ensure an abundance of food.[13] He supervised the activities of the officials of wheat (blado), punishing them for trying cases that overstepped their jurisdiction.[14] By 1415, this criminal function had been transferred from the Captain to the Podestà. More and more of the specific spheres of criminal responsibility held by the Captain in the early fourteenth century were no longer his exclusive responsibility by 1415.

By 1415, the functions and purposes of the Captain had changed a great deal. He was still charged with some duties that were related to his original functions, but many of these original areas of jurisdiction had been transferred to the court of the Podestà. In the statutes of 1415, there were very few rubrics that singled out the Captain as the exclusive prosecuting official; rather, he was frequently mentioned as sharing the power to prosecute crimes with the Podestà and the Executor. By 1415, the Captain mainly prosecuted crimes that the other two rectors could have treated equally well. However, his authority in criminal matters had actually increased, since he was newly empowered to treat any kind of serious crime, a power he did not possess in preceding eras. He had one judge entirely devoted to criminal matters, whereas previously one of his judges had handled all ordinary civil and criminal cases under his purview. Like the other two rectors, he was also the recipient of greater and greater powers of *arbitrium* (discretion) over an ever-growing number of criminal cases.

If the specific rubrics treating a crime and naming a rector to handle it were the only sources of information that could be found on the Captain for the early fifteenth century, little could be concluded concerning his major functions. Fortunately, the functions of the judges and notaries subordinate to the Captain supply information. By 1415, the Captain was in charge of the extraordinary civil jurisdictions, that is, the small claims cases, the treasury and gabelle cases, and appeals, through his judge of camera and gabelle and through his judge of appeals. The judge of appeals was subordinated to the Captain in the process which put all judicial power into the hands of the regular court system in order to centralize power. The Captain was chosen to supervise the judge of appeals because the Captain's civil court, the court of camera and gabelle, did not try cases that could be appealed. The process of sorting and shifting jurisdictions was making the jurisdictions of the rectors more coherent and logical. Most of the Captain's effort was employed in these areas of extraordinary civil jurisdiction. The subordination of the judge of appeals to the Captain gave the Captain a very powerful impact on civil material.

Most of the exclusive criminal duties of the Captain extant in 1415 appear to have originated in a much earlier time. Almost all the rubrics pertaining to his criminal duties appearing in the statutes of 1415 had previously appeared in the statutes of 1322–25.[15] These statutes indicate that some of the traditional attributes of the Captain continued to be his specialties in the early fifteenth century. The Captain, for instance, continued to safeguard important and constitutional parts of the statutes against changes by the Priors and the Gonfalonier.

The Captain had few criminal duties in the period 1322–25 when he performed the specialized functions of Captain of the People, Defender of the Guilds and Guildsmen, and Conserver of the Peace. By 1415 he had not acquired any additional specific criminal assignments but had received general criminal authority. Because the offices and the functions of the offices that the Captain had held in the thirteenth and fourteenth centuries were obsolete in 1415, some of his criminal jurisdictions were transferred to the Podestà when they fit more logically into the Podestà's jurisdictions. In some cases, the Captain continued to exercise the same functions in 1415.

One power that seems to have remained exclusively his in 1415 was the power to guard against magnates' taking over the government or disrupting the city through partisan warfare. The Captain could punish any popolano who went to the house of a magnate during a disturbance or time of sedition, especially if the magnate was involved in the disturbance. Usually he sent such an offender outside the borders of Florence.[16] Likewise, he punished any magnate who went to another magnate's house during a disturbance, especially if the magnate owning the house was involved in a quarrel with other magnates.[17] Anyone who impeded the Executor when he was leading his foot soldiers to the site of a disturbance for the purpose of repelling magnates or other rebels was punished

The Captain of the People

at the discretion of the Captain. No one could gather men to act in the service of a magnate during the time of a disturbance. Anyone throwing stones from his house at the Executor or at the soldiers of the Societies of the People during a disturbance was condemned by the Captain at his discretion, even to corporal penalties. No count or baron could march on the city at the time of a disturbance under threat of corporal punishment. No one from among the foot soldiers of the societies could use his weapons except in the defense of the people. All of these crimes were punished by the Captain at his discretion.[18] The origin of this power to prevent the magnates from instigating factional conflict is plain. As Conservator Pacis the Captain was in charge of keeping the peace among magnates who were aligned in the Ghibelline and Guelf factions.[19] This duty surfaced in the subsequent versions of the Ordinances of Justice in the three rubrics prohibiting polarization into factions around powerful magnates. The Captain shared jurisdiction over other political crimes with the Podestà.

In addition, the Captain retained a number of jobs in 1415 that continued from a previous era and centered around his responsibilities as Defender of the Guilds and Guildsmen and Captain of the People. His charge to defend the previously defenseless survived to some extent in the statutes of 1415. For instance, no one could prohibit another from washing or leading animals to drink in the rivers, or the Captain condemned.[20] Likewise, no corporation or popolo of the county could create ordinances that impeded or prevented taxpayers from cultivating crops or vines. If any organization or person acted against this rubric, the Captain could void the new ordinances and impose fines, damages, and interest.[21] The Captain was responsible for the defense of *inquilini* and *coloni*, that is, agricultural tenants. Anyone, especially any magnate, who did injury or violence to the possessions, homes, or lands of *inquilini* or *coloni* was to be denounced to the Captain.[22] In connection with his duties as Defender of the Guilds and Guildsmen, the Captain was the head of the system of syndics of the guilds. The syndics were officials within each guild who helped guildsmen harmed by magnates to take their cases to court and who made sure justice was done. The syndics fulfilled many other functions within the guilds.[23]

In 1415, the Captain had the very important duty of monitoring the legislative activities of the Priors and the Gonfalonier of Justice. There were several areas of the statutes that had a constitutional character, that is, they were considered essential and were made difficult to emend. The Priors and the Gonfalonier of Justice were prohibited from holding a council to discuss abolishing the statutes concerning the syndication, arrival, stay, election, *divieti*, or salaries of the Podestà, Captain, any of their *familia*, or any other foreign official, nor could they annul statutes concerning the duties of these offices. During the early fifteenth century, the rule concerning divieti waffled back and forth between unalterability and a requirement of thirty-six out of thirty-seven votes among the Priors, the Gonfalonier, and the colleges to allow exceptions to the divieti regulations. The Priors and the Gonfalonier of Justice had no right to hold a council to change the statutes concerning defaulting and fleeing or those concerning the conceding of licenses of reprisal, especially those statutes requiring the consent of the Councils of the People and of the Commune for the conceding of these licenses. Nor could the Priors and the Gonfalonier of Justice change the statutes for the purpose of giving their scribe an extension of the term for handing in the acts to the camera of the acts. If the Priors and the Gonfalonier of Justice did any of the above, the Captain condemned. If the Captain failed to fulfill this duty, he was removed from office (*Stat.* 5.1.23). This rubric also appeared in the statutes of 1322–25.[24] The function and power displayed in this rubric, certainly of a very important nature, had their origin in the late thirteenth century. Other evidence in the statutes indicates that the Captain played an executive role akin to that of the Priors at the time that the office of the Priors was created.[25] The Captain was sometimes said to be the head of the Priors, probably because he was Defender of the Guilds and Guildsmen and the Priors were originally representatives of the guilds.[26] His role in guarding the constitutional parts of the statutes, which originally reflected his political authority, continued in 1415 despite the termination of his political authority. The task of monitoring the Signoria remained with the Captain because the regular court system was becoming the central element in the system of checks and balances which guarded against corruption in the government. The Executor monitored the legality of the performance of many of the other officials. The power of the Podestà frequently was concurrent with that of other agencies in order to keep tabs on their performance.

The Captain was a functionary of the central government in 1415, carrying out many of the same duties as the other rectors. His distinctive duties were coordinated with those of the other rectors, not redundant. He had lost many of his traditional attributes and his ties with distinctive groups within the government, those ties had made him the defender of the powerless classes and the guilds. Lorenzo Cantini had difficulty explaining why the office of the Captain, which he characterizes as a bastion of democracy, was not suppressed until 1502. According to Cantini, despite the patriciate's constant effort to suppress this office, they were not able to do so until 1502. However, in the fifteenth century the office of the Captain was no longer the bastion of democracy and the threat to patrician government that Cantini imagines it to have been.[27] It was the Captain of the People who was granted the balia to punish the enemies of the Medici regime in 1434.[28] In fact, there is evidence that the character of that office underwent a sharp change in 1434. The Captain became the rector in charge of punishing political crimes, political crimes as seen from the vantage point of the Medici regime, and crimes the punishment of which benefited the Medici patriciate, such as rural crimes. Zorzi estimates that from 1476 to 1478, half of the sentences imposed by the Captain's court were received by bullectini from the Otto di Guardia.[29] While, in the latter half of the fourteenth century and the early fifteenth century, the Captain had lost his parochial character and become a part of a centralized bureaucracy, after 1434, as the character of the judicial system changed, the courts, and especially the court of the Captain, underwent a process of specialization.

6

THE EXECUTOR OF THE ORDINANCES OF JUSTICE

THE EXECUTOR of the Ordinances of Justice differed from the other foreign rectors in that he was required to be a *popolano* and not a knight. His popolano status reflected his function as a protector of the position of the *popolo* in the government. His office was created just after *il secondo popolo*, a period lasting roughly from 1286 to 1295, in which the popolo not only gained representation in the government but became its principal constituent, excluding the magnates from a significant part in ruling.[1] From 1282 to 1292, the upper guilds thoroughly dominated the Priorate, which had become the chief organ in the government. After 1292, election reforms resulted in a more broad-based government in which the upper and middle twelve guilds were dominant.[2] Throughout the fourteenth century, the Executor contributed to the creation of the territorial state. He restricted the lawless elements in society, enforced the *divieti* laws, and guarded against corruption of officials and usurpation of communal goods, all duties that aided in the building of the territorial state. Some of these functions continued to be important in the early fifteenth century.

The Executor was especially important in the early fifteenth century in the development and continuation of the territorial state in his capacity as head of syndication, the most important restraint in the system of checks and balances. Syndication (i.e., trying officials for committing crimes or neglecting their duties) formed a very powerful restraint on the foreign rectors and judges themselves, assuring their adherence to statute and to the rules of inquisition procedure. Syndication transformed the judicial system, forcing accurate record keeping, full disclosure of testimony, the justification of decisions and penalties, and the observance of safeguards for the defendant. It necessitated the basing of decisions on full proof, pressuring judges to obtain confessions or to combine sufficient partial proofs. The effect of political influence on the court system was thwarted by the need to ground decisions firmly in proof. Likewise, the syndication laws made other officials of the government accountable for decisions and actions taken in office. In all of these offices, better record keeping, better documentation of financial activities, and more rigorous accountability were mandated through syndication. The Executor headed this effort. Divieti laws, which the Executor was in charge of enforcing, likewise guarded against patrician influence.

The Ordinances of Justice

The office of the Executor of the Ordinances of Justice was not created until 1307, even though the Ordinances of Justice were written in 1293. This office was created to implement the political and social program outlined in these ordinances. When the Ordinances of Justice were written, the office of the Gonfalonier of Justice was created to execute the ordinances and was given the same authority as the Priors. The functions created by the ordinances were at first very revolutionary and were intended to handle an emergency situation: They provided for convoking the popular militia, arresting magnates for crimes, judging magnates, and destroying their towers and palaces. When it became apparent that executing the Ordinances of Justice would not be a one-time job but would require continuous surveillance of the magnates, and when the Gonfalonier of Justice became an executive official much like the Priors, the position of Executor of the Ordinances of Justice was created.[3]

The purposes of many of the Executor's activities were closely identified with the purposes of the Ordinances of Justice. The ordinances embodied the popular constitution of Florence, ensuring the position of the popolani in the government while restricting and excluding the magnate class. While these regulations were modified throughout the late thirteenth and fourteenth centuries, their original purpose remained intact in all of the subsequent editions. The Ordinances of Justice sought to make the communal government sovereign by enforcing law-and-order measures on the lawless magnates and drawing most of the magnates, except for a few very powerful counts, within Florentine domination for purposes of law and taxation. All of the twenty-one guilds banded together to promote the authority of the central government, in which they became a very powerful interest group. The number of politically enfranchised guilds was decisively fixed at twenty-one.[4] Communal offices were subjected to a strict system of monitoring to assure that communal authority promoted, not harmed, public well-being. Emphasis was placed on recovering communal offices and lands from private ownership.[5] The Societies of the People were created to defend the government against magnates and other rebels. Under the supervision of the Executor, all of these measures fostered the growth of a strong territorial state.

The Ordinances of Justice were continuously renewed until the 1340s and 1350s. In the 1380s, another movement was mounted to end feudal prerogatives by subjecting the domains of even the most powerful counts to communal taxation, breaking treaties formerly established between the commune and the feudatories, and by reclaiming communal goods from private hands.[6] In the early fifteenth century, when the magnate problem became much less acute, the sections of the Ordinances of Justice relating to sanctions against the magnates began to fall into desuetude. Although the acts of the rectors of the late fourteenth century contain many instances of gangs of magnates pillaging, burning fields, assaulting people, and committing other crimes, fifteenth-century records do not indicate the same prominence of magnate crime. As a result, magnates were no longer tried under the Ordinances of Justice in the fifteenth century.[7] Along with the diminished use of the rubrics pertaining to magnates, there was a parallel decline in the use of those pertaining to the citizen militia. The militia, which on occasion displayed *popolo minuto* sentiments, was no longer convoked. Although these parts of the ordinances were now rarely used, the ordinances pertaining to syndication, divieti, and subordination of all elements to the communal government remained important throughout the period of the early fifteenth century. The Ordinances of Justice appeared in the 1415 statute compilation.

The Ordinances of Justice were composed of rubrics enacted from 1282 to 1293. They were collected for the first time in 1293, just before the Priorate of Giano della Bella, during whose Priorate a predominantly popolo minuto government ruled Florence.[8] A temporary coalition between the popolo minuto and the *popolani grassi* (wealthy commoners, usually guildsmen from the upper guilds), who united to wrest power from lawless groups of magnates who perpetrated crimes openly without restraint, brought this popolo minuto government to power. The version of the Ordinances of Justice redacted under the popolo minuto government contained the most severe sanctions against the magnates. When the power of the popolo minuto waned after the exile of Giano della Bella in 1295, the Ordinances of Justice were softened but retained the same general goals.

While most Florentine ordinances had to be renewed periodically, often annually, to be valid, the Ordinances of Justice transcended the renewal process because they had a more general validity. Although the ordinances were frequently renewed, renewal stressing the determination of the government to execute them, execution took place whether renewal occurred or not. Likewise, revisions constituted elaborations of the program of the Ordinances, not changes. They were renewed for most of the first half of the fourteenth century, revisions being made in 1294, 1295, 1297, 1300, 1301, 1306, and 1323.[9] In 1378, execution of the Ordinances of Justice was given priority in order to thwart the Parte Guelfa's abuse of its power of *ammonizione* (i.e., proscribing and disenfranchising citizens as

Ghibellines), which was undermining the republican nature of the government. The Ordinances of Justice were included in the statutes of 1415. Because they were important laws that had been created throughout a general period from 1282 through the early fourteenth century, they had a general validity. In fact, they embodied philosophies so basic to the commune that they can be considered constitutional. The 1415 version of the Ordinances of Justice emphasized this constitutional character. Starting in the 1297 version and extending through the 1415 version, the Ordinances of Justice were given full strength and validity, prevailing over any other statutes and reforms.[10] They could not be removed or diminished for any reason. It was illegal to hold councils concerning their removal or suspension.[11] The fullest statement of the constitutional character of the Ordinances of Justice was made in 1415. To treat these ordinances like other ordinances, which needed to be renewed, is to misunderstand their fundamental nature and timeless quality, which embodied so much of the essential philosophy of republican Florence.

The program outlined in the Ordinances of Justice put public good above private interests and articulated a system and a structure to ensure that this purpose was carried out. The reaffirmation of the continued validity of the Ordinances of Justice, shown by their inclusion in the 1415 statutes, demonstrates the continuation of the territorial state in that period. The structures articulated in the ordinances were designed to prevent corruption, misappropriation of power, lack of accountability, and use of government offices to promote private benefits. The Executor, who compelled the application of these laws, continued to be a major guardian of the territorial state. Despite the diminishing value of the sections of the Ordinances of Justice on magnates and on the military aspects of the Societies of the People, the rest of the ordinances remained active and pertinent in 1415.

The Ordinances of Justice went through many revisions in the late thirteenth and early fourteenth centuries, but the underlying principles remained unchanged. To some extent, the versions that were redacted after the fall of Giano della Bella were less severe in their treatment of the magnates. Whereas his government had excluded all magnates from the office of the Priorate, subsequent versions of the ordinances admitted *scioperati*. *Scioperati* were those, often of the magnate class, who belonged to a guild for the political privileges membership brought but who carried on no commercial activities. After the list of those ascribed magnate status was increased to seventy-two families under Giano della Bella, the list changed little until the 1340s and 1350s.[12] At that time, the ordinances were considerably moderated to incorporate the concept that there were leaders or captains of crimes and only these captains deserved to receive full punishment. Likewise, only magnates intentionally committing grave crimes deserved to be tried under the Ordinances of Justice.[13]

The correspondence between crime and punishment was an area of the Ordinances of Justice that had gone through many revisions and adjustments. The version of the ordinances which was redacted by the popolo minuto–dominated government of 1293–95 called for severe sanctions against any magnate who committed an offense against a popolano. The Podestà and the Captains, intimidated by the potential repercussions that would befall them if they did not mete out severe penalties, and by the accusations of partiality toward the magnates which would be made against them, prescribed the severest penalties for the slightest crimes. This evident inequity was corrected when a government composed primarily of members of the upper guilds came into power. A scale of crime and corresponding penalties graduated by severity was created within the Ordinances of Justice, just like the scale of penalties in the rest of the statutes, only much more severe.[14]

The post-1293 revisions put the program of the Ordinances of Justice into action. The number of popolani in the citizen militia was increased. A troop of carpenters was organized to dismantle the houses of offending magnates.[15] A system of syndics and procurators was established throughout the city and the contado to report magnate offenses and bring them to court. In the offices that magnates traditionally held, such as the custodianships of castles, the punishment for corruption was increased. Magnates were initially excluded from many communal offices; later, this ban was extended to include the Priorate.[16] An important change was the substitution of the Executor for the Gonfalonier of Justice as the official in charge of executing the Ordinances of Justice.

The version of the Ordinances of Justice contained in the 1415 statute compilation included the original Ordinances of Justice of 1293 plus all of the additional ordinances redacted in succeeding years up to the 1350s. The only updating done in the early fifteenth century increased the penalties for magnates who committed crimes against communal officials, particularly the Priors.[17] The 1415 version included severe sanctions against rectors who neglected to apply the Ordinances of Justice. It continued to include a liability system for magnates which extended to relatives of several grades of affinity.

Executing the Ordinances of Justice—The Magnates

Although the Executor had acquired additional spheres of jurisdiction in 1415, his duties in applying and executing the Ordinances of Justice remained the same. The ordinances were in part created out of a pact between the guilds. All of the twenty-one guilds benefited from the privileges and were obligated by the responsibilities agreed upon in the Ordinances of Justice. When through the ordinances the guilds assumed authority as the chief component of the communal government, they took on the responsibility of putting public good ahead of their private interests. From this time forth, membership in the guilds became a prerequisite to communal officeholding. To meet this public function, the guilds assumed a public attitude. The prohibitions against monopolies in the guilds date from this time. Not only the guilds, but also the Societies of the People agreed to foster public good. Although this cannot be considered as the creation of the territorial state, because the groups involved acted as intermediaries between the individual and the state, it was, at least, the creation of the concept of a public good which transcended class and corporate divisions. When the corporate groups that had composed the government diminished in importance, parts of the Ordinances of Justice continued to remain important for their deference to public well-being and their establishment of structures which ensured public well-being, such as the syndication procedures, the divieti laws, and the antimonopoly laws. The Executor was put in charge of these bulwarks of the territorial state, and he continued in this capacity in the early fifteenth century.

The Ordinances of Justice contained more than a program to put the guilds into power, even limiting their power. The guilds were not allowed to form monopolies, pacts, or agreements.[18] The guilds had positive responsibilities toward the commune and functioned as an integral part of the commune. Both the neighborhood organizations and the magnates were subordinated to the commune.[19] The magnates could no longer decline the jurisdiction of the commune.[20] The great power of the magnates and feudal lords had to be bridled before the commune could carry out its basic functions, such as maintaining law and order. Securities were taken from all magnates as a precaution against their lawless behavior (Tract. Ord. Iust. 33). One of the main thrusts of the Ordinances of Justice was to increase the effectiveness of the reporting and trying of magnate crimes and to elevate the penalties for these crimes to discourage magnate violence. Activities of the potentially troublesome magnates were closely monitored. Magnates were limited in the amount of power they could possess in the government, only being allowed to hold certain offices (Tract. Ord. Iust. 93). The divieti laws contained in the Ordinances of Justice, by prohibiting more than one member of a house from holding office concurrently, affected the magnates with their extended family structure more adversely than they did other groups.

Likewise, officials in Florence were regarded as a potentially oppressive class. Negligence by the Podestà or the Captain, for instance, was seen as damaging to the citizens, *contadini,* and *districtuali* of Florence (Tract. Ord. Iust. 17). The Ordinances of Justice attempted to quash abuses perpetrated by officials. Measures were taken to free communal offices from any kind of quasi-ownership. The responsibility of syndicating was given to the Executor of the Ordinances of Justice. A mandatory general inquisition was conducted for each official as he left office (Tract. Ord. Iust. 3). The communal government could not hope to spread its power if the oppressive actions of its officials were undermining trust in the government.

The Executor carried out the Ordinances of Justice, safeguarded them from alteration or cancellation, and ensured their application in the courts (Tract. Ord. Iust. 1). He often executed sentences imposed for infractions; and, because those sentenced were likely to be powerful and armed, he used, besides his own retinue, the soldiers of the societies (Tract. Ord Iust. 14). However, the Executor was not the main official to try magnates and others violating the Ordinances of Justice. The Podestà and the Captain conducted most of the trials of Ordinances of Justice crimes and most trials of magnates (Tract. Ord. Iust. 14). The Executor was said to put the Ordinances of Justice into effect through the Podestà and the Captain and their judges; that is, he monitored the trials of these crimes in their courts. The syndics of the *popoli* or *plebatu* and the syndics of the guilds helped to bring cases against magnates to the courts of the Podestà and the Captain (Tract. Ord. Iust. 20).

The Podestà and the Captain condemned magnates who conspired against the state. They split the jurisdiction of first instance against magnates, the Podestà trying cases in which magnates offended popolani in their persons and the Captain trying cases in which magnates offended popolani in their possessions (Tract. Ord. Iust. 68). The injured person was obligated to denounce the crime to either the Podestà or the Captain, whichever had jurisdiction. Sometimes these rectors were intended to execute the cases they tried. The Executor made all executions of condemnations against magnates of the city, county, and district, if the condemnations were not exacted through the Podestà or the Captain within fifteen days (Tract. Ord. Iust. 14). When the Podestà or the Captain condemned magnates who conspired against the state, the Podestà executed the sentence, even collecting the fine from the relatives and consorts, if necessary. If he failed to do so, it fell to the Executor (Tract. Ord. Iust. 71). In serious personal assaults, the Podestà was given a term in which to execute before the Executor took over (Tract. Ord. Iust. 80). If the execution took longer than the period given the Podestà or the Captain, this probably indicated some kind of difficulty in accomplishing it. Where power was an issue in the execution, the Executor assumed the responsibility. Often no mention is made of a term for execution for the Podestà or the Captain, which means that the Executor was assigned the task from the beginning. The Executor devastated the houses of magnates if this was called for in the penalty (Tract. Ord. Iust. 71; 75). Usually it was the foot soldiers of the societies who were called on to follow the Executor to perform executions and devastate houses. They maintained and defended the state, repelled magnates and other rebels and enemies of Florence, and made just vendettas against these rebels and enemies for the state. However, the Ordinances of Justice did not suppress magnates alone but anyone who acted counter to the interests of the state. Anyone acting in a violent, unruly way could be considered a magnate (Tract. Ord. Iust. 24). The Executor carried out sentences against rebels and political criminals.

The job of executing the sentences of the Ordinances of Justice was not just a matter of riding out to destroy houses and confiscate goods. Decisions had to be made concerning what goods a magnate or rebel owned, and claims against these goods had to be adjudicated (Tract. Ord. Iust. 87). The Executor also watched the performance of the Podestà and the Captain in their offices, seeing to it that they were not influenced by fear of the magnates and ensuring that they followed statute. He took petitions against the Podestà and the Captain from litigants in cases in which these litigants felt the statutes had not been observed (Tract. Ord. Iust. 17).

Another kind of execution of the Ordinances of Justice performed by the Executor was in defense of officials or popolani who were burdened or wrongly convicted by a foreign government, especially the pope. Here again the Executor defended the popolani against oppression by the powerful. The Executor received this claim and presented it to the Priors and the Gonfalonier of Justice, who decided on the justice of the claim (Tract. Ord. Iust. 2). If oppression was present, they notified the Executor to defend this Florentine in whatever manner possible at communal expense. This was done partly in a legal manner through syndics who defended these cases in foreign courts, the Executor monitoring the progress of these cases, and partly in a physical manner, by not allowing foreign powers to damage the goods or persons of Florentines. When strong-arm measures were necessary, execution was left to the Executor.

Besides the Executor, the Priors and the Gonfalonier of Justice also had certain responsibilities and powers in implementing the Ordinances of Justice. The Priors and the Gonfalonier had the power to declare people magnates, that is, to decide that they should forever bear the stigma, penalties, and legal prejudices of having magnate status. The Priors and the Gonfalonier tried magnates or popolani for crimes, the serious and violent nature of which made them atrocities, and bestowed magnate status on those they found guilty. In addition to directly trying these crimes, the Priors and the Gonfalonier monitored the process of recognition in the courts of the foreign rectors in cases against magnates or concerning Ordinances of Justice crimes. I discuss the importance of these crimes to the power of the Priors and the Gonfalonier in Chapter 7. The jurisdiction given to the Priors and the Gonfalonier over crimes warranting the bestowal of magnate status was the only large class of crimes they were empowered by statute to try directly. These trials were important in the fourteenth century but were of negligible importance in the early fifteenth century. Here interest centers around an assessment of the cases that would seem to be a part of the Executor's jurisdiction over magnates but that were instead assigned to a different court. The Executor, who was devoted to the supervision of Ordinances of Justice and magnate cases, had a significant counterbalancing power over cases tried by the Priors and the Gonfalonier.

The Priors and the Gonfalonier were empowered by statute to try a large number of serious crimes that were most likely to be committed by magnates, crimes like homicide, seizing land by force, kidnapping for ransom, detaining someone in a private prison, and making a vendetta against someone other than the principal person. These crimes were usually tried in the courts of the foreign rectors, but it was possible to air them before the Priors and the Gonfalonier, if the accuser desired to do so and if the crimes were truly atrocities. These cases were accuser-initiated, petitions being received from popolani against popolani or magnates, or from magnates against other magnates, for serious crimes. The people being tried were not exclusively magnates in the beginning. The Priors and the Gonfalonier tried cases in which discretion had to be used to decide whether the bestowal of magnate status was warranted. Crimes for which the culprit was automatically attributed magnate status were tried in the courts of the foreign rectors.

The bestowal of magnate status was a devastating event for the condemned person as this status carried many legal handicaps and inconveniences. Magnates had to give securities to the commune so that if they committed a crime, the penalty could be partially offset by the security (Tract. Ord. Iust. 33). Magnates could not live in the same quarter in the city or *plebatu* in the county as other members of their lineage (Tract. Ord. Iust. 23) and were restricted from holding certain communal offices (Tract. Ord. Iust. 89; 90; 91; 93; 94). Magnates could not bear testimony against popolani nor make accusations against them unless the accusing magnate was the one offended (Tract. Ord. Iust. 43; 61). Magnates could be accused more easily, condemned with less proof, and assigned elevated penalties (Tract. Ord. Iust. 23; 72; 78; 79). The attribute of magnate status that may have been the most prejudicial and harmful was the mutual liability among magnate relatives and magnate consorts for securities and penalties (Tract. Ord. Iust. 36; 56; 58; 59). Also, when a magnate committed a crime, the injured person was obligated to accuse (Tract. Ord. Iust. 68).

Those having magnate status included more than just feudal lords and their families, but all feudal families were not considered magnates. Originally, thirty-six families within the city and many more in the contado were so designated, the popolo minuto government of 1294–95 elevating this number to seventy-two within the city, including in this number all of the families that had any members who were *cavalieri* (knights). Gradually, exceptions were made for branches of families known to be faithful to the government. The Ordinances of Justice, as they appear in the 1415 statutes, enumerate by quarter the magnate houses and the members of their houses that were affected (Tract. Ord. Iust. 32). Beyond this, anyone who committed an act of a very violent nature was subject to becoming a magnate. Anyone who acted in a way that jeopardized the stability of the commune was legally limited in his participation and his effect on the commune. While the power of the Priors and the Gonfalonier to bestow magnate status may seem to have been autonomous enough to promote abuse, infringing upon the powers of the rectors enough to interfere with the courts of the rectors, and devastating enough to a person's political status to be used in a strictly political way, this was not the case. The Priors and the Gonfalonier did not circumvent the rectors' courts at will in magnate crimes. First, trials of these crimes were required to be accuser-initiated. Furthermore, the Executor checked on the adherence of the Priors to the Ordinances of Justice in the same way that he checked on the adherence of the other rectors to the ordinances. Lack of conformity to the ordinances by the Priors and the Gonfalonier was punished either through capital punishment and confiscation of goods or through a 500-lire fine and a permanent incapacity to hold office, with no appeal permitted (Tract. Ord. Iust. 3; 12; 5.1.14). The Priors and the Gonfalonier similarly were tried by the Executor for crimes that might bear on the Priors' performance of magnate trials. The Executor tried the Priors for falsity, bribery, extortion, receiving communal goods, and fraud, punishing these crimes with a 500-lire fine and incapacity to hold office, appeal again being barred (Tract. Ord. Iust. 15; 5.1.14). Besides being able to try these cases in summary trials before syndication, the Executor syndicated the Priors and the Gonfalonier for these crimes. Sentences delivered by the Priors and the Gonfalonier were not valid unless the ordinances were observed. Many other officials were involved, along with the Priors and the Gonfalonier, in cases in which the bestowal of magnate status could issue.

The power over making magnates that was ascribed to the Priors and the Gonfalonier does not provide an example of executive encroachment on the regular court system in the early fifteenth century. These powers were used much less in the fifteenth century than in the fourteenth. In the 1350s, the trend in the changing of status was going in the opposite direction. The list of magnate families was created in the 1290s and changed little until the 1350s, when branches of magnate houses were allowed to change their status to popolano. The list of magnates appearing in the 1415 statutes is composed of those who had had magnate status for a century, no new large blocks of families having been added. The Ordinances of Justice were used to proscribe individual criminals and sometimes small groups of relatives in the late fourteenth century. Examples of punishment by the bestowal of magnate status can still be found in the last decade of the fourteenth century. The 1380s and 1390s witnessed the territorial state making its final settlement with the magnates and feudal lords, retracting most of the remaining privileges, jurisdictions, and immunities.[21]

While this may seem surprisingly late for the resolution of this problem, it must be remembered that J. Plesner places the heyday of feudalism in Tuscany in the late thirteenth and early fourteenth centuries.[22] However, the criminal archives of the Podestà from the early fifteenth century show that magnate violence against popolani had disappeared (see Chapter 8, below). In the criminal sentences of the mid-fifteenth century, crimes perpetrated by magnates cease to receive special prosecution.[23] When magnates ceased to be treated differently by the court system, the Priors and the Gonfalonier ceased to create magnates. The power of the Priors and the Gonfalonier to create magnates fell into desuetude in the early fifteenth century.

The Priors and the Gonfalonier of Justice also took part in supervising magnate trials, checking on the process of recognition that went on in the courts of the Podestà, Captain, and Executor by examining the cases in which the rectors decided not to proceed. The Priors and the Gonfalonier of Justice were looking for cases in which fear of proceeding against a powerful magnate unjustly prevented a case from being recognized, not cases in which insufficient evidence or some other appropriate reason prevented recognition. When an accusation was extended or an inquisition was initiated against a magnate for a crime committed against a popolano, the rector to whom the accusation was extended or by whom the inquisition was initiated convoked the other two rectors to decide whether they should form a trial. If they decided to proceed, the rector to whom the accusation was extended formed an inquisition, proceeded, and terminated. But if they decided not to admit the accusation or form the inquisition, the case was turned over to the Priors and the Gonfalonier of Justice, who convoked the Gonfalonieri, the Buonuomini, the captains of the Parte Guelfa, the Otto di Guardia, the six counselors of the Mercanzia, and the twenty-one captains of the guilds, who deliberated whether the case should be continued or not. If they decided not to proceed, the case was dropped. If they decided to proceed, the case was returned to the appropriate rector, who was required to try the case.[24] Although the Priors and the Gonfalonier were given important supervisory powers in checking the process of recognition, their powers were not independent of the regular court system. They reassessed only those cases that the rectors had decided not to treat, and returned the cases to the rectors for trial if they deemed them worthy of prosecution.

In terms of magnate trials that he conducted from start to finish, the Executor punished those who tried to exempt themselves from communal jurisdiction while living in communal territory. In the early days of the commune, when individual magnate families had their own separate treaties with the commune, permitting them to maintain private courts and jurisdictions, this problem must have been more acute. If any magnate said to have committed a crime against a popolano attempted to decline the jurisdiction of the commune, impede the execution of a sentence, annul a process or sentence, or force officials to abstain from a process, the Executor proceeded against this magnate and his consorts, who should have corrected the magnate and prevented him from declining the jurisdiction of the commune.[25] The Executor corrected those who believed their rights were such that they could pose an exception *fori declinatoria* because they had their own courts.

The Executor was also involved in the effort to guard communal property when he monitored the activities of the Priors and the Gonfalonier of Justice in protecting communal property from private appropriation. The Executor exacted a fine from the Priors and the Gonfalonier of Justice for negligence in giving aid to officials who protected communal goods from private usurpation (*Stat.* 3.55). He could condemn the Priors and the Gonfalonier of Justice, the Buonuomini, or anyone else for intentionally usurping communal property. If the Priors and the Gonfalonier of Justice sold land near the city walls, the Executor condemned.[26]

Syndication

But by far the greatest sphere of jurisdiction of the Executor at first instance was over crimes committed by officials in office, known as syndication. This jurisdiction was treated most fully in the Ordinances of Justice but was cross-referenced in many other parts of the statutes, indicating the actual use of the power. While one could make a case that the Ordinances of Justice were kept in 1415 only because it was illegal to get rid of them, the general appearance of a jurisdiction in several parts of the statute compilation shows active use. This was probably the most quotidian area of activity of the Executor. Like many functions, syndication passed from one official to another and went through many changes through the centuries. However, syndication had a somewhat stable history for the fourteenth and early fifteenth centuries, remaining active throughout this period. Gino Masi has studied syndication for the fourteenth century, drawing information from communal statutes and from the trial records of syndications which he and Antonio Anzilotti collected and organized in the Archivio di Stato in Florence. He presents a history of the institution.

During the time that bishops controlled the administration of many of the cities in Italy, including Florence, before the advent of the commune, the power to syndicate belonged to the *episcopalis audientia*.[27] As governmental power passed slowly from the bishop to a communal government, in the tenth to thirteenth centuries, so did the power to syndicate officials. This passage was achieved by the *visdomini* and buonuomini, officials who participated in the administration of the bishop but later freed themselves from him and became part of the communal government. By the fourteenth century, syndication was carried on by two officials, a major syndic and a minor syndic, the major syndic syndicating the more important officials and the minor syndic the less important officials. The major syndic was usually the Executor, while the minor syndic was usually the judge of appeals. For most of the fourteenth century, the major and minor syndics were accompanied by a college of syndics that received the accusations and voted in the *partito* deciding the sentence. In the major syndications in the fourteenth century, part of the performance of the syndication, particularly the examination of the witnesses, was carried out by an assessor, usually the judge attached to the Executor, on behalf of the Executor (pp. 87–88).

According to the statutes of 1415, by the fifteenth century the minor syndic had disappeared, leaving the whole process of syndication to the Executor. The judge of appeals no longer had any part in syndication. The college of syndics, who were extracted citizen popolani, continued to do a large portion of the activities of syndicating. The interplay between the Executor and his judge seems to have changed; there was almost never any mention of an assessor who participated in any part of the process. The Executor's judge was, perhaps, more involved in general criminal trials in the fifteenth century. The Executor, on the other hand, was active in most of the process and could personally vote on the sentence along with the syndics. Although in most rubrics of the statutes, when a rector was named, either he or his judge was intended, in this case, where voting practices were being discussed, it is less likely that the rector and judge were considered as interchangeable.

According to Masi, extortion was the crime most commonly treated in the syndication process (p. 70). Unfortunately, he does not support this with any statistical data drawn from the cases but with a rubric from the statutes of 1415 which does not say that most syndication trials treated extortion. Much more telling is Masi's list of crimes of which rectors were commonly accused. Rectors could be accused of neglecting to pursue banned people and rebels, neglecting to punish them within five days after their capture, neglecting to arrest criminals *in flagranti,* neglecting to proceed against those receiving banned people and rebels, and neglecting to take action against popoli and plebatu who were negligent in apprehending rebels. This list shows the emphasis that was placed on police matters and the imperative treatment police matters received. The rectors were expected to act aggressively in forming inquisitions. Further, rectors could be accused of many other crimes: involving themselves in matters not proper to their office; extorting money; neglecting to investigate those out past curfew or involved in gambling; committing acts of violence or injury; neglecting the duties of their office; failing to return to the commune the communal property pertinent to their office; and being absent from the city for fifteen days. Preventing the usurpation of communal property continued to be a priority for the rectors (p. 101). Much of the syndication process involved duties omitted and neglected besides actual crimes committed in office. Certain documents were always present at syndication which allowed the Executor to determine whether officeholders had fulfilled their duties. He used the acts of the foreign rectors to review the cases tried by them. He could check up on the pecuniary condemnations that the foreign rectors had collected in the books of the treasury of *entrate* (income) (p. 349). The books of the Officials of Condotta, that is, the *conducte et reasignationum,* showed the times worked and the duties fulfilled by the officials of the county and district. The books of consignment of the *massaio* of the treasury recorded the communal goods that had been returned by officials. While extortion trials may have been many, especially given the preponderance of private accusation in syndication trials, Masi especially demonstrates the side of syndication that involved omission.[28]

While petitions of accusation from private individuals were the most common, there were other sources of petitions. Petitions of accusation were also taken from retinue members against their head and from other communal officials.[29] Masi does not mention the initiation of syndication by public fame but the extensive use of public fame in other kinds of trials and the great reliance of *ex officio* trials on public fame would indicate public fame as an indispensable mode of accusation in any kind of judicial procedure in Florence, even *ex officio* syndication trials.

Most of the syndication trials that Masi has examined resulted in absolution. Masi attributes the high absolution rate not to corruption but to the need of the commune and the official to come to an amicable agreement in which the official saved face. Many of these officials were, after all, members of a professional cadre of rectors and officials who served in many Italian cities. Their dignity could not be offended outright by the commune. According to Masi, where officials were justly accused by private accusers, accuser and official privately negotiated an agreement preventing the embarrassment of the official.[30]

Trials of officials were handled in two ways: through regular criminal procedure and through syndication. Regular criminal procedure was used when the crime was of such a serious nature that the punishment could not be deferred until the time of syndication. For instance, the *miles* and notaries of the Executor took accusations against the officials of the county and district out of a *tamburo* box located in the main church of the town in the county and district. The accusations were brought to the Executor, who decided whether the crimes were so serious that punishment should be levied immediately. If so, the Executor carried out a summary inquest and condemned to the penalties ordered in the statutes. If the charge could be deferred, the Executor held the accusation secretly in a certain book and waited for the time of syndication, after the official's term of office had ended (*Stat.* 5.4.68).

Extortion was one of the main crimes that the Executor punished immediately. It was tried during office before syndication; if the officeholder was condemned, he lost his office immediately (*Stat.* 5.4.70). The Executor tried extortion committed by any official; for instance, the vicars, captains, podestà, and other officials of the county and district were condemned for extortion by the Executor when they received money for absolving or condemning unjustly. The condemnation was done according to regular procedure (*Stat.* 5.4.70). If these officials accepted money for trying civil cases or for performing any action in civil cases, such as exaction of debt, detention, or *staggimento* (sequestration), for which they were not supposed to exact a fee, this was considered a kind of extortion which could be punished by the Executor. The vicars, captains, and podestà could not keep animals that had been confiscated during illegal exportation through their territory but had to send them to Florence. Laws concerning salaries of these officials could not be changed. All of these extortion-related crimes were reported by citizens putting *cedule* (written accusations or notations) in a box located in the major church of the place in the county and district; the boxes were opened by the Executor's miles and notaries. The Executor inquired, punished, and immediately removed the offending official from office. In his duties pertaining to supervising county and district officials, the Executor was sometimes aided by the *paciales* (a group of six citizens elected by the Priors, the Gonfalonier, and the colleges), who monitored the Executor's criminal trials of the county and district officials, made sure they were prosecuted, and helped to protect the citizenry from oppressive officials (*Stat.* 5.4.68). The paciales, who were stationed in the county and district, participated in the adjudication of cases that were reported in their area. They observed the vicars, captains, podestà, and other officials of the county and district, making sure that they did not make illicit extortions or otherwise burden the people. The paciales helped to decide whether the matters reported by cedula were urgent enough to try immediately. Citizens were linked with the regular court system in these trials. However, if an accusation was placed by tamburo at the Executor's home in Florence instead of in the town in the county and district, the paciales played no part. In these cases, the Executor acted alone. For instance, in cases in which a vicar, captain, or podestà received too much *directura* (i.e., received more than the normal fees for processing a case), the tamburo could be placed at the Executor's home, and the subsequent trial was conducted by the Executor (*Stat.* 5.4.85).

The Executor tried other officials for extortion according to regular procedure before syndication. The Executor recognized cases of extortion or bribery, receiving communal goods, fraud, and falsity committed by the Priors, the Gonfalonier of Justice, the gabelle officials, or any other officials.[31] His jurisdiction was very extensive, covering as it did every communal official for the most common crimes committed in office. These crimes warranted immediate expulsion from office. The Executor performed the whole trial, from recognition to condemnation.

Besides extortion, the Executor tried officials for many crimes before syndication and according to regular procedure. The Executor monitored the treasurers of *entrate ed uscite* (incomes and expenditures) to see if they performed their duties themselves and not through substitutes, and he carried out the ensuing trials. For this crime, the Executor inquired by examining people who were appointed to watch gabelle and treasury officials and by receiving accusations from any other people.[32] The Executor was similarly in charge of checking whether the scribes, notaries, treasurers, and accountants stayed at their offices. He did this through one of his notaries who checked twice a day. If he discovered them absent, he charged them an *appuntatura* (a fine) (*Stat.* 1.59). These fines were exacted during the offender's term of office, although there was no actual trial involved. The Executor checked regularly on the Officials of Grascia, inquiring, condemning, and punishing, to make sure they exercised their offices faithfully and legally.[33] Violators of the divieti laws, even the Podestà and the Captain, were tried before syndication because the officeholders were forced to leave office before their term ended for divieti infractions.[34] Those who assumed offices illegally or assumed offices that were illegal for them to assume were dismissed from office before their term expired. For instance, buyers of gabelles or collectors of gabelles were not allowed to be Tower Officials, the officials who supervised the collection of the gabelles. If any buyer or his relative was elected to the Office of the Tower, the Executor could fine him 1,000 lire without any condemnation.[35] Those people who received communal offices that were not legal for them to assume were immediately removed from office, as were those who overstepped the authority of their offices. In these cases, the Executor recognized and tried according to regular procedure.[36]

The jurisdiction over people who assumed offices that were not legal for them to assume was taken over from the Executor by the office of the Conservatori di Leggi in 1429. When the Executor handled these matters, that is, until as late as 1429, there was rarely any attempt to use the power of examining the qualifications of officeholders as an instrument of factional conflict. The great power that the Executor wielded over this very sensitive material was rarely abused. With the creation of the Conservatori di Leggi, the situation quickly changed. The Conservatori branded their political opponents as bastards, bankrupts, malfeasants, and tax delinquents, thereby excluding them from officeholding. The decisions of the Conservatori were biased by factional and class affiliation.[37]

In terms of the first instance, regular procedure jurisdiction of the Executor, the crimes that pertained to his office were usurpation or appropriation of communal goods; challenges to the authority of the commune; serious crimes committed by officeholders by which people were oppressed; and violations of the rules of officeholding enabling families or individuals to become overpowerful through monopolizing offices.

The other method of trying crimes that officials committed in office was syndication. Criminal condemnations of officials were carried out just like other criminal trials, but syndication trials had their own procedure. However, the penalties were the same as those meted out in regular criminal trials.[38] Syndication trials by the Executor always took place in Florence and were mainly used to discover and try defects, omissions, and commissions, as the statutes say. An official was considered deficient when he showed up for office without the proper equipment or retinue: for instance, if he did not have sufficient men, horses, and arms to staff a castle. Omissions were duties assigned to an official that he neglected to perform. Commissions were wrongful acts committed while carrying out the duties of office; usually, but not always, crimes that his office put him in a unique position to perpetrate, such as extortion. Commissions were also the subjects of regular criminal trials, but defects and omissions usually were not. Crimes of officials that were tried in regular criminal condemnations were so serious that they came to the notice of the rectors before the general inquisition starting the syndication process was even held. Included in this category were crimes such as assault or homicide, which were not uniquely affiliated with officeholding. Syndication was almost exclusively the realm of the Executor.[39] The other rectors could be involved in the prosecution of such crimes committed by officials, although these were mainly assigned to the Executor.

Another difference between syndication and criminal condemnation was that syndication was a mandatory process that officials were required to go through at the end of their term in office, while regular criminal trials were conducted in an ad hoc manner. Against every official, even if he was not suspected of being guilty of any crime, a general inquisition was formed. For every official, a time was designated in which people could come and complain about his behavior. An accusation once lodged was not retractable.

All communal officials, both foreign and citizen, seem to have been subjected to the syndication process. The statutes specifically mention the syndication of the Podestà, the Captain, the preceding Executor, their judges, their retinue members, the judge of appeals, the judge of camera and gabelle, the officials over the goods of rebels, the judge of the Mercanzia, and all the remaining foreign officials for things neglected, omitted, and committed.[40] Probably all citizen officials were syndicated, too. There are specific rubrics discussing syndications of specific officials but no general rubric naming all the citizen officials who were to be syndicated. When all of the citizen officials mentioned as syndicated are added together, a picture of their general syndication emerges. The treasurers of *entrate ed uscite* were syndicated.[41] The treasury officials were syndicated, not for money that needed to be restored to the commune, but for other failures in office, presumably things omitted, neglected, or committed. Trials for failing to restore communal money were conducted months after the close of the official's term of office (*Stat.* 1.17; 1.60). Any official who dealt with communal money was syndicated, including extracted officials, deputed officials, or any members of the councils (*Stat.* 1.17). Even the Priors and the Gonfalonier of Justice were put under the Executor's perusal, along with their scribe and notary (*Stat.* 1.62). County and district officials, even the notaries who were officials with a competence of up to forty soldi, were syndicated by the Executor.[42] These officials carried on many of the ordinary jobs in these places, such as organizing guards to patrol at night, compelling tax payments, and compelling the pursuit of outlaws. All of the podestà, captains, and vicars; all the other officials of the county and district of Florence who exercised office in any city or place of the county and district; and all of their subordinate officials and retinue members were syndicated by the Executor.[43] These were all the major officials of the county and district. They were syndicated first by a judge attached to one of the other Florentine rectors, at the location they governed, and then again in Florence by the Executor. The treasurers of whatever popolo of the county and district, or the syndics or rectors of the popolo, appeared before the Executor in Florence to be syndicated. They were first syndicated in their locations and then again in Florence by the Executor when the accountants reviewed their books (*Stat.* 1.60).

Very infrequently were rectors other than the Executor ascribed the power of syndication. However, any of the rectors who found that one of the Priors or the Gonfalonier of Justice had committed falsity or bribery/extortion could try him, when his term of office had ended, through a summary trial that had to be finished in ten days.[44] All of the rectors shared the duty of supervising the performance of the Officials of Grascia.[45] When the office of the Executor was vacant, either of the other two rectors was empowered to assume his syndication duties. All of the rectors were empowered to condemn officials in trials before syndication. The Podestà and the Captain sent judges to locations in the county and district to syndicate.

It was rare for officials to be exempt from syndication. However, the officials over the goods of rebels, while they were specifically mentioned as being among the syndicated officials, were exempted for decisions they made concerning claims against goods confiscated from rebels, or concerning goods confiscated against the form of the statutes, so anxious was the commune to make confiscations permanent.[46]

While it is certain that all of the foreign officials underwent the syndication process under the Executor, it also is probable that all citizen officials were syndicated. Masi says for the fourteenth century that all officials were syndicated.[47] Even the offices that Martines singles out as the executive offices with judicial duties were subjected to the syndication process. These are the offices that, according to Martines, the oligarchy used to control the government, the executive offices that supplanted other more representative parts of the government. But the powers that the executive offices wielded were regulated by statute and monitored by a system of checks and balances of interlocking duties of other officials, usually the officials of the regular court system. Executive powers were further checked in the syndication process. The foreign official of the Mercanzia was specifically named by statute as being subjected to syndication concerning things neglected, omitted, or committed.[48] The statutes state unequivocally that any citizen officials extracted, elected, or otherwise deputed, especially if they dealt with any communal money, were to be syndicated (*Stat.* 1.17). Other executive officials were syndicated, like the Priors and Gonfalonier of Justice (*Stat.* 1.62).

Besides being enmeshed in a system of checks and balances, the Tower Officials must have been syndicated. The Tower Officials existed in the fourteenth century, when Masi reports that all officials were syndicated, but they were not yet known by that name. They were called the *sei sui diritti del comune* until 1328, when they moved into the tower of the Palace of the Podestà and changed their name to the Tower Officials.[49] They did not have much in common with the executive officials with judicial power created in the 1380s and 1390s, such as the Otto di Guardia. Since the Tower Officials were syndicated in the fourteenth century, they must have been in the fifteenth century. Their actions were certainly well enough documented, and this documentation was the usual material on which to base syndication trials. The condemnations by the Tower Officials were written in acts and given to the treasury of the acts. All communal goods were listed in one register, all the rental agreements made by the commune with private cultivators in another, and all the goods of the rebels, banned, and condemned in another, called *Lo Specchio*. Every facet of the Tower Officials' duties were recorded ready to be checked. The Tower Officials were subjected to the divieti regulations, the regulations of officeholding paralleling the syndication regulations also contained in the Ordinances of Justice.[50] The officials over the goods of rebels, who were subordinated to the Office of the Tower, were syndicated, even though they were exempted from syndication concerning some major tasks that they performed, such as confiscation of goods for the commune. This was not done to allow them to act corruptly, but to allow liberal and permanent confiscation of goods.[51] Their duties were frequently interlocked with those of the foreign rectors in order to prevent corruption. Once property had been incorporated into the fisc, the possibility of claiming it back into private hands was rendered remote by the government. There are many other rubrics demonstrating this impulse to make confiscations irreversible.[52]

References to the syndication of the Otto di Guardia are much less certain, although the Otto was very likely syndicated. The Otto was interlocked with the regular court system, the Otto investigating and the rectors performing the trials. The Otto kept records of its activities. For instance, if the Otto monitored the foreign officials and their retinues for defects, the fines for the defects uncovered were recorded in a book held by the provisors of the treasury of Florence (*Stat.* 1.37). The records on which the Otto could be syndicated existed, but specific reference in the statutes to its syndication does not exist.

While the Executor was the major official who syndicated, he did not always take part in all the stages of the syndication process, and he did not syndicate alone. He shared this function with citizen popolani officials who were extracted and who were called syndics. The syndication process incorporated the participation of regular lay people with that of the rectors of the regular court system. The instances in which the syndics were present were the most important syndication responsibilities. When the Executor syndicated the Podestà, the Captain, and the preceding Executor, for instance, he was aided by eight popolani citizens who actually performed most of the functions.[53] When he syndicated the judge of appeals, the judge of camera and gabelle, the officials over the goods of rebels, the judge of the Mercanzia, and all the other foreign officials, he acted with four citizen syndics (Tract. Ord. Iust. 10). The reason for having these popolani syndics must have been similar to that for employing the paciales in the trials of county and district officials. The Ordinances of Justice stipulated that popolani participate to ensure that due procedures were taken against officials and to monitor the Executor's performance. Other syndications must have been handled by the Executor alone. He alone appears to have syndicated county and district officials when he received accusations at his palace in Florence, and to have acted with a great deal of personal discretion (Tract. Ord. Iust. 8). If no penalty was stated in the statutes, he could penalize at his own discretion. Summary procedure was specified with no mention of a *partito* (a vote) being taken as in the trials where the syndics were present. The Executor alone syndicated the treasurers, the syndics, and the rectors of the popoli of the county and district. They were first syndicated in their commune and then in Florence by the Executor when the accountants reviewed their books (*Stat.* 1.60).

The syndics played a major role in procedures that included them. They were able to form the inquisition on their own or with the Executor, while they alone conducted most of the process and decided the sentence. The majority of the syndics with the Executor, or six syndics without the Executor, formed the inquisition against a rector. This was a general inquisition in which people with complaints could lodge them during a certain period of time. The length of the period in which people could

The Executor of the Ordinances of Justice

place accusations, if not stated in the statutes, was determined by the majority of the syndics with the Executor or by six syndics without him. The syndics and the Executor received accusations in an appointed place. The officials being syndicated had to report there, to respond to the inquisition and defend themselves before the syndics and the Executor. The syndics examined the allegations of omissions and illegal acts, consulting a lawyer on points of law when necessary. They absolved or condemned the official by putting the verdict to a partito and gaining two parts (i.e., two-thirds) of the votes of the eight syndics. The Executor and the syndics notified the treasury of any condemnation, while the Executor alone sent the condemnation to execution within three days, usually by having the treasury retain the official's last salary installment or part of it (Tract. Ord. Iust. 10; 1.62). Although the Executor and the syndics formed the inquisition and heard the defenses together, the syndics alone carried on most of the process and reached a sentence, the Executor alone executing. The Executor must have had a supervisory role to assure adherence to statute. Whether the Executor participated in every facet or was only witness to some facets of the syndication trial, he was intimately connected with and physically present at the scene of all syndication trials.

Wrongdoing by communal officials could be redressed either through criminal condemnations or through syndication. Although the spheres of the crimes treated with these two methods overlapped, criminal condemnations mainly concerned serious crimes, while syndications dealt with things neglected, omitted, or committed.

The podestà, captains, vicars, and other officials of the county and district were syndicated for things committed, omitted, or neglected. These syndications were held in Florence, since treasurers and accountants could check on many of these things there. However, accusations concerning the actual perpetration of crimes could be more easily collected at the officeholding location in the county and district. Accusations were no doubt taken in Florence, too. Before being syndicated in Florence, these officials had already been inspected in their location in the county and district by one of the judges of the other rectors for crimes committed against the local people. Rather than defect of duty crimes, these were crimes against people, such as extortion or abuse of power. The Captain of Arezzo, the Captain of Pisa, and the officials of Volterra were syndicated on location for bribery or extortion, theft, debt, divieto infractions, and intervention in civil causes overstepping their delegated power.[54] While syndication mainly involved things omitted or neglected, syndication could treat very serious crimes. Officials, even the very important foreign officials, could be accused during syndication of crimes for which corporal penalties were imposed (*Stat.* 1.62).

Officials were syndicated to make sure they carried out the duties of their office and observed the prohibitions of their office, as they swore to do when they took their oaths (*Stat.* 1.18). For the podestà, captains, vicars, and other principal officials of the county and district, there was a whole host of positive and negative duties. The officials had to arrive on time and live in the place they administered. They had to retain the proper officials and retinue the whole time. None of these officials could return to Florence, even after their term of office was finished, until their successor arrived. They had to govern their city, land, or castle honorably, not diminishing the possessions of this place but protecting them, conserving the rights of the residents, and returning whatever local goods had reached their hands. The law had to be administered according to the local statutes approved by Florence. The condemned and banned of Florence could not be received or given safe conduct. No podestà, captain, or vicar of the county and district could retain with them in office any official who had a divieto to that office (i.e., who held the office illegally). All civil, criminal, and mixed causes and sentences given by them had to be put in writing and ordered in books by the proper notary. The podestà, captains, and vicars, and their retinue members, were not supposed to accept contributions of money, goods, or services, unless the statutes permitted it. Concerning all these things, the officials of the county and district had to be syndicated in Florence (*Stat.* 1.18).

The foreign rectors were syndicated concerning things omitted, neglected, and committed, like most officials (*Stat.* 3.154). They especially could be condemned in syndication if they neglected to pursue and capture criminals (*Stat.* 3.154). Great importance was placed on their performance in police matters, which showed the vitality of inquisition procedure. In every syndication inquisition against the foreign rectors, there had to be a *capitulum* treating their performance in this capacity. The rectors could be syndicated for not sending out retinues to catch people playing prohibited games.[55] In addition, the Podestà was supposed to keep the peace by compelling hostile parties to make pacts and leave securities.[56] If someone feared harm from another, the Podestà ordered the latter to pledge no harm and to leave a security. All of the retinue members of the foreign rectors were syndicated. The criminal notaries were syndicated twenty-five days from the end of their office for not writing accusations in the communal records when they received them (*Stat.* 3.8).

The trials conducted against the Priors and the Gonfalonier of Justice, besides treating things omitted, neglected, and committed, dealt especially with finding falsity, extortion, and bribery.[57] The major subject of investigation was the performance of the Priors and the Gonfalonier in the sphere of administration of justice (Tract. Ord. Iust. 12; 5.1.45). The syndication duties of the Executor over the Priors, as well as over the other officials, acted to counter corruption and overstepping the powers of office in the Florentine government. Syndication continued in this capacity in the early fifteenth century.

The Executor and the Societies of the People

The Executor had jurisdiction over affairs that pertained to the societies of the *gonfaloni* and *contrata* (divisions) of the city, county, and district. These societies, descended from the *societas peditum*, were strongly reinforced in the Ordinances of Justice, their principal task being to guard the popolani from attacks by the magnates and to guard the communal government from treasonous plots designed mainly by magnates. These societies were of military importance in the fourteenth century but were of little importance, especially in regard to their duties in guarding against magnate disturbances, by the early fifteenth century. When they were active, the societies were composed of popolani, those between the ages of fifteen and seventy living within a popolo. No magnate or servant of a magnate, and no foreigner or Ghibelline, could be part of any society (*Stat.* 5.1.325). There were sixteen societies, one per gonfalone, there being four gonfaloni in each quarter of the city (*Stat.* 5.1.324). The societies were organized citizen militias, and each had its own flag and flag bearer. In case of outside incursions, the societies manned and defended the fortifications. Each society had eighty heavily armed soldiers with heavy military machines, like *ballistas* (which threw heavy stones), who followed the Executor to the place of the disturbance or to the fortifications, and other soldiers more lightly armed, who stayed in the neighborhood and defended it (*Stat.* 5.1.326). The arms for the eighty were kept in a special arms shop in the neighborhood. When the Priors and the Gonfalonier of Justice rang their bell, the eighty followed the society's flag to the designated place. During a disturbance in the city, the Gonfalonier of Justice would send these men to close the gates and guard them. The rest of the men of the society who stayed in the neighborhood were only armed to whatever extent they were able to arm themselves. They stayed in the *contrata* to defend it so that magnates could inflict no injury or property damage (*Stat.* 5.1.327).

Belonging to a society had certain benefits. If a popolano had been harmed by a magnate, the Gonfalonier (Vexillifer), or standard-bearer, of the society accompanied him to court to ensure that justice was done. If the popolano was a pauper, the society paid the court costs (*Stat.* 5.1.333). The Gonfalonier of a contrata or popolo afforded protection to the members of the societies by stopping crimes in progress and apprehending criminals. Similarly, three hundred guards per night from the societies watched the city for the perpetration of any kind of crime. If they found a broken window or a ladder positioned for entering a home, they investigated (*Stat.* 5.2.3). In these cases, the societies were combating ordinary crime; the offended was not necessarily a popolano and the offender was not likely to be a magnate. The Gonfalonier, who was required to go to the scene of the crime to aid a popolano harmed by anyone, was similarly fulfilling an ordinary criminal duty, since the offender was not necessarily a magnate (*Stat.* 5.1.334). The local Gonfalonier, along with the men of the society, went to the defense of a popolano being offended, capturing the assailant and leading him to the fort (*Stat.* 5.1.334).

The Executor, as protector of all the popolani against overbearing and lawless magnates or other rebels, was head of all the societies and leader of their military expeditions. If any unrest were anticipated in Florence, the Executor gathered all the Gonfalonieri and led them with their societies to the fortifications (*Stat.* 3.64). While the Executor was not the official who ordered out the troops, this being done by the mandate of the Podestà, Captain, Priors, and Gonfalonier of Justice, he led the heavily armed sections of the societies both in the city and in the county. The Executor led the foot soldiers on expeditions even outside Florentine territory (Tract. Ord. Iust. 85).

The Executor monitored the members and officials of the societies to keep them faithful to the commune and ready to bear arms. The purpose of the societies was to protect the city against plots formed by magnates. But the Executor did not primarily try the magnates involved in these plots; instead, he tried the popolani involved in the plots, and those members or officials of the societies who failed to arm during a disturbance or followed a magnate in a rebellion (*Stat.* 5.1.329). The magnates involved in such plots were usually tried by the Podestà and the Captain. However, the Executor, because he commanded the armed societies, frequently captured criminals who took part in the disturbance, even if these criminals were magnates. There was, therefore, an area of jurisdiction that was held by the Podestà and the Captain, on one hand, and the Executor, on the other. For instance, while the Captain usually punished those who impeded the foot soldiers, those impeding being mainly magnates, the Executor was also said to punish those impeding (Tract. Ord. Iust. 82; 5.1.328).

Usually the Executor was concerned with punishing the members and officials of the societies. The Executor punished, completely at his discretion, those of the societies, including the Gonfalonieri, who did not convene when summoned to go to the site of a disturbance (*Stat.* 5.1.327). No one from any society was supposed to go to a magnate's house during a disturbance or he would be punished through the Executor, who inquired, proceeded, and condemned at his complete discretion (*Stat.* 5.1.329). He condemned Gonfalonieri who failed to help popolani go to court against offending magnates or failed to pay court costs for poor popolani (*Stat.* 5.1.333). The Executor condemned Gonfalonieri who went to a magnate's council. The *praepositi*, or head Gonfalonieri, monitored the activities of the Gonfalonieri to make sure they did not attend such a council. If the *praepositi* did not properly watch the Gonfalonieri, the Executor condemned them at the denunciation of three counselors of the societies (*Stat.* 5.1.338). The Executor punished the Gonfalonier, counselors, and *restringitores* (the Gonfalonieri's helpers) if they were remiss in their duty of administering the arms shop for their society (*Stat.* 5.1.341). The Gonfalonier, counselors, and *restringitores* could order any members of the society to perform any tasks needed for the society; those who failed to respond were fined twenty soldi. The Gonfalonieri condemned in this case, but the Executor compelled payment (*Stat.* 5.1.343). The Executor had full discretion in punishing the three hundred night guards of the societies for neglecting to patrol the city at night for crimes in progress. He kept a constant check on their performance through his retinue (*Stat.* 5.2.3). No Gonfalonier was to betray his obligation to protect popolani in court by going to court in favor of a magnate, or the Executor condemned and exacted payment (*Stat.* 5.1.339).

The Executor used the societies to arrest those who committed crimes during a disturbance: popolani who went to a magnate's house during a disturbance (*Stat.* 5.1.329); anyone bringing horsemen or foot soldiers through the city during a disturbance (*Stat.* 5.1.330) and magnates or others, not members of the societies, who carried arms in public during a disturbance (*Stat.* 5.1.331). He could hardly have done these things without troops. The Executor monitored the readiness and loyalty of the societies, making sure all of the officials did their jobs and made no overtures to magnates or rebels (*Stat.* 5.1.325). He was empowered to see that all of the ordinances of the societies were executed (*Stat.* 5.1.348).

Although all of these functions of the Executor were detailed in the 1415 statute compilations, the actual tasks performed by the Executor for the societies must have assumed a different shape by the early fifteenth century. The societies themselves had changed a great deal by this time, their military importance becoming negligible. Because the magnate problem was no longer troublesome by the fifteenth century, measures treating this problem were falling into desuetude. The roles played by the Gonfalonieri within the societies gave way to more important roles that they filled in the central government. However, the political importance of the societies was greatly diminished.

At the time when the Ordinances of Justice were created, the societies were important components of the government because they formed part of the forces which wrested power away from the magnates. Throughout the fourteenth century, the societies played a major role in elections of the communal government. In the first half of the fourteenth century, the societies were represented in the communal government by the Sixteen Gonfalonieri, whose power was rapidly increasing. But during the course of the fourteenth century, the Gonfalonieri became a college of the central government, severed from the societies of the gonfaloni. They became a regular organ of government, dealing with general governmental matters, and not strictly, or even principally, with military matters or matters pertaining to their duties in the societies.

From 1350 on, the Sixteen Gonfalonieri attended to governmental affairs of a general and public nature.[58] They were no longer elected by the societies but were chosen from the *borse* of the major offices. By 1387, twelve of the Gonfalonieri were chosen from the major guilds and only four from the minor guilds. Despite the rubrics indicating functions within the gonfalone, their real sphere of activities within the gonfalone must have been small. The Sixteen had transcended their position in the gonfalone to become one of the executive colleges of the central government that voted on most important matters of state and that shared in most of the decisions made by the Priors. Measures concerning spending, taxes, and new laws all needed the approval of the Sixteen Gonfalonieri. Even though the Sixteen Gonfalonieri had become extremely important, the societies did not profit from their rise to power because the connection of the Gonfalonieri with the societies had been severed.

By the early fifteenth century, the military importance of the societies of the people had dwindled to nothing. This citizen militia had not been called to arms since 1393. During the Ciompi revolt, the citizen militia had not provided protection for the Signoria. Many of the members of the militia joined the forces of the guildsmen who were overthrowing the regime. From this time forth, the citizen militia was deemed untrustworthy by the government, foreign mercenaries being hired in their stead to protect the security of the government.[59] Because the magnate problem no longer existed in 1415, the main military function of the Executor had disappeared.

By 1415, the societies of the people were much reduced in power. The gonfaloni had become units of taxation and of regular police duty. The system in which the Gonfalonier or some member of the society accompanied a popolano to court was no longer used. The societies of the people no longer functioned as intercessors between the individual and the state. The regular police duties of the three hundred guards of the night probably did continue. Although the *cappellani,* officials who reported crime, disappeared between the 1322–25 compilation and the 1415 compilation, the three hundred guards of the night were still present in the 1415 compilation.

The Executor's Jurisdiction over Prison

The Executor of the Ordinances of Justice had jurisdiction over crimes perpetrated in the communal prison. This was not just an extension of his jurisdiction over officials. While all of the officials of the communal prison were under his regulation concerning defects and crimes, the Executor's jurisdiction further extended to those detained in the prison, to the crimes and relations among them. This was another category of crimes that the Executor and his judge handled at first instance.

The Executor's criminal judge was in charge of making visits to the prison to monitor prison activities. He visited the prison at least once a month to see if the *superstiti* (the supervisors) were committing crimes against prisoners or were neglecting their duties in such a way that the prisoners were being harmed. The Executor further monitored the behavior of the superstiti and the guards through the provisors of the prison. The provisor's job was to keep the prison clean, to monitor the behavior of the guards and superstiti toward the prisoners, to monitor the performance of the treasurers and notary, and to buy provisions for the prison. The provisors could enter the prison whenever they wanted, since they had their own key, and could stay in whatever part of the prison they liked, to inquire if anything illicit, any crimes, or any injuries were being perpetrated. The provisors denounced to the Executor anything they discovered (*Stat.* 1.72). Their denunciations were probably the Executor's best and most constant source of knowledge of activities within the prison. The reports of his own criminal judge, who was required to view the prison at least once a month and could go more often if any suspicion arose, were also a direct source of knowledge. The regulators of *entrate ed uscite* reviewed the books of the prison and reported any fraud discovered to the Executor (*Stat.* 1.71). The Executor had to rely heavily on the denunciations of officials instead of private accusations because the prisoners could not legally accuse.

The Executor or his criminal judge could try any of the officials who served in the prison—the superstiti, provisors, guards, treasurers, or notary. The Executor had no jurisdiction over the presbyter of the prison, but the presbyter, besides being a cleric, had no duties that would have enticed him into abuses since he mainly gave the sacraments of the Church to the prisoners (*Stat.* 1.74). For extortion or fraud, the judge could try the superstiti, the treasurer, the provisors, or anyone connected with the prison, even the prisoners. The Executor and his judge tried the superstiti and the prison guards for anything illegal, especially extortion, acting with great discretion in condemning (*Stat.* 1.72). The podestà of the prison, the official who collected money from the prisoners for lights and other necessary items, could be tried by the Executor for any crimes committed in office (*Stat.* 1.73). The Executor and his criminal judge were appointed to try the treasurers of the prison for fraud or for failure to spend the money they collected from the prisoners for buying provisions deemed necessary by the provisors. The notary and treasurer of the prison were required to present a *cedula* written in their own handwriting to the regulators of the entrate ed uscite. The cedula had the names of all the prisoners who had paid some quantity of money toward their pecuniary condemnation and the amounts they paid. If any fraud was discovered, the regulators notified the Executor, who investigated. The provisors could also turn in the treasurer to the Executor for fraud or any other crime (*Stat.* 1.72). The Executor also had jurisdiction over prisoners, trying them for extortion and fraud, and recognizing and judging in cases concerning debts between prisoners (*Stat.* 1.24).

Extortion was the main concern of the Executor in his prison duties. Since some of the officials were assigned to collect money from the prisoners for various necessities and some of the officials were assigned to collect money toward gaining a release, extortion must have been a natural and common abuse. In addition, the superstiti could exact money for *agevolatione* (comforts), such as the right to walk about freely within the prison. The opportunities for extortion under these circumstances were many. Money could have been exacted from prisoners hoping to receive better treatment or early release. Very little was said in these rubrics about assault by guards on prisoners or between prisoners. Only once were the provisors enjoined to guard against injuries, seemingly injuries inflicted by the superstiti and guards upon prisoners (*Stat.* 1.72). Still, assaults of all kinds must have been common, especially since there were only five superstiti and three guards to guard the entire prison. Although many prisoners were detained for debt, more were detained for assault.

Unlike the Podestà and the Captain, the Executor fulfilled several distinct functions despite his parity of authority in criminal matters with the other rectors. Most were tied to his origins in the Ordinances of Justice. He executed in cases involving crimes by magnates and most other Ordinances of Justice-related crimes, except for declining the jurisdiction of the commune and usurping communal goods and rights, which Ordinances of Justice crimes he tried at first instance. He tried at first instance cases involving officials, either through regular condemnation or

The Executor of the Ordinances of Justice

through syndication. He tried at first instance any cases involving crimes perpetrated by members and officials of the societies. All crimes that took place in the communal prison, whether between prisoners or between prisoners and officials, were under the Executor's jurisdiction.

In 1435, the office of the Executor was eliminated. His spheres of jurisdiction were transferred to the Podestà.[60] Some of his functions, such as his jurisdiction over magnates, had become irrelevant or obsolete. Others, such as syndication, were, perhaps, unpalatable to the Medici government.

7

THE EXECUTIVE OFFICES

Since it has been posited that in the early fifteenth century the executive branch of the government dominated the other parts of the government, such as the judicial branch, it is necessary to examine the activities of the executive branch, particularly of those executive offices that had judicial duties, in order to determine if the relationship was one of domination. This chapter discusses the main executive offices and the offices of the executive agencies. The main executive offices were the Priors, the Gonfalonier of Justice, the Sixteen Gonfalonieri, and the Twelve Buonuomini. The Councils of the People and of the Commune are also considered here, since they frequently had the right to reject or accept executive measures. The executive agencies discussed are the Tower Officials and their subordinate officials—the officials over the goods of rebels, the banned, and the condemned, and the governors of the gabelles; and the other agencies not connected to the Tower Officials—the Otto di Guardia, the Conservatori delle Leggi, the Onestà, and the Ufficiali di Notte.

First, I briefly discuss the origins and history of the main executive offices. Then, I examine the tasks not connected to the judicial system, which were performed by the Priors, the Gonfalonier, and the colleges, with or without the councils. Next, I examine the judicial tasks of the executive branch, with emphasis on those tasks performed by the Priorate without the colleges and councils, or by the Priorate and colleges without the councils, because it is of particular interest to know to what degree major governmental powers, especially those affecting the judicial system, could be wielded by a small, or relatively small, number of people. I also concentrate on the amount of influence that the executive branch wielded over the judicial branch. The sections on the executive agencies will follow.

The offices of the Priors and the Gonfalonier of Justice, the heads of the executive branch, were founded at different times. The office of the Priors was founded in 1282, during the rule of Cardinal Latino, while the office of the Gonfalonier of Justice was established in 1293, during the period of the redaction of the Ordinances of Justice. The office of the

The Executive Offices

Gonfalonier of Justice was established for the purpose of executing the Ordinances of Justice, but was subsequently changed into a more general executive office paralleling the functions and powers of the Priors. The office of the Priors was created during the rule of Cardinal Latino as a means of achieving greater unity.

The government of Cardinal Latino was installed in 1280 as part of the plan instated by Pope Nicholas III to keep central Italy Guelf. The constitution of Cardinal Latino's government was a peace agreement imposed on the contending Guelf-Ghibelline factions and enforced by the government. The government of Cardinal Latino, however, was based on an abstraction and brought little real unity. Public order was continually violated, corruption was common in the financial administration, and the attitudes of the groups composing the state were conflicting. The organization of the guilds became important as a stabilizing and unifying force in this power vacuum. At first, the influence of the guilds was recognized by the government's extending an invitation to the captains of the seven major guilds to take part in discussions of important political questions. From 1281 on, the captains of the seven major guilds, and sometimes the captains of the twelve guilds, were included in all political discussions. They also participated in the election of the executive officials, the Quattordici. The guilds were quickly becoming the center of the commune.

In 1282 the Priorate was created; by 1283 it had supplanted the lifeless institutions of Cardinal Latino's government and was offering some solution to the internal discord. There were, at first, three Priors chosen from the guilds in general. The installation of the Priors was not a triumph of the democratic movement, as the Priors were uniformly important men from the major guilds. These men were by and large Guelf partisans who had ties to the class of Guelf magnates. Against the backdrop of Ghibelline successes in many cities in Italy, Florence moved toward a more Guelf stance. Despite the major guild status of the Priors, they represented not just the major guilds but all of the guilds. The popular class had already won its place in the government, being represented in the councils, the Quattordici, and the Sapientes. The movement of the guilds into the center of the government continued with the creation of the Defender of the Guilds and the Council of the Defender. The Conservator Pacis, whose job under Cardinal Latino had been to enforce the peace between Guelfs and Ghibellines, was merged with the Defender of the Guilds, thus changing the whole political orientation of the office of the Conservator to one affiliated with the guilds.[1]

The Priors, who continued to be important men from the major guilds, representing all of the guilds, continued to dominate the government almost up until 1293. In that year, they were joined by a new official, the

Gonfalonier of Justice. The initial stages of popular participation began in 1289, with the increasing role of the twelve major and middle guilds in the government and with some role also being played by the minor guilds. The broad-based government under the Priors spearheaded a movement to get rid of sloppy and privilege-oriented government, make all officials accountable, and tighten the financial administration. The movement against the magnates in 1293, culminating in the Ordinances of Justice, was part of this restructuring. The government of Giano della Bella was the high-water mark of the popular movement in these years. In the early fourteenth century, the power of the Priors was mitigated by the addition of the two colleges, the Sixteen Standard-Bearers (Gonfalonieri delle Compagnie) and the Twelve Good Men (Dodici Buonuomini).

The Priorate, or Signoria, composed of the eight Priors of the guilds and the one Gonfalonier of Justice, was the executive branch of the Florentine government. Most of the executive, legislative, or judicial decisions made by the Priorate were made in conjunction with the two colleges. Some executive, legislative, or judicial decisions made by the Priors, the Gonfalonier of Justice, and the colleges also required the consent of the two councils: the Council of the People and the Council of the Commune, both very numerous bodies.

In matters in which the Priorate alone, or the Priorate and the colleges, deliberated and decided by themselves without the councils, the Priorate was at its most influential. All of the *tre maggiori* offices were chosen from special *borse* and had a greater percentage of members from the patriciate than the Council of the People and the Council of the Commune had, although the membership of the councils and the tre maggiori offices was drawn substantially from the same class.[2] Partisan politics and favoritism did not triumph when the councils were involved in decisions. The councils were the bulwark of the republican constitution. There was a greater chance of partisan politics and favoritism when the Signoria, or the Signoria and the colleges, acted on their own.

The Priors, the Gonfalonier, and the colleges, as the executive body of the commune, were very involved with the supervision of the *stipendiarii* and with all functions having to do with the making of war. They were given some power to regulate communal funds allocated to the fortification of castles (*Stat.* 5.1.72). They could increase the number of soldiers in the castles and, therefore, increase the amount of funds channeled in this direction (*Stat.* 5.1.75). They decided what arms the *castellani*, the *stipendiarii*, and the retinues of the county and district officials needed to retain, and what penalties were levied for the defects of these officials as well as for the defects of the retinues of the foreign rectors, even removing them from office.[3] The Priors, the Gonfalonier, and the colleges sent an extracted citizen who checked on defects to accompany the foreign rectors' notaries of consignment on their regular rounds, and sent the Officials of Condotta, who checked on defects at their request (*Stat.* 5.1.78). They set the salaries of the castellani (*Stat.* 5.1.65; 5.1.72). They provided for the manning of communal forts, deciding which forts to use to defend the commune (*Stat.* 5.1.64). However, they did not have any power independent of the councils to make war.

But the councils gradually lost their power over war. After 1384, during times of war, the power to hire mercenaries and to conduct strategy was delegated to an executive commission, the Dieci di Balia, or the Dieci di Guerra. The system whereby decisions concerning war were voted on by the Signoria, the colleges, and the councils was too ponderous to be practical. The councils reserved the right to vote to convoke the Dieci until 1393, but subsequently lost this power. The Priors, the Gonfalonier, and the colleges retained power over foreign policy, including the power to decide when to go to war, and the legislative councils retained some right to intervene in the formulation and execution of foreign policy.[4] In 1411, the legislative councils helped pass a provision that curtailed the executive's power to engage in military campaigns beyond the borders of the territory, creating the Council of Two Hundred. The approval of the Council of Two Hundred was needed to commence a military campaign, annex territory, or create a war *balia*. According to Brucker, it was hoped that this large assembly could resist intense pressure from the executive to pass legislation desired by the leadership and opposed by the guild community. The councils were assuming more power over military enterprises, curtailing the executive's authority and diminishing the independence of the executive in these matters.[5]

The Priors, the Gonfalonier, and the colleges were limited in their power over the budget, acting in most instances in conjunction with the Council of the People and the Council of the Commune. Any petition or proposal that conceded over 200 lire from communal money was required to receive a *partito* of twenty-eight beans from the Priors, the Gonfalonier, and the colleges (there were thus thirty-seven officials in these offices, with twenty-eight in this case being required to cast their beans, or votes, in favor in order for the measure to pass), and to be approved by the councils (*Stat.* 5.1.214). The councils were often reluctant to approve taxes, especially for war. Frequently, the Councils of the People and of the Commune voted down *prestanze* (forced loans to the government) that the Priors, the Gonfalonier, and the colleges championed, therefore having a decisive effect in this forum.[6] The intransigence of the councils posed a major problem during times of financial crisis, such as 1393–1404 and the mid-1420s. In the 1393–1404 period, this problem was met by giving all powers over the levying of prestanze bearing interest and prestanze with no return (in effect, direct taxes) to the standing balia of the Ottantuno, although the legislative councils retained some control over assessments and interest rates paid out on the shares of the Monte, the communal funded debt. The Ottantuno, composed of the executive officeholders, proved to be willing to tax themselves and to reduce the interest rate on the Monte. They also helped to create a system of tax assessments that was so complex that corruption and favoritism were rendered nearly impossible.[7] In 1404, after the return to constitutional forms, the councils again were empowered to vote on prestanze and *estimi*, and again frequently rejected tax measures even with the enemy at the gates.[8] Although the Priors could not by themselves enact tax measures, they were the primary officials in handling the exaction of taxes, deciding penalties for defaulting, and determining what goods tax debtors owned. Also, the Signoria and the colleges had great power over the collection of gabelles, powers that they delegated to the Tower Officials and the governors of gabelles and that they supervised in the hands of these officials.[9]

During the early fifteenth century, two new councils were created, the Council of One Hundred Thirty-One and the Council of Two Hundred. These councils are hardly mentioned in the statutes of 1415. The Council of One Hundred Thirty-One was composed of the Priors, Gonfalonier, colleges, captains of the Parte Guelfa, Ten of Liberty, six counselors of the Mercanzia, twenty-one consuls of the guilds, and forty-eight *arroti* (chosen electors). The number of arroti was successively raised several times. The character of the Council of Two Hundred is debated. Guidi states that the Council of Two Hundred was composed of two hundred members of the upper *reggimento* (patriciate). Those who were eligible for this office were those who had been *seduti* or *veduti* (either actually seated in one of the offices or extracted for an office but barred because of a divieto, and so put back into the borsa; either one is an honor) for the major offices after 1381.[10] In contrast, Brucker states that the Council of Two Hundred was more representative of the guild community and was created to strengthen the guild community's resistance to reggimento-sponsored measures.[11] These two councils voted on measures, such as taxes, prior to the voting of the Councils of the People and of the Commune. Whether created as a tool of the reggimento or as a tool for combating it, the Council of Two Hundred did not seem to strengthen the hand of the reggimento leadership. Because the Councils of the People and of the Commune were never suspended, bills favored by the patriciate still had to be passed by these councils. The Council of Two Hundred proved to be nearly as intransigent as the regular councils anyway, rejecting the renewal of a war

The Executive Offices

balia and voting down taxes intended to pay mercenaries.[12] Probably the enactment that created the new councils indicated that wherever the Council of the People and the Council of the Commune were mentioned in statute, the new councils were also meant.

The Priors, the Gonfalonier, and the colleges performed the major governmental function of settling discords among officials, even judicial officials, because they were heads of every branch of the government, including the judicial branch. There was no special official within the judicial system to perform the function of settling discords among officials, since not even the judge of appeals had this within his competence. The Priors, the Gonfalonier, and the colleges resolved disputes, particularly jurisdictional disputes among the Podestà, the Captain, the Executor, and other officials. If the officials did not accept their resolutions, they forfeited 500 lire from their salaries (*Stat.* 5.1.17). The Priors, the Gonfalonier, and the colleges had always served in this capacity.[13] Although Martines regards the exercising of the power to decide conflicts of jurisdiction as an example of executive aggressiveness, there is nothing either new or necessarily abusive in the exercising of these powers.[14] In none of Martines' examples do the Priors attribute jurisdiction to themselves.

In these ways, the Priors, the Gonfalonier, and the colleges, sometimes with and sometimes without the councils, handled the executive jobs of the government. Their executive duties, as established in the statutes, included overseeing the judicial system. They ensured that the Podestà and the Captain recognized, punished, and condemned in a manner that upheld communal honor. They made sure that the Podestà, the Captain, and the Executor, and their famiglia, punished crimes and exacted condemnations according to statute, as well as defending and maintaining the jurisdictions and rights of the commune. Judges, milites, and notaries from the famiglia of the foreign rectors who acted otherwise could be removed by the Priors, the Gonfalonier, and the colleges (*Stat.* 5.1.17).

The Priors, the Gonfalonier, and the colleges performed many good and necessary tasks for the court system. It should not be assumed that any interference on the part of the Signoria was unwarranted and abusive. It is necessary, therefore, to separate the good and useful tasks performed by the Signoria in the judicial system from abusive interference that promoted oligarchic benefit and factional interests. This difference is difficult to delineate because useful power was not that power given to the Priors by statute and abusive power that power seized extrajudicially by the Priors. *De iure* and *de facto* power had no significance in this context because so much power was given to the Signoria in the statutes that there was little need to exceed these powers. While modern concepts of justice disapprove of the arbitrary element which influence by the executive branch introduces into the judicial branch, Renaissance Florentines did not conceive of this influence as resulting in injustice. After all, in the late twelfth and early thirteenth centuries, the Consuls, the earliest executive officials of the commune, performed both executive and judicial duties.[15] The Podestà and the Captain had both executive and judicial functions until 1373. The statutes of 1415 assigned many judicial duties to the Priors, the Gonfalonier of Justice, and the colleges. The judicial system had a system of checks and balances which thwarted use of these powers for purposes for which they were not intended. The question is whether the Priors, the Gonfalonier, and the colleges were able to use these powers to further partisan interests.

The Priors, the Gonfalonier, and the colleges received sufficient power through the statutes to manipulate the judicial system in many different ways. Although their ability to manipulate legislation or to perform first-instance trials was limited, they had an almost unlimited power of interference through bullectini. While Martines goes far afield looking for the sources of power which justified the judicial activities of the Signoria and the colleges, justification can be found in the statutes for all of the examples of judicial activity that he cites.[16] Where the exercising of power was not permitted to the Signoria and the colleges in the statutes, few examples of the illegal usurpations of these powers exist. Direct trial of very few kinds of cases was permitted to the Signoria and the colleges; thus, few examples of direct trial can be seen. Because appeal was never delegated to the Signoria, none of this can be seen in the early fifteenth century. Great powers of interference through bullectini were given to the Priors, the Gonfalonier, and the colleges mainly for fulfilling real needs in the judicial system. The overstepping of these powers was thwarted by a system of checks and balances. Interference in the judicial system was only permitted when the Signoria, or the Signoria and the colleges, reached a total or near unanimous consensus. Therefore, it is necessary not only to locate the foci of power of the Signoria in the judicial system but also to determine to what ends the system of checks and balances permitted them to use these powers and to what ends the Signoria attempted to use them. The Priors, the Gonfalonier, and the colleges could interfere a great deal in the judicial system and still be only fulfilling the tasks assigned to them, or they could try to use the courts for the benefit of the patriciate in a manner that was not intended by statute. Interference was present but was not frequently used in corrupt ways. The Signoria and the colleges mainly stayed within the limits imposed and were forced to do so by the safeguards incorporated into the statutes. To investigate this question, the powers given to the Signoria and the colleges by statute

The Executive Offices

must be elucidated, as well as the ways that the Signoria and the colleges were made accountable for what they did with these powers.

There were four major ways that the Signoria affected criminal justice: election, legislation, direct trial, and bullectini. I discuss each of these methods in turn. In order to evaluate the opportunities for abuse and undue interference on the part of the Priors and the Gonfalonier, I pay special attention to the degree of autonomy that the Priors and the Gonfalonier possessed over exercising the judicial functions attributed to them by statute. In a few special cases, these officials could act alone. Often they acted either in conjunction with the colleges or in conjunction with the colleges and the Councils of the People and of the Commune. I also pay special attention to other factors thwarting the possibility of corruption.

Powers over Election

The Priors and the Gonfalonier exercised some influence over the government in general and the judicial system in particular through their participation in elections. Their influence was great in the early fourteenth century but became more restricted as time progressed. In the early fourteenth century, the Priors and the Gonfalonier, in various combinations with other officials, elected many governmental officials. After 1355, the Priors, the Gonfalonier, and the colleges lost most of the power that they formerly had over elections, more and more officials being elected through scrutiny and succeeding extraction. In this system, lists, or *recate,* of people being nominated for office were drawn up by various groups. Those nominated were then voted on and required to receive a certain number of votes to be eligible for office. The names of those who attained eligibility were put in a bag, or borsa. When new officials were needed, names were drawn by lot from the election bags. This was the system of election prescribed for more and more of the officials after 1355. The Priors and the Gonfalonier could exercise little influence when officials were chosen in this way, especially since there was usually a long passage of time between when the *borse* were filled and when used for elections.[17]

Between 1328 and 1352, the Priors and the Gonfalonier made up one of the recate, or nomination lists, but this practice stopped in 1352. After that, they had no part in selecting the names of those who were potentially eligible for office. They no longer had the possibility of influencing this choice. Likewise, the Twelve Buonuomini no longer made up the list for the election of the Gonfalonier. The Societies of the People, the guilds, and the Parte Guelfa drew up these lists (p. 155). Nor did the Priors and the Gonfalonier have decisive authority in the next stage of election, the scrutiny (*squittino*) stage. In this stage, more than one hundred people, usually the Priors, Gonfalonier, Gonfalonieri, Twelve, twenty-one consuls of the guilds, and eighty arroti (chosen electors) voted on those nominated. Sometimes the captains of the Parte Guelfa or the six counselors of the Mercanzia voted too, depending on the office being filled. A certain number of votes had to be attained in this process in order for those nominated to become eligible for office and, therefore, put into the borse. The Priors and the Gonfalonier had one vote apiece, as did every other member of the scrutiny commission. The extraction process was outside the influence of any state officials, since the names were drawn randomly. After 1352, new officials called *accoppiatori* conducted a new stage of the election procedure which followed the scrutiny stage. The *accoppiatori* went through the borse selecting out the names of those whom they deemed to be the best citizens, putting these names into other borse, which were exclusively designated for the offices of the Priors and the Gonfalonier. Thus, the process was random within each borsa, but the borse had been ranked.

In 1355, not all officials were elected by the scrutiny and succeeding extraction process, but more and more became elected in this way as the century progressed. Before 1355, the Priors and the Gonfalonier had much greater influence in elections. The rules for election were more inconsistent. Many elections were performed by the Priors, the Gonfalonier, and the Twelve Buonuomini, these elections needing the approval of the Councils of the People and of the Commune. In 1325, often the Priors and the Twelve Buonuomini performed the scrutinies for these offices, assigning those elected to the various posts throughout the territory (p. 165). The statutes of 1355 still specified that the Priors, the Gonfalonier, and the colleges should establish the manner of election for some offices. The rules that they established were to be valid as if they had been made by the Councils of the People and of the Commune. The Priors and the Gonfalonier, in conjunction with different organs of the government, still performed many of the elections in 1355 (pp. 167-70). The importance of the Priors and the Gonfalonier in elections diminished after 1355 because scrutiny and extraction procedures were extended uniformly to almost all offices. In 1355, the Priors, Gonfalonier, Sixteen Gonfalonieri, and Twelve Buonuomini were first chosen by scrutiny and extraction. In 1401, several important offices were added to the list of offices elected by scrutiny and extraction, among them the Tower Officials, the officials of abundance of grain, the Officials of Pupilli, many gabelle officials, and the Officials Castrorum (p. 244). Election by the Priors, the Gonfalonier, and the colleges was rare after this time. However, the Priors and the Gonfalonier did retain some sway over elections, even in the early fifteenth century. Throughout the fourteenth and early fifteenth centuries, the scrutinies for the Councils of the Commune and of the People were performed by the Priors, the Gonfalonier, and the colleges (p. 247). Even in 1415, the consuls of the guilds that took part in the scrutiny, as well as the arroti, were elected by the Priors, the Gonfalonier, and the colleges, giving them indirect influence (p. 317). The Dieci di Guerra were appointed by the major offices and approved by the councils. The Priors, the Gonfalonier, and the colleges could elect the six officials of the Monte, an important power (*Stat.* 5.1.163).

Before the mid-fourteenth century, elections were administered variously and inconsistently. In the 1322–25 statutes, elections for the county and district officials were done case by case with no guiding principles applied. For instance, greater care was not taken to ensure the fairness of election of more important officials than less important officials (p. 165). The coming of the territorial state is evidenced by greater systemization in elections.

The addition of the accoppiatori was an important innovation in the election process, biasing election of the Signoria in favor of the patrician class. However, there was no monetary standard, class standard, or major guild membership posed as a criterion for selection to the borse of the Signoria. The system of accoppiatori was created in 1352 and thus was not a new addition or corruption of the election system invented in the early fifteenth century. Until 1390, the accoppiatori were elected by the tre maggiori officials, but after 1390 they were more democratically elected. The accoppiatori were the most voted for in the maggiori elections from each quarter (pp. 287–94). The power of the accoppiatori to eliminate names from the borse was only assigned to them in 1434. Perhaps the Signoria's loss of the power to elect the accoppiatori more than anything else diminished the influence of the Signoria over elections. Elections in the early fifteenth century were particularly free from undue influence by the Priors and the Gonfalonier. The laws concerning elections were conspicuously enforced during this period (pp. 241, 244, 266). Because the borse were used as much as twenty years after they were made, the Priors and the Gonfalonier were further distanced from elections (p. 277). Although the Priors, the Gonfalonier, and the colleges made the scrutinies for the Councils of the People and of the Commune, this partial control of the election of these bodies did not result in the election of people to the councils who were in sympathy with the wishes of the Priorate or the executive branch of the government. Throughout the late fourteenth and early fifteenth centuries, the Priors and the councils were constantly in conflict. The trend toward the scrutiny and extraction method of election included almost all offices by the early fifteenth century, diminishing the influence of the Priorate and the colleges.

The Priors had little influence over the election of judicial officials in 1415. Foreign officials, like the foreign rectors, were elected by electors (not the arroti, however) who were extracted from borse. The Priors could replace any of the famiglia of the rectors only if they were behaving improperly or illegally (*Stat.* 5.1.23; 5.1.17). If the office of one of the foreign rectors was vacant, the Priors, the Gonfalonier, and the colleges could appoint a foreign rector of their choice. The foreign criminal notaries were elected by a scrutiny of the Priors, the Gonfalonier, and the colleges (p. 329).

In the early fifteenth century, new election rules increased the influence of the patrician class but not of the major offices. These new rules placed a fiscal requirement on those holding office and a lineage requirement on those becoming arroti. Both of these new regulations were approved by the Councils of the People and of the Commune. In 1404, a provision was enacted stipulating that only those members of the major guilds who had personally paid prestanze in the city for thirty years, or whose father, grandfather, great-grandfather, or brother had done so, would be admitted to offices of the commune. Those from the minor guilds were required to have paid prestanze personally or through their family for twenty-five years. Notaries were required to have paid for twenty years before they could enter any notarial post. The head of a *consorteria* enfranchised the entire *consorteria* through paying his prestanze. A provision of 1406 enacted the requirement that arroti involved in electing the Priors, the Gonfalonier, or the colleges must have a father, paternal grandfather, great-grandfather, or brother who had held one of these offices or had been a captain of the Parte Guelfa (pp. 105–7). Although the patriciate was becoming more powerful in the government in the early Quattrocento, there was no faction that was sufficiently organized or powerful to use government offices to its own benefit. Not until the Medici could elections be manipulated to ensure some continuity in the election of one particular faction. Even after 1434, Medici control of elections was tenuous.

Besides having power in elections in this way, the Priors and the Gonfalonier had the capacity to create extraordinary officials, that is, officials that were not envisioned in or regulated by the statutes. Usually these extraordinary officials were created in areas in which the Signoria had a special interest, such as enforcement of sumptuary laws. Because the power was delegated from the Signoria, the Signoria retained some supervisory powers over these officials. The Priors and the Gonfalonier could create officials on their own only if these officials were appointed for a period of less than two months. These extraordinary officials were often appointed to fill some temporary need, such as overseeing repair of the banks of the Arno or of the city walls (*Stat.* 5.1.89). In conjunction with the colleges, the Signoria could appoint other kinds of officials with longer terms of office.

In the late fourteenth and early fifteenth centuries, there was some proliferation of these commissions receiving delegated power from the Priors and the colleges. Martines has pointed to a number of offices that he considers to have been commissions of the Signoria: the Dieci, the Otto, the Monte, the Six of Mercanzia, the Tower Officials, the regulators, the Defenders of the Laws, and the accoppiatori.[18] According to Martines, this proliferation of commissions increased the power of the Priors because the Priors exercised power over these commissioned offices and because the men filling these offices were from the upper ranks of the patriciate like the Priors. An investigation of these offices reveals that some of them that he names were not created at this time, such as the Office of the Tower and the Mercanzia; some of them had only a remote connection to and subjection to the Priors, such as the Mercanzia; and some of them did not wield powers that would enhance the powers of the Priorate to any great degree. Guidi posits that the proliferation of offices at the top had the opposite effect. In his opinion, spheres of activity were being separated from the Priors and given to offices with some degree of autonomy, such as the assigning of military matters to the Dieci.[19] As the territorial state was organizing and centralizing, the Signoria was receiving power over a number of new areas and from a number of new sources, such as the newly captured towns in the territory. The Signoria became overburdened with tasks and was forced to delegate some of its powers.

The offices to which the Signoria genuinely delegated power were the Otto, the Dieci, the Office of the Tower, the Office of Condotta and Defetti, the Ufficiali di Notte, and the Onestà. The areas of competence of these offices were the same areas in which the Priors could exercise direct power and competence and to which the Priors devoted particular attention. The Priors, the Gonfalonier, and the colleges delegated power and closely supervised these offices but were not usually in control of them or in control of the elections to these offices. The nexus between the Priors and these offices was not close enough to permit control by the Priors.

The Priors, the Gonfalonier, and the colleges had a special interest in the enforcement of sumptuary laws and could make sumptuary provisions without the councils. The Priors, the Gonfalonier, and the colleges without the Councils could elect extraordinary officials in this area, four citizens with a term of office of less than one month dedicated to repressing and punishing infractions of the sumptuary laws. Those appointed could make provisions and put them into effect even if this entailed spending communal money. These provisions and allotments had to be approved by a partito of the Priors, the Gonfalonier, and the colleges (*Stat.* 5.1.139). The appointment of these officials to handle this function of the Priorate did not enhance the power of the Priors, since the sphere of interest was not one of great political importance. The enforcement of the sumptuary laws was used to bring in revenue.

The 1322-25 statutes empowered the Priors, the Gonfalonier, and the Twelve Buonuomini to depute officials, as many and as often as they wanted, for supervising prostitution.[20] Their main job was to discover prostitutes who worked outside the permitted brothels. The appointment of officials to supervise prostitution led to the establishment of a permanent office of Onestà in 1403.

The Priors were closely connected to the Otto, whose job was to uncover conspiracies against the Priors. Accusations concerning these conspiracies could be given to one or the other interchangeably, but trial of these political crimes took place in the courts of the foreign rectors. The Priors had little power in the election of the Otto. The Priors, the Gonfalonier, and the colleges were permitted to substitute one or more members of the Otto when they were in unanimous agreement that this must be done (*Stat.* 5.2.56). However, whereas from 1379 to 1406 the Priors, the Gonfalonier, and the colleges elected the Otto, from 1406 on the Otto were elected by scrutiny and extraction.[21] This was the method of election specified in the 1415 statutes (*Stat.* 5.2.61).

The powers of the Dieci di Guerra to create leagues and make war were direct delegations of the powers of the Priors and the colleges. The Dieci was a provisional office that only came into existence when necessary. The functioning of the Dieci was very closely tied to that of the Priorate. The Dieci were never elected by scrutiny and imborsation; however, they were frequently elected with the participation of a great number of officials as in 1386, 1389, 1405, 1413, 1414 and probably for most of the years in between. Usually at least the Priors, Gonfalonier, colleges, captains of Parte Guelfa, six of Mercanzia, Otto, Ten of Liberty, and twenty-one arroti participated. In some years, the Dieci were elected by the Council of Eighty-One, of which the Priors, the Gonfalonier, and the colleges were a part.[22] The Dieci only appear to have had judicial power in conjunction with the Otto and in areas in which the Otto had judicial power.

The Priors supervised the tasks of the Tower Officials, making sure they spent communal money for necessary things and monitoring their performance in office (*Stat.* 5.1.126). The powers of the Priors overlapped the powers of the Tower Officials. The Priors had a direct interest in the judicial duties of the Tower Officials in safeguarding communal property. The Priors, the Gonfalonier, the colleges, and the regulators could make regulations concerning the sale of the goods of rebels, the banned, and the condemned, and declarations as to what goods belonged to them (*Stat.* 5.1.122; 5.1.123). However, the Signoria had little influence over the election of the Tower Officials, since they were elected by scrutiny and extraction from the ordinary borse.[23] The Priors, the Gonfalonier, the colleges, and the regulators could reduce the number of the Officials of Condotta, Officials of Defetti, Officials of the Tower, and lords of all gabelles (*Stat.* 5.1.114). For these offices, the Priors, the Gonfalonier, the colleges, and the regulators approved the election or extraction (*Stat.* 5.1.118). The Priors and the Gonfalonier were closely tied to the Officials Castrorum, the Officials of Condotta, and the Officials of Defetti, all of which were interrelated. Many of the activities of the Officials Castrorum were carried on in collaboration with the Priors, but the Officials Castrorum were extracted from borse (*Stat.* 5.2.149). The Officials of Condotta began to be elected by scrutiny and extraction in 1345.[24] The Priors, the Gonfalonier, and the colleges could order the Condotta Officials to review stipendiarii for deficiencies (*Stat.* 5.1.78). The Priors were closely involved in the functions of the Officials of Defetti.[25] The Priors, the Gonfalonier, and the colleges could make provisions concerning the deficiencies of stipendiarii and of county and district officials. The Officials of Defetti were elected through scrutiny and extraction.

Thus, in many of the offices with which the Priorate was involved and to which they had delegated power, they had little control over elections. Some of these offices had no political content, like the Onestà. All of them enjoyed a certain amount of autonomy from the Priorate despite supervision by the latter.

Powers over Legislation

The Priors had opportunities to interfere in the judicial system through their powers over legislation. The Priors and the Gonfalonier very rarely legislated by themselves; usually the colleges acted in conjunction with them, and usually the participation of both the Councils of the People and of the Commune was required. All of these bodies, even the two councils, were needed to make statutes (*Stat.* 5.1.139). The power of the Priors and the Gonfalonier of Justice was greatly tempered by the required participation of the two councils, both of which were great in number, the Council of the People numbering 285, and the Council of the Commune numbering 192. After 1410, the participation of the Councils of Two Hundred and of One Hundred Thirty-One was also required in every matter in which the Councils of the People and of the Commune acted. The Priors and the Gonfalonier of Justice normally initiated legislation, being able to convoke the councils to reform the laws whenever it seemed suitable to them (*Stat.* 5.1.17). This undoubtedly gave them some control over what kinds of laws were deliberated, some power of manipulation of the criminal justice system.

There were special classes of provisions and ordinances that could be enacted without the consent of the councils, with only the participation of the Priors, the Gonfalonier of Justice, the Gonfalonieri, and the Twelve. The logic behind the selection of these areas of enactment is difficult to decipher. They were not always areas of little importance, nor were they areas that might require great expediency of action. On the other hand, they were not areas of political importance, either. They seem to have been merely a hodgepodge of areas of enactment which had somehow come under the direct influence of the Priorate and the colleges. The Priors, the Gonfalonier of Justice, and the colleges could make regulations for repressing homicides, assaults involving the use of arms, and infractions of the sumptuary laws controlling luxury. They could act without the councils even to create penal ordinances in these areas (*Stat.* 5.1.139). The Priors, the Gonfalonier of Justice, and the colleges could make provisions concerning gabelles levied on luxury items, ornaments, and precious vestments (*Stat.* 5.1.139). They were empowered to make provisions concerning diminishing the useless expenses, deceptions, and frauds committed in the Office of the Tower, as well as provisions, even penal ones, which aimed at assuring that the rights of the commune were preserved by the Tower Officials, including provisions that regulated the defenses that were alleged by private people wishing to claim communal property as their own (*Stat.* 5.1.126).

There were two areas over which the Priors, the Gonfalonier, and the colleges could legislate which were of some political significance. These officials could act alone in deciding which societies were permitted to congregate and what penalties were levied on societies which were disbanded and meeting illegally. They could make provisions, even penal ones, for destroying unwanted societies (*Stat.* 5.1.136). Both religious and trade conventicles had posed problems throughout Florentine history because of their political activities. Balia over illegal congregations was attributed to the Priors, the Gonfalonier, and the colleges in the statutes of 1322–25 as well as in the statutes of 1415, so was not a new power.[26] In the early fifteenth century, private conventicles at which government business was discussed and government elections were arranged were one kind of congregation which could be treated by this law. Balia was also given to the Priors, the Gonfalonier, and the colleges to combat the dissemination of defamatory or seditious literature. The rubric bestowing this power was new to the statutes of 1415. The Priors, the Gonfalonier, and the colleges could provide that the revealers of those writing and disseminating defamatory literature against the regime, against certain citizens, or against the rectors receive rewards of up to 500 gold florins. They could make regulations that would combat this crime (*Stat.* 5.1.137). This new rubric addressed the problem of the constant conspiracies, especially those created by exiles, in the early fifteenth century.

There were many more instances in which the Priors, the Gonfalonier of Justice, and the colleges could act without the councils, but all of them were of minor importance. In these areas, the Priors and the Gonfalonier of Justice had greater freedom to promote the political and social program of the patriciate because of the absence of the tempering influence of the councils. However, the lack of coherence of these areas of direct influence militates against thinking that the law allowed manipulation of legislation by the executive branch to implement government policies and prejudices. Rather, the legislative system posed safeguards against exclusive direct influence by the executive branch. The Priors and the Gonfalonier did not control legislation in all areas of political significance. In fact, they were barred from suggesting changes in the laws affecting the judicial system, such as laws concerning syndication; divieti; salaries of the Podestà, the Captain, or the Executor; election laws for these offices; or the regulations regarding their performance. In 1408, this changed for the divieti regulations, but a very high consensus was still required. The Priors and the Gonfalonier could not propose that the laws concerning defaulting and fleeing be changed nor that licenses for reprisal be conceded without the participation of the councils (*Stat.* 5.1.23). The Priors, the Gonfalonier, and the colleges could not make ordinances in favor of named individuals or in regard to war (*Stat.* 5.1.27).

Powers of Direct Trial

The Priors, the Gonfalonier, and the colleges could affect criminal justice through the cases they directly tried, but there were only a few types of these cases. They were permitted to try serious crimes committed by magnates but not other kinds of political crimes. They could not directly try those political crimes the trials of which could be easily manipulated for use against partisan opposition, such as treason. The laws were not structured to surrender control of the judicial system to the Priors. The statutes were very clear in reserving direct trial for the foreign rectors except in a few very well-defined instances. Rather, the rubrics permitting the Priorate and the colleges to try crimes directly were aimed at arming the Priorate and colleges with the weapons to safeguard the commune against its age-old enemies, the magnates. The fact that these were accuser-initiated crimes and not crimes that could be brought *ex officio* militated against the Priorate using direct trial as a political tool.[27] The petition had to be presented by the injured person. Also, because direct trial by the Priors, the Gonfalonier, and the colleges was limited to real magnates after 1382, excluding popolani who were treated as magnates, it was a poor tool for seizing power.[28]

Petitions were accepted by the Priors, the Gonfalonier of Justice, and the colleges to try crimes that were atrocities or enormities. Those who were convicted of these crimes suffered a change in legal status, a popolano becoming a person treated as a magnate and a magnate becoming a person treated as a supramagnate. The Priors, the Gonfalonier, and the colleges could try homicide, poisoning, plundering, robbery, expelling anyone from his home or land, theft, vendetta against a person other than the principal offending person, incest, adultery, rape, sodomy, abduction of a woman, assassination or assault by an assassin, detention of anyone in a private prison, detention for the purpose of extorting ransom, compelling anyone to be a witness, prohibiting anyone from being a witness, compelling anyone to make or revoke any last will, and, generally, whatever personal offense for which a corporal penalty was imposed by statute.

Any one of these crimes could also be tried in the court of one of the foreign rectors. The choice of whether the crime was tried before the Priors or before the rectors was made by the accuser. Any trials of these crimes which were initiated *ex officio* or by denunciation of another official were aired in the courts of the rectors. If the accuser chose to bring his case before the Priors, the Gonfalonier, and the colleges rather than the rectors, it was because of the elevated penalties that the Priors and the Gonfalonier of Justice could dispense. If an accuser thought the level of violence and abuse of power of the crime perpetrated against him was great, he might try to secure the damages against his offender that the Priors and the Gonfalonier of Justice could inflict. If his case failed to meet the requisite levels of violence and abuse of power, he took the chance of having his case fail completely. Defendants not convicted in the court of the Priors, the Gonfalonier of Justice, and the colleges were not handed over to the courts of the rectors but were completely absolved.[29]

A petition from a private accuser was extended either to the Priors and the Gonfalonier or to the collateral (civil judge) of the Podestà to give to the Priors and the Gonfalonier. On the day when the petition was exhibited or the following day, the Priors and the Gonfalonier were required to have the party cited against whom the petition was exhibited so that he should appear in their presence within the third day or in a shorter term from the day of the citation. Simultaneously, the Priors and the Gonfalonier of Justice convoked the Gonfalonieri and the Twelve, before whom and in the presence of the parties, if they came, or in their absence, if they didn't come, the petition was read. This congregation decided whether the crimes contained in the petition should be considered enormities and atrocities and whether the crimes deserved to be treated in this fashion. If it was decided that the crime was an atrocity, the defendant was cited to the actual trial of the crime to defend himself. The Priors, the Gonfalonier of Justice, and those assembled examined the proof and listened to witnesses as in trials in the courts of the rectors (Tract. Ord. Iust. 101). Then the Priors, the Gonfalonier of Justice, and the colleges decided by partito whether the defendant was guilty and deserved to be treated as a magnate or a supramagnate. If the defendant was found guilty, they summoned the consuls of the guilds to help vote on whether the person incriminated should be considered a magnate. If so, all the statutes applying to magnates applied to him, his sons, and their descendants. If his guilt was not proven or his crimes did not justify his gaining the status of magnate, he was completely absolved (Tract. Ord. Iust. 24).

The crimes enumerated were crimes likely to be associated with magnates and their level of violent behavior. The involvement of the Priors, the Gonfalonier of Justice, and the colleges in making and controlling magnates is evident in the Ordinances of Justice. They had complete control over the bestowing of magnate status, which carried with it a host of legal handicaps. Further, they decided how much security magnates needed to give to the commune to ensure that they would not commit crimes (Tract. Ord. Iust. 57). Better control was sought through the system of securities and the diminished proof needed to convict magnates, as well as the increased penalties meted out to magnates, means by which the commune sought to discourage and contain magnate crime. Control over the bestowal of magnate status gave the Priors the political weapon of keeping certain people out of public office but only by reason of their lawless behavior. For several crimes, such as committing homicide in the Piazza Signoria or the Mercato Nuovo, bestowal of magnate status with all of its legal handicaps was automatic. These crimes were tried by the rectors (Tract. Ord. Iust. 26; 28). But in any instance in which the bestowal of magnate status was discretionary, the Priors, the Gonfalonier of Justice, and the colleges decided (Tract. Ord. Iust. 24). Relatives and consorts of those condemned to death for committing homicide in the Piazza Signoria or the Mercato Nuovo could be declared magnates (Tract. Ord. Iust. 26). The county-dwelling relatives and consorts, as well as those giving aid and favor to county dwellers who killed citizens, were put to partito. Often the Priors, the Gonfalonier of Justice, and the colleges put to partito the relatives of those being made magnates for crimes to see if these relatives also should be incriminated. For the culprits themselves, magnate status followed automatically (Tract. Ord. Iust. 27). When anyone offended the Gonfalonier of Justice or one of the Priors, the Gonfalonieri, or the Twelve with arms and with effusion of blood but did not kill him, these officials decided whether the crime was an atrocity warranting the bestowal of magnate status or not (Tract. Ord. Iust. 29). For this crime, the trial took place in the court of the Podestà or the Executor, but the Priors, the Gonfalonier of Justice, and the colleges sent a bullectino stating whether the crime should be punished as an atrocity.

However, the trial of magnates according to the Ordinances of Justice was only important until the late fourteenth century, after which time special treatment of magnates by the court system ceased. The question becomes whether the Priors used the power given them over atrocious crimes to achieve ends not intended by the bestowal of this power. They could have used direct trial of these crimes to disenfranchise political enemies. After 1352, popolani as well as magnates committing atrocities were subject to these special regulations and to becoming magnates.[30] However, in 1382, the legislation providing for the conferral of magnate status on popolani found guilty of atrocious crimes was annulled, limiting the uses to which the Priors and Gonfalonier could put this legislation.[31] The Priors did not abuse these powers by censuring political enemies. The use of the rubrics of the Ordinances of Justice to bestow magnate status appears to have stopped by the fifteenth century, so that they were no longer used against anyone, even magnates.[32] During the fifteenth century, magnates purchased their popolani status in order to be enfranchised. Law, public opinion, and the system of checks and balances prevented the Priors from using the Ordinances of Justice in ways not intended by statute.

While some historians posit that the Priors, the Gonfalonier, and the colleges could try political cases, examples of them directly trying political crimes are rare. The statutes placed the trial of political crimes squarely in the courts of the foreign rectors, particularly the Podestà.[33] The acts of the foreign rectors reflect this encumbrance, a sizable number of political cases appearing in the acts of almost all years.[34] Even the Otto di Guardia, the commission of the Signoria investigating sedition, was not trying political crimes in the early fifteenth century. We have no examples of these crimes in the courts of the Otto and no statutes empowering the Otto to try them. This implies that the source of the delegated power of the Otto, the Signoria, did not possess such power either.

Political crimes in the early fifteenth century frequently were conspiracies organized by members of the patriciate who had been exiled to other Italian cities.[35] Sometimes they had been exiled in the first place for some kind of illegitimate political activity. They continued this activity wherever they were, attempting to inspire rebellions in Florence which would bring them back from exile. Often the attempted conspiracies crossed class lines. Sometimes the conspiracies had some relationship to the Alberti, Albizzi, and Medici factional disputes. Florence was involved in many external conflicts in the early fifteenth century, being embroiled with the Dukes of Milan, King Ladislaus, and almost all of its neighbors, thus exacerbating the conspiracy problem and providing a larger forum for conflict and more opportunities for illegal alliances and defections. All of these cases were tried in the courts of the foreign rectors, although the Signoria exercised influence on the trials through the use of bullectini, the next type of influence of the Signoria on the judicial system discussed. The political conflicts of 1393 and 1433 provide examples of factional conflict. But because of the constant changes of the membership of the Signoria and because of the desire of many Florentines to safeguard republican institutions, political vicissitudes of this type did not succeed in making any political faction triumphant until the takeover by the Medici in 1434.

An example of a political trial frought with factional implications is the trial of Giovanni Guicciardini in 1431.[36] Giovanni Guicciardini was a long-time member of the aristocracy and a constant officeholder. His political affiliations were with the Albizzi faction, at a time when the Medici were consolidating their power. The Medici faction, in order to discredit the Albizzi, attempted to make him a scapegoat for the mismanagement of the war against Lucca. He was framed for extorting supplies from the war while he was serving in his post as *commissario al campo* in charge of provisions. He was tried before the Captain of the People, but because the Captain of the People was under the strong influence of the Medici party, a most unfair trial was commenced. The Signoria and the colleges, when they sensed that the Captain was not being fair, assigned members of the colleges to sit in on the trial and a bodyguard to protect Giovanni Guicciardini during the trial. The Captain tried to dispense with these guards in order to torture Giovanni. At this juncture, the Signoria took the case out of the court of the Captain and assigned it to the Executor. Giovanni was acquitted in the Executor's court. However, shortly after the trial, Giovanni was named as a *scandalosi*, and again was acquitted. In 1429 a law had been passed called *"degli scandalosi,"* intended as a measure to heal the divisions among the citizens and reduce the power of the factions. However, the inexact wording of the law allowed the law to be used as a tool for factional conflict by the contending factions. This law required that certain citizens name other citizens that they considered to be scandalous people who worked against the interests of the government. The four citizens most commonly named were put to partito, those receiving a two-thirds vote being subjected to a penalty, such as exile. No crime was alleged and no procedural safeguards were observed. This law was a sure sign of the government's desperate attempts to keep control of the situation and the impending breakdown of republican values.

Assessing the dynamics of this case, the executive branch was not using the judicial system to further factional ends. While the Medici were successful in influencing the Captain of the People, they were not successful in influencing the Signoria and colleges. The Signoria and colleges were steadfast in promoting a fair trial and intervened with bullectini to this end. The Signoria never attempted to take the case out of the courts of the foreign rectors. Giovanni was acquitted and continued to hold offices in Florence.

Thus, the Priors, the Gonfalonier, and the colleges had the power to try magnate crimes, but this power had fallen into desuetude in the early fifteenth century. Political crimes were not within their jurisdiction. The only other kind of direct trial over which they may have had jurisdiction were the crimes, deficiencies, and omissions of stipendiarii. They closely regulated the stipendiarii in every detail and may have made judgments in these matters (*Stat.* 5.1.83). In this area, the Signoria delegated their powers to the Otto di Guardia, as n. 10 Otto di Guardia, the only surviving deliberations record of the Otto from the early fifteenth century, shows. The Priors, therefore, tried very few crimes directly. The Priors, the Gonfalonier, and the colleges were forbidden to try any criminal cases other than the ones specifically assigned to them by statute.[37]

Bullectini

The Priors, the Gonfalonier, and the colleges could further influence the criminal law system by intervening in cases conducted by the foreign rectors. Instead of directly trying the cases, they superseded the powers of the rectors and altered the process of justice through the use of bullectini, which were executive orders to the foreign rectors. A bullectino could take the form either of simply an order to proceed in a particular case or of a letter of instruction specifying either the outcome or the penalty. The Priors and the Gonfalonier of Justice could use the bullectini to cancel condemnations or lay them aside after they were partially paid. They could even send people to prison without trial, circumventing the whole criminal justice system. The Priors had much more latitude in interfering

The Executive Offices

through the mechanism of bullectini than they did through direct trial, because the bullectini were not limited in use to any particular crimes but were generally applicable. The Priors, the Gonfalonier of Justice, and the colleges could order the rectors to proceed or to condemn; they could set the penalty or could cancel all or part of a condemnation that a rector had made. For instance, they could order the Podestà, the Captain, or the Executor to proceed when a magnate was suspected of offending a popolano. When one of the rectors received an accusation that a magnate had offended a popolano but decided not to recognize it, the Priors, Gonfalonier, Gonfalonieri, Twelve, captains of the Parte Guelfa, Otto di Guardia, and six counselors of the Mercanzia together could send a bullectino ordering the rector to proceed, if they felt that it was warranted.[38] When a member of the Priorate or the colleges was assaulted, the Priors, the Gonfalonier of Justice, and the colleges sent a bullectino to the Podestà or the Executor directing him to condemn the assailant. Condemnation automatically carried the penalty of magnate status.[39] If magnates or anyone else had perpetrated violence or extortion against guildsmen or others, the trial was carried out before either the Podestà or the Captain; however, the Priors and the Gonfalonier of Justice could intervene if they thought that the decision did not uphold communal honor (*Stat.* 5.1.17). However, the power of the Priors, the Gonfalonier of Justice, and the colleges to regulate magnates and to bestow magnate status was used much less in the fifteenth than in the fourteenth century.

There were cases in which the rectors conducted trials and issued condemnations, but in which the Priors, the Gonfalonier of Justice, and the colleges stepped in to determine the amount or severity of the penalties. They could impose whatever penalties they liked, however grave, against those who did not pay their condemnations, fines, or gabelles (*Stat.* 5.1.120). This was a helpful clause when the government coffers were approaching empty. Since the government employed much of its money for hiring mercenaries in circumstances of grave danger, tax defaulting could be considered a very serious offense tantamount to treason. This gave the Priors great power, especially over the wealthier segments of society, to bleed Florentines mercilessly for taxes. In cases in which someone was caught buying more grain than his family could use, trial took place in the courts of the rectors but the Priors, the Gonfalonier, and the colleges sent a bullectino ordering the amount of the penalty.[40]

The Priors and the Gonfalonier, acting without the colleges or the councils, set the penalty in another case: they had the power to exile people to designated places outside the territory of Florence without any condemnation being reached and even without any crime having been committed or alleged. The Podestà, the Captain, and the Executor executed these commands of exile without seeing any proof except the bullectino from the Priors and the Gonfalonier of Justice (*Stat.* 5.1.25). This was done on the occasion of war or discord among the magnates or others, or on the occasion of any threat to the good and pacific state of Florence. Those who appeared to be inciting the discord or disturbance were exiled. The Priors and the Gonfalonier sent notaries to the places of exile to ensure that the exiles stayed in their designated places. The notaries reported this information to the Podestà and the Captain. Those breaking the terms of their exile received that penalty which had been established by the discretion of the Priors and the Gonfalonier at the time of the confinement according to the quality of the disobedience. The flexibility of the criminal charges as well as the permitted independence of action of the Priors and the Gonfalonier make this stand out from the rest of their powers, which were tempered by first instance judicial decisions by the foreign rectors and the necessity to attain a high percentage of the votes of the Priors, the Gonfalonier, and the colleges. Here the Priors and the Gonfalonier were permitted to act in an extraordinary way on account of reason of state. While there is nothing new about these powers, existing as they did in the 1322–25 statutes of the Captain, they may have been used in a new way or to a new degree in the late fourteenth and early fifteenth centuries.[41] Perhaps this rubric is the legal basis for the events that occurred in 1393, 1433, and 1434, when one faction, temporarily gaining an upper hand, exiled another.

Further, the Priors and the Gonfalonier by themselves, with a partito of eight votes, could send someone to prison. This power could be invoked even if there was no disturbance (*Stat.* 5.1.26). The Priors and the Gonfalonier did not need to allege that any crime had been committed. A case of this sort appears in Brucker's *The Civic World of Early Renaissance Florence*.[42] Here a man was seized by the Executor and interrogated concerning the killing of a usurer. Although he was acquitted in this court, he was imprisoned by the Signoria, only being released when a petition for release sent by him was approved by the councils. While only eight votes were needed to imprison someone, it was more difficult to get someone released from prison. This required a partito of twenty-eight votes from among the Priors, the Gonfalonier, and the colleges (*Stat.* 5.1.26).

The Priors, the Gonfalonier of Justice, the Gonfalonieri, and the Twelve, together with the Tower Officials, could revoke sentences made by the foreign rectors against the commune, that is, sentences awarding what was formerly thought to be owned by the commune to a private person.[43] Although this was not interference in a criminal condemnation, this power to revoke illustrated the special commission of the Priorate to defend communal goods and to make sure the rectors did so as well, even if this meant intervening in the decisions of the rectors.

The Priors, the Gonfalonier, and the colleges could interfere in the judicial system through their power to cancel condemnations. Cancellation was very much like another form of interference, oblation, which will be discussed subsequently. Oblations were the permanent releases of prisoners from prison during religious holidays as an offering to God. Cancellations also were orders to release prisoners, but there was no religious purpose. Both cancellation and oblation were methods of emptying the overcrowded prisons. When people condemned for crimes could not pay their condemnations or their private debts, they were detained in the communal prison until they paid. Many of those who could not pay in the first place, especially the poor, had little chance of paying once in prison. Since the prisons could not continually be filling up without emptying, people had to be pardoned through cancellation and oblation, and then released. Cancellation and oblation differed in another respect: the councils had to approve cancellations, once they were passed by the Priors, the Gonfalonier, and the colleges, but not oblations. Oblations were limited in number, but cancellations were not. Cancellations sometimes involved releasing people from exile, as well as from prison. When a great number of people exiled from Florence gathered in given locations, unrest and conspiracy festered. Cancellations were necessary to quell this unrest and end factional fighting.

Condemnations made by the rectors could be canceled by the Priors, the Gonfalonier, and the colleges with the approval of the councils. This power, described in the 1322–25 statutes as well as those of 1415, had undergone changes in this period. In the 1322–25 statutes, obtaining a peace from the injured party was a requisite step in obtaining a cancellation, although other conditions also had to be met.[44] In 1415, obtaining a peace was not as important. In the 1322–25 statutes, all those receiving cancellations had to pay part of their condemnation. For serious crimes, the whole condemnation had to be paid, but the cancellation meant a return to a pristine state in which no record of the condemnation remained and no stigma preventing officeholding existed. In the 1415 statutes, the law had changed to some extent. Less payment had to be made, but the permanent consequences were greater.[45] While some requirement of partial payment appeared in the 1415 statutes, the new consequence of condemnation was a perpetual stain and some legal incapacities for holding office.[46] The feeling was no longer that a private matter had been justly settled but that a public crime deserved to be treated in a public way and not with such leniency. It had been found that the extension of this kind of leniency promoted favoritism and flagrant disregard for law and order. The 1415 statutes amended this situation with a perpetual ban from officeholding for serious crimes.

While the requisite number of votes among the Priors, the Gonfalonier, and the colleges was the same for the cancellation of condemnations of all crimes in the 1322-25 statutes, only the cost of the cancellation being graduated according to the severity of the crime, in the 1415 statutes the number of votes necessary to obtain the cancellations was sharply higher for serious crimes—in particular, treason, rebellion, and other political crimes. It was, therefore, more difficult to get a cancellation of a political crime in the early fifteenth century than in the fourteenth.

In 1325, the cancellation of condemnations of political crimes required a two-thirds vote of the Priors, the Gonfalonier, and the colleges. A provvisione of 1381 changed the requisite number of votes to a unanimous vote of the Signoria and colleges, that is, thirty-seven votes. This provision appears in the 1415 statutes. However, alongside this statute appears a revision of 1404 which changed the requisite number from thirty-seven to thirty-four for granting cancellations from condemnations for political crimes (*Stat.* 5.1.200). This is possibly because some measure had to be taken to alleviate the problem of the gathering of exiles in other Italian cities who then promoted political agitation in Florence. While clemency had to remain difficult to attain, it could not be impossible while conspiracies promoted by exiles were being uncovered. The Priors, the Gonfalonier, and the colleges could lighten penalties with a smaller partito than was necessary to cancel them. When someone gathered an army or conspired against the Florentine state, capital punishment was mandatory, the rectors having no discretion to give out a lesser penalty. However, the Priors, the Gonfalonier, and the colleges with a partito of thirty-two votes could mandate punishment other than capital.

According to the statutes of 1322-25, anyone committing any crime was eligible for a cancellation if he gained approval for his petition from the Priors, Gonfalonier, colleges, and councils, and if he paid the amount required. For most crimes, the requisite amount was three soldi per lire. However, for the most serious crimes, the whole condemnation had to be paid before the person could be canceled from the book of the banned. The crimes in this category were homicide, falsity, inciting castles to rebel, sodomy, collecting tolls, robbery on the streets, violation of possessions, land, or homes, assaulting someone carrying grain, offending through assassins, breaking instruments of peace, making a vendetta against someone other than the principal person, and extortion. Likewise, magnates could only have their condemnations canceled if they paid the whole condemnation. These crimes mainly outline a profile of magnate crimes. In 1322-25, when a cancellation was granted, the name of the person was canceled from the book of the banned and no legal handicaps remained.

A provvisione of 1371 changed the laws concerning cancellation and documented a change in the manner in which cancellations were given.[47] In 1371, those condemned to death, amputation of a member, or a fine of 1,000 lire or more could not have their condemnations canceled except by a unanimous vote of the Priors, Gonfalonier, colleges, and twenty-one consuls of the guilds, with the approval of the councils. This provision appears in the statutes of 1415, except that the consuls of the guilds no longer voted (*Stat.* 5.1.197). Especially included in this category of serious crimes were condemnations for rebellion. If the condemnation to be canceled was for under 1,000 lire, twenty-eight votes of the Priors, the Gonfalonier, and the colleges were required. A 1404 statute, also contained in this compilation, gave a new payment scale for different condemnations. Those condemned to death paid only 100 lire, not the full penalty, as was paid for serious crimes in the 1322–25 compilation. The rate on pecuniary condemnations was changed from three soldi to two soldi per lire. While it may seem that the lower payments for serious crimes made cancellation in these cases easier to attain, the requirement of such a high degree of consensus among the Priors, the Gonfalonier, and the colleges decreased the likelihood of the opportunity to pay the reduced fine which accompanied a cancellation.

However, in 1404, another new law concerning cancellations was enacted, which also appeared in the statutes of 1415 (*Stat.* 5.1.200). This again altered the number of votes necessary to attain cancellations. In this version, rebellion, political agitation, and subversion of the state were singled out as the most serious crimes, the crimes for which cancellation was most difficult to attain, although the number of votes needed to cancel condemnations in these cases was reduced from thirty-seven to thirty-four, still a high level of consensus. For any crime other than rebellion for which the punishment was death, a cancellation required thirty votes. For any crime for which the punishment was amputation of a member or a fine of 100 lire or more, the cancellation required twenty-eight votes. For other crimes, the votes remained as before.

As noted above, oblations were cancellations of condemnations granted by the Priors, the Gonfalonier, and the colleges for religious reasons, the released prisoners being given to God as an offering or oblation. On religious holidays, particularly the festival of St. John the Baptist, the Priors, the Gonfalonier, and the colleges released many people from prison for the honor of God, the festival, and the city. Oblation was, as we have seen, a means of emptying the prisons. Many who were detained in prison for debt or for pecuniary penalties that they could not pay were not violent and dangerous criminals who had to be separated from society. Releasing prisoners was conceived of as an oblation because the poor were the usual recipients of this grace. The statutes of 1322–25 required that the poorest and most destitute be considered first. The length of time served was also used as a criterion. This guideline was specified in the rubric treating oblations used before 1325, but it disappeared in 1325. Oblations, in some small way, acted to combat the built-in inequities to the poor of a system of primarily pecuniary penalties. The Priors, the Gonfalonier, and the colleges used oblations to rectify injustices. When it came to the notice of these officials that an inequitable judgment had been made which was caused by the rigidity of the law, they lightened the penalty through granting an oblation. Thus, the Priorate could better take intent, for instance, into account than the regular court system, which was quite strictly tied to statute.

There were several distinctive characteristics of oblation that made it different from cancellation. Oblation was aimed at the poor. The criminal spent a good deal of time in prison before he was released, at least six months but usually much longer. In 1415, the Priors, the Gonfalonier, and the colleges chose the recipients and performed the oblations without needing to obtain the consent of the councils. In 1325, the Special Council of the Captain voted along with the Priors and the Gonfalonier on oblations. The colleges had not yet attained sufficient power to vote along with the Priors and the Gonfalonier on executive matters. In 1415, the consent of the councils was not needed. Those eligible to be *oblati* were brought to the attention of the Priors, the Gonfalonier, and the colleges by the superstiti of the prison, who kept track of the causes for incarceration, the amount of time served, and other parameters of eligibility. Cancellations were requested from the Priors, the Gonfalonier, and the colleges through private petitions.

The institution of oblation existed in Florence before the 1322–25 statutes. While the giving of oblations was initially unrestricted and completely at the discretion of the Priors, the Gonfalonier, and the colleges, greater restrictions and regulations were added. Before the 1322–25 statutes, no limit was placed on the number of oblations that could be granted. The Priors, the Gonfalonier, and the colleges abused the institution of oblation by granting too many oblations and by granting them regardless of the seriousness of the crime committed. For instance, in 1298, 168 condemned people were liberated during the festival of St. John the Baptist alone.[48] The rubric concerning oblation appearing in the 1322–25 statute compilation redressed these abuses. The Priors, the Gonfalonier, and the Special Council of the Captain could only give oblations three times a year, at Easter, Christmas, and the festival of St. John the Baptist; at each

The Executive Offices

holiday, only fifty people could be offered. All people who received oblations had to have been imprisoned for six months. In 1325, magnates who committed crimes against popolani and people who had already been liberated through oblation once before were barred from eligibility. Political criminals, those committing treason or sedition, were required to pay their whole condemnation to receive an oblation. Those making a vendetta against someone other than the principal person or violating property were required to serve two years in prison before they were eligible for oblations. Debtors were required to have the license of their creditors before they could seek oblations. New citizen officials who did not vote were chosen to assist the Priors, the Gonfalonier, and the Special Council in choosing the oblati. When the oblations were bestowed, the recipient was completely absolved.[49]

In the 1415 compilation, further restrictions were placed on oblations. Those who were involved in a homicide but did not strike a blow or those giving aid to murderers were required to be detained in prison for four years. Those disrupting divine offices must first serve two years before being eligible. Theft of 200 lire or more meant at least one year in prison. No one committing a crime against persons could be granted an oblation for one year. More classes of criminals were required to be detained for longer than six months in the communal prison before oblation, and more classes of criminals were barred from oblation altogether. Those offending another prisoner were detained a mandatory period of one year; those committing rape, adultery, kidnapping, or serious assault served two years; those committing theft or blasphemy served three years; those gambling or carrying illegal arms served one year, one month, and one day; and those perpetrating a vendetta against other than the principal, a violation of a peace, or a violation of possessions still served two years. Another option for fulfilling the required penalty for these crimes was a detention of six months accompanied by a payment of three soldi per lire. However, those who had been granted an oblation previously were allowed to be granted another if they received a partito of thirty-two votes from among the Priors, the Gonfalonier, and the colleges.

More serious criminals were barred from oblation. The most important example of this trend toward restriction was the barring of political criminals. Oblations were not used to mend factional fighting but were strictly for liberating the poor. Furthermore, no *maleabbiatus* (a person who was banned for a crime and could be offended with impunity), no magnate who offended a popolano, and no magnate who failed to pay a condemnation for his consort, could be granted an oblation. No one who injured a Prior, a Gonfalonier, a Podestà, a Captain, or an Executor could receive an oblation. No one causing a political disturbance, committing sedition, setting the official palaces on fire, rebelling, making war against the commune, or causing a castle to rebel could enjoy the benefit of oblation. Hired assassins were barred. Newly prescribed was the exclusion from office of anyone who had received an oblation (*Stat.* 1.83). Eight officials, extracted from borse to aid the Priors, the Gonfalonier, and the colleges, read the names of those eligible for oblations to these officials, who voted on those to be released. The collateral of the Podestà was also required to be present during this procedure (*Stat.* 1.84). The presence of these additional officials put a further check on the activities of the Priors and further assured that those who were being voted on were eligible and appropriate for receiving this benefit.

Therefore, cancellation and oblation gave the Priors some power to interfere in the judicial system, but the restrictions involved limited this power. The question of how the Priors, the Gonfalonier, and the colleges used cancellation and oblation remains important. The amount of freedom that they had, in terms of both statutory restrictions imposed and permitted independence of action, affected the latitude of applications from which they had to choose.

Neither cancellation nor oblation was newly created in the early fifteenth century as a political tool for the patriciate. Both of these institutions hailed back to the fourteenth century and were traditional powers attributed to the Priors and the Gonfalonier of Justice. Oblation was a completely inappropriate tool for showing factional favoritism or granting waivers from political crimes. Oblations were intended for the poor, and no people committing political crimes were eligible for them. The powers of the Priors, the Gonfalonier, and the colleges over oblations diminished as more and more restrictions were placed on their bestowal. Although approval of the councils was not required for the granting of oblations, watchdog officials participated and the number of oblations was restricted. Oblations required a high degree of consensus, two-thirds of the votes or more.

The power of the Priors, the Gonfalonier, and the colleges to cancel condemnations was used more frequently as a political tool and an instrument of illegitimate influence on the judicial system than their power over oblations. Still, there were restraints on the use of cancellations for these purposes. Cancellations had to be approved by the councils. Cancellations of serious crimes, particularly political crimes, required a high degree of consensus among the Priors, the Gonfalonier, and the colleges.

Both oblations and cancellations fulfilled real needs in the judicial system and were not just means given to the executive branch to interfere. Both alleviated overcrowding in the prisons. The executive branch could act as a court of equity through both of these devices, since the

Priors could act with greater freedom than the regular courts, which were tied to statute. Further, the executive branch could make this system of pecuniary penalties more equitable to the poor through the use of oblations. The executive partially defused the faction-ridden political scene through cancellations of condemnations. The Signoria needed some powers of interference in a totally foreign-staffed judicial system.

The most common task of the Signoria and the colleges was deliberating petitions requesting favors. These petitions mainly contained requests for reductions of tax assessments, relief from taxes already owed, and clemency from creditors. For instance, the Priors, the Gonfalonier, and the colleges could issue a bullectino excusing someone from a debt owed to the commune. If a person owing a debt to the commune received a bullectino or a license for a delay of payment from the Priors, the Gonfalonier, and the colleges, but failed to give security to the commune within a month, the bullectino was revoked and another could not be obtained except through a partito of thirty-six votes from among the Priors, the Gonfalonier, and the colleges (*Stat.* 5.1.48). An exemption or immunity from paying communal taxes required a partito of thirty-four votes (*Stat.* 5.1.207). The Priors could certainly influence justice through these bullectini, giving benefits to those in favor with the reggimento; however, the high degree of consensus needed to issue them foiled attempts at factional favoritism. Bullectini directed to the courts of the rectors were rare even in the early fifteenth century. Zorzi records no bullectini in his sample of court cases for the year 1400, and only two were recorded in this study for the Podestà's court in the 1426–28 period.

The Tower Officials

The Tower Officials were responsible for the maintenance of all kinds of communal possessions, such as piazze, roads, bridges, agricultural possessions that had been confiscated, and the rights of gabelle collection. While formerly the care of these possessions had been divided among several offices according to the type of goods involved, by 1415 it was subsumed under one office, the Office of the Tower, which supervised all of them. The major previous offices that were united were the Tower Officials; the lords of all gabelles; the officials over the goods of rebels, the condemned, and the banned; and the Quinque Rerum.[50] Some of these offices and some of the minor offices subsumed under the Tower Officials and contained in the tract devoted to the Tower Officials ceased to exist, and some continued to operate under the supervision of the Tower Officials. The office of Quinque Rerum, a predecessor form of the Tower Officials, had supervised gabelles, goods of rebels, bridges, piazze, streets, and mills. However, the Quinque Rerum no longer existed once the Tower Officials were formed. In the early fourteenth century, the fourteen good men had been in charge of renting communal lands to tenants and providing loans to them. The fourteen good men had passed out of existence, their job having been taken over by the Tower Officials.[51] In contrast, the lords of all gabelles as well as the governors of the various gabelles were ongoing; and the officials over the goods of rebels, the condemned, and the banned remained a very important office under the supervision of the Tower Officials.

The evolution of the organization of the Office of the Tower could serve as a model for that of the territorial state. The Office of the Tower, even in the fourteenth century, was a key post in administering the possessions and rights of the commune. It was strengthened under the popular government of Walter of Brienne in 1342 in order to combat the usurpation of communal goods by the rich and powerful men of the city and the contado. This was part of the movement toward impersonal and efficient government. The Office of the Tower initiated better systematization of communal goods—for instance, initiating the procedure of keeping one comprehensive record of communal property and rights. The Tower Officials instigated legal action against the rich and powerful usurpers of communal property. Becker relates some interesting examples of actions taken in support of the war against the usurpation of communal property that began in that year.[52] Throughout the second half of the fourteenth century and the early fifteenth century, the Office of the Tower continued to be expanded and systematized, paralleling the continued development of the territorial state. Many offices were subordinated to the Office of the Tower in a logical process by which all offices with any competence pertaining to communal goods were united. Another great stage of growth occurred in 1364, when the lords of all gabelles; the officials over the goods of rebels, the condemned, and the banned; the officials of the mills; the officials of the streets, bridges, and walls; and the officials of the sea became subordinated to the Office of the Tower. As late as 1415, additional tasks were still being attributed to the Tower Officials. In 1415, the office over the streets of the contado and district was terminated, its tasks being given to the Office of the Tower. Just as the territorial state continued to systematize, so did the Tower Office.

The Tower Officials were more closely aligned with the Priors and the Gonfalonier of Justice than with any of the rectors because the executive branch was in charge of all efforts to preserve communal goods. The Priors, the Gonfalonier of Justice, and the colleges set the rules for how the Office of the Tower had to operate. The administration of the goods of rebels, the condemned, and the banned was overseen by the Priors, the

The Executive Offices

Gonfalonier of Justice, and the colleges. These same officials monitored the Office of the Tower for deceptions, frauds, and unnecessary expenses. They made provisions concerning the manner of the registration of the goods coming into the commune and over the defenses that could be alleged by private people concerning these goods (*Stat.* 5.1.126).

The operations of the Tower Officials were completely submerged in the system of checks and balances. All communal lands and property were registered in one book, and the Tower Officials were required to have this property publicly announced throughout the city by banners. Nothing could be canceled from this book except through the legal judgment of the rectors and with the express consent of the Priors and the colleges.[53] Only city lands which lacked buildings could be sold and alienated from the fisc, with the approval of the Council of the People and the Council of the Commune (Off. Turr. 1). The Tower Officials rented out communal goods and kept registers of all the goods rented out and the oathswearers who backed up these rental agreements (Off. Turr. 20). The foreign rectors compelled any person to pay who defaulted on the rents owed on communal property (Off. Turr. 7). The process of confiscating land was a joint effort between the Tower Officials and the officials over the goods of rebels, on one side, and the foreign rectors, on the other. The rectors made the condemnations requiring confiscation of goods. Together the Tower Officials, the officials over the goods of rebels, and the foreign rectors investigated to determine the property of condemned people (Off. Turr. 10).

The tasks of the Tower Officials and the governors of gabelles, who were subordinate to the Tower Officials, likewise were coordinated with the competence of the judge of camera and gabelle. A party wishing to protest the payment of a gabelle placed a deposit with the governors of gabelles but litigated in the court of the judge of camera and gabelle.[54] The sphere of competence of the judge of camera and gabelle transected the sphere of competence of the Tower Officials, since they could both try gabelle collectors for fraud, extortion, and bribery (*Stat.* 1.16). The Tower Officials and the governors of gabelles, on the one hand, and the judge of camera and gabelle, on the other, shared the competence over standardized weights and measures. The judge of camera and gabelle judged cases of merchants selling bulk goods without using the official communal measures set up by the Tower Officials and the governors of gabelles.[55]

The Tower Officials were required to send whatever condemnations they made to the treasury of the acts within ten days. Sale of the right to collect a gabelle took place in a public auction.[56] A register had to be kept of all communal property that was rented out to tenants, giving information concerning the property, the name of the renter, the amount for which the oathswearers had obligated themselves, and the successive quantities that were paid.⁵⁷ If any of these things were neglected, especially the information concerning the oathswearers and the registration of payments, the regulators of the commune discovered this when they reviewed the books. They withheld the pecuniary condemnation from the salary of the officials responsible. The Tower Officials kept a register of the gabelles sold. Four men from the colleges and two of the regulators of the commune reviewed the contracts of sales and reported their findings to the Priors, the Gonfalonier, and the colleges, who, along with the regulators of the entrate ed uscite, had to approve the contract. The Tower Officials were subject to the divieti laws and very probably to the syndication laws, as were the officials over the goods of rebels, the condemned, and the banned. Furthermore, the Tower Officials were not likely to be exclusively members of the upper reggimento. They were chosen through scrutiny and extraction, being extracted from the ordinary borse, not the borse of the tre maggiori.⁵⁸

Public goods such as piazze, streets, and bridges were maintained by the Tower Officials. The Tower Officials distributed the responsibility for repair and maintenance of the streets and bridges of the county and district among the communes and popoli of the county and district.⁵⁹ They spent communal money on the repair of the Ponte Vecchio (Off. Turr. 21). The Tower Officials supervised the renting of communal agricultural land to tenants. Most of this land came into communal possession through the confiscation of lands of rebels, the condemned, and the banned, although some came from communal purchases which had taken place in an earlier period. The Tower Officials had to discover and recuperate any communal lands, goods, and rights (Off. Turr. 1). They incorporated the possessions of rebels, the condemned, the banned, and defaulters from taxes into the communal goods, and kept *Lo Specchio,* the register of all goods incorporated into the commune (Off. Turr. 2). An evaluation of the land was carried out by the Tower Officials to facilitate the renting to tenants (Off. Turr. 8), usually for a price based on the productivity of the land (Off. Turr. 3; 8). The *coloni, fictaiuoli,* and *pensionari* (agricultural workers) of the condemned became tenants of the commune when the land was confiscated (Off. Turr. 4). The Tower Officials compelled rent payments from communal tenants (Off. Turr. 1). Most land could only be rented for a three-year term and could not otherwise be alienated, but land in the city over which there was no structure could be sold by the Tower Officials (Off. Turr. 1).

The Tower Officials also managed the communal rights of collecting some of the gabelles. The Tower Officials and lords of all gabelles sold the rights to collect some of them: the gabelle of nuntii, the gabelle of the seven piazze, the gabelle of *pollaiolorum, treccarum, trecconum* (ambulating vendors who sold chicken, fruit, and vegetables, the gabelle being charged on the product sold), the gabelle of beasts, the gabelle of the piazza of grain, the gabelle of mills and *gualchiere* (machines in the textile industry), and the gabelle of horned animals and game (Off. Turr. 29). They also sold the rights to collect the annual gabelle on weights and measures (Off. Turr. 1). They sold the rights to collect all these gabelles in an auction to whoever bid the highest. The buyer of the gabelle, who managed the actual collection, hoped to collect more money than the amount he had spent buying the right to collect. Further, the Tower Officials fulfilled some functions pertaining to weights and measures. Once a year they approved the barrels for selling wine and oil (Off. Turr. 42; 43). By the early fifteenth century, the practice of selling gabelles had fallen into desuetude. Communal officials collected them, which was a move toward greater efficiency, greater revenue production, and greater public control of public functions.

The Tower Officials had a court and conducted certain kinds of trials related to their spheres of interest. Much of the bulk of their case load must have been civil, since cases concerning claims against lands and goods confiscated by the commune from the goods of rebels, the condemned, and the banned were conducted in their court. The Tower Officials were aided in this task by the officials over the goods of rebels, the condemned, and the banned (Off. Turr. 4; 5; 2.77). First the Tower Officials established what lands and possessions belonged to the condemned and banned, mainly by meeting with the rectors and syndics of the county or the *cappellani* of the city from those places where the condemned was reputed to have lands and goods. After the foreign rectors condemned someone for a crime for which the punishment was confiscation of goods, the foreign rectors, along with the Tower Officials, met with the rectors, syndics, and cappellani, who reported on the lands and goods possessed. After this, those who had claims against the goods came to allege before the Tower Officials (Off. Turr. 10; 5.2.77). The claims could not be initiated by the condemned nor be made in favor of the condemned. The person bringing the protestation, as the claim was called, had to provide a deposit before the case could begin. The officials over the goods of rebels, the condemned, and the banned estimated the worth of the goods claimed, set the amount of the deposit according to the worth of the goods, and accepted the deposit. They investigated carefully to ascertain whether the protestation was made on behalf of the condemned or banned or whether the instruments brought in defense of the goods were simulated or fictitious. If either of these was discovered to be true, the deposit was confiscated by the commune. Sufficient proof of the falsity of the claimant's protestation was provided by proof that the instruments were fictitious or by three witnesses of public fame saying that the claim was on behalf of the condemned or that the instrument was fictitious (Off. Turr. 4).

Not all cases against the commune, that is, cases in which someone claimed land already confiscated by the commune, were tried directly by the Officials of the Tower. Some were tried before the foreign rectors and monitored by the Tower Officials. An official called a syndic formed a liaison between the rectors and the Tower Officials. Whenever any judicial cause, litigation, question, or controversy arose brought by anyone against the commune in the presence of a rector or judge, the syndic had to be cited to defend the interests of the commune. If a sentence was about to be given against the commune, the syndic notified the Officials of the Tower. The syndic made an automatic appeal to the judge of appeals and notified the Priors and the Gonfalonier of Justice, so that in his prosecution of the appeal, he could consult with them and could execute their mandate (Off. Turr. 11). Even if the party making a claim against the commune won in the trial of the appeal, the sentence was not valid unless it was approved by the Priors, the Gonfalonier of Justice, the colleges, and the Officials of the Tower (Off. Turr. 5; 2.77).

Obviously, it was difficult to win a case against the commune. Once land that was confiscated became part of the fisc, it was difficult to get it back. This strong concept of the fisc reflects the advanced development of the territorial state. Again, the state's great need for revenue was a primary motivation for strong legislation. The Tower Officials did not use their power to interfere in the judicial system to the benefit of a patriciate. Strict legislation against the usurpation of communal land mainly discouraged the rich and powerful from this activity.

Besides this civil jurisdiction over claims to communal goods, the Tower Officials had some minor jurisdictions in criminal cases. They decided summarily and *de facto* who was in default on their rent payments for communal lands and levied penalties automatically. They, as well as the Podestà and the Captain, were responsible for compelling tenants of communal lands to pay their rent (Off. Turr. 1; 8; 16). All those who did not pay in the agreed-upon term owed one-quarter of the rent more if the payment followed within thirty days and double rent if the payment was later than thirty days. However, possession of communal goods by renters was protected in the same way that possession was protected for all other tenants and owners; that is, through the foreign rectors. The Podestà and the Captain could recognize and punish anyone who occupied or destroyed lands, trees, or houses on communal possessions, or set fire to the homes of communal agricultural tenants (Off.

Turr. 7). The Podestà, the Captain, and the Executor were responsible for protecting the possession of communal goods for communal renters as long as these individuals paid their rents (Off. Turr. 8).

Those who bought the rights to collect gabelles were under the jurisdiction of the Tower Officials. The Tower Officials could proceed against buyers who violated pacts or ordinances concerning gabelles. The Tower Officials had balia in examining and recognizing complaints against buyers of gabelles or complaints of one buyer against another. They could quash and annul any trial against anyone concerning a gabelle. The Tower Officials did not execute their own sentences but relied on any of the Florentine officials established for justice (in other words, the rectors and their retinues) to send their sentences to execution, even starting with the capture of the person (Off. Turr. 32). The Tower Officials had a court but had no police retinue to carry out their condemnations. They had only a notary, an accountant, and two nuntii (Off. Turr. 1). When the buyers of the gabelles did not pay the commune the amount for which they had purchased them, the Executor proceeded against them at the request of the Tower Officials (Off. Turr. 33). If the crime for which the buyers or collectors were being tried was collecting more than they should, they were punished by the Podestà or the Executor (Off. Turr. 34).

Other than their jurisdiction over communal tenants and over gabelle buyers, the Tower Officials had two very minor spheres of judicial interest over which they did not try directly. They supervised all the trials of weights and measures. No Podestà, Captain, Executor, *iudex rationum*, official of *blado*, or any of their retinue could inquire into weights or measures or make any process concerning these without license of the Tower Officials.[60] Further, the Tower Officials inquired after those selling fish in illegal places. They denounced them to the rectors, who could inquire, proceed, punish, and condemn.[61]

Besides the Tower Officials, who sold the rights to collect gabelles and tried gabelle-related cases, the governors of the gabelles also tried gabelle-related cases, but those cases of gabelles that were not sold but managed by the commune. There were some similarities between these two kinds of officials. The Tower Officials managed the gabelles that were sold by the commune to buyers of gabelle collection rights with their subordinate collectors. However, the rights to collect some gabelles were not sold but were managed by governors who collected them. Mainly, these were the gabelles of wine and gates, and, most importantly, the gabelle of contracts. These important gabelles had their own governors. There were also general governors of gabelles for lesser gabelles. All these governors had the same job. Both the Tower Officials and the governors of gabelles did estimates of the values of lands and other possessions. The Tower

Officials, however, mainly estimated communal land in order to establish what rents would be due. The governors of gabelles estimated the goods of those delinquent in paying their gabelles when goods were about to be confiscated or pawned to pay the gabelles. Both the Tower Officials and the governors of gabelles tried complaints concerning the gabelles. The major complaints tried by the Tower Officials were complaints against the gabelle buyers and collectors, or claims (protestations) concerning confiscated lands. The complaints received by the governors of gabelles were complaints that the gabelles were collected in instances where they were not owed.

There were three kinds of governors of gabelles mentioned in the statutes: the governors of all gabelles, the governors of the gabelles of wine and gates, and the governors of the gabelle of contracts. Each of the governors had the same job in relation to his own gabelle. The governors had two basic functions: they exacted the gabelles and they tried cases related to their gabelles.

The governors exacted delinquent gabelles by compelling payment without figure of a judgment or solemnity of statute. They discovered who was delinquent; for example, who had carried out a transaction for which a gabelle was supposed to be paid, and declared this person delinquent in payment. They investigated to discover those delinquent in paying their gabelles.[62] The governors of the gabelle of contracts investigated through examining parties said to have made a contract. It was relatively easy to figure out some of the people who owed the gabelle of contracts, since the notaries drawing up contracts were required to keep official records that verified transactions.[63] Payment could be exacted either through the governors themselves or through other communal officials at the instance of the governors, after a determination had been made by the governors.[64] The governors could either direct the nuntii of the commune and the berrovarii of the rectors to compel payment or could direct the rectors or other communal officials to compel through the nuntii or berrovarii.[65] The governors compelled payment in several ways. They sent the nuntii and berrovarii to break into the houses of gabelle debtors to take goods to be pawned or sold to pay off their debts.[66] At the instance of the governors, nuntii and berrovarii could capture, detain, and put gabelle debtors in prison until their debt was paid.[67] Nonpayment for a contract could be punished as gabelle fraud.[68]

The governors tried by partito some kinds of cases pertaining to gabelle collection. The governors of all gabelles met two times a week to determine justice,[69] while the governors of the gabelle of contracts met either morning or evening every day for this purpose.[70] Summarily and without figure of a judgment they determined who owed gabelles in various kinds of cases (Tract. gab. contract. 5). They heard complaints concerning these gabelles, probably coming from those who felt they were either overcharged based on faulty estimates or were charged for kinds of contracts for which a gabelle need not be paid. Gabelles did not need to be paid on contracts between family members or on loans from the guilds to their members (Tract. gab. contract. 13; 20). Like the Tower Officials, the governors could condemn exactors and nuntii summarily, but these exactors were communal officials, not hirelings of the gabelle buyers. The rectors exacted these fines for the governors (Tract. gab. contract. 7). Further, the governors could condemn notaries for fraud. Notaries, who drew up documents and contracts, were supposed to report all contracts for which a gabelle should be paid. Failure to do so was considered intentional defrauding (Tract. gab. contract. 26). Some of the cases handled by the governors must have involved some amount of complexity, since the governors were encouraged to use knowledgeable counsel to decide difficult cases.[71]

Therefore, the Tower Officials were organized throughout the fourteenth and the early fifteenth centuries, certainly not precipitously formed in the late fourteenth or early fifteenth centuries. This organization was intended to create impersonal and efficient management of communal property. An efficiently run Tower Office reduced the possibility of aristocratic usurpation of communal goods. The Office of the Tower was a fully accountable office of administration, working in conjunction with other officials, such as the rectors and syndics of the county and district, the judge of appeals, and the foreign rectors.

Otto di Guardia

The office of the Otto di Guardia was an executive commission wielding some judicial powers. Created in 1378 by the Ciompi government to protect it from conspiracies by those formerly holding posts but displaced by this popolo minuto revolution, it proved to be so useful that successive governments, despite their differences in political philosophy and constituency, continued to employ the Otto. Originally conceived of as a temporary measure, the Otto became a permanent organ of the government. However, the judicial role of the Otto in the early fifteenth century has been greatly exaggerated because the Otto became so important in the late fifteenth century. After 1434, the Otto began to invade areas of civil and criminal litigation. In 1453, it was admonished for interfering in civil cases over which it had no legal jurisdiction. In 1471, all the areas in which the Otto had no jurisdiction were stipulated in order to try to restrict it from acting in these areas. By this time the Otto had become the major criminal court, destroying the courts of the foreign rectors. Without evidence from the early fifteenth century, the characteristics that the Otto acquired in the late fifteenth century have been projected back onto the early fifteenth century, where they do not belong.

The court of the Otto was a court of summary procedure, proceeding through partito without regard for statute or any of the solemnities of inquisition procedure. The extension of the Otto in the late fifteenth century brought an end to the sophisticated development of inquisition procedure. Thus, the early fifteenth century is the period of the greatest development of inquisition procedure in the courts of the foreign rectors, making it a period of particular interest to the study of legal history. In the late fifteenth century, the summary procedure of the Otto required no real defense, no real assessment of evidence, and no extensive testimony from witnesses.[72] However, in the early fifteenth century, the Otto had a very restricted jurisdiction. It had not supplanted the regular judicial system to any degree and did not try any regular civil or criminal cases.

There are a few records indicating the sphere of activity of the Otto before 1434: one record of its judicial activities in 1406, the statutes of 1415, some provvisioni, and scattered references in the *Giudice degli appelli: Condanne proferite dagli ufiziali intrinseci* records. Most material on the Otto comes from the period after 1460, when it was most powerful. An assessment of the activities of the Otto before 1434 must be based on the limited documents from this period. Then the degree to which the Otto had invaded the court system can be evaluated.

The original purpose of the Otto was to safeguard the government from sedition. It formed a political police force, taking denunciations, sending out spies, investigating, and capturing suspected political criminals. Undoubtedly they carried out some interrogation of the defendants because they were in touch with the investigation and because they needed to further the investigation by attempting to ascertain the names of others involved. With this compiled, cases were turned over to the foreign rectors, usually the Captain, for trial. Initially, the Otto had no power to try rebels, only to arrest them and send them to the rectors. The first interrogation which they made would have been very important for the formation and outcome of the trial.

However, the primary duty of the Otto, as it appears in the 1408–9 record of their judicial cases, was to manage the troops in the castles and fortifications. These troops prevented rebellion initiated from within or without. The Otto made sure the fortifications were in good repair and were sufficiently manned, hired additional troops if necessary, and investigated for infractions perpetrated by the stipendiarii. Typical infractions were leaving their posts or exercising a trade in the place where they were stationed. The Otto were included in all councils because their opinions on foreign policy were so valued. The Otto did not try rebels at this time but investigated for conspiracy or rebellion. It could demand the appearance of anyone and could mete out penalties for noncompliance. When the Otto found infractions, it notified a foreign rector, if the culprit was a rebel. Occasionally the Otto seemed to try stipendiarii directly. Usually, however, it notified a vicar of the county and district by sending a bullectino. These bullectini were not *instructoria*, or letters demanding that an already determined sentence should be reached. Instead, they ordered the rector or vicar to proceed against a suspect. The Otto was responsible for authorizing societies to meet, this being a safeguard against conspiracies against the state. Meetings of societies were illegal unless authorized.

The Otto was very closely affiliated with another office, the Dieci di Balia. The Dieci di Balia managed the troops during wartime, the Otto during peacetime. When the two existed concurrently, the Otto was more involved in monitoring the numbers of supplies and troops, while the Dieci conducted the war and controlled troop deployment. Often, because the two offices were so redundant and because an urgent situation might not permit elections, the Otto simply became the Dieci with the addition of two more men. By the middle of the fifteenth century, the Otto had changed functions and the Dieci was left with the care of the troops.

The statutes of 1415 continued to link the Otto with the supervision of the stipendiarii and repair of the fortifications. The money paying the salaries of the Otto came from the *appuntatura* (fines levied for defects in office, like not appearing on time or not being armed properly) collected from the stipendiarii, one job of the Otto being to check for these defects and levy the fines (*Stat.* 5.2.57). The Otto was also in charge of guarding the Arno and the entrances it created into the city. If they elected guards for this purpose, the prospective guards had to be approved by the Priors, who undoubtedly checked their loyalty to the government (*Stat.* 5.2.58). The Otto, along with the Priors and the colleges, was responsible for managing the office of the Six of Pistoia, the Florentine officials who had custody of the citadels around Pistoia. The Priors, the colleges, the Dieci di Balia (if this existed, or the Otto di Guardia, if it did not), could restrict or broaden the powers of the Six of Pistoia. The Dieci was still interchangeable with the Otto. The Otto, besides monitoring the defects of the troops, monitored the defects of the foreign officials and their retinues. The Otto or the Officials of the Condotta required all the foreign officials to make a *monstra*, or show, of their retinues. The Otto fined the foreign officials who had defects in their retinues, making decisions concerning these fines through voting by partito (*Stat.* 1.37). The Otto, likewise, examined the foreign rectors and their retinues for infractions of the divieto laws (*Stat.* 1.3).

There was some connection between the breaking of the divieto laws and the Otto's quest to thwart any disruption of the government. The divieto laws prevented foreign officials who had any connection with cities inimical to Florence from serving in Florence. Further, they prevented any group from a given city or family from being overpowerful in Florence by forbidding officials from the same city or family from serving in Florence either simultaneously or too frequently. This function of the Otto can be seen as part of its duty to thwart foreign interference. A provvisione of 1421 reaffirmed the Otto's right to investigate foreign officials for infractions of the divieto laws. In 1429 this power was taken from the Otto and given to the Conservatori delle Leggi.[73]

Another function of the Otto evident in the statutes of 1415 was its authority to award damages to those harmed by the banned or condemned. The Otto decided on damages awarded to contadini who had their homes burned, crops destroyed, beasts killed, or vines cut, or were captured by a condemned or banned person. The person suffering the damages had recourse against the *liga* in which the crime was committed or against the consorts and relatives of the condemned or banned person, both of which were partially responsible for not restraining the banned person or for not capturing him and turning him over to the authorities. The complaints were taken by the Otto, who decided and terminated the cases by partito within a month. It had full authority to decide the damages and to execute its decision. Here was a definite judicial activity requiring the substantiation of facts and the formation of a judgment. This duty fell to the Otto because it was responsible for capturing the banned and condemned or for keeping them outside Florentine territory.

The kind of burning and devastation described in the 1415 statutes was most likely to occur during a war or uprising, the cutting of vines being particularly associated with tumult. Many laws in Florence were aimed at keeping farmland under cultivation despite any kind of disaster (*Stat.* 2.78). Martines discusses a case of this sort in which the Otto was called on to force a liga to pay damages. Between 1386 and 1390, the Liga of Antella suffered extensive losses of buildings and farms from thefts and damage. One of the *pivieri* (parishes) of Antella would not pay its share of the losses. The Otto decided to force payment on all of the pivieri in accordance with the laws of Florence and the duties of office of the Otto. Martines regards this as the beginning of the development of the Otto's jurisdiction over civil disorder, and I would concur that, perhaps, this is some attempt to force a rebelling district to pay for its destructive activity. At this initial stage of development, the Otto's activities in this area can also be closely linked with the need to keep farmland under cultivation and the need to find someone to foot the bill when war or tumult disrupted agriculture.[74] The Otto, the Priors, and the foreign rectors all monitored seditious activity. Anyone gaining knowledge of a conspiracy was required to report it to the Otto di Guardia or to any one of several officials, such as the Priors and the foreign rectors (*Stat.* 3.60). The foreign rectors conducted these trials. There were many officials working against sedition at this time, the foreign rectors being among them. The closest example to counterrevolutionary activity carried on by the Otto was the powers it was given in 1412 over the Alberti to enforce their exile from Florence.[75] The Otto was given such power because it was in charge, in general, of monitoring the banned and condemned. The increased budget to carry on this activity which was given to this office in 1412 was one step in assigning it some power over civil disorders. Its activities in banning the enemies of the Medici in 1434 are closely linked with the power it was given over the Alberti in 1412.

In 1420, the Otto was given jurisdiction over public officials and private citizens who embezzled money from the government. The Otto could accept *tamburazioni* (anonymous denunciations) regarding this crime and could proceed summarily against those accused. It issued a *declaratio* that a particular sum had to be paid back to the commune. Either the rectors or the Otto could execute the sentences.[76]

When all of the areas of competence attributed to the Otto before 1434 are considered, there is little of what can be called real judicial activity and certainly nothing resembling the arbitrary justice that the Otto could dispense in the later fifteenth century. The declarationes that the Otto could send out before 1420 enjoined the foreign rectors to proceed against suspects, with the Otto investigating and compiling evidence for their use. The provvisione of 1420, while it empowered the Otto to send out a declaratio containing a sentence, did not call for any kind of real judgment on the part of the Otto di Guardia. Instead, the Otto used the conclusions of the communal accountants to determine whether a crime had been committed. Nevertheless, the declaratio was a precursor to the kind of bullectini that it sent out after 1434. The bullectini or *instructoria* after 1434 contained a sentence or condemnation already determined by the Otto di Guardia, which it enjoined the regular court to pronounce. By the second half of the fifteenth century, only the structure of the regular court system was preserved. The powers given in the statutes of 1415 and the provvisione of 1421 concerning the divieto laws, likewise, did not call for the Otto to make a real judgment, although it could send out a declaratio containing a sentence. Infractions of the divieto laws, such as being under age or being disqualified because of nonpayment of taxes or too recent officeholding, required few leaps of judgment, and thus could easily be verified. The demands for emendation of damages, which the Otto could send out in declarationes, did call for some kind of substantiation and judgment. Facts and testimony were collected to determine the existence of damage, the amount of the damage, and the verifiability of a condemned or banned person in the area. Then a declaratio, containing the amount of damages to be paid, was sent to the *liga* or to the consorts and relatives.

None of these examples of the judicial powers of the Otto di Guardia before 1434 have any resemblance to the judicial powers wielded by the Otto under the Medici. The areas in which the Otto could send out declarationes containing sentences had little political content. Although the Otto di Guardia had the power to investigate for sedition, the declarationes sent out concerning this crime commanded the regular court officials, the foreign rectors, to proceed against a certain person, without instructing them further. Before 1434, the Otto were important investigatory officials in the criminal justice system, as heads of the stipendiarii and as consultants on foreign policy. They were also important as a political police force, but they did not yet try political offenders, nor did they have any general competence in criminal matters.

In the 1433–34 period, this was beginning to change. In 1433, the Signoria gave the Otto the power to send out *instructoria* to the foreign rectors concerning crimes committed at night. In 1434, the Otto carried out the famous exile of the opponents of the Medici. Here the Otto determined the condemnations and called on the Captain to pronounce them. This is an example of a strictly political judgment being substituted for a legally valid one, as well as of the use of bullectini to circumvent the regular court system. 1434 was the first time the Otto had ever been granted balia, full powers to proceed against political offenses. The Captain was also granted balia at this time. Even after 1434, the Otto did not normally possess balia.[77]

Other Executive Agencies

Other executive agencies with judicial powers were created before 1434. The Conservatori delle Leggi (Defenders of the Laws) was created in 1429. This agency, monitoring those taking office, enforced the qualifications for officeholding. Minors, bastards, bankrupts, malfeasants, tax delinquents, and anyone who had not paid their *prestanze* continuously for thirty years or more were weeded out in accordance with already existing laws. The proscriptive power of this agency was used as an instrument of partisan repression but equally by all factions.[78] The Conservatori became an extremely powerful agency after 1434 with a much expanded sphere of competence. The Onestà, or Morals Commission, another creation of the Quattrocento, was an executive agency. The Onestà was especially commissioned to treat cases involving pimps and prostitutes. Another court, the Ufficiali di Notte (Officials of the Night), was created sometime during the early fifteenth century. This court was an investigative body and a court of summary process; it tried cases of sodomy.

The above analysis does not show a rapacious and unaccountable executive branch crushing an enfeebled judicial branch. Direct trial was very rarely conducted by the Priors, the Gonfalonier, and the colleges; instead, cases were uniformly sent to the regular courts of the foreign rectors. The great amount of interference in the judicial system permitted to the Priors, the Gonfalonier, and the colleges through bullectini was tempered by statutory limitations and the requirement of a near consensus among the executive officials. The Tower Officials, although they handled a great deal of property and fulfilled some very important functions, did not decide whose property to confiscate. These decisions were made by the regular court system of the foreign rectors. Usurpation of communal property was prevented through very strict rental regulations, especially those demanding prompt payment, and regulations that were almost prohibitive concerning the alienation of communal property. The efficiency and organization of the Tower Office further prevented usurpation. The Office of the Tower continued to organize in the early fifteenth century. The Otto di Guardia tried very few cases during this period but acted in conjunction with the regular court system in cases of sedition. The Otto was still closely tied to the supervision of the stipendiarii and the monitoring of the banned. It had not yet begun to invade the territory of the criminal courts. The institution of the Conservatori delle Leggi and laws such as *"degli scandalosi"* promoted factional fighting and favor-mongering but, as no faction decisively had the upper hand, and no faction successfully manipulated the Conservatori or the cases tried under the "degli scandalosi" laws, all factions were equally damaged in the resulting mud-slinging. At any rate, this development did not take place until 1429. Neither the Onestà nor the Ufficiali di Notte had jurisdiction over any material of political importance.

8

THE CASES: PHILOSOPHIES OF PROSECUTION AND PROFILES OF CRIMINALITY

AFTER HAVING examined statutory evidence, I will now assess evidence from criminal cases. In order to draw conclusions about criminality and the criminal law system of the early fifteenth century, I examined a three-year series of condemnations, from mid-1425 to mid-1428, from the Podestà's court. I then employed conclusions drawn from the cases to test conclusions drawn from the statutes. Analyses of both cases and statutes yielded similar conclusions. In addition, the cases verified the preceding chapters in a general way by showing that the statutes were actually applied law. Correspondence between the statutes and the cases was very close. Inquisition, not summary, procedure was clearly being employed by the courts of the foreign rectors. Both the characterizations of criminality and of the philosophy of prosecution demonstrated in the statutes were verified by the cases. By comparing cases from the 1425–28 court of the Podestà with samples from other periods, I was able to show that the character of criminality and prosecution changed throughout the period.

The statutes of 1415 were employed in the courts of the foreign rectors, which were the major courts of law, until at least 1433. Inquisition procedure, as detailed in the statutes, was followed exactly by the courts, as was demonstrated abundantly in the acts of the courts called the books of the process and the books of the condemnations. The foreign rectors who came to serve in Florence were allotted time to study these statutes, which they were required to use to make their decisions or they risked severe punishment. Many of my major conclusions drawn from the statutes are supported by information from the cases. In conformity with the statutes, the cases demonstrate an increasing reliance on public initiation. Testimony was the major mode of proof, elicited, according to the legal method, by asking the witness to address consecutively each *capitulum* of the accusation or inquisition, or of the *defensiones*. The cases were based on this evidence. Torture was applied in conformity with the rules of the statutes and only in cases allowed by the statutes. All impor-

Philosophies of Prosecution and Profiles of Criminality

tant debt cases were prosecuted in the court of the Podestà, having been referred from other courts, such as those of the guilds, that lacked this jurisdiction. Important debt cases were tried according to the statutes pertaining to defaulting and fleeing. Changes and refinements in these laws were reflected in the cases.

The trials of officials that were conducted in regular court proceedings, that is, outside syndication, conformed to the statutes governing these trials. Political crimes were tried in the courts of the rectors, as specified in statute, and the very rare bullectini that affected these cases corresponded to instances allowed by the statutes of 1415. Issuance of these bullectini was governed and limited by the statutes, especially those concerning the required consensus among the Priors and the colleges.

Statutes and cases agree closely in the early fifteenth century because the major changes that took place in society, the judicial system and the political system occurred later. The early fifteenth century was more akin to the period that preceded it than the one that followed it, especially in criminality and philosophy of prosecution. Crimes symptomatic of class conflict were not yet dominant in the 1425–28 cases, as they would become in the late fifteenth century. Class-biased justice was not prevalent in the 1425–28 series of cases, as in late fifteenth-century cases. Lower-class assaults against lower-class victims were prosecuted in the early fifteenth century but ignored later. Since criminality and the goals of prosecution had not yet changed, the 1415 statutes continued to be suitable.

However, the traditional nature of early fifteenth-century law, the criminal justice system, and crime did not mean that this period was retrogressive in these areas. The early fifteenth century marked the furthest development and refinement of inquisition procedure before this relatively sophisticated procedure was replaced by summary process, with its perfunctory assessment of evidence, minimal safeguards to the defendant, and complete arbitrariness of the fullest discretion of the deciding body. The late fifteenth century was retrogressive in political philosophy and jurisprudence. The dampening of the republican spirit, as occurred in successive stages from 1434 on, contributed to retrogression in these areas. The early fifteenth century was the culmination period for law. The fortuitous combination of the territorial state (including its increased ability to compile evidence, protect witnesses, and apprehend criminals) with the relative refinement of inquisition procedure, especially in the area of examining witnesses, led to some success in ensuring justice. However, the heavy reliance on torture and public fame witnesses revealed the shortcomings and limitations of the Florentine system.

I examined and analyzed 177 condemnations and absolutions from the court of the Podestà.[1] A sample of cases from the court of one of the foreign rectors should be fairly representative of criminality, since the jurisdiction over very few kinds of cases had been removed from these courts and sent to other courts, and the criminal responsibilities of the rectors were becoming more similar. The Onestà had claimed jurisdiction over prostitutes and the Tower Officials over weights and measures. The Ufficiali di Notte, formed sometime in the first half of the fifteenth century to try cases of sodomy, was apparently not operative by 1428, since sodomy cases appeared in the courts of the foreign rectors. The Otto had not yet taken away any cases from the courts of the foreign rectors, much less co-opted the criminal court system. Although each foreign rector had areas of specialization, as public initiation and police apprehension became more common, the rector who gathered the information or whose retinue interrupted the crime became the proper rector to try the case, despite jurisdictional lines. Still, since I limited my survey to the Podestà's court, I would not expect to find cases of syndication against officials or cases brought for or against prisoners, both of which were areas of specialization of the Executor. A greater number of debt cases may have appeared in the court of the Podestà than in the other courts.

Even though cases of prostitution and weights and measures were removed from the courts of the foreign rectors, these courts remained vigorous in the early fifteenth century. Because of new powers of *arbitrium* and an enhanced role of public officials in combating crime, the rectors were becoming more powerful. The Signoria and the Otto deferred to the first-instance criminal jurisdiction of the foreign rectors.

I chose to examine the years 1425–28 because of their temporal proximity to the return of the Medici in 1434 and because the documents were fairly complete and in good condition. In analyzing the cases, I paid special attention to those facets of crime that shed light on the development of inquisition procedure and the territorial state. The characteristics of some kinds of crime, such as debt, assault, and theft, illuminate the relationships between different classes. Trials of political crimes demonstrate the characteristics of prevalent political crime and attitudes of the state in prosecuting political crime. Both debt and political crimes provide some indices of the advancement of the takeover of the state by the patriciate or some patrician faction. Throughout this chapter, I compare the statistical analysis derived here for the years 1425–28 to two other analyses, one provided by Dorini and the other by Cohn. Dorini has analyzed two fourteenth-century case samples, one from 1352–55 and another from 1380–83. Cohn has analyzed case samples from three periods, 1344–45, 1374–75, and 1455–66.[2] By comparing data from the early fifteenth century with data from all of the above periods, I can draw some conclusions concerning the profile of criminality for an extended period.

Philosophies of Prosecution and Profiles of Criminality

A statistical analysis of the cases from 1425–28 shows an advanced stage of development of inquisition procedure. Cases initiated through inquisition outnumbered cases initiated through private accusation even more than they did in the two fourteenth-century periods studied by Dorini.[3] The higher rate of conviction for inquisition-initiated cases than for accusation-initiated cases demonstrates the increasing effectiveness of inquisition procedure. The reduction in the contumaciousness rate points to greater effectiveness in the reporting and interrupting of crime, an important part in making inquisition procedure function properly.

Trials could be initiated several different ways, but all of them fall into one of two groups: private and public. There were three methods of public initiation: denunciation by a rector or syndic from the county or district, public fame, and *ex officio*. All three had existed since the rebirth of the concept of public crime. The only kind of private initiation was private accusation, and sometimes the right to accuse was restricted to close kin.

Table 1 shows the percentage of cases initiated by each method compared to the total number of cases. The effectiveness of each kind of initiation is measured by the conviction rate for each and appears in Table 2.

Table 1 demonstrates that the number of cases initiated by some form of public initiation greatly predominated over the number of cases initiated by private accusation, 71.8 percent to 28.2 percent. Dorini has noted that public initiation was in the process of supplanting accusation throughout the fourteenth century.[4] While in the 1352–55 period, 545/1057, or half of all condemnations, were initiated by accusation, between 1380 and 1383, 223/793, or one-third of all condemnations, were initiated by accusation. Table 1 indicates that the number of private accusations compared to the total decreased again in the early fifteenth century, falling to just over one-fourth. The continued strengthening of the efforts of the judicial system to bring cases to trial even as late as 1428, that is, its efforts to enforce law and order, rest by necessity on a strong, effective judicial system and a strong, effective state. On a theoretical level, public initiation was gaining ground because the concept of crime as a public matter was growing stronger. Consequently, on a practical level, public initiation was permitted by statute to be used in an increasing number of crimes because more private crimes came to be considered public matters, allowing the intrusion of public officials into more areas of crime. Here, the dialogue between the statutes and the cases was the pivotal point in the introduction of change. Potential accusers, on the other hand, allowed the state to prosecute their cases because of the effectiveness of state prosecution and the diminished personal risk. While it is impossible to determine whether statute influenced practice, or practice statute, both are

Table 1. Case Initiations

Case Initiations	Initiation/Total	% of Total
Public		
Public fame	68/177	38.4
Denunciation of a rector	31/177	17.5
Inquisition *ex officio*	28/177	15.8
Private		
Private accusation	50/177	28.2

Table 2. Conviction Rates

Case Initiation	Convictions/Cases Judged	Conviction Rate (%)
Public		
Public fame	55/68	80.9
Denunciation by a rector	17/31	54.8
Inquisition *ex officio*	13/28	46.4
Private		
Private accusation	33/50	66.0
Private accusation without debt defaulting cases	13/30	43.0

likely. The close dialogue between statute and practice validates the statutes and indicates their current use.

In the 1425–28 period, not only was public initiation becoming numerically preponderant over accusation, it was proving to be more effective. Table 2 presents the conviction rates for all four kinds of initiations. When the figures are at first considered, public initiation does not seem to be an improvement over accusation. If the conviction rate for the three kinds of public initiations taken together, 85/127, or 66.9 percent, is compared to the conviction rate for accusation, 33/50, or 66 percent, not much difference appears between the two. However, these figures mask real effectiveness. When it is considered that of the 33 cases initiated by private accusation and resulting in convictions, 20 of them were cases of defaulting and fleeing debt that had a 95 percent conviction rate, the effectiveness of accusation appears to have been quite different. Defaulting and fleeing debt cases were always initiated by creditors and almost always ended in conviction because the defendant had fled and was contumacious. These cases had almost always been tried in another court where debt had already been proven. That all of these defendants were convicted because contumacious does not prove the effectiveness of private accusation. Without these cases, the conviction rate for private accusation was 13/30, or 43 percent, far different from 66 percent.

According to Dorini, publicly initiated cases had a better rate of conviction than accusation-initiated cases in the fourteenth century. Unfortunately, it is impossible to compare the effectiveness of public initiation in the two centuries because Dorini attempts to prove his thesis by selecting two crimes that were predominantly accuser-initiated in the fourteenth century and tabulating the conviction rates for these crimes: simple theft at 50 percent and verbal injury at 30 percent. Dorini does not generate any conviction rates for public and private accusation with which to compare the 1425–28 conviction rates. The success of public initiation must also be measured against the degree to which public initiation had to overcome traditional feelings of honor and private rights to vengeance or prosecution, against which it was competing. It must also be considered that accusation was given every advantage over inquisition, since the state preferred to transfer the effort and expense of a case to the private sector, if possible. Even while the rectors were given power to initiate trials in more and more cases, private accusation was encouraged, especially as a supplemental source. The state would not initiate a case unless all logical accusers had been asked to accuse. Despite these counteracting factors, a conviction rate of 66.9 percent made inquisition an effective method in combating crime.

Another index of effectiveness is the rate at which reluctant witnesses were prosecuted, an index for which Dorini provides fourteenth-century evidence. The dramatic slowdown in the rate of reluctant witnesses demonstrates that the effectiveness of the court system was improving through its extension of better protection to witnesses. Witnesses did not appear in court when they feared the court would not adequately protect them against the opposing party. While Dorini records 140 condemnations for reluctant witnesses between 1352 and 1355 for all three courts, by 1380–83, this figure was reduced to approximately 47 cases.[5] In the records of the single court investigated here for 1425–28, only one instance of a reluctant witness is found.[6] Since the effectiveness of inquisition procedure rested on the ability of the courts to collect evidence independently, this demonstrated ability of the court system to compel witnesses also proves success, here an improvement over the fourteenth century.

Tables 1 and 2 show that of the kinds of initiations used to report crimes—accusation, denunciation, public fame, and *ex officio*—public fame was both the prevalent form of initiation and had the highest conviction rate. Public fame initiation was the most successful because the initiation itself provided the proof—that is, the public fame witnesses that were required to initiate a case counted as part of the number of witnesses required to convict the defendant, or may have even been the same number, although usually fewer witnesses were required to initiate and sufficient proof could be attained by combining public fame witnesses with other forms of proof. Proof exacted under torture was frequently used to support public fame proof. For some crimes, the number of public fame witnesses required to convict was specifically regulated by statute. For other crimes for which public initiation was permitted but no number of public fame witnesses was mentioned, the number of witnesses required to initiate an inquisition and to convict the defendant was probably four.[7] It is of great significance that public fame witnesses alone could be sufficient to convict. If, however, public fame accusations also provided the proof, it would seem that public fame initiation would have a 100 percent conviction rate instead of a 80.9 percent conviction rate. When the cases are examined, almost all the public fame cases that did not end in convictions stressed that the defendant had provided proof in his defense, either through witnesses or through documents.[8] Witnesses were a means of defense in all kinds of cases. In cases of officials, successful defenses against public fame inquisitions could rely on the records of the office.[9] Therefore, in public fame-initiated cases, successful conviction was likely, since the accusing witnesses also supplied the proof, unless the defendant denied in court and supplied supporting evidence.

Public fame initiations were entirely different from *tamburazioni* (secret accusations). Tamburazioni were notes containing accusations which were placed in a tamburo box, which was located near the office of an official, usually the Executor. The accusations were anonymous but suggested witnesses who could prove the allegations. If the rectors could find enough proof to form a case, they did so; but lacking proof, the case was not required to be pursued. Before 1434, very few tamburazioni collected by the Executor ever resulted in proceedings.[10] The accusers in public fame initiations were always identified. They did not claim to have any direct knowledge of the case, testifying only to what they knew to be rumors in Florence.

Despite the evident shortcomings of public fame inquisition, having people testify to rumors, it did represent an independent avenue of investigation. Public fame accounts could be recorded at the bench from those reporting information, or statements could be gathered from public fame accusers at the scene of the crime. Berrovarii must have interviewed people in the vicinity of the crime, compelling those with any information to appear in court. These witnesses must have known enough about the crime to supply the court with the name of a suspect but not enough to act as real witnesses. Enough concordance in these statements led to the initiation of a proceeding. The great drawback to this kind of testimony was that no one was really responsible for his or her statements. In public fame cases, the witnesses were not required to reveal their sources of information.

Inquisitions initiated *ex officio* had the lowest conviction rate of all. These were cases in which the victim did not want to accuse or was not sure enough of his case to do so, and in which a sufficient number of public fame witnesses were not forthcoming. The court system had enough evidence to determine that a crime had been committed and to name a suspect. While *ex officio* cases included some strong cases, such as those in which the berrovarii had interrupted crimes *in flagranti*, they also encompassed those in which evidence was lacking. The kinds of cases that are found to have been initiated *ex officio* are rather surprising. They were exactly the same kinds that Cohn states were missing from the courts between 1455 and 1466, reinforcing the conclusion that the court system of the early fifteenth century was more aligned with the court system of the period that preceded it than with that of the period that followed it. In other words, the kinds of cases that the early fifteenth-century court system wanted to prosecute and prosecuted on its own despite obstacles were the same kinds of crimes ignored by the mid- and late fifteenth-century courts.

One common kind of case initiated *ex officio* in the early fifteenth century was assault involving friends, neighbors, or relatives, in which the victim was not willing to accuse. Some of these cases even involved mutual assaults, and both participants were criminally charged. Cohn asserts that these cases were not prosecuted in the mid- and late Quattrocento. Because of changes in settlement patterns which concentrated the poor in ghettos by the late fifteenth century, crimes that affected ghetto dwellers and no one else, such as assaults among the poor, were not prosecuted.[11] The courts had become reserved for cases that advanced the interests of the rich and powerful.[12]

In the early fifteenth century, the opposite circumstance occurred. Public initiation had reached its furthest extension. The concept of crime as an offense against the public rather than as simply a private matter was dominant. Inquisition brought crimes that had formerly been considered private matters to court for the first time. The 1322–25 statutes paid much more attention to instruments of peace and their benefit to the defendant than did the statutes of 1415, although instruments of peace remained an important resolution. The history of the litigation of the kind of cases that Cohn describes can be traced back to the thirteenth century, when the court system was little interested in deliberating over assaults and insults between friends, neighbors, and relatives. If the offended party agreed to a peace, court proceedings were halted. By the early fifteenth century, the attitude of the courts—the philosophy of prosecution—had come full circle concerning the prosecution of assaults between *propinqui*. Although the court system may not have been as successful in forcing information from unwilling victims and witnesses as it was in obtaining information in other cases, it prosecuted assaults between *propinqui* in the early fifteenth century. The success of the territorial state promoted an environment in which the state was able to foster public order and promise protection to its citizens. In the mid- and late fifteenth century, when the government began to bestow its benefits mainly on the members of the patriciate, the government no longer promised protection to all classes or was interested in affording this protection.

When the cases initiated *ex officio* are examined, assault cases are very prominent. Nineteen out of 28 *ex officio* cases, or 67.9 percent, were assault cases. Some cases stated that the victim and other suitable accusers refused to accuse.[13] Many of the cases involved people who were obviously friends or had some other bond of affinity,[14] and many involved victims and assailants of like social class, usually the lower class.[15] Assaults were traditionally cases in which the victims and assailants were of the same social class. The cases in which the victim or suitable accusers failed to accuse were bound to have a low conviction rate. The conviction rate for the assault cases in the 1425–28 sample was 36.8 percent, very low. Another class of *ex officio* cases of the same character were crimes similar to assault, in which the victim also did not want to accuse: threatening and slander. These represent 3/28, or 10.7 percent of *ex officio* cases. Taken together with assault, these 3 crimes comprise 22 out of 28 cases, or 78.5 percent of all *ex officio* cases. Other crimes initiated *ex officio* were crimes interrupted by berrovarii: bearing prohibited arms, going out past curfew, and gambling. There were 3 cases of this kind. When one reflects on how frequently these crimes were mentioned in the statutes, these 3 cases out of 177 total represent a very small part of the crimes being prosecuted. The statutes mention these crimes so frequently because the power to prosecute them became synonymous with the power and duty to conduct regular police investigations and present these authoritatively in court. All 3 cases resulted in convictions.

The cases that came to the court of the Podestà through denunciation by a rector of the county and district were cases of crimes perpetrated in the county and district in places in which no official in this location in

Philosophies of Prosecution and Profiles of Criminality

the county and district had a high enough jurisdiction to try the cases. The local rector, variously known as the consul or syndic, the head of the popolo, had responsibility for the division of the *estimo* and the division of the repairs of streets and bridges, besides his judicial duties. All of the members of the popoli were responsible for reporting crimes and helping to apprehend criminals and were collectively liable for fines for not doing so. The rector gathered information from members of the popoli and denounced to the local podestà, if there was one superior to the rector, or to the Podestà in Florence, if not. The Podestà drew up the inquisition, cited the witnesses, and conducted the case. It is likely that much of the information came from the local rector, since the members of the popolo were held so strictly responsible for reporting to the rector what they knew concerning crimes and the whereabouts of banned people in the contado and district. Since these cases were reported by a locally elected official, the selection of cases for prosecution was not biased by oligarchical influence.

Of the total of 177 cases, only 2 were initiated by bullectini. These cases are categorized as *ex officio*-initiated cases because the rectors formed the inquisitions after receiving the bullectini. There was no large influx of cases coming from the executive or any of its agencies. No bullectini originated with the Otto, but since the Otto and the Dieci di Guerra were nearly identical at that time, the one case that originated with the Dieci may be presumed to have been interchangeably from the Otto. The Otto had greater judicial responsibilities than the Dieci. In the case from the Dieci, the custodian of a castle, while possessing a great deal of Florentine money given him for supplies, defected to the Duke of Milan, surrendering his castle and all of the money. The defendant was a foreign stipendiarius under contract to the Dieci di Guerra.[16] The other bullectino was sent by the Priors. In this case, four members of upper-class houses—two Tornaquinci, one Billiotti, and one Bardi—were condemned for treason. Their treasonous activity consisted of defaulting on their taxes for over four years. All four were convicted and sentenced to capital punishment.[17] This sounds very serious and smacks of factional conflict, but, in fact, this kind of case was part of a game played by the government in a desperate attempt to increase tax revenues. At the first sign of any willingness to pay or leave a deposit, the case would be completely dismissed. No one was ever decapitated for tax defaulting.[18] Neither the case against the foreign stipendiarius nor the case against the tax defaulters that was destined to be dropped had any political content despite their origin in executive bullectini.

Despite the evolution toward a public concept of crime, the judicial system continued to seek help from the private sector. Private accusation

Table 3. Responses of the Defendants

Response	Response/Total	% of Total
Contumaciousness	75/177	42.4
Negation	64/177	36.1
Confession	38/177	21.5

was the method preferred by the court system, since it was useful to have the accuser gather the evidence. The victim and his relatives were always asked to accuse before the court system would begin a publicly initiated case. The court system demonstrated the same attitude when it continued to allow vendetta against the principal offender and when it continued to rely heavily on banning criminals who then could be offended with impunity.

Table 3 demonstrates the responses of defendants and ranks them numerically. Among the three possible responses, both contumaciousness and confession led to automatic conviction. Unlike our judicial system, when a defendant was contumacious from court, the trial was conducted in his absence and a guilty charge was issued. Confession also warranted a guilty charge, but many confessions were elicited under torture.

The predominant response to criminal charges in the early fifteenth century was contumaciousness. While this seems to speak ill for the effectiveness of the courts and the police system, the early fifteenth century contumaciousness rate was a vast improvement over what went before. In any system where torture was used as a means of exacting information from the defendant, the contumaciousness level can be expected to be very high. Innocent as well as guilty can be expected to flee from such a trial procedure. Dorini notes some improvement in the contumaciousness level between his two sample periods for the fourteenth century, citing a contumaciousness level of 920/1578, or 58.3 percent for 1352–55, and a level of 663/1192, or 55.6 percent for the years 1380–83.[19] Therefore, for the sample years in the early fifteenth century, a contumaciousness rate of 75/177, or 42.4 percent, records a sizable reduction in this response. The reduction can be attributed to a more effective police force. Presumably, the more serious the charge, the greater the contumaciousness rate.

Besides contumaciousness, a large number of convictions, 21.5 percent, were reached through the confession of the defendant. Courts in Florence, or in any premodern system, preferred to exact confessions from defendants because confessions were thought to be a definite kind of proof, relieving the judge of the responsibility of making a conviction based on the assessment of evidence. Sometimes confessions could be of benefit to the defendant, prompting a reduction of the penalty (*Stat.* 3.2). However, although confessions were sometimes motivated by the prospect of a reduced penalty, usually confessions were exacted under torture. Torture was a basic part of inquisition procedure used when cases lacked decisive evidence. In a system that relied more and more on the state's gathering evidence and less and less on the accuser's furnishing all the evidence, torture, like public fame, became more important.

When the confessions are examined to determine how many were exacted under torture, it is difficult to know in which cases torture was used. The cases never state that torture was used, since confessions given at the site of the torture were not admissible in court. Only confessions that were reaffirmed at the bench were admissible as evidence (*Stat.* 1.61). In either case, whether the confession was given spontaneously at the bench or whether it was exacted under torture and then reaffirmed at the bench, the acts read that the confession was *sponte facta*, made spontaneously. Therefore, from the wording of the cases, no difference is apparent, since all of the acts read that the confessions were *sponte facta*. However, one can usually tell from the crime being tried whether torture would have been applied or not. There were a limited number of crimes in the trial of which the judge and rector were allowed to torture the defendant to attain additional information or a confession. In the cases of many of these crimes, torture had to be preceded by *inditia*, other evidence, although these safeguards were not necessary in all cases.

The basic crimes, enumerated in the general rubric on torture, for which torture could be employed were robbery by a habitual thief, robbery at night, falsification, fraud, arson, devastation at night (usually destroying crops at night), kidnapping, transmitting letters to the enemy, and homicide. In all these cases, inditia had to precede (*Stat.* 3.110). Torture was allowed in kidnapping cases in order to get information leading to the whereabouts of the victim. However, there were many other crimes, named in the specific rubrics describing crimes, in the trials of which torture was permitted without inditia. Torture could be administered to sodomy suspects at the discretion of the rector, even without inditia preceding (*Stat.* 3.115). In cases of harming a foreign rector or his goods, torture could be administered with no preceding inditia (*Stat.* 3.101). In cases of defaulting and fleeing debt, the rectors could order whatever kind of torture they liked, however much they liked, in investigating suspected defaulters who had been detained in the fort and against whom there was some amount of proof, such as the books of their creditors.[20] The usual reaffirmation of the creditors' books came from the contumaciousness of the defendant. Crimes of stipendiarii could apparently be investigated through torture, since the Vicar of Valdarno Inferiore and S. Miniato, the Vicar of Valdinievole, and the Vicar of Anghiari were allowed to use torture, and their jurisdiction was exclusively over stipendiarii.[21] The foreign rectors could torture at their discretion in cases of people exporting foodstuffs from Florence.[22] Torture could be used against gamblers to ascertain the names of those hosting the games.[23] The Executor could torture with only one piece of public fame evidence preceding in cases in which members of corporations of the guilds set prices or formed monopolies (*Stat.* 3.87). Those who were suspected of invading monasteries and nunneries and raping nuns could be tortured (*Stat.* 3.53). Those who clipped or falsified money could be tortured without preceding information (*Stat.* 3.130). The rectors could employ torture to investigate cases of escaped slaves (*Stat.* 3.186). In cases of seditious activity in the city, county, district of Florence, or even outside the district, torture could be applied in whatever manner seemed suitable to the rectors (*Stat.* 3.66). People suspected of being involved in any kind of conspiracy would be put to torture without preceding inditia (*Stat.* 3.61). These were the cases in which torture was allowed by statute.

When attention is turned to the cases in which the defendant confessed, the cases of confessions to serious crimes mirror the cases in which torture was permitted by statute. Again, statute is seen to be strictly followed in the cases, the dialogue between the two being important for the validation of the statutes. Since the statutes specified the instances in which torture could be applied, the cases in which the defendant responded with a confession because of torture can definitely be determined. The cases can be divided into those in which torture was applied and those in which confessions were truly given spontaneously. Of these confessions, 25 out of 38, or 65.8 percent, were prompted by torture. While ascertaining convictions through torture does not particularly inspire confidence in the criminal law system, it should be remembered that each of these supposed culprits was apprehended by the police forces of the central government. Each of these suspects would have undoubtedly preferred to be contumacious had they not been apprehended. When the character of these torture-induced confession cases is examined, robbery on the streets, or robbery by a professional and habitual thief, stands out as the major crime treated in this manner. In these cases, the culprit was reputed to have committed many thefts, often in other cities. Condemnations for theft and sentences of banning may already have been handed out in these other cities. Through improved methods of investigation, the Florentine police had located and apprehended these wanted criminals. Cases of sedition and rebellion formed another large group of torture-induced confession cases. In all of the torture-induced confession cases, the penalty was very high, often capital punishment. No one would confess to these crimes unless tortured. When we look at all convictions, 25/118 or 21.2 percent were motivated by confessions exacted under torture.

In the other 34.2 percent of confession cases, those not induced by torture, confessions were usually motivated by certainty of conviction or the petty nature of the crime. Confessions occurred in cases in which the criminal was caught *in flagranti*.[24] Petty crimes with light penalties, such as petty theft and insult, prompted confessions, especially considering that reduced penalties were given when confessions were spontaneous. In one interesting case, the defendant confessed without being subjected to torture because he possessed proof of mitigating circumstances that warranted a reduction in the penalty.[25] Those who came to court to defend themselves usually escaped conviction: 91.9 percent of the time, those who presented a defense of witnesses or documents were able to triumph over their accusers, even if these accusers were the state officials. In inquisition procedure, the contested litigation part of the trial was sophisticated: testimony was freely admitted for both defense and prosecution. Denials ran the gamut of all crimes.

In order to draw a profile of criminality, the prevalent crimes from the court of the Podestà from 1425 to 1428 must be determined and examined. Table 4 enumerates the prevalent crimes, tells what percentage of the total crime each represented, and gives the conviction rate for each crime. The remainder of this chapter is organized around discussions of each of the prevalent crimes and what they reveal about early fifteenth-century society, political environment, and philosophies of prosecution.

The most prevalent crime in the early fifteenth century was assault. Table 4 demonstrates that thefts were only half as frequent as assaults in the early fifteenth century. For 1352–55, Dorini finds that there were 229 assaults per 100,000 as compared to 150 thefts per 100,000, or 65.5 percent as many thefts as assaults, and for the period 1380–83, there were 154 assaults per 100,000 as compared to 40 thefts per 100,000, or 25.9 percent as many thefts as assaults.[26] Thus, for all of the fourteenth century and the early fifteenth century, crimes against persons greatly predominated over crimes against property. In the periods examined by Dorini, one-fourth to one-third of all crimes were assaults. In the sample presented here for 1425–28, 30 percent of all crime, or nearly one-third, were assaults.

In the world of Renaissance crime, people assaulted friends, neighbors, and relatives but stole from people to whom they were not related. Cohn proves the first proposition and Dorini the second. In Cohn's Trecento samples, assaults nearly always involved litigants of similar social status, 84 percent of the time in 1344–45, and 91 percent of the time in 1374–75.[27]

Table 4. Composition of Criminality

Crime	Crime to Total	% of Total	Convictions/ Judged	Conviction Rate (%)
Assault	53/177	30.0	30/53	56.6
Theft	27/177	15.2	16/27	59.2
Debt defaulting and fleeing	22/177	12.4	21/22	95.5
Political crimes	18/177	10.2	14/18	77.8
Crimes by officials	10/177	5.6	4/10	40.0
Homicide	9/177	5.1	9/9	100.0
Breaking tenant pacts	3/177	1.7	2/3	66.7
Crimes against good morals	6/177	3.4	4/6	66.7

In the majority of Dorini's samples, people were robbed by absolute strangers.[28]

In all of Cohn's and Dorini's samples from the fourteenth century and in the sample presented here for 1425–28, crimes against persons predominated over crimes against property. However, in Cohn's sample from 1455–66, the opposite appears to be true: crimes against property predominated over crimes against persons. In Cohn's statistics, assaults made up 39 percent of all crime in 1344–45 and in 1374–75, fell precipitously to 18 percent in 1455–66. This also shows a change from the prevalence of crimes involving litigants of like social class to the prevalence of crimes involving litigants of unlike social class. Crime in the mid- to late fifteenth century demonstrated greater class conflict than crime in the fourteenth and early fifteenth centuries. Assault prosecutions declined while prosecutions of interclass crimes increased.

Cohn believes that the courts of the mid-Quattrocento were used by the patriciate to further their own private ends, collect their debts, and punish their contadini. Many cases of theft, debt, rural trespass, poaching, and neglecting to work the land were found in his sample.[29] However, the defaulting and fleeing debt cases that he uses to support his thesis of class conflict are not suggestive of class conflict, since these cases exclusively involved merchants. But for assaults, Cohn shows that in cases between parties of unequal social status, in the fourteenth century, lower-class accusers more frequently prosecuted members of the upper class; whereas in the mid-Quattrocento, upper-class accusers more frequently prosecuted members of the popolo minuto or contadini. The prominence of theft during this period was a sign of atomized class conflict. Because collective forms of political dissidence, like the Ciompi revolt, were suppressed, class conflict surfaced in an unorganized form.[30]

When the 1425–28 sample is assessed considering the characterization of criminality for the period that preceded it and the period that followed, it is clear that crime in the early fifteenth century was more similar to crime in the fourteenth century than it was to crime in the mid-fifteenth century. In this sample, assault clearly predominated over theft and over other interclass crimes such as those involving tenancy. The change from the prevalence of intraclass crimes to the prevalence of interclass crimes had not yet occurred. The courts were not instruments by which the rich furthered their private interests and oppressed the poor.

The early fifteenth-century information on a crime related to assault—homicide—shows homicide to represent 5.1 percent of total crime. This is consistent with all of Cohn's samples but not with Dorini's. In both of Dorini's periods, 15 percent of all crimes were homicides. Cohn posits that the relationship between the rate of homicides committed and the rate of assaults committed is always the same because homicides are just assaults in which the victim happens to die. Therefore, when the proportion of homicides reported to assaults reported changes in a way that homicide represents a high proportion of assaults, he concludes that some assaults were not being prosecuted by the courts. In the late fifteenth century, assaults between members of the popolo minuto were selectively ignored because the court system was only interested in prosecuting cases that benefited the rich and powerful. The selective ignoring of popolo minuto assaults was possible because of changes in the residential pattern of the popolo minuto which took place after 1383 but before the late Quattrocento. While the popolo minuto were distributed citywide in the Trecento, by the late Quattrocento 80 percent of the poor lived in ghettos on the city's periphery.[31] Residential segregation made ignoring popolo minuto crime easier. Cohn demonstrates that residential patterns remained the same until at least 1383 but had changed by the late Quattrocento. Until the eve of the period studied here, residential patterns remained traditional. Cohn records the proportion of homicides to assaults to be 3.7 percent for 1344–45; 9.9 percent for 1374–75; but soaring to 34 percent for 1455–66.[32] The 1425–28 sample shows the proportion of homicides to assaults to be 9/53 or 16 percent. However, Dorini's samples show a much higher proportion even than Cohn's fifteenth-century sample; 47 percent for 1352–55 and 38 percent for 1380–83.[33] While Dorini's homicide rates seem unrealistically high, he is operating with by far the largest samples, and so there is no room for casting aspersions on his results. Since the periods he studies are not known to be the periods in which the social gulf between rich and poor was the widest among all the periods being compared, Cohn's thesis concerning the meaning of the ratio between homicide and assault is not borne out by the evidence. However, Cohn's general conclusions concerning residential patterns and philosophies of prosecution are not damaged much by the elimination of this thesis.

For 1425–28, assaults and homicides had very different conviction rates: 56.6 percent for assault and 100 percent for homicide. The high conviction rate for homicide can be accounted for by the clear-cut nature of the evidence but not by any greater willingness on the part of the relatives of the victim to accuse. Only 9.4 percent of assault cases were initiated by the victim or his relatives, the remaining 90.6 percent being initiated through some form of public initiation. Only 1 out of 9 homicide cases, or 11 percent, was initiated by a relative of the victim, the remaining 89 percent being initiated by public means. Public initiation was making great inroads even into cases of a traditionally private nature. Sixty-seven percent of all *ex officio*–initiated cases (19/28) were assaults. These cases had a very low conviction rate, 7 out of 19, or 36.8 percent, because no accuser stepped forward and victims and witnesses gave information unwillingly. These were the cases of assaults between friends, neighbors, and relatives that those involved never wanted to see prosecuted. Unlike the mid- to late Quattrocento sample, assaults between lower-class litigants were frequently prosecuted.[34] Not only were these cases prosecuted, they were mainly initiated *ex officio*. Even mutual fighting was prosecuted *ex officio*.[35]

After assault, theft was the next most prevalent crime. According to Dorini, theft was interclass and was commonly perpetrated by women and foreigners, as well as by other classes of culprits. Theft committed by *robbatores stratorum* (professional thieves) was a common kind of theft which was dealt with particularly harshly by the criminal system. The information contained in the acts that pertains to these cases has a strange character, different from the character of information in other cases.[36] Bits and pieces of information concerning innumerable instances of theft are strung together, perhaps without the name of the victim, or the location of the crime, or the worth of the goods. These theft cases provide the best picture of the quality of hearsay information. The list of crimes enumerated in the acts is a composite of information gathered from the public fame accusers and the culprit himself during torture. The incidents of theft known in a hearsay fashion to the public fame accusers were used to form the capitula of the inquisition, to which the witnesses and the defendant were asked to respond, capitulum by capitulum. All eight of the cases of *robbatores stratorum* were initiated by public fame accusation. The defendant, as he was tortured and questioned concerning the *articula*, supplied additional information. Seven of the 8 defendants were convicted through confessions that were very likely to have been exacted under torture, since robbery on the streets was a case in which torture was allowed; the other was convicted through contumaciousness. The *robbatores stratorum* were the true dregs of society: vagabonds, servants, wandering children, and foreigners. All of the convicted received either capital punishment or corporal punishment followed by a prison term, except in the case of a minor whose age mitigated his penalty. It is easy to imagine that with each city in Italy having many criminals who were either contumacious or banned, a great number of criminals already convicted in various cities were wandering about the peninsula.

In the 1425–28 sample presented here, theft represents 15.3 percent of all crime. This is roughly the same figure that Dorini reaches for his two fourteenth-century samples, showing, again, the traditional quality of the profile of criminality of the early fifteenth century.[37] The incidence of assault and the incidence of theft stayed roughly the same throughout the fourteenth century and into the early fifteenth century, interclass crime not yet having made inroads into the predominance of intraclass crime.

The communal courts handled many debt cases in the early fifteenth century, signifying either that the patriciate used the court system to extort payments from the debt-ridden popolo minuto or that the communal courts had seized jurisdiction over all important debt cases. Debt is of interest if we wish to gain insight into society. The acts detailing other crimes, too, such as breaking tenant pacts, poaching, entering into possession, and disturbing possession, indicate the relationship between the patriciate and the popolo minuto.

Of the crimes that yield information concerning the relationship between the upper and lower classes, debt was far and away the most important. The debt cases that the court of the Podestà prosecuted from 1425 to 1428 were all cases of defaulting and fleeing debt. The very high conviction rate of 95.5 percent can be attributed to the fact that the defendants had defaulted and fled and were, therefore, guilty through contumaciousness. Of the 21 defendants convicted, 20 were contumacious and 1 confessed. Defaulting and fleeing cases involved sums of 100 lire or more. Of the 22 debt cases, 21 were litigations involving amounts over 100 lire just as the statutes specified, and many involved much larger amounts. In the one case involving an amount under 100 lire, the debtor was a member of the Bardi family.[38] The size of these debts indicates that they could rarely have been sums owed by members of the popolo minuto and were usually debts between merchants. Of the 22 debt cases, all of which were cases of defaulting and fleeing debt, only 2 involved artisans and merchants from the lower guilds.[39] One of these cases was a landlord-tenant dispute. In all the other cases, the defendant was either a merchant from one of the major guilds or a relative or business partner of the accuser and creditor.[40] None of these cases, therefore, demonstrates class conflict or the patriciate's use of the court system to oppress debtors.

Many of these defaulting and fleeing debt cases had already been tried as simple debt cases in other courts. This topic has been discussed extensively in Chapter 4. By the early fifteenth century, the centralization of the communal court system and the diminution of other competitive corporate bodies allowed the commune to transfer some important kinds of cases, such as defaulting and fleeing debt, into the exclusive jurisdiction of its courts. By this means, the courts of the foreign rectors seized all important debt cases and reviewed the decisions of the lesser courts before executing their sentences. That cases were transferred to the communal courts from the guild courts does not signify that the major guildsmen used the communal courts to exact their debts from the popolo minuto. In 10 out of the 22 debt cases, the cases had first been tried as simple debt in another court, either a guild court or the court of the Mercanzia. Debt cases seem frequently to have been tried in the defendant's guild, since the creditor was trying to force that guild to hold its member responsible, so were less susceptible to oppression.[41] Debt cases, too, were frequently tried in legally binding private arbitrations in which the parties chose the arbitrators. Once a public instrument concerning the decision was drawn up, the arbitration was as binding as a decision from another court. Unfortunately, there is no opportunity to tell whether the courts of the foreign rectors frequently overturned the decisions of the guild courts, the Mercanzia court, or the arbitrators, since 20 out of 22 defendants were contumacious and automatically convicted. All of the debt cases were initiated by the private accusation of the creditor or his heirs.

Only 3 cases of tenants having broken pacts were prosecuted in the Podestà's court from 1425 to 1428, 1.7 percent of all crime. This was a low percentage, considering that war disrupted agricultural activities and put pressure on the agricultural class to produce food for troops. In this era, in which the plague had devastated the population, agricultural laborers were a scarce commodity. The agricultural laws attempted to keep agricultural workers cultivating the land under the same conditions as previously. In one of these cases of breaking tenant agreements, the agricultural worker had gone to work for someone else.[42] In another case, the agricultural laborer, accused by the land owner, was acquitted.[43]

While in cases of breaking agricultural pacts one expects to see the rich prosecuting the poor, in cases of entering property of another, destruction of property, and not quitting property one expects to see the poor prosecuting the rich. Dorini states that in the fourteenth century, disturbing or entering possession was a crime frequently perpetrated by the powerful against the weak or by one faction of the powerful against its adversaries. In Dorini's samples, almost all of these cases ended in absolutions, because witnesses, even public fame witnesses, were reluctant because they feared the powerful. Villages became collectively responsible for destruction of property if a culprit was not found and convicted, because they had failed to come forward to accuse and condemn. In these crimes, in which fear prevented the injured party from accusing and the witnesses from testifying, the *arbitrium* to initiate the case *ex officio* was extended to the rectors, as was the right to use public fame proof to support an accusation made by the injured party.[44] The 1425–28 sample includes 6 cases of entering or disturbing property. Two of these cases were disagreements between farmers, 3 were disagreements between upper-class litigants, and 1 was a case of an upper-class person wresting a piece of property away from a member of the popolo minuto. In this last case, which exemplified aristocratic usurpation, the court decided in favor of the popolo minuto possessor.[45] Class conflict was not present to any significant degree in these cases either.

While disturbing possession was a common crime in Dorini's periods, in this respect the early fifteenth century proves to have differed from what went before. Because of greater clarification and systematization of legal titles to land and better law enforcement, usurpation was less tempting and less likely to be successful. Such lawlessness, especially perpetrated by magnates, ended around the turn of the fifteenth century.

Table 4 demonstrates that political crimes represented a good portion of total crime, 10.2 percent. When this percentage of total crime is compared with the percentage from other eras, political crimes from the early fifteenth century seem to have been of middling volume. Cohn gives no statistics for political crimes. For Dorini's two sample fourteenth-century periods, he records that political crime composed 4.5 percent of the total of those condemned in the 1352–55 period but had jumped to 18.6 percent of those condemned in the 1380–83 period.[46] The period after the Ciompi had an elevated rate of political trials because the government was changing hands, returning to a more upper-class orientation, in a reaction against the popolo minuto government that followed the Ciompi.

The statistics on political crime do not tell the whole story. The character of the cases needs to be examined in order to know the nature of political crime, since political crime was a relative matter. Most of the political crimes in the court of the Podestà between 1425 and 1428 pertained to conducting war against the Duke of Milan. They were not internal conspiracies or dissensions per se, although the attempted manipulation of external political affairs, such as helping a foreign enemy to take control of Florence, sometimes accompanied the activities of a faction agitating to gain power in Florence. Most of the cases of political crime involved the surrendering of castles and lands in the district to the Duke of Milan, helping him to capture these regions. The background of the defendant in these cases was an important variable. Some of these rebels and traitors were foreign stipendiarii who were in Florentine employment and had defected to the Duke of Milan, but whose defection made no statement concerning Florentine political unrest. Florentine subjects were also in the employment of Florence as stipendiarii. In the contado and district, where castles were being lost to the Duke of Milan, many Florentines were stationed as *castellani* and *commissarii*, which usually were upper-class offices. Also in the district were feudal magnates who were under Florentine dominion but switched sides when advantage dictated.

Fourteen out of 18 political cases were war-related, and 12 out of these 14 were convictions. Some of these convictions had only a remote relationship to Florentine factional conflicts. In some, foreign hired stipendiarii, usually leaders, were convicted of defecting to the Duke of Milan. Presumably money, not loyalty, was the deciding factor in these cases. One was a case initiated by bullectino from the Dieci. The Dieci would be the natural source of the accusation, since they had the best access to the information.[47] In other cases, the people condemned were Florentines from the city or contado who were employed as stipendiarii in armies that had defected or who had fought among the troops of the Duke of Milan.[48] In still other cases, Florentines who served as commissarii or as other officials in the contado and district had defected and surrendered their castles to the enemy.[49] These cases may really have been investigations of those who through incompetence or misfortune had lost the castles they were in charge of to the enemy. In 1425, for instance, there was a rash of nonaristocratic Florentine officials holding offices in the contado and district who lost their castles to the Duke of Milan, reputedly through inexperience and incompetence. These castellani were convicted of treason and sentenced to death *in absentia*.[50] In other cases, local inhabitants of newly captured places, such as Arezzo, rebelled. Remote Tuscan feudal lords who wanted to escape Florentine suzerainty took advantage of the proximity of the Duke's armies to defect.

Four out of 18 political crimes had only an indirect connection with Florence's wars; of these, 2 were acquittals. Of the 2 condemnations,

Philosophies of Prosecution and Profiles of Criminality

1 was a trivial case of insult to an official and the other was the case, already discussed, of the tax defaulters, sentenced to capital punishment, who would undoubtedly come to some fiscal compromise with the communal government. This case was sent to the court of the Podestà by bullectino from the Priors.[51] The Priors had the power to invoke whatever sanctions they liked against tax defaulters because the success of Florentine wars depended on the commune's capacity to pay mercenaries. The generation of taxes to meet war needs was the all-consuming problem of the early fifteenth century. The crushing and inequitable taxes of the early fifteenth century caused tax defaulting.[52] Although the Catasto of 1427 did not solve Florence's tax problems, it was unquestionably an attempt at efficiency and equitability of taxation. The Catasto, taking place as late as 1427, shows the great effort that continued to be made by the territorial state toward greater efficiency. One of the 2 acquittals was also of great interest. In this case, it was alleged that a crowd of members of the popolo minuto and of the patriciate attacked the berrovarii and familia of the Podestà when they tried to arrest a member of the Spini family for a debt owed to a member of the Peruzzi.[53] Considering the state of the Florentine economy, the shortage of money, and the vigor employed in debt collection, this case probably represents a whole genre of like cases.

Although there are cases that may have had factional connotations among this sample of political cases, no wholesale use of the court system to conduct factional warfare was present. As yet, no forum other than that of the foreign rectors had developed a criminal jurisdiction over political matters.

While in the first two decades of the early fifteenth century, conspiracies against the government, especially plots instigated by Florentine exiles, were common, by the 1420s conspiracies of this sort were infrequent. The political climate had changed, and those who had created political strife were anxious instead to reconcile themselves with the government. The Florentine government of the 1420s adopted a policy of treating political crime with moderation in order to foster civic unity. The Priors frequently canceled sentences of exile in the 1420s.[54] The class that constituted the councils was successfully expressing its opposition to policies promoted by the patriciate and policies that enhanced the power of the patriciate through voting down these measures in the councils.[55] This class was mollified by a fair adherence of the government to constitutional republican forms. Neither this class nor the popolo minuto was active in dissent. Crimes committed by the popolo minuto, such as conspiracy or assault on officials, were not apparent in the 1425–28 sample. There were no large-scale insurrections from the time of the Ciompi to the time of the Medici. Political crime in the 1420s mainly involved either rebellion of subjects in the territory, especially in areas near the communes, such as Pistoia, that attempted to withdraw from Florentine dominion, probably because of the crushing tax burdens; or tax defaulting, caused by the same problem.

Class conflict was not a predominant theme of the early fifteenth century. People of all classes were aware of the growth of factions and of the enormous personal power of certain individuals who frequently held office and always took part in the *pratiche* (informal meetings of the most powerful people in the government that influenced government policy). But during the early fifteenth century, the efforts of all citizens were consumed by the wars of defense and expansion, which forged an atmosphere of civic unity. The popolo minuto would not rebel when the enemy was at the gates. The low level of political dissension of the 1420s was not caused by successful suppression by police forces, such as the Otto di Guardia. If that were so, the evidence would look different. Cases of attempted political activity aborted by the Otto would appear in the records of the Podestà, sent by bullectini from the Otto and tried in the court of the Podestà.

The high conviction rate in the sample of political crimes, 77.8 percent, can be attributed to a high rate of contumaciousness. Many of the defendants had defected to or been captured by the Duke of Milan and were not easily retrievable for their trials. Dorini records much higher conviction rates for his two periods, 94 percent for 1352–55 and 94.8 percent for 1380–83.[56] The likelihood of biased prosecution probably increases with the increase in conviction rate. The crimes prosecuted at that time did not reflect political dissension or class conflict.

The 1425–28 sample indicates that only a small number of crimes were committed by officials and tried in the court of the Podestà. Crimes committed by officials were usually tried in syndication in the court of the Executor. Any of the rectors, however, were empowered to try officials in a regular court proceeding even before the end of the official's term of office, if the crime was serious or disqualified the official from holding office. The Executor's court predominated even in regular trials of officials. Although the Podestà's court may have tried only a small number of cases of crimes by officials, this is not an indication that few officials were tried or that few had committed crimes. Many more crimes of officials were tried by the Executor during syndication and by the Executor and the Captain in regular court trials.

The cases against officials recorded in the acts conform to statutory guidelines, showing that the statutes were used. All of the cases in the Podestà's court were either for serious crimes, usually extortion, or for ineligibility to hold office. Six out of 10 cases involved extortion, showing that extortion was often tried in a regular court procedure before syndication. Trials of citizen officials for extortion were specially assigned to regular trial in the court of a foreign rector (*Stat.* 3.75). Almost all of the officials tried in the Podestà's court from 1425 to 1428 were citizen officials, showing that the statutes were being followed here to the letter.

The conviction rate for crimes committed by officials was very low, 40 percent. Dorini attributes this same phenomenon, which he also notes in his samples, to attempts to maintain the dignity of the foreign officials, whose cases predominated in the syndication trials that he examines. Because syndication trials must not become a source of international conflict, crimes committed by foreign officials were punished privately to save face. The low conviction rate for the citizen officials cannot be accounted for in the same way. However, since there was such an aggressive policy toward collecting accusations and trying officials, it is unlikely that the courts were unduly lenient. An examination of the nature of the cases points to the visibility of officials: their position made them scapegoats for innumerable frustrations. A common kind of case ending in acquittal was one in which entire cadres of officials were accused of extortion and failure to perform the duties of office. People were inclined to become incensed at officials for inconveniences, legitimate expenditures, and any punitive action. The new invasion of the formerly private world of private crime by public officials caused resentment against officials. All accusations against officials seem to have been investigated, no matter how unlikely.

Prosecution of officials continued to be active in the early fifteenth century. In the Podestà's court, 5.7 percent of all crimes were crimes of officeholders, although this was not the court predominantly interested in these crimes. Eight out of 10 cases were initiated by public fame initiation, in other words, through public means. The rectors had great discretion in increasing the penalties. In cases culminating in convictions in the 1425–28 sample, the penalties were severe, even corporal, and always included exclusion from future officeholding, usually permanently. This, too, corresponds with statute.[57]

While it is surprising how late magnates continued to act in a reckless and lawless fashion on occasion, magnates no longer posed a significant threat to the commune by 1425. At some point around the turn of the fifteenth century, magnates ceased to be tried according to the Ordinances of Justice. The appearance of the Ordinances of Justice in the statutes was justified by current usage. Sometimes, even after 1400, parties attempted to have their adversaries declared magnates.[58] But the era of the Ordinances of Justice had passed. Brucker gives examples of magnates being prosecuted by the Ordinances of Justice until 1392[59] but being prosecuted according to regular procedure after 1400.[60]

While Dorini derives rates of 3.6 percent in the 1352–55 period and 5.2 percent in the 1380–83 period for crimes perpetrated by magnates and prosecuted according to the Ordinances of Justice compared to total crime, the 1425–28 sample presented here includes only one defendant of magnate status, who was tried for assaulting a tax collector who tried to capture him for tax defaulting. The court of the Podestà was an appropriate court to try crimes perpetrated by magnates, using the Ordinances of Justice. However, this magnate was not being tried according to the Ordinances of Justice but instead was acquitted in a regular inquisition proceeding.[61]

Offenses classified as crimes against good morals were committed at a fairly constant rate throughout the fourteenth and fifteenth centuries. This category of crime included rape, adultery, pandering, sodomy, and invasion of a monastery.[62] The 6 cases in the 1425–28 sample include 2 cases of rape, 1 of adultery, 1 of sodomy, 1 of invading a monastery, and 1 of pandering. The sodomy case was a typical representative of fourteenth- and early fifteenth-century sodomy cases, not at all resembling cases prosecuted in the mid- and late fifteenth century.[63] In the fourteenth and early fifteenth centuries, sodomy charges were brought against those who through violence, threats, or allurements committed homosexual rape, especially against minors. In the mid- to late fifteenth century, however, the state intruded on private life to too great a degree, homosexual relationships of long standing becoming matters of prosecution.[64] The presence of sodomy cases in the court of the Podestà demonstrates that the Ufficiali di Notte had not taken this jurisdiction away from the regular court system even by 1428. The court of the Ufficiali di Notte became a very powerful court of summary procedure in the mid- to late fifteenth century. In the early fifteenth century, the system for treating sodomy remained as it was in the fourteenth, which was already aggressive enough. Throughout this period, because the character of the crime made discovery difficult, proof was made easy despite the very serious nature of the prescribed penalty. Acting in a manner that aroused suspicions of sodomy, such as being in a covert place with a boy, was enough to condemn.

The determination of the punishment for rape depended on the means used to subdue the victim and the condition of the victim. Where soothing and deceptive words were used to conquer the victim, the penalties fell below 500 lire, which was the normal penalty for rape.[65] A successful defense against rape charges, not one that gained acquittal but one that sizably reduced the penalty, was proof, usually through testimony, that the victim was of low moral standards.[66] The rape of prostitutes was not punished (*Stat.* 3.112).

Examination of the cases yields several important conclusions. Criminal cases from as late as 1428 demonstrate that the statutes were applied exactly. The courts of the foreign rectors remained very important and active, having exclusive jurisdiction over almost all crimes. Their power was still increasing as the territorial state continued to strengthen in the early fifteenth century. Defaulting and fleeing debt cases were newly being funneled into the courts of the foreign rectors. Cases from wherever Florence spread its dominion over newly subjected territory also came to their courts.

Inquisition procedure was used as specified in the statutes. The cases verify the spread of public initiation and, therefore, the increase in the state's responsibility to collect evidence for the cases tried in its courts. This increased responsibility was met through more effective police work as well as an increased reliance on torture, public fame initiation, and public fame proof. The improved effectiveness of police work is reflected in the reduction of the contumaciousness rate, while reliance on torture and public fame is demonstrated by their very frequent usage in the cases.

From the cases that were tried in the Podestà's court, there is little indication of the imminent Medici takeover. Class conflict appears to have been minimal. Intraclass crime remained predominant. Although there was a plethora of debt cases, all of them occurred between merchants. Very few tenancy disagreements were prosecuted. The patriciate was not using the court system for its own benefit. While factional conflicts of an indecisive nature took place in the first two decades of the fifteenth century, these gave way to civic unity in the 1420s. Almost all political crimes were war-related and not particularly suggestive of dissent. All in all, prosecution does not indicate much about the solidifying of factions in this era or the widening of the economic gap between rich and poor. Either prosecution was not affected by these movements or the movements themselves had not yet solidified into abusive forms.

9

CONCLUSION

THE CENTRAL INSTITUTIONS of the Florentine criminal law system in the early fifteenth century were still the medieval courts of the three foreign rectors, the Podestà, the Captain of the People, and the Executor of the Ordinances of Justice, just as they had been throughout the fourteenth century. Similarly, criminal trials were conducted using inquisition procedure just as they had been from the late thirteenth century. Important changes, however, had taken place and were continuing to take place in the offices of the rectors and in inquisition procedure that greatly enhanced the effectiveness of this system. The fortuitous confluence of a strong state with improvements in inquisition procedure and the court system led to a strongly self-reliant court system that could, for the first time in the early fifteenth century, fully implement inquisition procedure by arresting criminals *in flagranti,* initiating cases through public initiation, gathering evidence independently, compelling witnesses, and successfully convicting. Because the political and social atmosphere influenced the effectiveness and the philosophies of prosecution of the criminal law system, a study of this system must include some consideration of political and social influences. Conversely, a study of the judicial system supplies a great deal of evidence about the government and society. When this interrelated sphere is regarded as a whole, the early fifteenth century is seen to have been dominated by three closely related developments: the full implementation of inquisition procedure; the continued development of the territorial state, which made this possible; and the struggle between republican institutions and the nascent patriciate.

A territorial state is a sovereign state in which the central government has authority over most of its territory and its people, although a medieval or a Renaissance state was capable of achieving only a moderate level of authority. The government is run by a bureaucracy, which seeks to work efficiently in the public interest. No one class controls the government for its own benefit, because the government holds public good to be superior to the rights of any person or any group. The people of the state have a direct relationship with the state, not through any group that intercedes between the people and the state. The government functions

Conclusion

impersonally according to rules, the statutes, and has some capability of enforcing its rules on its constituency. The Florentine territorial state began to form in the 1340s and continued to develop along these lines throughout the early fifteenth century until the recall of the Medici from exile in 1434. The existence of this strong, impersonal, centralized state temporarily thwarted the development of a ruling oligarchy. Although an aristocracy was most certainly forming, this aristocracy was only minimally successful in manipulating the criminal court system. Class-biased justice was not present in the early fifteenth century.

The major sources that I used to examine the criminal law system were the statutes of Florence of 1415 and the cases tried in the court of the Podestà from 1425 to 1428. Other samples of criminal cases with which to compare this sample can be found for the fourteenth century in Umberto Dorini's *Il diritto penale e la delinquenza in Firenze nel secolo quattordici* and Samuel Cohn's *The Laboring Classes in Renaissance Florence*, and for the mid- to late fifteenth century in Cohn's *The Laboring Classes*. The statutes of 1415 have been largely ignored as a source for examining the law, politics, and society of the early fifteenth century because some historians, mainly Kohler, have regarded these statutes as anachronistic and antiquated before their redaction. This is a priori unlikely, given that a full-scale revision was authorized in 1415 and that the work was carried out by the eminent jurist Paolo di Castro.

A comparison of these statutes with the cases from the 1425–28 period indicates a close correspondence. Many of the most recent changes in the law were reflected in the court cases. For instance, changes in the law concerning defaulting and fleeing debt, the most important kind of debt cases, which removed these cases from the courts of the guilds and transferred them to the courts of the foreign rectors, were apparent in the court cases. In the same way, recent changes in the law that increased the types of cases in which some form of public initiation was permitted were reflected in the court cases as an increase in public-initiated cases. There is also a correspondence between the very small number of cases which were initiated by *bullectini*, that is, by order of the executive branch, and the limitations set by the statutes for the issuing of bullectini. Finally, torture was applied in conformity with statute and only in cases allowed by statute. The foreign rectors were required to study these statutes before they took office and to base their judgments on them. Statutes and cases agree closely because the early fifteenth century preceded major changes that took place in the social, political, and legal systems.

The early fifteenth century has been misrepresented by historians who wish to include it in the period after 1434 when the Medici returned to Florence to become its leading citizens. In this view, Florence was already dominated by an oligarchy that had terminated republican institutions. In a seminal work that has overturned the conceptualization of the mid-fifteenth century, Nicolai Rubinstein has demonstrated that even after the Medici recall, republican institutions were resilient, while slight changes in the election procedures maintained the tenuous hold of the Medici on their unofficial leadership. The citizens who participated in the colleges and councils valued this participation so highly that a Medici despotism would not have been successful. The early fifteenth century was not a part of the late fifteenth-century Medici despotism.

Those who believe that a patriciate ruled Florence in the early fifteenth century have posited that the courts of the foreign rectors were becoming supplanted by executive agencies with judicial duties and that this movement spearheaded the patrician takeover. However, there is no evidence of the attrition of the rectors' courts until financial necessities in the mid-1420s mandated cuts in funding in all facets of the government. The importance of the courts of the foreign rectors continued to increase as the government took power away from the courts of the corporate entities that formerly composed the state and attributed them to the foreign rectors. In the medieval Florentine commune, individuals belonged to strong corporate organizations, such as the guilds and the Parte Guelfa, which composed the state. In the early fifteenth century, these corporations lost some crucial areas of jurisdiction to the state's courts. The growing use of public initiation of cases also gave greater responsibility and authority to the courts of the foreign rectors. As the concept of crime changed from crime as a private matter to crime as a public matter, the public institutions became responsible for more and more parts of the procedure.

Inquisition procedure had been employed in the Florentine courts since the late thirteenth century. Borrowing from Langbein, who borrows from Schmidt and Millar, inquisition procedure, as opposed to private prosecution, is defined as the ability of government organizations to initiate and conduct the entire proceedings of the trial, or at least to conduct all of the proceedings except initiation, *ex officio*; and the ability of government organizations to investigate judicially and to establish the substantive facts and objective truths. The success of inquisition procedure rested on its capability of being self-reliant in most parts of the trial, a self-reliance increased by the use of public initiation. The statutes of 1415 greatly increased the number of crimes in which public initiation was permitted. In the 1352–55 period, half of all trials were initiated by private accusation; in 1380–83, one-third were initiated by private accusation; and in the 1425–28 period, 28.2 percent, or just over one-fourth, were so initiated. Inquisition procedure greatly eroded the concept of justice as a private affair.

Conclusion

Increased public initiation brought greater success to the court system because cases that were initiated through one of its three public forms—public fame, *ex officio*, or denunciation by a public official—had a higher conviction rate than cases initiated by private accusation. The success of the early fifteenth-century criminal justice system is also demonstrated by a drastic reduction in the contumaciousness and reluctant witness rates. The contumaciousness rate, which was 58.3 percent between 1352 and 1355 and 55.6 percent between 1380 and 1383, was reduced to 42.4 percent in the 1425–28 period. Any system using torture as part of the procedure would have a high contumaciousness rate under any conditions. As for reluctant witnesses, there were 140 cases of prosecution in the courts of the three foreign rectors from 1352 to 1355, and 47 cases from 1380 to 1383; only 1 such case is found in the court of the Podestà from 1425 to 1428, which shows better protection and more effective compulsion of witnesses. These improvements can be attributed to better surveillance, better apprehension of criminals, and better gathering of proof. The early fifteenth-century police forces of the rectors were larger in proportion to the population than they had been in the past.

But besides these improvements, the more self-reliant and public the criminal law system became, the more it employed independent avenues of investigation, such as torture, public fame initiation, and public fame proof, which were juridical methods of questionable value. In the 1425–28 period, 21 percent of all convictions were brought about by confessions exacted under torture. Public fame initiation is that initiation in which the accusers identified themselves but attested to having only an indirect knowledge of the case, testifying only to what they knew to be rumors in their neighborhood in Florence. Thus, no one was really responsible for their statements. Public fame initiation was very successful because the initiation itself provided part of the proof; that is, when a sufficient number of public fame accusers were found to initiate the case, this provided part of the proof to convict. Often confessions exacted through torture supplied the rest of the necessary proof. However, successful defense was possible if the defendant presented proof. Public fame initiation was the predominant form of initiation in the early fifteenth century, representing 38.4 percent of all case initiations. That the most common kind of crime initiated by *ex officio* initiation was assault, exactly the kind of crime that previously would have been initiated by private accusation, illustrates the strengthening of the public aspects of crime.

The growing importance of public initiation forced changes in the judicial system, breaking down the jurisdictional specialties of the rectors. Whereas previously the rectors had been specialized according to function and according to the constituency that they represented, by 1415 they were very much alike. Because the police of the rector who arrived at the scene of a crime were not necessarily the police of the rector who had competence over that particular crime, the lines of competence between the rectors became blurred. For the first time in the 1415 compilation, the rector who interrupted a crime was given the right to try the case, despite any divisions of competence. For the first time in 1415, all the rectors were given equal authority and *arbitrium*, or discretion, and were permitted to try all crimes. As the territorial state took power away from the constituent corporate groups and forged the state into one unit, the rectors lost their parochial character and became uniform officials of the state. The strength of the criminal justice system supports my thesis that the territorial state continued.

The Captain is a telling example of this transition from parochial responsibilities to general competence. In the late thirteenth and the early fourteenth centuries, the Captain was head of the *popolo*, the collectivity of all classes of people other than the feudal nobility and commercial nobility. He extended special protection to guildsmen and tried crimes that pertained to those duties and that constituency. By 1415, however, the Captain was no longer the usual rector to try guild-related crimes. This sphere of competence had been replaced by a general criminal purview. This phenomenon, which is observable in the criminal law system, was symptomatic of movements in the government as a whole, which contributed to the development of the territorial state. The corporate constituents of the state gave way to a unified, centralized state.

Early fifteenth-century crime resembled that of the fourteenth century rather than that of the mid- to late fifteenth century; this was one reason that the statutes remained applicable. In the early fifteenth century, as in the fourteenth, intraclass crimes such as assault greatly predominated over interclass crimes such as theft. In contrast, in the later fifteenth century, interclass crimes predominated, showing greater class conflict and a philosophy of prosecution that benefited the rich. Assaults between members of the lower class were ignored because prosecuting them was of little value to the patriciate, and the philosophy of extending protection to all classes had been forgotten. In the early fifteenth century, however, not only were these cases prosecuted, they were prosecuted *ex officio* after the victims refused to accuse. One reason for this difference was a change in residential patterns. Cohn has demonstrated that in the 1380s the poor had a citywide distribution, while in the late fifteenth century their residential patterns resembled ghettos. In the early fifteenth century, the court system was not yet geared to benefiting the rich. Almost all the debt cases in early fifteenth-century criminal courts were cases between merchants, not cases of the rich prosecuting the

Conclusion

poor. Class conflict was not a prominent component of early fifteenth-century crime.

The traditional nature of early fifteenth-century criminality and philosophies of prosecution was not retrogressive. The early fifteenth century showed considerable development and refinement of inquisition procedure before this relatively sophisticated procedure was disposed of in favor of summary process with perfunctory assessment of evidence, minimal safeguards for the defendant, and the complete arbitrariness of the fullest discretion of the deciding bodies. It was the mid- to late fifteenth century that was retrogressive in political and juridical philosophy, when republican institutions gave way to oligarchic government.

The territorial state began to develop in the 1340s when the financial needs of the state militated against the continuation of a privilege-oriented government that failed to tax the rich and allowed extensive usurpation of communal property. In the Middle Ages, the state in Florence, the commune, was definitely not a territorial state. It was composed of several corporate groups loosely held together by the government. These groups held the allegiance of their members and acted as intercessors between the individual and the state. Thus, many privileged groups existed whose interests were not subordinated to those of the state. In the late fifteenth century, a territorial state, likewise, did not exist, since an oligarchy ruled the state for its own benefit. In order to show a territorial state still developing in the early fifteenth century, it must be demonstrated that the medieval corporate intercessors lost power, giving way to a centralized state, and that the oligarchy did not yet rule for its own benefit.

The three major corporate groups that composed the state and acted with public power—the guilds, the Societies of the People, and the Parte Guelfa—began a process of subjection to the state and diminution of power that continued throughout the early fifteenth century. Concomitantly, the state was centralizing, systematizing, and becoming more efficient. The Societies of the People, which were the citizen militia and political organizations of the different geographic sections of the city, were last called out on a military expedition in 1393; in the same year, the power of the Parte Guelfa to disenfranchise citizens was terminated; in the statutes of 1415, the guilds could no longer restrict their members to litigating in the guild courts, the state courts being provided as an alternative. Some important types of cases that were pertinent to the guilds, such as falsity and defaulting and fleeing debt, were barred from the guild courts and transferred to the foreign rectors' courts. Similarly, fraud was increasingly assigned to the rectors' courts. The Wool Guild's foreign judge lost much of his power, while the Silk Guild's foreign judge disappeared altogether. The Mercanzia, the court serving the whole merchant community, which formerly had a great deal of power over foreign affairs, was stripped of this power, including the power to grant reprisals. Reprisal was the right, conceded by the government to one of its subjects, to capture a citizen of a foreign state and seize his goods up to a certain sum, until the subject, who had suffered an offense at the hands of another citizen from that foreign state, had obtained the satisfaction that he deserved. This power was taken away from the Mercanzia in 1408 and transferred to the Signoria. Reprisal, a sort of miniature declaration of war, fit more properly into the duties of the executive.

The territorial state continued to develop in the early fifteenth century; its crowning achievement, the tax reform known as the Catasto, a system of taxation graduated according to wealth, took place in 1427. The changes in the power and position of the foreign rectors as well as the reorganization of the statutes demonstrate centralization, systematization, and increased efficiency. The Office of the Tower, the office that administered public goods and protected them against private usurpation, continued to organize; the office dealing with the streets of the contado and district were added to its purview in 1415. An articulation of all the government officials reveals a working bureaucracy regulated by a system of checks and balances that assured impersonal and accountable government. For instance, no public goods could be canceled from the books of the Office of the Tower without a judgment of the foreign rectors. Similarly, syndication, the mandatory trial of officials concerning their performance in office, continued to make officials accountable, even those officials of the executive branch.

Besides implementing inquisition procedure, the continuation of the territorial state thwarted aristocratic control of the government and the judicial system. The Signoria continued to change its viewpoints and policies every two months with the change of membership. When the Medici took over the government, they used the vehicle of alterations in election procedures. Electoral irregularities were few in the early fifteenth century. The councils continued to thwart aristocratic attempts to dispose of constitutional forms. According to theories that posit an oligarchic takeover in the early fifteenth century, the oligarchy used the executive offices of the state to control every part of the state, including the judicial branch; extraordinary executive offices with judicial duties were created and given important duties and extraordinary power to circumvent the need for the approval of the councils, which had a less aristocratic makeup and a more republican orientation. These executive offices with judicial duties supposedly supplanted the regular court system. The executive branch was accountable to no one, and frequently acted with *de facto*, not *de iure*, power.

Conclusion

An examination of the judicial system shows this to be incorrect. The courts of the rectors remained vigorous: the only cases removed from them concerned prostitution and weights and measures. Political cases were tried in the courts of the foreign rectors. The Otto di Guardia, the court that eventually supplanted the rectors' courts in the mid-Quattrocento by invading both their civil and their criminal jurisdictions, did not conduct criminal trials, except of mercenaries, in the early fifteenth century. The Signoria acted within its *de iure* powers. The executive branch was subjected to the syndication laws and was included in the system of checks and balances.

The Signoria was given by statute a great deal of power to intervene in the judicial system. This power was not new, existing as it did throughout the fourteenth century. Throughout the medieval period until 1373, there was no separation between judicial and political officials. The foreign rectors themselves were the heads of the major councils and had important political duties until 1373, when they became strictly judicial officials. Thus, the judicial branch was separated from the executive branch, not invaded by it. When these two branches were separated, the Signoria, as head of all branches of government, still retained a good deal of power over the judicial system.

The power of the Signoria over the judicial system was mitigated by rules and regulations. The influence of the Signoria on election of judicial and of governmental officials was continuously diminished from the 1350s through the early fifteenth century, since the system of scrutiny and extraction had been extended over almost all officials. Legislative measures were proposed by the Signoria but needed the participation of the two colleges and the consent of the very numerous Councils of the People and of the Commune. The need for the consent of these councils, the bulwarks of republicanism, was not rescinded until 1471. The Signoria very rarely tried any criminal cases directly: whereas, in the fourteenth century, they tried atrocious crimes, in the fifteenth century, this jurisdiction atrophied to nothing. The 1415 statutes forbade the Signoria to try criminal cases other than those specifically assigned to them by statute. The trial of political crimes was assigned by statute to the foreign rectors, who appear to have been the ones actually trying these crimes in practice.

The real avenue of interference that the Signoria had into the judicial system was the sending of bullectini—that is, executive orders—to the courts of the foreign rectors. These bullectini could be of several different types, but most of these types were limited by statute in some way that disqualified them as vehicles of patrician control or bias. For example, the Signoria, together with the colleges, could cancel condemnations, but cancellation required a near consensus of the Signoria and colleges and the consent of the councils, particularly for political crimes. Penalties could also be canceled through oblations, which were permanent releases given to prisoners as part of the celebration of religious holidays, but oblations provided releases for the poor only. The Signoria and colleges were not given these methods of cancellation so that they could arbitrarily influence the judicial system. Cancellations fulfilled a real purpose, the emptying of the overcrowded prisons. Because many people were in prison for debt or pecuniary penalties that they had no hope of paying, the prisons could not be allowed to fill up and never to empty. Cancellations and oblations alleviated this problem. They also helped rectify the injustices to the poor of a penalty system that was mainly pecuniary. Both of these powers belonged to the executive throughout the fourteenth century, so were not new. Finally, the Signoria, acting without the colleges or the councils, had the power to exile people during times of political disturbance. The Signoria held this power throughout the fourteenth century; it was the legal basis for the large-scale exiling of the Alberti in 1394, the Medici in 1433, and the Albizzi in 1434. However, the Signoria's judicial powers usually were used as instruments of equity to counteract injustices caused by the rigidity of statute. Bullectini played a minor role in the criminal cases of 1425–28. Only 2 cases out of 177 were initiated by bullectini, both of which conformed to statutory limits and were devoid of political content.

The judicial role in the early fifteenth century of the executive commission, the Otto di Guardia, has been greatly exaggerated because the Otto became so important in the late fifteenth century, subsuming all criminal jurisdiction. However, the Otto was mainly concerned with administering the mercenaries and monitoring banned and condemned Florentines in the early fifteenth century.

Thus, when the early fifteenth century is examined through evidence from the period, a different characterization arises than the traditional one. Major changes had occurred in a judicial system formerly thought to be static; inquisition procedure had been refined and fully implemented. The ongoing efficient bureaucracy of the territorial state, replete with checks and balances, impeded patrician takeover.

According to Nicolai Rubinstein, 1434 marks a change of regime, when the Albizzi, who had been the dominant power, decisively gave way to the Medici, whose party became ascendant.[1] Through patrician networks the Medici family had accrued much support and power. In 1434, the Otto di Guardia e Balia and the Captain of the People were given extraordinary powers to consolidate the regime—to carry out, for example, the purging of the other party (p. 111). From this point forth, a rapid accretion of the role and impact of the Medici in the government occurred. Through alter-

Conclusion

ations in election procedures, the Medici assured themselves predominant influence in the government and some continuity of membership for themselves and their affiliates. They were not able to dispose of some real constitutional elements, such as the Councils of the Commune and of the People, nor did they attempt to discard some superficial attributes that retained the appearance of constitutionality, although Florentines often demonstrated that they knew the difference between the two (p. 145). In 1459, the Council of One Hundred, intended to be an arm of the Medici, superseded the Councils of Two Hundred, One Hundred Thirty-One, and One Hundred Forty-Five, but still was constrained to work alongside the resilient ancient councils, showing even then the continuation of the concept of the necessary collaboration of these councils (pp. 114–15). Florentines were not yet willing to accept exclusive recourse to personal power.

Throughout this period, the Otto was gaining in power and taking over an ever greater portion of all civil and criminal jurisdiction. This transition was accomplished through removing important cases from the courts of the Podestà and the Captain and placing them in the court of the Otto.[2] The Executor was eliminated altogether in 1435, perhaps partly because he monitored the adherence of officials to regulations. The Podestà and the Captain persisted, but their offices were desiccated. In addition, the expertise in these offices was diminished, necessitating the rule that rectors had to have had experience in being rectors one time in another location, a rule that previously had been unnecessary.[3] By the mid-fifteenth century, the Otto had wide *de facto* powers, the expansion of which continued under Medici patronage, despite the protests of those seeking a return to limits for the Otto.[4] The Otto paid little attention to statute, procedure, and jurisdictional boundaries. When the government was threatened, the practically unlimited powers of the Otto were increased to include greater powers over political crimes.[5]

The transition from all power in the court system being in the hands of the three foreign rectors to all power in the hands of the Otto was accomplished by various techniques.[6] The Otto was able to employ *de facto* powers that it did not constitutionally have because it was the Medici-backed court. It began dominating the rectors' courts through the use of bullettini, commanding the rectors to reach a certain sentence and mete out a certain penalty, until the rectors were an executing arm of the Otto.[7] The Otto began initiating important cases *ex officio* and leaving only accusation-initiated cases to the courts of the foreign rectors.[8] Because cases in the courts of the rectors became predominantly initiated through accusation and accusation-initiated cases always had a low conviction rate, these courts became ineffective. The Otto used its power to issue orders and then punish those disobedient to increase its jurisdiction. It became ever more repressive, with power to enforce the regime juridically against any kind of dissent and to punish, for instance, disturbances protesting Medici-biased scrutinies, as in 1453.[9] It could judge without giving any reason and with the greatest arbitrium, taking into account the quality of the delinquent, as well as the quality of the crime. The new judicial balance was a part of the new political regime. By 1478, the Otto was given the power to punish any crime, mete out any penalty in whatever manner, and proceed in whatever manner it liked.[10] The judicial powers and competence of the executive were generally increased after 1434, especially for political offenses. Judgment by the Otto was arbitrary justice, the result of the transfer of judicial power from the judicial branch to the executive. The powers of the judiciary were easily wielded for personal and class ends.[11]

Throughout this period, too, elections, and therefore control of who held power in the government, was brought under the control of the Medici.[12] Finally in 1471 the legislative Councils of the Commune and of the People met their end when Lorenzo gave power to the Council of One Hundred, making the ancient councils unnecessary. At this point, Lorenzo was powerful enough that popular opinions in favor of republicanism could be ignored and institutions could be altered at his will. The One Hundred gained exclusive powers in political, military, financial, and legislative decisions. The ancient councils had always been able to keep limits on the One Hundred and the Balia because the assent of the councils was needed, for instance, to extend the duration of the Balia. They had consistently opposed Medici policy.[13]

In 1477, as the power of the Otto was being increased and the office of the Captain was abolished, the Podestà then became the major criminal court, outside of the all-powerful Otto, and the Signoria and the Mercanzie became the predominant civil courts.[14] The powers bestowed on the One Hundred and the Otto became infinitely extended throughout the time of Lorenzo.[15] But, clearly, the fall from power of Lorenzo's son, Piero, in 1494, because of his own administrative and diplomatic ineptitude, ended one period and initiated another.

In the 1490s, the attempt to introduce, once again, institutions with a broader base into Florence was a failure. Principles from the republican era, such as rapid rotation in office, produced instability and inefficiency when applied to recently resuscitated or created institutions, such as the Consiglio Maggiore. Institutions with such a broad membership completely immobilized the government. During this period, there was talk of reforming the court system to make it less arbitrary and less dependent on the decisions of so few, such as the Otto, who could wield the power of life and death and were not even legal experts. There was even talk of reviving the foreign rectors, revered as symbols of republicanism and popular government. Suggestions like these were never adopted because of the chaos within the political system, rebellions in the territory, and dangers from without.[16]

This situation of ineffectiveness and instability was partially resolved in 1502 by the creation of a Gonfalonierato for life, the office held by Piero Soderini, and reforms within the administration and judicial system. These reforms foreshadowed the Grand Ducal government with great personal power at the top, citizen agencies that formed a direct link from the will of the executive to the rest of the government, and a working bureaucracy that was not upper class and was somewhat removed from the political fray. The Gonfalonier at the top was able to initiate cases and intervene in judicial decisions. In 1502, the Quarantia was created, which made control of penal matters by the executive more direct, as did the Otto (p. 104). The Quarantia tried only cases remanded to it by the Signoria, and its decisions were appealable. The Podestà and the Ufficiali di Notte, the court with jurisdiction over sodomy, were abolished and their jurisdictions transferred to the Otto di Guardia and the Conservatori delle Leggi (p. 103). The confusion of magistracies was simplified. The Ruota, which consisted of foreign juristic experts, was organized: it centralized many of the functions of the judicial system and took over the place of the Podestà and Captain in civil matters, criminal matters, and appeals. The Otto di Guardia and the Conservatori delle Leggi continued to be the major criminal courts. From 1512 on, the Medici family again began to accrue power and get control of the Otto and the Signoria. By 1530–31, a repressive movement had initiated the authoritarianism of the Grand Ducal period (p. 107).

The Grand Ducal period, that is, the period from 1537 to 1609, encompassed the reigns of Cosimo I, Francesco I, and Ferdinando I. This was a period, especially the reign of Cosimo I (1537–74), characterized by the Duke's great personal power and involvement in the judicial system and in administration in general, but fairly efficient and extensive bureaucratic, judicial, and administrative institutions. Government was divided into two levels of activity: the part of the state that pertained to Cosimo and the other dukes was absolutist, but the administration and bureaucracy had republican elements. The bureaucrats were chosen from outside the aristocratic class.[17] Cosimo was very interested in intervening in judicial matters and in reforming various problems within the judicial system, some of which were genuine (p. 136). Many of the problems he reformed with his own personal imput, for instance, taking all appeals into his own hands and monitoring his courts and justice in this way. The

Conclusion

Magistrato Supremo, founded in 1532 as an aristocratic representative council, became an instrument of the Duke's will. The Magistrato had no autonomous jurisdictions, but became the Ducal prerogative court handling the special categories of cases that the Duke wished to handle as prerogative cases: cases of sovereignty, poverty, and petitions for grace (pp. 142–43). The Duke was interested in the poor and exercised *tutela* over them. Some problems were addressed by a return to institutions that had some resemblance to republican institutions.

Cosimo aimed to address the salient problems of his judicial system: inequality, failure to execute punishments, and lack of systematization and continuity between the different parts of the judicial system. The inequality of treatment problem, in terms of both class and the dichotomy between dominant city and subject territory, was inherited from the court system of Lorenzo, which had given free rein to arbitrium, not requiring adherence to either the statutes or procedure. The Otto was a particular offender of ignoring the law, acting with complete arbitrium and meting out unequal justice (p. 137). In 1543, Cosimo decreed that many major crimes had to be judged according to the law and statutes, and in 1556 he canceled the use of arbitrium and balia in the courts of all magistrates and rectors, a significant step in restoring equality (p. 138). Greater adherence to statute enforced greater equality. The Otto and the Conservatori were given the power in 1549 to review the decisions of other courts in order to standardize justice, but the main result of this change was to give the Dukes a further method of manipulating the court system (pp. 139–40). Penalties were changed from pecuniary to corporal, allegedly to further equality. Greater equality of judicial treatment was, in fact, partially achieved among the classes and various locations, but the insinuation of the Duke's personal power into the courts introduced new criteria of inequality. Personal ties to the Duke became the greatest source of privileged treatment.[18]

Another problem prevalent in the Grand Ducal court system that was corrected by Cosimo was the lack of severity of punishment. Many judgments were reached, but few were properly executed.[19] The Otto was particularly culpable in favormongering. In 1558, Cosimo reformed the court of the Otto, no longer permitting aristocrats to hold these offices, and substituted men of legal training, who were not as amenable to facile acquittals and sentence reductions.[20] Disorganization, overlap, and lack of continuity in the judicial system were corrected through centralization, which meant both putting institutions under the personal power of the Duke as well as integrating them into the government. The judicial system was centralized around the Otto; and, in 1563, the position of fiscal auditor was created to supervise all criminal institutions and to act

Conclusion

as a direct agent of the Duke.[21] Cosimo took over large sections of the law himself.[22] In 1543, the territory was united under Florentine law in grave criminal matters, with much of the legislation being valid for the whole territory. The judicial system of the territory was centered around the Otto and the Conservatori.[23]

Although Roman law remained the basis of the summary procedure that was employed at this time, maintaining such elements as the recording of testimony and the use of reports of officials, like berrovarii, as proof, the return to a fully articulated procedure that made complete use of the learned law tracts was never again effected. Republicanism continued in the Grand Ducal period in the form of employing legal experts, maintaining some adherence to codes of law that helped promote greater equality, organizing the territory into a more consistent unit, and continuing to use the statutes of 1415, but the republican elements were overpowered by the personal power and the patrician networks of the Dukes.

BIBLIOGRAPHIC ESSAY

A DISCUSSION OF WORKS on both the territorial state and the judicial system will place this book within the context of other work. Several books on the Middle Ages and Renaissance have dealt with the formation of the territorial state: Marvin Becker's *Florence in Transition*, Lauro Martines' *Lawyers and Statecraft in Renaissance Florence*, Gene Brucker's *The Civic World of Renaissance Florence*, and Guidubaldo Guidi's *Il governo della città—repubblica di Firenze del primo Quattrocento*, among others. The works that will be discussed here pertaining to some aspect of the judicial system are Antonio Pertile's *Storia del diritto Italiano dalla caduta dell'impero romano alla codificazione*, Kohler and G. degli Azzi's *Das Florentiner Strafrecht des XIV Jahrhunderts*, Umberto Dorini's *Il diritto penale e la delinquenza in Firenze nel secolo XIV*, Guidi's *Il governo della città—repubblica di Firenze del primo Quattrocento*, Samuel Cohn's *The Laboring Classes in Renaissance Florence*, and Andrea Zorzi's *L'amministrazione della giustizia penale nella repubblica Fiorentina*.

In this book, I have advanced the thesis that the traits characteristic of the formation of the territorial state were visible in the judicial system and continued to be in evidence through the early fifteenth century. This thesis concerning the formation and continuation of the territorial state is most at variance with that of Martines in *Lawyers and Statecraft*. Martines believes that Florence became an oligarchy in the 1380s and 1390s. He defines oligarchy as "government where only the few have a voice and where among these the rich tend to hold the most authoritative positions."[1] According to Martines, the oligarchy came to power by creating new executive agencies within the government with extraordinary powers and reserving places in these agencies for themselves. They fostered greater centralization and efficiency in these posts to better control the state and even the judicial system for their own benefit. The agencies had their own areas of judicial competence composed of the most important cases, those of a political nature and those of benefit to oligarchs. According to Martines, the growth of these agencies with judicial powers was partially a response to the decay of the regular judicial system. In the 1380s and 1390s, the rise of the oligarchy was inextricably connected to the creation and advancement of these agencies and the centralization of the state. The agencies were outgrowths of an executive branch that was dominating and stifling the other parts of the government. This process continued until 1434, when the agencies were reabsorbed into the main executive offices of the Priors and the Gonfalonier, which continued to dominate all the other parts of the government and continued to be the domain of an even more exclusive oligarchy. The lawyers encouraged this process by giving legal advice that they knew would allow continuing usurpation of power by the oligarchy.

Martines' argument is based on several assumptions. First, it presupposes that centralization and the growth of the executive commissions occurred simultaneously with the usurpation and abuse of power by the oligarchy. Although Martines' definition of oligarchy fails to mention any element of successful control of the government, it is his assumption that the oligarchy was successful in its attempts at control. Second, it relies on the regular judicial system being dysfunctional in the early fifteenth century.

Centralization, however, antedated oligarchic hegemony. Most of the evidence presented by Martines inadvertently supports this viewpoint. His evidence for centralization and the creation of executive commissions points to the 1380s and 1390s, while his evidence for oligarchic takeover of the government and misuse of government commissions by oligarchs for their own benefit refers to a period after 1434. Martines warns the reader not to see the Medici return of 1434 as a dramatic event that produced great changes, but all of the information he cites on oligarchic usurpation of the government points to a period after this date. Martines admits that the tendency toward a declining number of men eligible for elections (which happens not to be true) was temporarily arrested in the beginning of the fifteenth century, a period of greater fluidity and easier entry into the government (pp. 133–35). After 1434, political power again began to concentrate (p. 389). He acknowledges that down to the fifteenth century, the court system was autonomous from the executive (pp. 124–25, 397). Martines states that the Signoria seldom accepted litigious petitions until the 1430s, meaning that the executive branch did not frequently intervene to remove cases from the regular court system to which they properly belonged, nor did it abuse the broad judicial powers that it was permitted to use by statute. Furthermore, the lawyers, who in a later period gave legal opinions to the government that aided the oligarchy in seizing power (dressing these justifications in legal language), did not give these kinds of opinions before 1434. Before then, the lawyers were concerned with correct interpretation of statute. As Martines states, "Up to about 1434 they [the lawyers] revealed no obvious inclination to strengthen the hand of the executive. As shown at the time of the Bastari (1387) and Moncione (1421) cases, lawyers seemed inclined to keep the authority of the Signory within existing bounds" (p. 402). The Bastari and Moncione cases are the most important cases he discusses. The Executor of the Ordinances of Justice, a *popolano* official whose job encompassed the regulation of the magnates and of others who displayed overbearing behavior, was suppressed in 1434, following the Medici recall.

It has already been demonstrated above that the executive agencies with judicial power were not promoting oligarchic power in the early fifteenth century. The formation of a territorial state, the promotion of centralization and efficiency, was not connected with the rise of the oligarchy. The territorial state began to be formed in the 1340s and continued along this vein through the early fifteenth century. The domination of the government by the oligarchy took place after 1434 with the political ascendancy of the Medici. Before 1434, the *reggimento* class was factionalized, no one faction successfully controlling, so that, as Martines asks, "Who could tell what the next group of Priors would do?" (p. 152). The Consulte et Pratiche from the early fifteenth century, as reflected in Brucker's *The Civic World of Early Renaissance Florence*, demonstrate that policy changed daily.

Martines' theme of the oligarchy's rise to power through the use of executive judicial commissions partly rests on his supposition that the regular court system was atrophying. According to Martines, the independent appellate judge was suppressed in a process that took place from 1410 to 1415, giving more power over appeals to the Signoria (p. 132). In fact, the appellate judge that existed after 1415 was more independent of the executive branch than the one that existed before 1410. The foreign appellate judge that existed before 1410 was elected by the Signoria and the colleges, while the foreign appellate judge after 1415 was chosen by the foreign Captain of the People and brought by the Captain in his entourage. Since there was one foreign appeals judge before 1415 and one after, there was no diminution of this office. The Signoria had virtually no say and apparently no interest in who was chosen. As has been previously stated, the Signoria tried very few appeals before 1434. Appeals were not permitted from criminal condemnations anyway (*Stat.* 2.127). Martines portrays the Podestà as well as the other two rectors as enfeebled magistrates in this period. While it is true that the Podestà and the Captain were no longer political officials as they had been a century before, their judicial power, as well as the judicial power of the Executor, was far from enfeebled. Because of the continued development of inquisition procedure, the rectors could initiate many more cases *ex officio*, without waiting for an accuser. Also, new powers of policing and surveillance through their retinues gave them increasing control in combating criminal activities in Florence. A perusal of the court records of the early fifteenth century shows a substantial case load in the courts of the foreign rectors. Martines' argument, as it pertains to the period before 1434, comes to rest on the reduction of the Captain's judges from three to two in 1425.[2] In fact, the office of the judge of camera and gabelle was not destroyed but was transferred under the supervision of the Officials of Grascia. The Captain had no real means of supervising this judge, since he had no other duties pertaining to gabelles, while the Office of Grascia was better suited to this task.[3] This was probably part of the strategy to increase the collection of gabelles during the period of economic crisis. The government was not too serious about this transfer, however. Several years elapsed before they even informed the Captain that he should not bring this judge in his entourage.[4] In the late 1420s, the government tried to cut the money allotment going to the judiciary, especially since an inquisition-based criminal law system was very expensive, but was not entirely successful in doing this either.[5]

Bibliographic Essay

Brucker's *The Civic World of Early Renaissance Florence* encompasses the years from just after the Black Death (1348) until 1434, but centers on the years from 1382, the fall of the guild regime, to 1434, the return of the Medici. The theme of Brucker's book is the struggle between corporate ethos and aristocratic values. According to Brucker, although the other corporations that composed Florence had lost cohesiveness after the Black Death, the corporate entities of the guilds continued to play a significant role in politics. The years from 1382 to 1434 were the years when the struggle between corporate entities and aristocrats molded history. This struggle manifested itself in the struggle between the councils, composed of guildsmen, and the Signoria, composed of aristocrats. The aristocrats were mainly wealthy guildsmen from the seven major guilds who had gained great political clout. Magnates did not figure prominently in their number. According to Brucker, the guildsmen in the councils were acutely aware of their position as representatives of the corporate ethos, but they did not have a community-wide identity, nor did they relate to the needs of the commune as a whole. The councils were intransigent and divorced from the public good. The councils voted against *prestanze*, taxes that took the form of interest-bearing loans borrowed from private citizens and that benefited the aristocrats, even when invading armies were at the gates of the city. They also consistently voted against measures that further restricted eligibility in officeholding and only grudgingly allowed the creation of *balie* that controlled the state and the fisc during times of crisis. The Signoria and the colleges, composed mainly of aristocrats, continually voted for prestanze to fight the many wars in which Florence was involved. The wars of the early 1380s were wars for survival, but the character of Florentine war soon became more imperialistic. Nonetheless, the *tre maggiori*, the three major offices of the Priors, the Gonfalonieri, and the Buonuomini, saw their promotion of these wars as motivated by the best interests for the public good, whether survival or trading rights were involved, according to Brucker. The funds for these wars were frequently extorted from people on the verge of starvation. Despite the obvious weaknesses in the fiscal system and the need for wholesale reform, the guild-dominated councils would only vote for gabelles on foodstuffs and for *estimi* (direct taxes) in the contado—in other words, for taxes that affected the lower classes, which had no money and were already driven to desperation. The guild-dominated councils were blind to public good.

Brucker sees the continuation of the corporate ethos manifested in the intransigence of the councils, their unwillingness to vote for prestanze to carry on wars for survival. The guildsmen composing the councils could not see beyond their own interests to the interests of the state as a whole. But perhaps the men who sat in the councils thought they were acting in the public interest and saw the threat to public interest coming from an aristocratic takeover, which would have destroyed the republican nature of the government. For this reason they voted against prestanze, which promoted the ownership of the government by the aristocratic class; against balie, which circumvented the republican constitution of the state; and against further restrictions on officeholding. The councils may have felt they were acting in the best interests of the state and not in a parochial manner.

Brucker sees the conflict between the corporate ethos, embodied in the councils, and the aristocratic ethos, embodied in the reggimento, as the major dynamic of this period. However, the councils were not really composed of a significantly different group than the group which belonged to the tre maggiori. Citizens from the old aristocratic families dominated the councils as well as the Signoria and the colleges.⁶ Brucker's sample shows roughly that of the citizens who composed the councils both in 1382 and in 1411, 70 percent were also selected as qualifying for the Signoria and the colleges. Since there seems to be little difference in the composition of the councils and of the tre maggiori, it is difficult to believe that the councils could represent corporate ethos and the Signoria elite mentality. According to Najemy, corporatism was dead and gone by 1400, if not earlier, having been replaced by attitudes of civic loyalty. Najemy states that after 1400 there was no longer any identification with corporatism.⁷ He draws this conclusion from analyzing systems for election, positing that these systems demonstrate both what Florentines conceived to be the basis of authority and to whom they believed this authority belonged. By 1390-1400, consensus politics was desired even by the guild community.⁸

According to Brucker, because of the intransigence of the councils, the form of politics changed. The aristocrats in the government championed an elite regime over corporate interests. They conceived of their own political wisdom as the correct repository of sovereignty. The forms of association changed, the reggimento circumventing the councils by ruling through balie, *pratiche,* and private political conventicles. Balie, extraordinary, temporary commissions appointed during crises, often possessed very great powers. Pratiche were sessions to sound out the opinions of the most important men in government, even if these men were not holding office at that time. The pratiche had no powers of decision making. However, since the men of true political experience were not always the ones extracted for office, the pratiche gave continuity to government by allowing the experienced politicians to be heard. Further, the most important members of the reggimento met in private conventicles outside government sessions to influence political decisions within the government. Government changed from being run according to the statutes to being run in an atmosphere of private wheeling and dealing, private alliances, and political favormongering. This was the new form of government, according to Brucker. But there are limits to this argument. The pratiche could not make decisions in government, only influence them. The pratiche could give advice, but the government was not constrained to follow it. Basic to the statutes is the philosophy that laymen, not experts, ought to be running the government. The balie were also limited in their power and influence, since they were temporary commissions in which the members were constantly changing. Florentines were suspicious of such balie and were always anxious to return to republican institutions, tolerating balie in periods of crises but returning to constitutional forms of government at the end of each crisis.⁹ The political conventicles held no real power, either, since before the Medici takeover no one could ensure the influence of the private conventicles through controlling the elections of officeholders. Furthermore, political conventicles were declared illegal, just as any move that threatened constitutional government met with stiff civic opposition.¹⁰

Brucker considers the developments that he sees as symptomatic of a territorial state. He sees in the reggimento's confident handling of some of the wars a growing expertise in government, the training of a class of expert politicians. The structure of the government was becoming centralized and rationalized. The regime possessed some awareness of the needs of the lower classes. The creation of the Catasto, the direct tax graduated by wealth, in 1427, was the ultimate sign of rationalized, benevolent, and efficient government.¹¹ Brucker comes very close to regarding the reggimento class as the guardians of the people.¹² According to Brucker, the reggimento class gained the political acumen to govern the state wisely, seeing the need for a reformed fiscal system, for decisive policies in governing, and for efficient handling of the wars. Is it conceivable that an unfettered reggimento would govern in the best interest of the state? It seems more likely that the system of checks and balances prevented the reggimento from ruling for its own benefit and restricted politicians to solutions that benefited the public interest. While there is merit in the argument that the reggimento class contributed to the fostering of public good, it could also be argued that the intransigent councils likewise contributed by guarding the republican constitution of the government. Brucker's portrait of the reggimento differs from that of Martines: to Martines the reggimento acted for its own benefit, while to Brucker it acted in the interest of the state.

While Brucker believes he portrays a territorial state in early fifteenth-century Florence, his thesis eliminates the existence of such a state on other grounds. To Brucker, the period of corporate ethos, which lasted until 1434, overlapped the period of reggimento government, which started in the first decade of the fifteenth century.¹³ The period when allegiances were held by corporations and only indirectly by the state only ended when the period of one-class government had already begun. There was thus no period of a territorial state.

Brucker's portrait of the corporate ethos is marred with conflicts. The strongest corporate survivor, according to Brucker, was the guild system. He agrees that the Parte and the Societies of the People had ceased to be important. But the corporate entities, the guilds, had undergone several changes in composition that were destructive to corporate ethos. Members of the highest guilds had transcended the guild system to become part of the reggimento. Those who had risen into the reggimento were not *scioperati*, people who joined the guilds only to be politically enfranchised, but successful merchants who continued to carry on mercantile activities.¹⁴ If only the people whose connection with the guilds was one of convenience and whose attachment to the work ethic was not strong had been severed as a class, the guilds could have survived with corporate ethos intact. But since the mercantile community was split, a corporation no longer existed. The highest class of the guild community had outgrown its dependency on the guilds and had developed a dependency on the state because of the state's ability to manipulate a large forum of economic factors. Further, Brucker shows that a divergence between the upper and lower guilds, which left the upper guilds in a much more politically important position than the lower guilds, began in the 1380s.[15] These divisions must have proved destructive to corporate ethos.

Lest we think that historians have reached a consensus that the patriciate ruled Florence with a relatively free hand in the early fifteenth century and that only the agency through which it achieved control is still in contention among historians, Guidubaldo Guidi's *Il governo di Firenze* extends what he calls the "democratic period" until 1434.[16] Guidi thinks that the balie and pratiche, Brucker's vehicles for the patrician takeover of the government, as well as the *parlamenti,* were pressure-release mechanisms to avert revolutions. The republican government existed from 1280 to 1434 with infrequent interruptions, revolutions being averted because the constitution allowed recourse to extraordinary measures (the balie, pratiche, and parlamenti) to make changes in the government. Thus, the government had enough elasticity to weather change. This argument somewhat resembles Becker's position that dictators or popular regimes were instituted when changes likely to produce unpleasant political repercussions had to be made.

Guidi denies that the patrician takeover took place before 1434, believing that the territorial state continued until 1434. He divides Florentine history into two periods: 1282 to 1434, the democratic period, and 1434 to 1480, the Medici period. Until 1434, the state was extending its power over particular interest groups, especially increasing its control of the guilds (vol. 1, p. 73). In the democratic period, Florentines were determined to preserve their republican institutions. Although for short periods the government was irregular, permitting extraordinary bodies to exercise great control over some facets of its functioning, it always reverted to republican institutions. Periods of irregularities in electoral procedures were always mixed with periods in which traditional forms were followed.

Guidi defines a democratic state as one in which several classes are represented through corporate representation with power proportional to the importance of the corporation (vol. 1, pp. 47–49). In his scheme, although the corporate entities were losing power in general, they continued to hold power in elections. The Parte, the societies, and the guilds made up the *recate,* the lists of nominees who must go through the scrutiny process to become eligible for office. Guidi posits that until 1434, social and economic pluralism existed in Florence, a pluralism that was reflected in officeholding, elections, and government actions. Guidi proves pluralism in officeholding in the 1400s by calculating the number of possible officeholders: 500 to 1,000 people on the recate lists to be voted on in the scrutiny for the major offices; 2,000 or more in the citizen offices *dentro e di fuori,* that is, in Florence and in the contado and district; 750 in the councils; 3,000 to 4,000 in the lesser offices, such as the nocturnal guards of the city. Fifteen hundred people participated in governing the guilds, the Parte Guelfa, and the societies. New people came into the government in large numbers (vol. 1, pp. 43–44). Furthermore, Guidi does not believe that power was being concentrated in executive officeholders who alone exercised real control. Rather, the Priors were diminishing in power as some of their tasks and authority were being parceled out to different offices. Because the Priors could not manage their workload, major executive powers and functions were assigned to the Dieci and the Otto. The overworked Priors were too busy to supervise the Dieci and the Otto in their performance of duties (vol. 1, p. 39).

Although an excess of *amor patriae* influences anyone who could call the period 1280 to 1434 the democratic period, Guidi's arguments are not without merit. Such a different definition of democracy tends to cloud rather than clarify the issues, to overstate rather than accurately state the argument. More than one class did participate in the government. Many features of horizontal rather than hierarchical government did remain. As Guidi maintains, little could be done without the Priors, but little could be done by the Priors alone. Although some officeholders that Guidi includes in his calculations of officeholders held offices of little political importance, some participants even in lesser offices, such as the nocturnal guards, did have an impact on the judicial system. The nocturnal guards decided who to arrest and controlled some of the preliminary trial information. John Najemy confirms that the political class continued to expand after 1378 when a much greater number of people were nominated for office than ever before. Nominations never fell below 5,000 after this, and in 1411 and 1433 exceeded 6,000.[17] Anthony Molho finds that in the decades 1393–1402 and 1410–19, the priorate was very widely shared: 480 posts were held by 431 people in the first period, and 480 posts by 433 people in the second period. Ronald Witt states that this distribution demonstrates a conscious effort to prevent the concentration of offices in the hands of a small leadership elite.[18] However, Najemy qualifies this by showing that after 1400, mobility was reduced, since only 91 new families entered the Signoria from 1402 to 1433; however, it was not eliminated. The leading families dominated the important positions in the government, even though different individuals from these families held office.[19]

Some of Guidi's conclusions should be tempered. The offices that had real political power, the *tre maggiori*, were few, and eligibility for these offices was restricted. Part of Guidi's argument for broad-based government rests on the continued participation of the corporate entities—the Parte, the societies, and the guilds—in elections. The captains of the Parte Guelfa, the Gonfalonieri of the societies, and the consuls of the guilds made up the recate lists, which nominated people to go through the process of *squittino*, or scrutiny. The squittino was performed by the Priors and the Gonfalonier of Justice, the Gonfalonieri, the Buonuomini, the captains of the Parte Guelfa, the officials of the Mercanzia, the proconsul of the Guild of Judges and Notaries, the consuls of the guilds, and the eighty *arroti*. As Guido Pampaloni has pointed out, this seems, on the surface, to indicate a wide base of electors, until it is revealed that the eighty arroti were chosen by the tre maggiori offices and were by and large of the same class. Then it appears that 117 out of 145 of those voting were chosen by the tre maggiori. Obviously, the contributions of the corporations were minor.[20] Since the Gonfalonieri of the societies were elected like the other tre maggiori offices, from the *borsa* of the major offices, there is no reason to think they represented the gonfaloni. The consuls of the guilds were chosen by the Priors, the Gonfalonier of Justice, the Gonfalonieri, and the Buonuomini. Although they were chosen from among the consuls within the internal governments of the guilds, if none of these could get sufficient votes from among the tre maggiori, the tre maggiori could elect anyone from the guilds.[21] Further, the office of the captains of the Parte Guelfa had been so altered by state interference that they no longer represented their constituency. In 1361, the commune of Florence enacted a law that the popolani captains of the Parte had to be part of the commission that carried out the squittino (vol. 2, p. 115). Despite the fact that the captains of the Parte Guelfa, the consuls of the guilds, and the Gonfalonieri of the societies made up the recate and voted in the squittino, they did not represent separate corporations, nor did they wield great power over elections. By the early fifteenth century, these officials were state officials like other state officials.

Guidi's work really centers on elections, a topic on which he has written a previous book. He traces the trends toward the uniform use of squittino and extraction and toward greater restrictions on eligibility for officeholding. From 1328 on, squittino and successive extraction were employed for more and more offices in the state. In the scrutiny process, lists were made up of worthy citizens, whose names were then submitted to a vote, or *squittino*, by the Priors, Gonfalonier of Justice, Gonfalonieri, Buonuomini, consuls of the guilds, captains of the Parte Guelfa, officials of the Mercanzia, and arroti. Those names that received sufficient votes were placed in a bag (imborsation) and extracted by lot when new officials were needed. From the beginning of the Quattrocento, more qualifications for officeholding were created; by 1415, almost all offices could be held only by those whose relatives had been *veduti* or *seduti*, that is, known to be in the borse or actually chosen for office previously. Three generations of residence and legitimate birth were necessary for admission to the highest offices.

The weakest parts of Guidi's book are the sections on the foreign rectors, which often break down into collections of undigested and assorted facts. For the years 1282–90, Guidi tells us that the Captain of the People had a very limited criminal jurisdiction because his true field of action was civil cases (vol. 2, p. 177). For 1328, Guidi states that the Podestà was mainly the civil judge, while the Captain particularly tried penal cases (vol. 2, p. 157). It apparently does not bother Guidi that the penal code in the statutes of 1322–25 is contained in the book of the Podestà. For roughly the year 1400, Guidi states that the Podestà handled all the civil cases (vol. 2, p. 170). There was never any point in time in which the Captain's court was the major penal court, nor was there any time at which the Podestà handled all civil cases. Guidi does not credit the Executor with having any judges in the 1322–25 period, when he had two judges; credits the Podestà with six judges, when he had eleven; and omits the important notary over the goods of rebels from the list of the Captain's retinue (vol. 2, pp. 159-61). Despite Guidi's use of the statutes as his major source, his interest in the judicial system is peripheral.

In order to put my work in perspective, the next group of books that I discuss are those that treat the judicial system. The major works are Pertile's *Storia del diritto Italiano*, Kohler and Azzi's *Das Florentiner Strafrecht des XIV Jahrhunderts*, Dorini's *Il diritto penale e la delinquenza in Firenze nel secolo XIV*, Guidi's *Il governo di Firenze*, Cohn's *The Laboring Classes in Renaissance Florence*, and Zorzi's *L'amministrazione della giustizia penale nella repubblica Fiorentina*. The legal material can shed light on the political scene as well as demonstrate independent developments in the legal mechanisms.

The classic work on the statutes of many Italian cities, written by Antonio Pertile, has already received the last word in historiographic criticism from Sarah Blanshei, in "Criminal Justice in Medieval Perugia and Bologna." Blanshei has pointed out that the entire conceptual framework of Pertile's six volumes was designed to trace late medieval and early Renaissance statutes back to their origins in either the Germanic codes or Roman law. No attempt was made to use the statutes to reveal social implications or principles of prosecution. This conceptualization, along with other inherent problems, has rendered an excellent piece of scholarship less useful than it ought to be. Perhaps it was necessary to separate out these traditional elements and influences before the parts of the statutes which were new and reflective of current social conditions could be recognized. Pertile's work is unable to generate any political or social conceptualization because of an inherent problem: the work has too great a scope both chronologically and geographically. Pertile treats the period 1200-1600 as if it were all one consistent period. Likewise, statutes from all of the geographical areas of the Italian peninsula and Sicily are indiscriminately drawn from as if there were some connecting factor among these very different communes, dictatorships, oligarchies, and kingdoms. When the statutes of the Kingdom of Sicily and the Commune of Florence are placed side by side in discussions with no attempt to contrast the materials, no theories of political or social developments can possibly arise out of the material.

Das Florentiner Strafrecht, by Kohler and Azzi, consists of two parts: a document pack and a commentary on the document pack. The document pack contains a selection of rubrics from the 1322-25 statutes of the Podestà and of the Captain, and a selection of parts of cases from the courts of these two foreign rectors, such as criminal condemnations from the Captain's court from 1343 and 1351, criminal condemnations from the Podestà's court from 1379, inquisition initiations from the Podestà's court from 1344, contested litigations from the Podestà's court from 1364-65, and so on. The purpose of the document pack is to familiarize students of Florentine history with a small sampling of documents pertaining to the judicial system. The commentary on the documents was written by Kohler. One would expect a commentary on selected documents to be piecemeal, and this it certainly is. Kohler manages to explain and tie together many of the documents presented, a feat in its own right, but anything more ambitious, such as an overview of the judicial system, is not attempted. The work appears to turn from topic to topic in an endless stream of unrelated dialogue and discrete pieces of information, never coagulating into an intelligible whole. Kohler covers the historical events leading up to the publication of the statutes of 1322–25 by lifting his account directly from Robert Davidsohn's *Storia di Firenze*, a reliable but not very ambitious practice. Kohler also makes several factual errors, such as stating that all witnesses in trials needed to be approved by the Signoria, when only magnate witnesses needed to be approved.[22]

Despite the disjointed quality of the work, which may have been unavoidable, Kohler presents two major theories. He believes that the last half of the thirteenth century was a formative period in Florentine law, one that witnessed the development of the law that was used in Florence for centuries. Related to this theory is his other thesis, that law remained changeless for centuries after this formative period.

According to Kohler, the most important advancement made in law in the thirteenth century was the introduction of inquisition procedure. The statutes of 1284 allowed the Podestà and his judges the right of initiating through inquisition in cases of theft, robbery, and murder.[23] This is consistent with the development of the other communes discussed in Blanshei's "Criminal Justice in Medieval Perugia and Bologna." Kohler apparently believed that once inquisition procedure was in place, no fundamental changes occurred. But the establishment of inquisition procedure in the late thirteenth century does not preclude changes or developments both in this procedure and in the law in general. The number of crimes for which trials could be initiated by inquisition greatly increased in the period ending in the early fifteenth century, as did the power of the state over its constituency and with it the power of the court system to implement inquisition process. The state vastly improved its capabilities to conduct surveillance and to exercise control. These kinds of developments had a great impact on the evolution of inquisition procedure. While it is true that the Florentine courts did not switch from inquisition to another kind of procedure in the fourteenth and early fifteenth centuries, the elaboration of inquisition procedure did occur. Since Kohler believed that the law was changeless, he felt free to draw indiscriminately from his documents and to discuss them in one dialogue, completely confounding sources from different periods.

Kohler further attempted to prove that Florentine law stayed the same from the thirteenth century to the early fifteenth century by citing similarities between the 1322–25 statutes and the 1415 statutes. This is a flawed method from the beginning. Even if Kohler found hundreds of similarities, unless he could show that either the similarities were of such a fundamental nature that differences were rendered unimportant or that differences were few and unimportant, he has not proved his thesis. Kohler's examples of similarities are not of such a fundamental nature. For instance, that decapitation was punishment for treason throughout the period is not too surprising. Nor is it surprising that an offense against the Captain or the Podestà, or resistance against them, was punished at the discretion of one of the rectors in 1322 and in 1415, since there could be so much variance in the degree of seriousness of this crime.[24] Proof that Kohler has not profoundly explored the similarities and differences in punishments is provided by the fact that he does not discuss any change in the worth of the currency in this period in which pecuniary penalties were the norm. While there is no question that the statutes of 1415 were based in part on the statutes of 1322–25, to say that few changes were made needs clearer demonstration than a number of discrete examples of similarities. Nevertheless, Kohler's work has led historians to believe that the laws and judicial system of Florence were changeless, and that the statutes of 1415, which were essentially from an earlier period, were not employed in the court system because they were already antiquated. Inherent in this idea is the notion that the political system was an obsolete superstructure and that real politics in Florence in 1415 were clandestine and private.

Umberto Dorini's *Il diritto penale e la delinquenza in Firenze nel secolo XIV* focuses on the same topic and is drawn from the same sources as Kohler and Azzi's work but is much superior and much more systematic and thorough. Instead of drawing conclusions from a random sample of the statutes, he systematically treats them. Dorini's book may even have been written as a corrective to Kohler's commentary. Dorini believes that changes occurred in the law from the thirteenth century to the early fifteenth century, concentrating on the changes introduced in the statutes of 1322–25. He also illustrates change by comparing all the criminal cases from the courts of the Podestà, the Captain, and the Executor for the triennia 1352–55 to all the criminal cases from the triennia 1380–83. The results are statistically quantified for greater exactness.

Dorini agrees with Kohler that the second half of the thirteenth century was a formative period in law, the period when crime began to be viewed as a public, not a private, matter. Unlike Kohler, Dorini sees the statutes as having a changing character responsive to the character of the period. Law is a reflection of prevalent crimes, and prevalent crimes are reflections of social conditions. He believes that criminality was elevated in the period after the plague as a result of chaotic conditions, while criminality was low in the period after the Ciompi revolt as a result of the establishment of a popular government.[25] Therefore, unlike Kohler, he sees changes occurring in the statutes and in the judicial system during the century and a half from the latter half of the thirteenth century to the early fifteenth century. Kohler's thesis that the criminal law was in stasis seems illogical, considering the amazing productivity of Florentines in other areas during this period.

Dorini believes that inquisition procedure was introduced in the period from 1250 to 1300 or earlier, and immediately began developing. The statute compilation of 1322–25 contained many rubrics from this earlier period which showed a preponderance of private over public concepts of law. Many of these rubrics were conveyed directly into the statute compilation of 1415, where they appear in Book 3, the criminal code. Indeed, even rubrics containing antique concepts of law survived in the 1415 redaction. However, changes in the law during the period from 1322–25 to 1415 were significant. For instance, in the statutes of 1322–25, rubrics pertaining to assault, which originated in a much earlier period, used the means of committing the assault as a major criterion for deciding the severity of the crime and thus the severity of the punishment. A culprit who used his bare hands to injure someone seriously could escape with a light penalty (p. 22). The statutes of 1415 put more emphasis on evaluating the results than evaluating the means (pp. 27–28).

Dorini describes the beginning of the process in which law changed from being a private concern to being a public concern. In the period surrounding the 1322–25 compilation, feudal procedures were abrogated in favor of communal ones. Vendetta was not outlawed by the state but regulated by it, usually by restricting the vendetta to the principal people involved. The law of 1322–25 aimed at limiting the disruptive effects of the magnates: their vendettas, their exaggerated sentiments concerning honor, their image of themselves as above the law, and their constant warfare in communal territory (pp. 10–12). Private instruments of peace extinguishing public penal actions, became less frequently employed after 1322–25, although still frequent even in the cases from the early fifteenth century (pp. 30–31, 37). A common crime, resisting arrest, often took place with the aid of relatives and friends (pp. 112–13). While defamation in 1322–25 usually consisted of one man's insulting another for not carrying out a vendetta, a provision of 1394, which appeared in the 1415 statutes, shows that defamation in the late fourteenth and early fifteenth century consisted of political insults (pp. 44–45). By 1352, social conditions had changed so that the concentration on battling magnate disruption was not as necesssary, although this problem persisted until the early fifteenth century. In 1352, the definition of magnate was altered to include even popolani who were violent and disruptive. After this time, prevalent class conflict was not between magnates and popolani but between members of the reggimento and the *novi homines* (new men entering the government—p. 234). Importance was placed on guarding the peaceful state of Florence against the incursions of any violent culprit. The 1415 statutes were a much more complete compilation than the 1322–25 statutes, showing the increasing grip of the state on its constituency. In 1355, a system of rewards was established to encourage members of the rectors' *famiglia* to capture people *in flagranti* (in the process of committing crimes), and in 1373 it was expanded (p. 214). The role of the state in interrupting crime and apprehending criminals was increasing, while private accusation was diminishing in importance.

Dorini points out the role of the Signoria as a promoter of equity. According to Dorini, the court system did not adequately take mitigating circumstances into account, especially the presence or absence of intent to commit a crime. In these cases, the Signoria and the councils sometimes intervened to give grace, that is, to lighten the penalty, as in a case of 1393 where an assailant causing an unintended miscarriage was convicted of homicide (p. 169). The Signoria used the so-called system of oblation, in which it permanently released many prisoners from prison as part of the celebration of religious holidays, to take into account poverty, infirmity, age, and excessively severe penalties not in concordance with the crime committed. The people released were those who had little chance of paying their way out (pp. 163, 180–82). Dorini's exposition of the Signoria's role in the judicial system is certainly vastly different than the accounts of the other historians whose works have been previously discussed.

Unlike Kohler and Dorini, Guidi centers his interest primarily on the statutes of 1415. He, too, is concerned with the similarities and differences between the different statute compilations. Guidi notes that whole new sections of statutes that had been separate from communal statutes in former eras appeared in the statutes of 1415, such as the material on gabelles, the tract on the guilds, the tract on the estimo, and minor tracts on matrimony, labor, and gambling.[26] This demonstrates that the state had increasingly subsumed formerly separate corporate entities and new functions in the process of centralization and systematization. Guidi also includes a table that shows the concordances he found among the different statute compilations, the statutes of 1322–25, 1355, 1408–9, and 1415.[27] The statutes of 1408–9 were similar to those of 1415.

Moving from the statutes to the criminal cases, Samuel Cohn's *The Laboring Classes in Renaissance Florence* presents a statistical analysis of court cases from the Trecento and the Quattrocento. Most of the book discusses the marriage and settlement patterns of the popolo minuto. Cohn discovers that the popolo minuto were evenly distributed throughout the city in the mid- and late Trecento, but by the late Quattrocento, over 80 percent lived in ghettos located at the city's periphery. According to Cohn, the formation of ghettos allowed the late fifteenth-century patriciate, which held sway over the judicial system, to ignore crimes in the ghettos among members of the popolo minuto. In his chapter on criminality, he analyzes court cases and comes to a similar conclusion.[28]

Cohn uses a one-year sample of criminal court cases that were tried in the foreign rector's courts from the year 1344–45, a one-year sample from 1374–75, and a twelve-year sample from the years 1455–66. There were fifteen times the number of sentences per semester for the earlier years than for the later period. Since a change in the judicial system that started sometime after 1434 and entailed greater oligarchic control has been posited here, Cohn's late fifteenth-century information is pertinent. It is worthwhile comparing the trends Cohn has perceived with trends described here for the early fifteenth century.

Cohn believes that the philosophies of prosecution held by the government and the judicial system have great impact on patterns of criminality. The philosophies that guide the decisions as to which cases will be prosecuted, especially if they are class-biased, affect the results of the analysis of court cases. Cohn believes that by the late fifteenth century, the patriciate con-

Bibliographic Essay

trolled prosecution and that prevalent crimes changed from crimes against persons to crimes against property. Thus, while he is suggesting that an important watershed in the history of crime occurred in the course of the fifteenth century, this conclusion is mitigated by the fact that crimes against persons in the ghetto were not prosecuted so do not figure into his analysis of criminality. Crimes against property were more vigorously prosecuted by patricians using the court system for their own ends, thus biasing the statistics. Cohn statistically demonstrates that crimes against persons were intraclass, while crimes against possessions were interclass. In the late fifteenth century, patricians frequently prosecuted members of the popolo minuto for debt, trespass, poaching, and agricultural crimes, using the court system to repress and fleece the lower classes. Assaults within the ghetto continued but went unprosecuted because patricians lacked interest in crimes that only affected ghetto dwellers. Since the living quarters of the poor were no longer distributed among those of other classes, intra-ghetto crime could be ignored. One wonders if it would not indicate the same patrician oppression if many cases of mutual assault among the popolo minuto had been prosecuted. While crime in the Trecento was reported 46 percent of the time by *cappellani*, who were elected officials of the popolo drawn predominantly from the minor artisan and even *sottoposti* classes, by the late Quattrocento these officials had disappeared; crime became mainly apprehended by the famiglia of the Otto. The vehicles by which the lower classes reported crime had disappeared, while upper-class means of reporting crime were prevalent.

Several aspects of Cohn's work have bearing on an investigation of the early fifteenth century. Cohn believes that crime had a traditional profile until at least 1374 and that the poor were not gathered into ghettos until sometime after 1383. This lends some support to the idea that the judicial system was not geared to benefit the rich until some period after the early fifteenth century. Cohn has indicated a broad-based involvement in apprehending criminals through 1375, crime frequently being reported by cappellani at this time. Further, he has stated that surveillance was a major part of the program in late fifteenth-century Florence which promoted patrician control of the popolo minuto, the growth of a class-segregated society, and the oppression of the popolo minuto through the court system. I posit that this surveillance was an extreme form of methods of policing and information gathering developed in the fourteenth and early fifteenth centuries. In the early fifteenth century, policing and information gathering were used to promote the successful functioning of the court system and may have been the key factor in the improved apprehension of criminals. The early fifteenth-century form of surveillance promoted law and order, not the neglect of law and order, and was material in making inquisition procedure work properly. When policing and information gathering, like the rest of the judicial process, became controlled by the patriciate, they became surveillance in an extreme form. The early fifteenth century was the seminal period for the growth of surveillance, when surveillance was primarily in the hands of the regular court system.

Lastly, I take exception to Cohn's conclusions concerning debt cases. Cohn shows that in the early period, 1344–45, 99 percent of all debt cases were brought to the courts of the rectors by private parties. But by 1455, only 37 percent of debt cases in the rectors' courts were brought by private parties; the remaining cases originated in the guild courts or the Mercanzia court, and were then brought into communal court. Thus, it seems to Cohn that communal criminal courts were reinforcing decisions made in the guild courts or the Mercanzia court. Cohn concludes from this that the courts of the rectors increasingly served the patrician mercantile class in collecting their debts. The power of the state was being used in a class-biased way to reinforce the wealth of the already wealthy. In fact, the opposite was taking place. The statutes on defaulting and fleeing debt show that in the 1322–25 period, the guild courts were in control of debt cases, while in 1415, the communal court system had seized control of the most important kind of debt, defaulting and fleeing. In the 1322–25 period, the twelve major guilds could make ordinances and statutes concerning defaulting and fleeing, and these ordinances were to be put into effect by the Captain of the People as if they were communal statutes. The twelve major guilds could make decisions in defaulting and fleeing cases that were executed without review by the communal rectors.[29] Thus, the guilds had sway over every kind of debt except for debt made by public instrument. People who belonged to the guilds had no need to pursue debt cases in communal courts, which also could try defaulting and fleeing cases, since they could accuse for the most serious kind of debt in the guild courts.

After 1415, the guild courts were no longer allowed to try cases of defaulting and fleeing; the courts of the foreign rectors and the court of the Mercanzia became exclusively responsible for this. Thus, when a merchant wanted the most serious sanctions invoked and wanted the aid of all of the communal police forces, he brought his case before the communal rectors. In 1415, before a case of defaulting and fleeing was brought before one of the rectors, simple debt was supposed to have already been proven in communal court, the guild courts, or the Mercanzia court. The courts of the rectors retried the case of simple debt and made sure fleeing had occurred. Thus, for a crime as serious as defaulting and fleeing, the commune did not rely on the decisions of the guilds without reviewing them. For simple debt, the communal rectors executed the decisions of the guilds automatically. For defaulting and fleeing, the rectors tried the case again. The evidence does not support the view that the communal courts simply served the patriciate. Decisions of the major guilds were more subject to scrutiny in 1415 than they were in the 1322–25 period. The bloodcurdling comminations of torture in debt cases were not new to the statutes of 1415, newly instituted to help patricians extort money, but were present in the 1322–25 redaction. The laws on defaulting and fleeing in the 1415 statutes with all of their severity were taken in the main from the 1322–25 statutes.

New work has been done on the Florentine judicial system by Andrea Zorzi. Zorzi has written about the late thirteenth and early fourteenth centuries (the communal era) and the fifteenth century.[30] He is knowledgeable

Bibliographic Essay

concerning the archival sources and adept at filling in lacunae in records with other archival records; for example, lacking the deliberations of the Otto di Guardia for all years in the first half of the fifteenth century except 1408–9, he uses the Giudice degli Appelli, Condanne proferite dagli Ufiziali intrinseci records to get some sense of the activities of the Otto. However, these records have scant information on the Otto, producing about one case per year starting in 1427. While Zorzi believes that each case represents an area of investigation that has been ceded *de facto* to the jurisdiction of the Otto, this remains, to some degree, a matter of conjecture.

Zorzi is principally interested in how political power and its vicissitudes affect the judicial system. Therefore, he is more interested in the citizen courts, like the Otto di Guardia and the Conservatori delle Leggi, which were much more susceptible to political influences, than in the courts of the foreign rectors, which were less responsive. His interest in political influence and corruption biases his portraits of the courts, casting them in a political light instead of highlighting their everyday functioning. His discoveries of corruption, infractions of the *divieti* laws, and the political ties of foreign rectors are very important to bring out, but his exclusive highlighting of these aspects tends to obscure the regular running of the court system. In the past, court records have been used to outline social trends without regard for the mechanisms of the legal system. With Zorzi there is some danger of seeing the court system as only an arm of the political system, instead of as a legal system with its own purpose of meting out justice and apprehending criminals. However, Zorzi is, in general, fair, attempting to balance this with more generalized statements: for example, that the court system of the foreign rectors functioned relatively autonomously from the political situation, the development of a new judicial order taking place in the 1430s and 1440s.[31]

Zorzi centers his interest on the court of the Otto di Guardia, a court that was very much a part of the government, its members sitting in the most important assemblies of the government. This court became an instrument of the will of the Medici. He is quite conscientious in showing the conflicts and obstacles to the Otto becoming a full court completely controlled by the Medici by the 1470s. He demonstrates the restricted nature of its jurisdiction in the early fifteenth century, the government's reluctance to accord the Otto the power to condemn, the Otto's slowness in obtaining its own police force, its lack of full court status until the 1450s, and the setbacks suffered by the court of the Otto and by the Medici in general during the republican resurgent movements of 1454–58 and 1465–66 (pp. 68–69). Conflicts occurred over whether the Otto should be elected by lot, as was the case after 1406, or by direct election of the Signoria, as was the case in 1433, the two systems alternating after this (p. 70). It is useful, too, to have Medici influence on the court system, which all historians have estimated as strong, thoroughly documented for the 1460s and 1470s.

Zorzi believes that some attrition of the courts of the foreign rectors occurred in the early fifteenth century, mainly starting in the 1420s, but some objection to his methodology should be made. He attempts to show a gradual and steady decay of these courts from 1400 through 1478 by showing samples from 1400–1401, 1433–35, and 1476–78. For the 1400–1401 sample he shows the foreign rectors receiving no bullectini from the executive offices, thus not being interfered with at all, and having an inquisition *ex officio* initiation rate, a barometer of the court system's efficiency and well-being, of 90.69 percent, which was very high. For the next sample he chooses the years 1433–35, which were particularly atypical years, and finds a bullectini rate of 9.13 percent, which, considering the political tumult and extraordinary stress on the court system during those years, is not that surprising; and an inquisition rate of 68.50 percent, which, considering the directives that poured forth from the executive branch to the courts concerning political trials, is not surprising either (pp. 53–56). It is difficult to detect at what point a downward trend started or occurred (perhaps in 1433–35), or if in fact it did occur, given the atypical nature of those years. Zorzi also documents a downward trend in the number of cases processed by the foreign rectors in the 1420s. But the 1420s represent a population nadir in Florence, a decrease in population so radical that even with the addition of all of the new territory incorporated into the Florentine state, the population still decreased.[32] Attrition, too, was related to spending cuts and took place across the government.

Zorzi documents the growth of the Otto, although he tends to give the impression that the Otto had a predetermined and steady rise to power. He fails to mention, for instance, that while the office of the Otto was created for the purpose of safeguarding the government from subversion, it was created by the guild government of 1378 to prevent subversion by aristocrats plotting against this more populist government. He does underscore that the Otto could not condemn, only investigate, and rightly demonstrates that its power to issue and enforce its own edicts was one of the vehicles that the Otto used to expand its power. It did not actually receive the power to condemn until 1478, although *de facto* it tried every conceivable kind of case before then.[33] Police powers continued to remain with the foreign rectors; the Otto only got a police force in 1463.[34] Bullectini from the Otto and the Signoria to the courts of the foreign rectors became very common and eventually undermined and destroyed these courts.

In conclusion, I hope that this work will contribute to the study of the history of Florence by documenting the normal functioning of the court system from the mid-thirteenth to the early fifteenth century. I have carefully explored the institutions, officials, and procedures of this system in order to add to the knowledge presented in the above-discussed works.

NOTES

Chapter 1. Introduction: The Judicial System and the Territorial State

1. Chittolini, *Stato regionale*, and Chittolini, *La crisi degli ordinamenti comunali*.
2. Becker, *Florence in Transition*, and Becker, "Florentine Territorial State," 109–39.
3. Becker, *Florence in Transition*, 2:204.
4. Chittolini, *Stato regionale*, 294.
5. Ibid., 296.
6. Podesteries were areas ruled by podestà. A podestà was a local official with judicial and other duties such as assessing and collecting taxes. The local podestà are to be distinguished from the Podestà, the foreign rector in Florence. Both terms appear throughout the text.
7. Chittolini, *La crisi degli ordinamenti comunali*, 37–40.
8. Provv. R. 118, fols. 365r–366v, e.g., cites a provvisione of October 1408. See also Provv. R. 118, fols. 394v–395v.
9. Martines, *Lawyers and Statecraft*, 162.
10. Dorini, *Notizie storiche sull'università di Parte Guelfa*.
11. Guidi, *Il governo di Firenze*, 1:212. The rest of the information in this paragraph comes from Guidi.
12. Ibid., 114–15.
13. Brucker, *Civic World*, 64–68, 73.
14. Ibid., 314.
15. Ibid., 94, 253.
16. Guidi, *Il governo di Firenze*, 2:50.
17. Becker, "Florentine Territorial State," 115; Brucker, *Civic World*, 283.
18. Najemy, *Corporatism and Consensus*, 3.
19. Becker, "Florentine Territorial State," 115.
20. Guidi, *Il governo di Firenze*, 1:347.
21. Ibid., 1:287; *Stat.* 5.1.4.
22. Salvioli, *Storia della procedura*, 99.
23. Brucker, *Civic World*, 52.
24. Guidi, *Il governo di Firenze*, 2:107.
25. Najemy, *Corporatism and Consensus*, 264.
26. Becker, "Florentine Territorial State," 115–17.
27. Ibid., 111–12.
28. Brucker, *Civic World*, 313.
29. Weissman believes that no confraternities were actually disbanded but

that all were required to have the approval of the Signoria (*Ritual Brotherhood*, 165–66).

30. Molho, *Public Finances*, 178. The rest of the information in this paragraph comes from *Public Finances*.
31. Ibid., 116–17.
32. Rubinstein, *Government of Florence*, 111.
33. The Dieci became less powerful in 1426, when, because of mismanagement of funds, their financial duties were taken away and given to the Ufficiali del Banco. Molho, *Public Finances*, 164–66.
34. Guidi, *Il governo di Firenze*, 2:208.
35. Martines, *Lawyers and Statecraft*, 136.
36. Zorzi, *L'amministrazione della giustizia penale*, 53.
37. Atti del Esecutore degli Ordinamenti di Giustizia (AEOG), no. 2075.
38. Rubinstein, *Government of Florence*, 70.
39. Molho, "Florentine Oligarchy and the *Balìe*," 42.
40. Ibid., 33.
41. Guidi, *Il governo di Firenze*, 1:229–40.
42. Brucker, *Civic World*, 245.
43. Guidi, *Il governo di Firenze*, 1:233.
44. Ibid., 1:265–66.
45. Molho, *Public Finances*, 73.
46. Najemy, *Corporatism and Consensus*, 277; Molho, "Politics and the Ruling Class," 412.
47. Rubinstein, *Government of Florence*, 76. The rest of the information in this paragraph comes from Rubinstein.
48. Becker, *Florence in Transition*, 1:152–53.
49. Atti del Capitano del Popolo (ACP) 2732, case of Johannes quondam Nicoli de Nursia.

Chapter 2. Inquisition Procedure and the General Powers of the Foreign Rectors

1. Vallerani, "Conflitti e modelli procedurali."
2. Zordan, *Angelo Gambiglioni*, 32–33, 58.
3. Provv. R. 123, fols. 14v–15r, 1432.
4. *Stat.* 1.3; 1.68; 3.61; 3.63; 3.68; 3.83; 3.115.
5. See Chapter 8. See, for example, *Stat.* 3.39; 3.51; 3.55; 3.61; 3.83; 3.87; 3.89; 3.90.
6. For example, *Stat.* 1.70; 3.164; 3, Tractatus Ordinamentorum Iustitiae, 23; 3, Tractatus Ordinamentorum Iustitiae, 49; 4, De Offitialibus Turris, 34; 4, Tractatus et materia Consulum Artium et Mercatorum, 138; 4, Tractatus et materia extraordinariorum: De laboratorum tractatu et materia, 11; 4, Tractatus et materia extraordinariorum: de laboratorum tractatu et materia, 12.
7. Dorini, *Il diritto penale*, 144–45.
8. Ibid., 231–32.
9. Zorzi, *L'amministrazione della giustizia penale*, 81–83.

10. Ibid., 53.
11. Kuehn, "Arbitration and Law in Renaissance Florence."
12. Pertile, *Storia del diritto*, 6, pt. 1:451–53.
13. *Stat.* 3.55; 3.61; 3.66; 3.101; 3.113; 3.115.
14. Dorini, *Il diritto penale*, 155.
15. *Statuti*, 2: Statuto del Podestà, 1325, 3.78.
16. For example, AEOG 1934, 1v; AEOG 1934, 2v.
17. For example, *Stat.* 3.71; 3.73; 3.101; 3.112; 3.113; 3.115; 3.130; 3.139.
18. *Stat.* 4, De Offitialibus Turris, 77.
19. *Stat.* 4, De Offitialibus Turris, 10.
20. Dorini, *Il diritto penale*, 170.
21. *Stat.* 3.61; 3.62; 3.63.
22. *Stat.* 4, De Offitialibus Turris, 77.
23. Cohn, *Laboring Classes*, 181.
24. *Stat.* 3, Tractatus Ordinamentorum Iustitiae, 12.
25. It has been necessary to coin new English terms, the noun *cognition* and the verb *to recognize* to translate the Latin *cognitio* and *cognoscere*. There are no existing English words for these Latin words. *Cognitio* is halfway between jurisdiction and indictment. When a rector is said to *cognoscere*, to recognize a case, he is accepting the case for trial. He is at once admitting that he has jurisdiction over the case while claiming to have seen sufficient proof to warrant a trial. Recognizing a case seems to involve a stage of procedure in which the evidence is reviewed to determine whether a crime was actually committed or not.
26. Dorini, *Il diritto penale*, 213, citing statutes of 1355, Pot. 3.157.
27. *Stat.* 3, Tractatus Ordinamentorum Iustitiae, 68.
28. *Stat.* 3, Tractatus Ordinamentorum Iustitiae, 62.
29. *Stat.* 4, Tractatus et materia extraordinariorum, 76.
30. *Statuti* 2: Statuto del Podestà, 1325, 3.75.
31. *Stat.* 4, Tractatus et materia Consulum Artium et Mercatorum, 104; 181; 182; 194.
32. Dorini, *Il diritto penale*, 143, n. 1.
33. Zordan, *Angelo Gambiglioni*, 58.
34. *Stat.* 3.63; 3.66; 3.71; 3.72.
35. *Stat.* 4, Tractatus et materia Consulum Artium et Mercatorum, 149.
36. Trexler, "Death and Testament."
37. Becker, "Three Cases," and Becker, "Nota dei processi."
38. Brucker, *Society of Renaissance Florence*, 240–41.
39. Becker, "Florentine Politics."
40. *Stat.* 4, De baptismate, 15.
41. Gene A. Brucker, "Sorcery in the Early Renaissance," *Studies in the Renaissance* 10 (1963): 7–24.
42. Cozzi, *Stato, società, e giustizia*, 17–24, and Ruggiero, *Violence in Early Renaissance Venice*, 21–22.
43. Ruggiero, *Violence in Early Renaissance Venice*, 20. The rest of the

information in this chapter comes from *Violence in Renaissance Venice*, chapters 1, 2, 4, 5, and 9.

Chapter 3. The Subordinate Officials of the Foreign Rectors

1. Gilmore, *Roman Law in Political Thought*, 15–44.
2. Martines, *Lawyers and Statecraft*, 30–31.
3. Ibid., 33.
4. Cohn's contention that the Executor's criminal judge tried no ordinary criminal cases is incorrect. See, Cohn *Laboring Classes*, 181–82.
5. *Stat.* 3, Tractatus Ordinamentorum Iustitiae, 25.
6. Atti del Podestà (AP), no. 4388, 23v–24v.
7. Franchini mistakenly identifies the *milites* as noblemen of great wisdom who gave wise counsel to the Podestà. See Franchini, *Saggio di ricerche sull'istituto del Podestà*, 155.
8. *Stat.* 4, De Offitialibus Turris, 29.
9. *Stat.* 4, De Offitialibus Turris, 65.
10. *Stat.* 4, Tractatus gabellae contractuum, 5.
11. *Stat.* 4, Tractatus gabellae contractuum, 13.
12. *Stat.* 4, De Offitialibus Turris, 42.
13. *Stat.* 2, 127; 3, Tractatus de cessantibus et fugitivis, 3.
14. *Stat.* 4, Tractatus et materia Consulum Artium et Mercatorum, 27.
15. *Stat.* 4, De Offitialibus Turris, 32.
16. *Stat.* 4, De Offitialibus Turris, 33.
17. *Stat.* 4, Tractatus gabellae contractuum, 4.
18. Similarly, in France, appeal involved a full retrial of issues of fact. See Langbein, *Prosecuting Crime in the Renaissance*, 214, citing Dawson, *History of Lay Judges*.
19. Kuehn, "Arbitration and Law in Renaissance Florence," 292–94.
20. Salvioli, *Storia della procedura*, 188.
21. Chittolini, *Stato regionale*, 300–301.
22. Martines is incorrect in saying that all appeals from the county and district went to the judge of appeals in Florence. There is a general rubric pertaining to the county and district to this effect, but exceptions are many. See Martines, *Lawyers and Statecraft*, 223.
23. *Stat.* 5.4.24; 5.4.25; 5.4.26.
24. *Stat.* 4, De baptismate, 3.
25. *Stat.* 4, De baptismate, 4.
26. For a history of appeals and of the other spheres of competence formerly possessed by the judge of appeals, see Davidsohn, *Storia di Firenze*, 4, pt. 1:163–65.
27. Martines, *Lawyers and Statecraft*, 132.

Chapter 4. The Podestà and Other Officials with Judicial Powers Affiliated with the Podestà

1. Lansing, "Nobility in a Medieval Commune," 7.
2. Lorenzo Cantini, "Dell'ufizio del Podestà di Firenze," 3.
3. Ibid., 60, 63, 66, 74.
4. Santini, *Studi sull'antica costituzione*, 26–31.
5. Plesner, *L'émigration de la campagne à la ville*.
6. Ibid., 106–7.
7. Ibid., 132.
8. Franchini, *Saggio di ricerche sull'istituto del Podestà*, 39–77.
9. Ibid., 93–94.
10. Cantini, "Dell'ufizio del Podestà di Firenze," 110.
11. Franchini, *Saggio di ricerche sull'istituto del Podestà*, 164.
12. Ibid., 140–41.
13. Cantini, "Dell'ufizio del Podestà di Firenze," 111.
14. Franchini, *Saggio di ricerche sull'istituto del Podestà*, 165.
15. Cantini, "Dell'ufizio del Podestà di Firenze," 117.
16. *Statuti*, 2: *Statuto del Podestà, 1325*, 3.76.
17. For the Captain's jurisdiction over foodstuffs, see *Statuti*, 1: *Statuto del Capitano del Popolo, 1322–25*, 1.16; 1.23. For the Captain's affiliation with the consuls, see *Statuti*, 1: *Statuto del Capitano del Popolo, 1322–25*, 2.14.
18. *Statuti*, 2: *Statuto del Podestà, 1325*, 2.9; 2.55; 2.57; 2.81.
19. *Stat.* 4, Tractatus et materia Consulum Artium et Mercatorum, 18.
20. Salvioli, *Storia della procedura*, 99.
21. *Stat.* 3, Tractatus de cessantibus et fugitivis, 1; 3. Consecutive references to this source appear in text.
22. *Stat.* 4, Tractatus et materia Consulum Artium et Mercatorum, 27, p. 183.
23. *Stat.* 3, Tractatus de cessantibus et fugitivis, 1.
24. Cohn, *Laboring Classes*, 191–92.
25. Bonolis, *La giurisdizione della Mercanzia*, 99. Here Bonolis cites all the guild statutes that show the consuls trying cases of defaulting and fleeing debt.
26. Cf. *Statuti*, 1: *Statuto del Capitano del Popolo, 1322–25*, 2.60, to *Stat.* 3, Tractatus de cessantibus et fugitivis, 16.
27. *Stat.* 3, Tractatus de cessantibus et fugitivis, 5.
28. For example, the Statutes of the Campsor Guild of 1291, cited in Salvioli, *Storia della procedura*, 99.
29. *Stat.* 3, Tractatus de cessantibus et fugitivis, 34. Consecutive references to this source appear in text.
30. *Stat.* 4, Tractatus et materia Consulum Artium et Mercatorum, 26. Consecutive references to this source appear in text.
31. Salvioli, *Storia della procedura*, 99.
32. *Stat.* 4, Tractatus et materia Consulum Artium et Mercatorum, 36. Consecutive references to this source appear in text.

33. Brucker, *Civic World*, 52; Doren, *Le arti Fiorentine*, 52–60; Rodolico, *I Ciompi*, 197–206; Rodolico, *La democrazia Fiorentina*, 457–58.
34. Bonolis, *La giurisdizione della Mercanzia*, 99.
35. *Statuti*, 1: *Statuto del Capitano del Popolo, 1322–25*, 2.50.
36. *Stat.* 4, Tractatus et materia Consulum Artium et Mercatorum, 33.
37. *Stat.* 4, Tractatus et materia Consulum Artium et Mercatorum, 33.
38. *Stat.* 3.141; 4, Tractatus et materia Consulum Artium et Mercatorum, 33.
39. *Stat.* 4, Tractatus et materia Consulum Artium et Mercatorum, 66.
40. *Statuti dell'arte del Cambio (1299–1316)*, Statuto dell'arte del Cambio (1299), 29.
41. *Stat.* 4, Tractatus et materia Consulum Artium et Mercatorum, 13. Consecutive references to this source appear in text.
42. Bonolis, *La giurisdizione della Mercanzia*, 26. The rest of the information in this paragraph and the one immediately following comes from Bonolis.
43. Salvioli, *Storia della procedura*, 343–45. The information in the next four paragraphs comes from Salvioli.
44. Del Vecchio and Casanova, *Le rappresaglie nei comuni medievali*, 2–3.
45. Ibid., 3.
46. Ibid., 31.
47. Bonolis, *La giurisdizione della Mercanzia*, 32–33. The rest of the information in this and the following two paragraphs comes from Bonolis.
48. Martines, *Lawyers and Statecraft*, 133–35.
49. Bonolis, *La giurisdizione della Mercanzia*, 129–31.
50. *Stat.* 4, Tractatus et materia Consulum Artium et Mercatorum, 24. Consecutive references to this source appear in text.
51. *Stat.* 3, Tractatus de cessantibus et fugitivis, 7; 12; 14; 5.1.248.
52. *Stat.* 3, Tractatus de cessantibus et fugitivis, 7.
53. *Stat.* 3, Tractatus de cessantibus et fugitivis, 12.
54. *Stat.* 4, Tractatus et materia Consulum Artium et Mercatorum, 27.
55. *Stat.* 4, Tractatus et materia Consulum Artium et Mercatorum, 27.
56. *Stat.* 4, Tractatus et materia Consulum Artium et Mercatorum, 7.
57. *Stat.* 4, Tractatus et materia Consulum Artium et Mercatorum, 104. Further consecutive references to this source appear in text.
58. *Stat.* 4, Tractatus et materia Consulum Artium et Mercatorum, 182. Further consecutive references to this source appear in text.
59. *Stat.* 4, Tractatus et materia extraordinariorum, 11.
60. *Stat.* 4, Tractatus et materia extraordinariorum, 22.
61. *Stat.* 4, Tractatus et materia extraordinariorum, 23.
62. *Stat.* 4, Tractatus et materia Consulum Artium et Mercatorum, 97; 104; 121; 186; 194; 195; 205; 215; 222; 258. Consecutive references to this source appear in text.
63. Fasano Guarini, "Giustizia, stato, e società," 145.
64. For example, *Stat.* 5.4.20; 5.4.21.

65. Fasano Guarini, *Lo Stato Mediceo di Cosimo I*, 78.
66. Connell, "Il commissario," 593.
67. Fasano Guarini, *Lo Stato Mediceo di Cosimo I*, 77.
68. Zorzi, *L'amministrazione della giustizia penale*, 22.
69. Connell, "Il commissario," 609.
70. Martines, *Lawyers and Statecraft*, 220–21.
71. Connell, "Il commissario," 609.
72. Zorzi, *L'amministrazione della giustizia penale*, 27.
73. Connell, "Il commissario," 597.
74. Ibid., 603–4.
75. For the opposite opinion, see ibid., 615.
76. Ibid., 609.
77. Connell, "Clientelismo e stato territoriale," 526–33.
78. Fasano Guarini, "Giustizia, stato, e società," 137.
79. Zorzi, *L'amministrazione della giustizia penale*, 28.
80. Chittolini, *Stato regionale*, 311.
81. *Stat.* 5.4.42; 43; 47; 50.
82. *Stat.* 5.4.59; 70; 95.

Chapter 5. The Captain of the People

1. Santini, *Studi sull'antica costituzione*, 130.
2. Ibid., 135–38.
3. Ibid., 151–52.
4. Kohler and Azzi, *Das Florentiner Strafrecht*, 183.
5. Davidsohn, *Storia di Firenze*, 4, pt. 2:151.
6. Cantini, "Dell'ufizio del Podestà di Firenze," 117.
7. *Statuti*, 1: *Statuto del Capitano del Popolo, 1322–25*, 1.2.
8. *Statuti*, 1: *Statuto del Capitano del Popolo, 1322–25*, 2.1.
9. *Statuti*, 1: *Statuto del Capitano del Popolo, 1322–25*, 1.53.
10. *Statuti*, 1: *Statuto del Capitano del Popolo, 1322–25*, 4.4.
11. *Statuti*, 1: *Statuto del Capitano del Popolo, 1322–25*, 2.14.
12. *Statuti*, 1: *Statuto del Capitano del Popolo, 1322–25*, 2.1.
13. See, e.g., *Statuti*, 1: *Statuto del Capitano del Popolo, 1322–25*, 1.17; 1.20; 1.22; 1.23; 1.24.
14. *Statuti*, 1: *Statuto del Capitano del Popolo, 1322–25*, 1.16.
15. For instance, *Stat.* 3, Tractatus Ordinamentorum Iustitiae, 21, of 1415, was the same as *Statuto del Capitano del Popolo* 2.4, of 1322–25; *Stat.* 3, Tractatus Ordinamentorum Iustitiae, 46, of 1415, was the same as *Statuto del Capitano del Popolo* 5.55, of 1322–25; *Stat.* 3, Tractatus Ordinamentorum Iustitiae, 47, of 1415, was the same as *Statuto del Capitano del Popolo* 5.56, of 1322–25; *Stat.* 4, Tractatus et materia extraordinariorum: De laboratorum tractatu et materia, 26, of 1415, was the same as *Statuto del Capitano del Popolo* 3.8, of 1322–25; *Stat.* 3, Tractatus Ordinamentorum Iustitiae, 82, of 1415, was the same as *Statuto del Capitano del Popolo* 3.3, of 1322–25; *Stat.* 3, Tractatus Ordinamentorum Iustitiae, 51, of 1415, was the same as *Statuto del*

Capitano del Popolo 2.12, of 1322–25; and *Stat.* 5.1.23, of 1415, was the same as *Statuto del Capitano del Popolo* 2.6, of 1322–25.

16. *Stat.* 3, Tractatus Ordinamentorum Iustitiae, 46.
17. *Stat.* 3, Tractatus Ordinamentorum Iustitiae, 47.
18. *Stat.* 3, Tractatus Ordinamentorum Iustitiae, 82.
19. Kohler and Azzi, *Das Florentiner Strafrecht*, 183.
20. *Stat.* 4, Tractatus et materia extraordinariorum, 110.
21. *Stat.* 4, Tractatus et materia extraordinariorum: De laboratorum tractatu et materia, 26.
22. *Stat.* 3, Tractatus Ordinamentorum Iustitiae, 67.
23. *Stat.* 3, Tractatus Ordinamentorum Iustitiae, 19.
24. *Statuti*, 1: *Statuto del Capitano del Popolo, 1322–25*, 2.6.
25. *Statuti*, 1: *Statuto del Capitano del Popolo, 1322–25*, 3.10.
26. *Statuti*, 1: *Statuto del Capitano del Popolo, 1322–25*, 2.3; Davidsohn, *Storia di Firenze*, 4, pt. 2:151.
27. Cantini, "Dell'ufizio del Podestà di Firenze," 162–70.
28. Rubinstein, *Government of Florence*, 3n.
29. Zorzi, *L'amministrazione della giustizia penale*, 73–74.

Chapter 6. The Executor of the Ordinances of Justice

1. Parenti, "Dagli Ordinamenti di Giustizia"; Lansing, "Nobility in a Medieval Commune," 21–22.
2. Najemy, *Corporatism and Consensus*, 17–42.
3. Davidsohn, *Storia di Firenze*, 4, pt. 2:160–61.
4. Najemy, *Corporatism and Consensus*, 23.
5. Salvemini, *Magnati e popolani*, 234.
6. Becker, "Florentine Territorial State," 112–13.
7. Cohn, *Laboring Classes*, 60–61.
8. Salvemini, *Magnati e popolani*, 194–98.
9. Bonaini, "Gli Ordinamenti di Giustizia."
10. Ibid., 30.
11. *Stat.* 3, Tractatus Ordinamentorum Iustitiae, 1; 3.
12. Bonaini, "Gli Ordinamenti di Giustizia," p. 22.
13. Salvemini, *Magnati e popolani*, 261–65.
14. Ibid., 239–41, 261–62.
15. Ibid., 224–29.
16. Ibid., 230–32.
17. *Stat.* 3, Tractatus Ordinamentorum Iustitiae, 28; 70.
18. *Stat.* 3, Tractatus Ordinamentorum Iustitiae, 21.
19. *Stat.* 3, Tractatus Ordinamentorum Iustitiae, 19; Martines, *Violence and Disorder*; J. K. Hyde, "Contemporary Views on Faction and Civil Strife in Thirteenth- and Fourteenth-Century Italy," in Martines, *Violence and Disorder*, 273–307, at 290.
20. *Stat.* 3, Tractatus Ordinamentorum Iustitiae, 60. Consecutive references to this source appear in text.

Notes to Pages 136–152

21. Becker, "Florentine Territorial State," 112–13.
22. Plesner, *L'émigration de la campagne*, 21–24, 28, 58–59, 79, 90.
23. Cohn, *Laboring Classes*, 61.
24. *Stat.* 3, Tractatus Ordinamentorum Iustitiae, 62.
25. *Stat.* 3, Tractatus Ordinamentorum Iustitiae, 60.
26. *Stat.* 4, De Offitialibus Turris, 1.
27. Masi, "Il sindicato delle magistrature comunali," 50–51. Information in the rest of this paragraph and in most of the two that immediately follow comes from Masi.
28. Masi, "Il sindicato delle magistrature comunali," 352.
29. Franchini's assertion that syndication was carried out for the purpose of compensating private damages does not conflict with my view of syndication. Duties neglected or omitted could cause private damages; see Franchini, p. 180.
30. Ibid., 61.
31. *Stat.* 3, Tractatus Ordinamentorum Iustitiae, 15.
32. *Stat.* 3, Tractatus Ordinamentorum Iustitiae, 7.
33. *Stat.* 4, Tractatus et materia Consulum Artium et Mercatorum, 279.
34. *Stat.* 3, Tractatus Ordinamentorum Iustitiae, 3.
35. *Stat.* 4, De Offitialibus Turris, 32.
36. *Stat.* 3, Tractatus Ordinamentorum Iustitiae, 16.
37. Brucker, *Civic World*, 489–93.
38. *Stat.* 1.62; 3, Tractatus Ordinamentorum Iustitiae, 16.
39. For somewhat of an exception, see *Stat.* 3, Tractatus Ordinamentorum Iustitiae, 7.
40. *Stat.* 3, Tractatus Ordinamentorum Iustitiae, 10; 11; 1.62.
41. *Stat.* 3, Tractatus Ordinamentorum Iustitiae, 7.
42. *Stat.* 4, De Arte Iudicum et Notariorum, 10.
43. *Stat.* 3, Tractatus Ordinamentorum Iustitiae, 8.
44. *Stat.* 3, Tractatus Ordinamentorum Iustitiae, 12; 5.4.45.
45. *Stat.* 3, Tractatus Ordinamentorum Iustitiae, 8.
46. *Stat.* 4, De Offitialibus Turris, 4.
47. Masi, "Il sindicato delle magistrature comunali," 85.
48. *Stat.* 3, Tractatus Ordinamentorum Iustitiae, 10.
49. Guidi, *Il governo di Firenze*, 2:285.
50. *Stat.* 4, De Offitialibus Turris, 20; 32.
51. *Stat.* 4, De Offitialibus Turris, 4.
52. *Stat.* 4, De Offitialibus Turris, 5; 11; 12; 13; 14.
53. *Stat.* 3, Tractatus Ordinamentorum Iustitiae, 10; 1.62. Consecutive references to this source appear in text.
54. *Stat.* 5.4.1; 5.4.19; 5.4.36.
55. *Stat.* 4, Tractatus et materia extraordinariorum: Tractatus contra ludentes ad ludum zardietalios ludos prohibitos, 27.
56. *Stat.* 4, Tractatus et materia extraordinariorum, 67.
57. *Stat.* 3, Tractatus Ordinamentorum Iustitiae, 12.
58. Guidi, *Il governo di Firenze*, 2:52.

59. Brucker, *Civic World*, 94, 253.
60. Martines, *Lawyers and Statecraft*, 137.

Chapter 7. The Executive Offices

1. Ottokar, *Il Comune di Firenze*, 3–33.
2. Brucker, *Civic World*, 253.
3. *Stat.* 5.1.69; 5.1.72; 5.1.78; 5.1.83.
4. Molho, "Florentine Oligarchy and the *Balie*," 30–33.
5. Brucker, *Civic World*, 245.
6. See, e.g., Brucker, *Civic World*, 333.
7. Molho, "Florentine Oligarchy and the *Balie*," 40–49.
8. Brucker, *Civic World*, 147–48, 161–62, 333–34; Molho, "Florentine Oligarchy and the *Balie*," p. 51.
9. *Stat.* 4, De Offitialibus Turris, 47; 5.1.108; 5.1.109; 5.1.110; 5.1.111; 5.1.114; 5.1.125; 5.1.320.
10. Guidi, *Il governo di Firenze*, 2:145–49.
11. Brucker, *Civic World*, 245.
12. Ibid., 384, 409, 432.
13. *Statuti*, 1: *Statuto del Capitano del Popolo, 1322–1325*, 2.3.
14. Martines, *Lawyers and Statecraft*, 161–66.
15. Santini, "Studi sull'antica costituzione," 32; Martines, *Lawyers and Statecraft*, 125.
16. Martines, *Lawyers and Statecraft*, 120–25.
17. Guidi, *Il governo di Firenze*, 1:29. Most of the information in the next six paragraphs comes from Guidi.
18. Martines, *Lawyers and Statecraft*, 95, 402.
19. Guidi, *Il governo di Firenze*, 1:39.
20. *Statuti*, 2: *Statuto del Podestà, 1325*, 3.115.
21. Guidi, *Il governo di Firenze*, 2:226.
22. Ibid., 2:204–9.
23. Ibid., 2:286.
24. *Stat.* 5.1.78; 5.1.83; 5.1.85; Guidi, *Il governo di Firenze*, 2:215.
25. *Stat.* 5.1.69; 5.1.77; 5.1.78.
26. *Statuti*, 2: *Statuto del Podestà, 1325*, 3.103.
27. *Stat.* 3, Tractatus Ordinamentorum Iustitiae, 24.
28. Brucker, *Civic World*, p. 63.
29. *Stat.* 3, Tract. Ord. Iust., 24. Consecutive references to this source appear in text.
30. Dorini, *Il diritto penale*, 234.
31. Brucker, *Civic World*, 63.
32. Cohn, *Laboring Classes*, 61.
33. *Stat.* 3.61; 3.62; 3.63; 3.64; 3.65; 3.66; 3.67; 3.68; 3.69; 3.70; 3.71; 3.72.
34. Brucker, *Civic World*, 56, 90, 93, 139, 140, 165, 171, 173, 250, 398; AP, no. 4377, unpaginated, case of Antonius Neri de Buccono, unpaginated, case of Antonius Francisci et Jacobus Costantini de Asisio, unpaginated, case of Jac-

obus Ciachi de Buchono, unpaginated, case of Ser Augustinus quondam Alexandri de Alferiis de Ponte Tre Milo, unpaginated, case of Antonius Thodertini de Giereta et Bartolomeus Nestelli alius el Barbiere de Montesaccho; no. 4380, fols. 11v–12r, 14v–15v; no. 4388, fols. 8v–9r, 10r–11r, 27r–30r, 34r–35v, 43r–44r.

35. Brucker, *Civic World*, 172–74.
36. Antonelli Moriani, *Giovanni Guicciardini*.
37. *Stat.* 3, Tract. Ord. Iust., 24.
38. *Stat.* 3, Tract. Ord. Iust., 62.
39. *Stat.* 3, Tract. Ord. Iust., 29.
40. *Stat.* 4, Tract. Cons. Art. Merc., 182.
41. *Statuti*, 1: *Statuto del Capitano del Popolo, 1322–25*, 5.18.
42. Brucker, *Civic World*, 259.
43. *Stat.* 4, De Offitialibus Turris, 12.
44. *Statuti*, 1: *Statuto del Capitano del Popolo, 1322–25*, 3.94.
45. Dorini, *Il diritto penale*, 184; *Statuti*, 1: *Statuto del Capitano del Popolo, 1322–25*, 5.62.
46. Dorini, *Il diritto penale*, 184.
47. Ibid., 180–81.
48. Ibid., 178.
49. *Statuti*, 1: *Statuto del Capitano del Popolo, 1322–25*, 5.1.
50. *Stat.* 4, De Offitialibus Turris, 1.
51. *Stat.* 4, De Offitialibus Turris, 8.
52. Becker, *Florence in Transition*, 1:152–55.
53. *Statuta*, IV, De Offitialibus Turris, 1. Consecutive references to this source appear in text.
54. *Stat.* 4, Tractatus gabellae contractuum, 13.
55. *Stat.* 4, De Offitialibus Turris, 42.
56. *Stat.* 4, De Offitialibus Turris, 1; 29.
57. *Stat.* 4, De Offitialibus Turris, 20.
58. *Stat.* 4, De Offitialibus Turris, 1; Guidi, *Il governo di Firenze* 2:285.
59. *Stat.* 4, De Offitialibus Turris, 22; 25. Consecutive references to this source appear in text.
60. *Stat.* 4, Tractatus et materia extraordinariorum, 76.
61. *Stat.* 4, De Offitialibus Turris, 26.
62. *Stat.* 4, Tractatus gabellae contractuum, 22.
63. *Stat.* 4, Tractatus gabellae contractuum, 19.
64. *Stat.* 4, De Offitialibus Turris, 66.
65. *Stat.* 4, De Offitialibus Turris, 66; Tractatus gabellae contractuum, 5.
66. *Stat.* 4, De Offitialibus Turris, 65.
67. *Stat.* 4, Tractatus gabellae contractuum, 5.
68. *Stat.* 4, Tractatus gabellae contractuum, 19.
69. *Stat.* 4, De Offitialibus Turris, 62.
70. *Stat.* 4, Tractatus gabellae contractuum, 1. Consecutive references to this source appear in text.
71. *Stat.* 4, De Offitialibus Turris, 67.
72. Martines, *Lawyers and Statecraft*, 135–36.

73. Antonelli, "La magistratura degli Otto."
74. Martines, *Lawyers and Statecraft*, 226–27.
75. Brucker, *Civic World*, 339.
76. Antonelli, "La magistratura degli Otto," 14.
77. Rubinstein, *Government of Florence*, 111. See also Becker, "Violence and Justice," for an analysis of the everyday functioning of the Otto after 1460.
78. Brucker, *Civic World*, 489.

Chapter 8. The Cases

1. AP, nos. 4377, 4378, 4380, 4384, 4388, 4392.
2. Dorini, *Il diritto penale*; Cohn, *Laboring Classes*, 179–203.
3. Dorini, *Il diritto penale*, 142–43.
4. Ibid., 142.
5. Ibid., 95.
6. AP, no. 4392, unpaginated, case of Checcus Buti, Checcus Losi, and Baldazar Marci.
7. Pertile, *Storia del diritto*, 6:455n.
8. AP, no. 4377, fols. 70r–70v; no. 4377, fols. 76r–78r; no. 4384, fol. 14v; no. 4392, unpaginated, case of Franciscus filius Jacobi de Vecchietis.
9. AP, no. 4392, unpaginated, case of Nobilis Vir Bartholomeus, Ser Bartholomeus olim Chechi, etc.; no. 4392, unpaginated, case of Nobilis Vir Jacobutus Gueriante, etc.; no. 4392, unpaginated, case of Nobilis Vir Franciscus Bartoli.
10. Dorini, *Il diritto penale*, 231.
11. Cohn, *Laboring Classes*, 115–28.
12. Ibid., 189–94.
13. AP, no. 4392, unpaginated, case of Martinus Zanardi de Vulterra; no. 4392, unpaginated, case of Michaelus Pieri vocatus Tagha; no. 4392, unpaginated, case of Jacobus Nardi alius Papi.
14. AP, no. 4380, fols. 10r–11r; no. 4380, fols. 22r–22v; no. 4384, fols. 27r–27v; no. 4388, fols. 8r–8v; no. 4392, unpaginated, case of Michaelus Pieri vocatus Tagha.
15. AP, no. 4380, fols. 4r–4v; no. 4380, fols. 10r–11r; no. 4384, fols. 27r–27v.
16. AP, no. 4377, fols. 9r–9v.
17. AP, no. 4380, fol. 36r.
18. There are many cases in AEOG, no. 2075.
19. Dorini, *Il diritto penale*, 154–55.
20. *Stat.* 3, Tractatus de cessantibus et fugitivis, 5.
21. *Stat.* 5.4.22; 5.4.41; 5.4.42.
22. *Stat.* 4, Tractatus et materia Consulum Artium et Mercatorum, 181.
23. *Stat.* 5, Tractatus et materia extraordinariorum, 34.
24. AP, no. 4377, unpaginated, case of Dolfus Benedicti Michi; no. 4377, unpaginated, case of Lupus Fei, Laurentius Ugolini, and Hammen Pieri; no. 4377, unpaginated, case of Silvestrus Antonii.

Notes to Pages 213–218

25. AP, no. 4384, fol. 13v.
26. Dorini, *Il diritto penale*, 28–29, 64.
27. Cohn, *Laboring Classes*, 189.
28. Dorini, *Il diritto penale*, 63.
29. Cohn, *Laboring Classes*, 189.
30. Ibid., 190.
31. Ibid., chap. 5, The Ecology of the Renaissance City; 201.
32. Ibid., 187.
33. Dorini, *Il diritto penale*, 28, 38.
34. See, for instance: AP, no. 4377, unpaginated, case of Checchus Bonii Luce segator popoli S. Petri Maiorus; no. 4377, unpaginated, case of Guidones Jacobi popoli S. Michaelis; no. 4377, unpaginated, case of Nicolaus Pieri de Troppo et Arriguis de Alamania; no. 4377, unpaginated, case of Domina Piera uxor Antonii Chechi et Domina Nanna uxor Antonii Ugolini; no. 4377, unpaginated, case of Silvestrus Antonii; no. 4380, fols. 8r–9r, 21r–21v, 22r–22v, 27r–27v, 27v–28r, 33r–34r; no. 4384, fols. 1v–2r, 10r–10v; 17r–17v; no. 4388, fols. 37r–37v; no. 4392, unpaginated, case of Piermaximus de Branchadius; unpaginated, case of Zenobius olim Macthei de Falconeriis; unpaginated, case of Vannes Marsilii de Vecchiectis et Corradus Silvus Jacobi.
35. AP, no. 4380, fols. 27r–27v; no. 4392, unpaginated, case of Dominicus Fani vocatus Cece et Domina Philipa.
36. AP, no. 4377, unpaginated, case of Andrea Nannis de Teranazzario; no. 4380, fol. 17r; no. 4384, fols. 21v–22r; no. 4384, fols. 31r–32r; no. 4392, unpaginated, case of Stefanus Aliecti; no. 4392, unpaginated, case of Martinus Agnelis; no. 4392, unpaginated, case of Johannes Granaldi; no. 4392, unpaginated, case of Lucus Angeli vocatus Paradisi.
37. To find the percentage of theft to total crime in Dorini's two samples, the figures for theft on p. 64 must be compared with the figures for total crime from pp. 142 and 155. Calculating with this method, theft represented roughly 15 percent in the 1352–55 period and 11.5 percent in the 1380–83 period.
38. AP, no. 4392, unpaginated, case of Anguelus Zenobii Andree de Bardis.
39. AP, no. 4377, unpaginated, case of Antonius Nicholai alius Belacqua; no. 4377, unpaginated, case of Berus del Bianco sartor.
40. AP, no. 4377, unpaginated, case of Diotavitus olim Bartoli; no. 4377, unpaginated, case of Allobranicus filius olim Labuzzi; no. 4377, unpaginated, case of Arrighus domini Colutii; no. 4377, unpaginated, case of Thomas olim Luce de Castro Montis Varchi; no. 4377, unpaginated, case of Vestgius olim Simonis Guiducci; no. 4384, fols. 15v, 20r–20v, 25r–25v; no. 4388, fols. 1v–2v, 3r–4r, 12r–13r, 13v–15v, 21v–22v; no. 4392, unpaginated, case of Santius olim Mentini; no. 4392, unpaginated, case of Anguelus Zenobii Andree di Bardis; no. 4392, unpaginated, case of Frosinus filius olim Ugolini; no. 4392, unpaginated, case of Bernardus quondam Duti; no. 4392, unpaginated, case of Marchus Nicolai Benocii; no. 4392, unpaginated, case of Bernardus dictus Filippus.
41. AP, no. 4377, unpaginated, case of Arrighus domini Colutii; no. 4388, fols. 3r–4r; no. 4392, unpaginated, case of Marchus Nicolai Benocii; no. 4392, unpaginated, case of Bernardus dictus Filippus.

42. AP, no. 4377, unpaginated, case of Macteus et Masinus fratres et filii quondam Christofori.
43. AP, no. 4380, fols. 5r–6r.
44. Dorini, *Il diritto penale*, 59–61.
45. AP, no. 4392, unpaginated, case of Julianus Bartholomei.
46. Dorini, *Il diritto penale*, 129.
47. AP, no. 4377, unpaginated, case of Rodoricus Johannis de Ispania.
48. AP, no. 4388, fols. 34r–35r.
49. AP, no. 4380, fols. 11v–12r; no. 4388, fols. 27r–29v.
50. Brucker, *Civic World*, 477.
51. AP, no. 4380, fols. 35r–36r.
52. Brucker, *Civic World*, 472, 475, 483, 502.
53. AP, no. 4388, fols. 41r–42r.
54. Brucker, *Civic World*, 500–501.
55. Ibid., 504.
56. Dorini, *Il diritto penale*, 129.
57. *Stat.* 3, 75; 76; 79.
58. Brucker, *Civic World*, 506.
59. Brucker, *Society of Renaissance Florence*, 111.
60. Ibid., 101.
61. AP, no. 4392, unpaginated, case of Franciscus Jacobi Manelli et Ser Pierus Johannis Becti.
62. For 1344–45, Cohn obtains a rate of 3.7 percent compared to the total; for 1352–55, Dorini finds a rate of 3.2 percent; for 1374–75, Cohn obtains a rate of 3.4 percent; for 1380–83, Dorini finds a rate of 4.2 percent; for 1425–28, I obtain a rate of 6/177, or 3.4 percent; and for 1455–56, Cohn finds a rate of 5.3 percent. I obtained the figures for Dorini by adding together Dorini's figures for adultery, rape, and sodomy and obtaining the rate. Dorini, *Il diritto penale*, 68–72.
63. AP, no. 4392, unpaginated, case of Guidus Antonii Guidi.
64. Cohn, *Laboring Classes*, 196.
65. AP, no. 4392, unpaginated, case of Marcus filius Mactei Orpillarius.
66. AP, no. 4384, fol. 13r.

Chapter 9. Conclusion

1. Rubinstein, *Government of Florence*, 1–2. The rest of the information in this paragraph comes from Rubinstein.
2. Zorzi, *L'amministrazione della giustizia penale*, 67–72.
3. Ibid., 75.
4. Ibid., 67; Rubinstein, *Government of Florence*, 145.
5. Rubinstein, *Government of Florence*, 111, 123.
6. Zorzi, *L'amministrazione della giustizia penale*, 67.
7. Ibid., 53–56, 72.
8. Ibid., 72–73.
9. Rubinstein, *Government of Florence*, 123.

10. Zorzi, *L'amministrazione della giustizia penale*, 71.
11. Rubinstein, *Government of Florence*, 145.
12. Ibid., 114–15.
13. Ibid., 184–85.
14. Zorzi, *L'amministrazione della giustizia penale*, 77–78.
15. Rubinstein, *Government of Florence*, 185.
16. Zorzi, *L'amministrazione della giustizia penale*, 93–100. Information in the next paragraph comes from *L'amministrazione della giustizia penale*.
17. Fasano Guarini, "Giustizia, stato, e società," 140, 147. Most of the information in this and the next paragraph comes from "Guistizia, stato, e società."
18. Brackett, *Criminal Justice*, 142.
19. Fasano Guarini, "Giustizia, stato, e società," 136.
20. Brackett, *Criminal Justice*, 140.
21. Fasano Guarini, "Giustizia, stato, e società," 140.
22. Ibid., 138.
23. Zorzi, *L'amministrazione della giustizia penale*, 111.

Bibliographic Essay

1. Martines, *Lawyers and Statecraft*, 387.
2. Martines, *Lawyers and Statecraft*, 137.
3. Provv. R. 111, fols. 262r–263r.
4. Provv. R. 115, fol. 141v.
5. Zorzi, *L'amministrazione della giustizia*, 54n. 160.
6. Brucker, *Civic World*, 253.
7. Najemy, *Corporatism and Consensus*, 304.
8. Ibid., 265.
9. Brucker, *Civic World*, 84.
10. Ibid., 283
11. Ibid., 181.
12. Ibid., 283–84. Hans Baron initiated this interpretation, that upper-class Florentines were committed to broad-based participation in politics, in "The Social Background of Political Liberty in the Early Italian Renaissance," and *The Crisis of the Early Italian Renaissance*.
13. Brucker, *Civic World*, 323.
14. Ibid., 270.
15. Ibid., 37–38.
16. Guidi, *Il governo di Firenze*, 1:5–6. Information in the next two paragraphs comes from Guidi.
17. Najemy, *Corporatism and Consensus*, 236.
18. Ibid., 294–95, citing Molho, "Politics and the Ruling Class," 409; Witt, "Florentine Politics and the Ruling Class," 248.
19. Najemy, *Corporatism and Consensus*, 295–97.
20. Pampaloni, "Il governo della Repubblica di Firenze," 553–67.
21. Guidi, *Il governo di Firenze*, 1:287. Information in the next two paragraphs comes from Guidi.

22. Kohler and Azzi, *Das Florentiner Strafrecht*, 137.
23. Ibid., 208–9.
24. Ibid., 201–2.
25. Dorini, *Il diritto penale*, 8. Information in the next three paragraphs comes from Dorini.
26. Guidi, *Il governo di Firenze*, 1:72.
27. Ibid., 1:75–83.
28. Cohn, *Laboring classes*, 179–203.
29. *Statuti della Repubblica Fiorentina*, 1: *Statuto del Capitano del Popolo, 1322–25*; 2: *Statuto del Podestà, 1325*, 1, *Statuto del Capitano del Popolo, 1322–25*, 250. This rubric is from the 1282–85 period.
30. Zorzi, *L'amministrazione della giustizia;* "I Fiorentini e gli uffici pubblici;" "Giustizia e società a Firenze in età comunale."
31. Zorzi, *L'amministrazione della giustizia*, 46–47. Most of the information in the next two paragraphs comes from *L'amministrazione della giustizia*.
32. Molho, *Public Finances*, 26.
33. Ibid., 42–43, 50–51.
34. Ibid., 45, 84.

SELECT BIBLIOGRAPHY

Manuscript Sources, Archivio di Stato, Firenze

Atti del Capitano del Popolo (ACP).
Atti del Esecutore degli Ordinamenti di Giustizia (AEOG).
Atti del Podestà (AP).
Giudice degli appelli, Condanne proferite dagli ufiziali intrinseci (GA).
Otto di Guardia della Repubblica.
Provvisioni, Duplicati (Provv. D.).
Provvisioni, Registri (Provv. R.).

Published Sources

Statuta Popoli et Communis Florentiae (1415). 3 vols. Freiburg: M. Kluch, 1778–83.
Statuti della Repubblica Fiorentina. Edited by Romolo Caggese. 1: *Statuto del Capitano del Popolo, 1322–1325*. Florence: Galileiana, 1910. 2: *Statuto del Podestà, 1325*. Florence: E. Ariani, 1922.
Statuti dell'arte del Cambio (1299–1316). Edited by G. Marri. Florence: Leo S. Olschki, 1955.
Statuto dell'Arte della lana di Firenze (1317–1319). Edited by A. Agnoletti. Florence: F. Le Monnier, 1940.

Secondary Sources

Antonelli, Giovanni. "La Magistratura degli Otto di Guardia a Firenze." *Archivio Storico Italiano* 92 (1954): 3–40.
Antonelli Moriani, Margherita. *Giovanni Guicciardini: Un processo politico in Firenze (1431)*. Florence: Leo S. Olschki, 1954.
Baron, Hans. "The Social Background of Political Liberty in the Early Italian Renaissance." *Society and History* 2 (1960): 440–57.
———. *The Crisis of the Early Italian Renaissance*. Princeton: Princeton University Press, 1966.
Becker, Marvin B. "Nota dei processi riguardanti prestatori di denaro dal 1343 al 1379." *Archivio Storico Italiano* 114 (1956): 93–104.
———. "Three Cases Concerning the Restitution of Usury in Florence." *Journal of Economic History* 17 (1957): 445–50.
———. "Florentine Politics and the Diffusion of Heresy in the Trecento." *Speculum* 34 (1959): 60–75.
———. "The Florentine Territorial State and Civic Humanism in the Early Renaissance." In *Florentine Studies*, edited by Nicholai Rubinstein, 109–39. London: Faber, 1968.

———. *Florence in Transition.* 2 vols. Baltimore: Johns Hopkins Press, 1967–69.

———. "Changing Patterns of Violence and Justice in Fourteenth- and Fifteenth-Century Florence." *Comparative Studies in Society and History* 18 (1976): 281–96.

Blanshei, Sarah R. "Perugia, 1260–1340: Conflict and Change in a Medieval Italian Urban Society." *Transactions of the American Philosophical Society,* n.s. 66, pt. 2 (1976).

———. "Criminal Justice in Medieval Perugia and Bologna." *Law and History Review* 1, no. 2 (1983).

Bonaini, F. "Gli Ordinamenti di Giustizia." *Archivio Storico Italiano,* n.s. 1 (n.d.): 1–93.

Bonolis, Guido. *La giurisdizione della Mercanzia in Firenze nel secolo XIV.* Florence: Bernardo Seeber, 1901.

Brackett, John K. *Criminal Justice and Crime in Late Renaissance Florence, 1537–1609.* Cambridge: Cambridge University Press, 1992.

Brucker, Gene A. *The Civic World of Early Renaissance Florence.* Princeton: Princeton University Press, 1977.

———, ed. *The Society of Renaissance Florence: A Documentary Study.* New York: Harper and Row, 1971.

Cantini, Lorenzo. "Dell'Ufizio del Podestà di Firenze." In *Saggi Istorici d'antichità toscane,* edited by Lorenzo Cantini. Florence: S. Maria in Campo, 1796.

Chittolini, Giorgio. *La formazione dello stato regionale e le istituzioni del contado, secoli XIV e XV.* Turin: Guilio Einaudi, 1979.

———, ed. *La crisi degli ordinamenti comunali e le origini dello stato del Rinascimento.* Introduction by Giorgio Chittolini. Bologna: il Mulino, 1979.

Cohn, Samuel Kline, Jr. *The Laboring Classes in Renaissance Florence.* New York: Academic Press, 1980.

Connell, William J. "Il commissario e lo stato territoriale fiorentino." *Ricerche Storiche* 18:3 (1988): 591–617.

———. "Clientelismo e stato territoriale: Il potere fiorentino a Pistoia nel XV secolo." *Società e Storia* 53 (1991): 523–43.

Cozzi, Gaetano, ed. *Stato, società, e giustizia nella repubblica veneta (sec. XV–XVIII).* Introduction by Gaetano Cozzi. Rome: Jouvence, 1980.

Davidsohn, Robert. *Storia di Firenze.* Translated by Eugenio Dupre-Theselder. Florence: Sansoni, 1962.

Dawson, J. P. *A History of Lay Judges.* Cambridge: Harvard University Press, 1960.

———. *Oracles of the Law.* Ann Arbor: University of Michigan School of Law, 1968.

del Giudice, Pasquale, gen. ed. *Storia del diritto italiano.* Vol. 3: Giuseppe Salvioli, *Storia della procedura civile e criminale.* Milan: Ulrico Hoepli, 1927.

Del Vecchio, A., and E. Casanova. *Le rappresaglie nei comuni Medievali e specialmente in Firenze.* Bologna: Zanichelli, 1894.

Select Bibliography

Doren, Alfred. *Le arti Florentine*. Translated by G. Klein. 2 vols. Florence: F. Le Monnier, 1940.
Dorini, Umberto. *Notizie storiche sull'Università di Parte Guelfa in Firenze*. Florence: L. Franceshini, 1902.
———. *Il diritto penale e la delinquenza in Firenze nel sec. XIV*. Lucca: Domenico Corsi, 1923.
Fasano Guarini, Elena. *Lo stato Mediceo di Cosimo I*. Florence: Sansoni, 1973.
———. "Considerazioni su giustizia, stato, e società nel Ducato di Toscana del Cinquecento." In *Florence and Venice: Comparisons and Relations*, edited by S. Bertelli, N. Rubinstein, and C. H. Smyth. Florence: La Nuova Italia, 1980.
Fraher, Richard M. "Conviction According to Conscience: The Medieval Jurists' Debate Concerning Judicial Discretion and the Law of Proof." *Law and History Review* 7 (1989): 23–88.
Franchini, Vittorio. *Saggio di ricerche sull'istituto del Podestà nei comuni medievali*. Bologna: Presso Nicola Zanichelli, 1912.
Gilmore, Myron. *Argument from Roman Law in Political Thought, 1200–1600*. Cambridge: Harvard University Press, 1941.
Guidi, Guidubaldo. *Il governo della città-repubblica di Firenze del primo Quattrocento*. 3 vols. Florence: Leo S. Olschki, 1981.
Herlihy, David, and Christiane Klapisch. *Les Toscans et leurs familles: Une étude du catasto florentin de 1427*. Paris: Editions de l'école des hautes études en sciences sociales, 1978.
Hughes, Diane O. "Urban Growth and Family Structure in Medieval Genoa." *Past and Present* 66 (1975): 3–28.
Kent, Dale. "The Florentine Reggimento in the Fifteenth Century." *Renaissance Quarterly* 28 (1975): 575–638.
———. *The Rise of the Medici Faction in Florence, 1426–1434*. Oxford: Oxford University Press, 1978.
Kent, F. W. *Household and Lineage in Renaissance Florence: The Family Life of the Capponi, Ginori and Rucellai*. Princeton: Princeton University Press, 1977.
Kirshner, Julius. "Paolo di Castro on *Cives Ex Privilegio:* A Controversy over the Legal Qualification for Public Office." In *Renaissance Studies in Honor of Hans Baron*, edited by A. Molho and J. Tedeschi. DeKalb, Ill.: Northern Illinois University Press, 1971.
Kohler, J., and G. degli Azzi. *Das Florentiner Strafrecht des XIV Jahrhunderts*. Mannheim: J. Bensheimer, 1909.
Kuehn, Thomas. "Arbitration and Law in Renaissance Florence." *Renaissance and Reformation, Renaissance et Reforme* 11, no. 4 (1987): 289–319.
Langbein, John H. *Prosecuting Crime in the Renaissance: England, Germany, France*. Cambridge: Harvard University Press, 1974.
———. *Torture and the Law of Proof*. Chicago: University of Chicago Press, 1977.
Lansing, Carol Leroy. "Nobility in a Medieval Commune: The Florentine Magnates, 1260–1300." Ph.D. diss., University of Michigan, 1984.

Martines, Lauro. *Lawyers and Statecraft in Renaissance Florence.* Princeton: Princeton University Press, 1968.
——, ed. *Violence and Disorder in Italian Cities, 1200–1500.* Berkeley: University of California Press, 1972.
Marzi, D. *La cancelleria della repubblica Fiorentina.* Rocca S. Casciano: L. Cappelli, 1910.
Masi, Gino. "Il sindicato delle magistrature comunali nel secolo XIV." *Rivista Italiana per la scienze giuridiche,* 1–2 (1930): 43–115, 331–411.
Molho, Anthony. "The Florentine Oligarchy and the *Balìe* of the Late Trecento." *Speculum* 43 (1968): 23–51.
——. "Politics and the Ruling Class in Early Renaissance Florence." *Nuova Rivista Storica* 52 (1968).
——. *Florentine Public Finances in the Early Renaissance, 1400–1433.* Cambridge: Harvard University Press, 1971.
Najemy, John M. *Corporatism and Consensus in Florentine Electoral Politics, 1280–1400.* Chapel Hill: University of North Carolina Press, 1982.
Ottokar, Nicola. *Il Comune di Firenze alla fine del Dugento.* Turin: Giulio Einaudi, 1962.
Pampaloni, Guido. "Il governo della Repubblica di Firenze del primo Quattrocento nella recente opera di G. Guidi." *Archivio Storico Italiano* 140 (1982): 553–67.
Parenti, P. "Dagli Ordinamenti di Giustizia alle lotte tra Bianchi e Neri." In *Ghibellini, Guelfi, e popolo grasso,* edited by S. Raveggi, M. Tarassi, D. Medici, and P. Parenti. Florence: N.p., 1978.
Pertile, Antonio. *Storia del diritto italiano dalla caduta dell'impero romano alla codificazione.* 2d ed. 6 vols. Turin: Unione tipografico-editrice, 1892–1902.
Plesner, J. *L'émigration de la campagne à la ville libre de Florence au XIIIe siècle.* Copenhagen: Gyldendal, 1934.
Rodolico, Niccolo. *I Ciompi.* Florence: Sansoni, 1945.
——. *Il Popolo Minuto: Note di storia Fiorentina (1343–1378).* 2d ed. Florence: Leo S. Olschki, 1968.
——. *La democrazia Fiorentina nel suo tramonto (1378–1382).* Rome: Multigrafica, 1970.
Rondoni, G. "I giustiziati a Firenze." *Archivio Storico Italiano,* 5th ser., 28 (1901).
Rubinstein, Nicolai. *The Government of Florence under the Medici (1434 to 1494).* Oxford: Oxford University Press, 1966.
Ruggiero, Guido. *Violence in Early Renaissance Venice.* New Brunswick, N.J.: Rutgers University Press, 1980.
——. *The Boundaries of Eros: Sex Crime and Sexuality in Renaissance Venice.* Oxford: Oxford University Press, 1985.
Salvemini, Gaetano. *Magnati e popolani in Firenze dal 1280 al 1295.* Florence: Carnesecchi e figli, 1899.
Santini, Pietro. *Studi sull'antica costituzione del Comune di Firenze.* Rome: Multigrafica, 1972.

Trexler, Richard C. "Death and Testament in the Episcopal Constitution of Florence (1327)." In *Studies in Honor of Hans Baron*, edited by A. Molho and J. Tedeski. DeKalb, Ill.: Northern Illinois University Press, 1971.

Vallerani, Massimo. "Conflitti e modelli procedurali nel sistema giudiziario comunale: I registri di processi di Perugia nella seconda metà del XIII secolo." *Società e storia* 48 (1991): 268–99.

Weissman, Ronald F. E. *Ritual Brotherhood in Renaissance Florence*. New York: Academic Press, 1982.

Witt, Ronald. "Florentine Politics and the Ruling Class, 1382–1407." *Journal of Medieval and Renaissance Studies* 6 (1976).

Zordan, Giorgio. *Il diritto e la procedura criminale nel "Tractatus de maleficiis" di Angelo Gambiglioni*. Padua: Cedam, 1976.

Zorzi, Andrea. "I Fiorentini e gli uffici pubblici nel primo Quattrocento: Concorrenza, abusi, illegalità." *Quaderni Storici* 66 (1987): 725–51.

———. *L'amministrazione della giustizia penale nella repubblica Fiorentina: Aspetti e problemi*. Florence: Leo S. Olschki, 1988.

———. "Giustizia e società a Firenze in età comunale: Spunti per una prima riflessione." *Ricerche Storiche* 18:3 (1988): 449–95.

INDEX

A

Accusation, xv, 22–24, 27, 203–5, 209–10; in syndication, 139–40
Acts (criminal records), 54
Angelo Aretino, xiv
Appeals, 33, 65–70; from county and district, 110
Arbitration, 28, 67
Arbitrium, 38–40, 51–52, 202, 230
Assault, 208, 213–16

B

Bailment, 27
Balie, xviii, 15–17; Council of Eighty-One, 16; Council of One Hundred, 17
Banning, 28, 32, 59–60
Becker, Marvin, xix, 2–3, 10, 17, 186, 241
Bella, Giano della, 128, 158
Brucker, Gene, 10, 178, 241, 244–47
Bullectini, xxi, 15, 22, 25–26, 111, 176–85, 201, 209, 227; cancellation and oblation, 179–85; imprisonment, 178; from the Otto di Guardia, 26, 125, 195, 197–98, 258
Bureaucracy, xiv, 4, 19, 226, 232

C

Cancellation of condemnations, 179–85, 221
Cantini, Lorenzo, 77, 124
Captain of the People, xi, 115–25; after 1434, 124–25; appeals, 49; as Conservator Pacis, 118, 120; criminal judge, 53, 62–63; as Defender of the Guilds and Guildsmen, 120; guilds, 90, 91, 120; judge of camera and gabelle, 63–65; judge of civil questions, appeals and nullities, 65–70; jurisdiction, 71, 79; magnates, 122, 132–33, 136–37, 150; as model of territorial state, 115–16, 230; notary of the *capsa*, 57; notary over the banned, 58–60; notary over consignment, 57–58; notary over the goods of rebels, 119–20; police, 49, 61, 71; and Podestà, 79, 116–17; and Priors and Gonfalonier, 123–24; protecting communal tenants, 190–91; subordinate officials, 50, 62, 70; syndication of county and district officials, 194. *See also* Foreign criminal notaries; Foreign rectors
Checks and balances, 17–19, 63–65, 93, 102–3, 126–27, 184, 187–88, 194, 232
Chittolini, Giorgio, xix, 2, 113
Ciompi revolt, 15, 88, 152
Citation, 26–27
Class conflict, 214–15, 222, 254–55; absence from early fifteenth-century cases, 201, 217–19, 227; debt, 83, 85; late fifteenth century, 230–31; patricians and guildsmen, 245
Cohn, Samuel Kline, Jr., xviii, 34, 83, 85, 202, 207, 208, 213–14, 216, 227, 241, 254–56
Condemnation, 32
Confession, 55–56, 210–13, 229
Confraternities, 12
Conservatori delle Leggi, 14, 26, 198–99; in Grand Ducal period, 237; officials, 108; power over *divieti* infractions, 142, 196
Consuls of the commune, 76–77
Consuls of the guilds, 86–92; debt, 80; election, 165; Officials of Grascia, 101–2; Podestà, 79
Contested litigation, 30
Contumaciousness, 28, 32, 59, 203, 210, 222, 229. *See also* Banning
Corporate state, 2–3, 7, 8–12, 47, 117–19, 228, 231, 244–49; elections, 3, 247–48; guilds, 83–85; rectors as heads of corporations, 33, 74–75. *See also* Guilds; Parte Guelfa; Societies of the People; Territorial state
Council of the Commune, 77–78, 116

281

Councils of the People and of the Commune, 169–70; dissolution, 17, 236; election, 165; fisc and war, 118, 159; republicanism, 235, 244–45; voting down *prestanze*, 160
Councils of Two Hundred and One Hundred Thirty-One, 159, 160, 169–70
County and district officials: accountability, 111–12; appeals from, 67–69; consignment to, 57–58; denunciation, 25, 107, 208–9; jurisdiction, 25, 33–34, 108–11; syndication of, 144, 147–48; trial before syndication of, 140–41. *See also* Notaries over consignment; *Stipendiarii*; Territorial state
County and district residents, legal handicaps, 112–13
Crimes, analysis of, xii–xiii, 200–225

D

Debt, 79–86; changes in legislation, 83–86; consent of creditor for bailment, 27; defaulting and fleeing, 82–86, 89–90, 98–99, 100, 204–5, 214, 217–18, 227, 256; Podestà, 53, 201; private document, 81–82; public instrument, 80–81; torture in defaulting and fleeing cases, 211
Degli scandalosi, 175, 199
Denials, 213
Denunciation, 22, 24, 25, 107, 208–9
Dieci di Guerra, 159, 209; competence, 14; delegated powers from Priors, 78; election, 165, 168; Otto, 195, 209
Diet of Roncaglia, 77
Disturbing possession, 219
Divieti laws: established, 4; for judicial officials, 8; Executor enforces, 126–27. *See also* Conservatori delle Leggi
Dorini, Umberto, xvii, 200–225, 227, 241, 252–54

E

Ecclesiastical jurisdiction, 40–43
Elections, 163–69, 247–49; *accoppiatori*, 16, 164–66; early fifteenth-century requirements, 166; irregularities, 16; scrutiny and extraction, 163–64
Exceptions (procedural), 27–28
Executive agencies, 167; after 1434, 12–15; judicial powers of, 17; Mercanzia, 93; as vehicles of patriciate takeover, 75, 241–43. *See also* Conservatori delle Leggi; Dieci di Guerra; Mercanzia; Onestà; Otto di Guardia; Tower Officials; Ufficiali di Notte
Executive Offices, 93, 156–99; relation to judicial branch, 156. *See also* Councils; Priors, Gonfalonier, and colleges (Priors of the Guilds, Gonfalonier of Justice, Sixteen Gonfalonieri of the Societies of the People, Twelve Buonuomini)
Executor of the Ordinances of Justice, xi, 79, 115, 126–55; appeals, 69; civil judge, 54; criminal judge, 53, 72; *divieti* laws, 142; executing condemnations against magnates, 132–33; *fori declinatoria*, 137; magnates, 127–37; monitoring the execution of the Ordinances of Justice, 135–36; notary of the *capsa*, 57; notary over the banned, 58–60; notary over consignment, 57–58; police, 49, 61, 73; powers over syndication, 49, 132, 137–49; prison, 153–55; Societies of the People, 149–53; subordinate officials, 50, 72; trials of officials before syndication, 140–42. *See also* Foreign rectors; Magnates; Ordinances of Justice; Prison; Societies of the People; Syndication
Exile, cancellation of, 179
Ex officio case initiation, 22, 24, 25, 207, 208
Extortion: syndication, 139, 148; trials before syndication, 140–41

F

Falsity, 86, 89–91
Foreign criminal notaries, 49–50, 55–56; monitoring torture, 30
Foreign rectors, 6–7, 20, 21, 33–40, 249–50; appeals, 49; attrition, 235–36, 257–58; checks and balances, 18;

Index

cornerstone of the regional state, 108–11; *imperium*, 34; jurisdiction, 14, 20–46, 33–34, 36–38, 47–48, 249–50; magnate trials, 173–74; relation to Otto di Guardia, 194; relation to Tower Officials, 187; subordinate officials, 47–73; syndication of, 148; uniformity of power but differentiation of function, 35, 37–38; vitality before 1434, 225, 228, 243. *See also* Captain of the People; Executor of the Ordinances of Justice; Podestà
Franchini, Vittorio, 77
Fraud, 89–91
Frederick I, Emperor, 77
Frederick II, Emperor, 116

G

Gabelles, 63–64, 95–96, 187–89, 191–93
Gonfalonierato for life, 237
Gonfalonieri of the Societies, 10, 152
Gonfalonier of Justice, 127, 156–58
Governors of gabelles: relation to the judge of camera and gabelle, 63–65; relation to the Tower Officials, 191–92
Grand Ducal reform program, 237–39
Guelf/Ghibelline conflict, 116–18, 157; Guelf black party, 120; *societates fidei*, 117
Guicciardini, Giovanni, trial of, 175
Guidi, Guidubaldo, 167, 241, 247–50, 254
Guilds: centrality to early commune, 116–17, 127, 131, 157; consuls of the guilds, 86–92; corporate ethos, 244–47; crimes outside jurisdiction of, 89–91; debt, 79–86; decline of, 10–12; fixed at twenty-one, 127; foreign official of Lana guild, 88–89; merchant account books, 87; necessities guilds, 91–92, 101–6; relation to Mercanzia, 96–98, 99–101; relation to Podestà, 75, 79, 86–92; role in elections, 248–49; subordination to state, 10–12, 75, 83–85. *See also* Consuls of the Guilds; Corporate state; Debt; Mercanzia; Officials of Grascia; Podestà

H

Homicide, 215–16

I

Imperium, 34, 51
Initiation of criminal cases, 22–27. *See also* Accusation; *Bullectini*; Denunciation; *Ex officio* case initiation; Public fame initiation and proof; *Tamburazioni*
Innocent IV, 116
Inquisition procedure, 20–46; as applied in the courts, 200–201, 203–4; definition, 21, 228; development, xii, xiv, xv, 6–7, 39–40, 226, 231, 251–52, 252–53; document to which the defendant responded, 27; effect on jurisdiction, 78, 79; end of development of, under Otto di Guardia, xviii–xix, 26, 194; institutions to facilitate, xi, 56–57; relation between secular and ecclesiastical inquisition procedure, xvi; syndication of, 126–27, 148

J

Judges: of camera and gabelle, 17, 63–65; civil, 53–54, 62–63, 65–70, 72, 119; of civil questions, appeals, and nullities, 62, 65–70, 138; over the collection of condemnations, 119; criminal, 52–53, 56, 62–63, 72, 119; number of, 48–49; relation to rectors, 34, 50–52; training, xi, 52

K

Kohler, Josef, xvii, 227, 241, 250–52
Kuehn, Thomas, 28

L

Latino, Cardinal, 156–57

M

Magnates, 37–38, 77, 135; accusations against, 23; end of special treatment, 26, 128, 136, 174, 223–24; Ordinances of Justice, 127–37; ramifications of status, 134–35; trials by foreign rectors, 132–33, 173–74; trials by Priors and Gonfalonier, 54, 172. *See also*

Magnates (*continued*)
  Executor of the Ordinances of Justice; Ordinances of Justice; Priors, Gonfalonier, and colleges
Martines, Lauro, xv, xvii, 8, 99, 44, 161, 162, 167, 241–43
Masi, Gino, 138, 139, 140, 144
Medici, xiii; control of elections, 166; end of republicanism, 236; Grand Ducal period, 237–39; Piero's fall from power, 236; political influence, 1–2, 12–13; surviving republicanism, 16–17; takeover, 19, 234–35
Mercanzia, 92–101; application of communal statutes, 96; debt, 80, 98–99; in early fifteenth century, 99–101; history, 94–98; relation to foreign rectors, 98–99; relation to state, 11, 75–76; reprisal, 94–99
Milites, 76–78, 116
Molho, Anthony, 248

N

Najemy, John, 10, 245, 248
Neighborhood, role in trial, 24
Nello da San Gemignano, 28
Notaries: over the banned, over the registers of the condemned and banned, and over extraordinary things, also known as the notary over the goods of the banned, condemned, and rebels, 48, 58–60, 70; of the *capsa*, 24, 48, 56–57, 60, 70, 72; Captain's notary over the goods of rebels of 1322–25, 119–20; civil, 54, 70–71, 72; common to all three rectors, 48; over consignment, 48, 57–58, 61, 70, 159; criminal, 55, 70. *See also* Foreign criminal notaries

O

Oblations, 111, 179–85
Officeholding, broad participation in, 248
Officials' crimes, 222–23. *See also* Syndication
Officials of Condotta, 159
Officials of Grascia, 20, 91, 101–7; checks and balances, 17–18; officials over abundance, 103–4; power to torture, 104
Officials over the goods of rebels, the condemned, and the banned, 189
Onestà, 26, 38, 168, 199
Ordinances of Justice, 127–53; against Parte Guelfa, 128–29; constitutional character, 129; exclusion of magnates from office, 129; Executor substituted for Gonfalonier, 130; feudal prerogatives, 127–28; history, 128–30; magnates, 127–37; Societies of the People, 149–53; syndication, 137–49
Otto di Guardia, xviii–xix, xxi, 13–14, 20, 108, 193–98, 209, 257–58; *balia* in 1434, 234; checks on the Otto, 18; election, 168; Grand Ducal period, 237; relation to Captain, 125; takeover of the court system, 235–36

P

Parte Guelfa, 8–9, 128–29. *See also* Corporate state
Patriciate: accountability as county and district officials, 111–12; definition, xx; political crimes, 174–75; political influence on the judicial system, xv, xvii–xviii, xx–xxi, 7–8, 12–18, 47, 49–50, 75, 161–63, 166, 214–15, 221, 227, 228, 232–34, 241–43, 254–56, 257; relation to Mercanzia, 93; usurping communal property, 14
Peace, instrument of, 27–28, 207–8, 253
Pertile, Antonio, xvii, 241, 250
Podestà, xi, 62, 74–114, 115; appeals, 68–69, 110; checks and balances, 184; civil judges, 53–54; criminal cases, 200–225; criminal judges, 52–53; debt, 79–86; history of office, 76–78, 116–17; jurisdiction over Officials of Grascia, 102–3; magnates, 132, 136–37, 150; notary of the *capsa*, 56–57; notary over the banned, 58–60; notary over consignment, 54, 57–58; police, 60–61; protecting communal tenants, 190–91; relation to Captain, 116–17; relation to consuls of the guilds, 86–92; relation to guilds, 74–76, 79–80, 86–92; relation

Index

to Mercanzia, 92–101; relation to Officials of Grascia, 101–4; subordinate officials, 50–62; supervision of county and district officials, 107–14; syndication of county and district officials, 144

Police, xv, xvii, 6–7, 21, 25, 32, 36, 208, 212; *berrovarii*, 56–57, 61, 71, 73; erasing jurisdictional lines, 36, 230; greater effectiveness, xv; growing number of, 48–49; *milites socii*, 56–57, 59–60, 60–61, 71; of Officials of Grascia, 104–5; statements of, as proof, 25, 61, 105; surveillance, 255; three hundred guards of the night, 152–53

Political crimes, 124–25, 180, 183–84, 197–98, 201, 209, 219–20, 222; torture in trial of, 212

Popolo: history of, 76–78; *il primo*, 116–17; representation, 116–17; *il secondo*, 126

Poverty, 182, 215, 238

Priors, Gonfalonier, and colleges (Priors of the Guilds, Gonfalonier of Justice, Sixteen Gonfalonieri of the Societies of the People, Twelve Buonuomini), 156–85; cancellation and oblation, 111, 179–85; checks and balances, 61–62; delegation of power, 78, 166–67; direct trial of atrocities, 171–74; fiscal matters, 159–60; guilds, 92; history of Priorate, 156–58; illegal conventicles and seditious literature, 170–71; interference in judicial system, 15, 161–62, 176–85, 233–34; legislation, 169–71; magnates, 133–37, 171–74; petitions to, 185; power over elections, 163–66; power over political crimes, 174–76; power over reprisal, 99–100; power to exile, 177–78; syndication of, 148–49; war, 158–59. See also *Bullectini*

Prison: Executor's jurisdiction, 72, 153–55; Priors and Gonfalonier's power over, 178, 179–85

Proof, 25, 28–32, 61, 95, 105. *See also* Public fame initiation and proof; Witnesses

Public fame initiation and proof, 6, 22, 24–25, 29, 31, 86, 201, 205–7, 212, 216, 229

Public initiation, xviii, 203–20, 258; increased use, 228, 229

Q

Quarantia (court), 237

R

Reluctant witnesses, 205
Reprisal, 94–101, 232
Republicanism, xxi, 1, 221, 226; after 1434, 16–17, 228, 235, 247, 257; councils, 158, 244–46
Responses (procedural), 210–13. *See also* Confession; Contumaciousness; Denials; Exceptions; Torture
Rewards for interrupting crimes and executing penalties, xvii, 33, 36, 253
Roman law influence on the judicial system, xi, xii, xiv, xx, 28, 29, 52, 66, 239
Rubinstein, Nicolai, 228, 234–35
Ruota, 237

S

Sex crimes, 224–25; sodomy, 24, sodomy and torture, 211. *See also* Onestà; Ufficiali di Notte
Signoria. *See* Priors, Gonfalonier, and colleges (Gonfalonier of Justice)
Societies of the People, 1, 3, 128, 129, 149–53, 231; as corporate component of the government, 9–10; as defense against magnates, 127, 133; relation to Gonfalonieri, 10
Specchio, Lo, 145, 188
Statutes, xvii, xix, 6, 26, 34–36, 38–40, 61, 69, 79, 99, 115–16, 201; anachronism, 74, 251–52; as applied law, 200, 227; as guarantors of equality, 21, 238; guild statutes, 87, 88; local, 112; Ordinances of Justice, 128; organizing the county and district, 5, 67, 107–8; *De Praeventione Iurisdictiones*, 36; regulating guilds, 75–76, 101; similarities between statutes of 1408–9 and 1415, 254; studied by for-

Index

Statutes (*continued*)
  eign rectors, 227; Tractatus et materia Consulum Artium et Mercatorum, 101; unified in 1415, 37
Stipendiarii, 13–14, 194–95, 220; and torture, 212
Summary procedure, 231; Otto di Guardia, 194, 199, 235–36
Syndication, 72, 126–27, 132, 137–49; of county and district officials by foreign rectors, 109–10; enforcing standards of proof, 29, 126–27; Executor's jurisdiction over, 72; extortion, 139; history of, 138; involvement of judge of camera and gabelle, 65; of judicial officials, 8; for neglect in police matters and in forming inquisitions, 139; officials' documents, 139; officials that were syndicated, 143–44, 144–45; *paciales*, 141; procedure, 146; trial of officials before syndication, 140–42. *See also* Executor of the Ordinances of Justice

T

Tamburazioni, 22, 25–26, 206; against officials, 140; Otto di Guardia, 197
Tax defaulting, 209, 221. *See also Divieti* laws
Tenant pacts, breaking, 97, 218–19
Territorial state, 1–19, 75–76, 83–84, 126–27, 225; Captain of the People as model, 115; *Catasto*, 221; centralization of officials, 35, 241–43; continued growth, 226, 231–32, 241; control of foreign policy, 100; effect on inquisition procedure, 201; Executor of the Ordinances of Justice promoting, 126, 131; expert politicians, 246; and the judicial system, 6; public nature of, xiii, 2–4, 76, 131; as regional state, 2–3, 4–6, 12, 67–69, 107–13, 220–21, 222; separation of branches of government, 78, 118; subordination of corporations, 75, 83–84; systematizing, 6, 21; systematizing of election, 165. *See also* Checks and balances; Corporate state
Torture, 6, 22, 29–30, 55–56, 64–65, 175, 200, 201, 216–17; crimes in the trial of which torture could be employed, 211–13; debt, 84; foreign official of Lana guild, 88; greater reliance on, 229; increased *arbitrium* over, 39–40; Officials of Grascia, 104; Vicar of Anghiari, 109. *See also* Confession
Tower Officials, 14, 20, 185–93; checks and balances on, 17; confiscation, 189–90; election, 164, 168–69; gabelles, 188–89, 191; governors of gabelles, 191–92; lords of all gabelles, 185–86; Lo Specchio, 188; officials over the goods of rebels, the condemned, and the banned, 185–86, 189; Quinque Rerum, 185–86; relation to foreign rectors, 190; relation to judge of camera and gabelle, 63–64, 187; relation to Priors, Gonfalonier, and colleges, 186–87; renting out communal lands, 187–88, 190; syndication, 145; weights and measures, 38

U

Ufficiali di Notte, 26, 199, 224
Usury, 41

V

Vendetta, xvii, 21, 28, 253
Venetian court system, 43–45; Avogaria, 43, 44; Council of Ten, 44–45; place of nobility in the court system, 43–45; Serrata, 43

W

Walter of Brienne, 4, 17, 186
Witnesses, 30–32, 54–56, 200

Z

Zorzi, Andrea, xviii, 185, 241, 256–58

KKH
9851.86
.S74
1994
66755f

DATE DUE